Functional Programming

Using Standard ML

KEE

D1395650

Prentice Hall International
Series in Computer Science

C. A. R. Hoare, Series Editor

BACKHOUSE, R. C., *Program Construction and Verification*
BACKHOUSE, R. C., *Syntax of Programming Languages, Theory and Practice*
de BAKKER, J. W., *Mathematical Theory of Program Correctness*
BJÖRNER, D., and JONES, C. B., *Formal Specification and Software Development*
BORNAT, R., *Programming from First Principles*
CLARK, K. L., and McCABE, F. G., *micro-PROLOG: Programming in Logic*
DROMEY, R. G., *How to Solve it by Computer*
DUNCAN, F., *Microprocessor Programming and Software Development*
ELDER, J., *Construction of Data Processing Software*
GOLDSCHLAGER, L., and LISTER, A., *Computer Science: A Modern Introduction*
HAYES, I. (Editor), *Specification Case Studies*
HEHNER, E. C. R., *The Logic of Programming*
HENDERSON, P., *Functional Programming: Application and Implementation*
HOARE, C. A. R., *Communicating Sequential Processes*
HOARE, C. A. R., and SHEPHERDSON, J. A. (Editors), *Mathematical Logic and
    Programming Languages*
INMOS LTD, *Occam Programming Manual*
JACKSON, M. A., *System Development*
JOHNSTON, H., *Learning to Program*
JONES, C. B., *Systematic Software Development Using VDM*
JONES, G., *Programming in Occam*
JOSEPH, M., PRASAD, V. R., and NATARAJAN, N., *A Multiprocessor Operating
    System*
LEW, A., *Computer Science: A Mathematical Introduction*
MacCALLUM, I., *Pascal for the Apple*
MacCALLUM, I., *UCSD Pascal for the IBM PC*
MARTIN, J. J., *Data Types and Data Structures*
POMBERGER, G., *Software Engineering and Modula-2*
REYNOLDS, J. C., *The Craft of Programming*
SLOMAN, M., and KRAMER, J., *Distributed Systems and Computer Networks*
TENNENT, R. D., *Principles of Programming Languages*
WELSH, J., and ELDER, J., *Introduction to Pascal, 2nd Edition*
WELSH, J., ELDER, J., and BUSTARD, D., *Sequential Program Structures*
WELSH, J., and HAY, A., *A Model Implementation of Standard Pascal*
WELSH, J., and McKEAG, M., *Structured System Programming*

Functional Programming Using Standard ML

Åke Wikström

Chalmers University of Technology
Göteborg, Sweden

PRENTICE HALL

London   New York   Toronto   Sydney   Tokyo   Singapore

KEELE UNIVERSITY
LIBRARY

2 3 JUL 1993

B | 25667

First published 1987 by
Prentice Hall International (UK) Ltd
66 Wood Lane End, Hemel Hempstead,
Hertfordshire, HP2 4RG

A division of
Simon & Schuster International Group

© 1987 Prentice Hall International (UK) Ltd

All rights reserved. No part of this publication may be
reproduced, stored in a retrieval system, or transmitted,
in any form or by any means, electronic, mechanical,
photocopying, recording or otherwise, without the
prior permission, in writing, from the publisher.
For permission within the United States of America
contact Prentice Hall Inc., Englewood Cliffs, NJ 07632.

Printed and bound in Great Britain at
the University Press, Cambridge.

Library of Congress Cataloging-in-Publication Data

Wikström, Åke, 1944–
    Functional programming using standard ML.
    Bibliography: p.
    Includes index.
    1. Functional programming (Computer science)
    2. ML (Computer program language)   I. Title.
QA76.7.W54   1987   005.13′3   87–17499
ISBN 0-13-331968-7

British Library Cataloguing in Publication Data

Wikström, Åke
    Functional programming using Standard
    ML. — (Prentice Hall International
    series in computer science).
    1.   Standard ML (Computer program
    language)
    I.   Title
    005.13′3   QA76.73.S6/

ISBN 0-13-331968-7
ISBN 0-13-331661-0 Pbk

To Maude, Cecilia, and Joel

Contents

Preface   xiii

1 Computers, Data, and Programs   1
 1.1 Symbols and Abstractions   2
  1.1.1 Data   2
  1.1.2 Names and concepts   3
 1.2 Numbers and Arithmetic   6
  1.2.1 Numbers and numerals   6
  1.2.2 Arithmetic and algorithms   7
  1.2.3 Arithmetic expressions   8
  1.2.4 Variables and formulas   9
 1.3 Modelling the Real World   10
 1.4 Computing Tools and Machines   11
  1.4.1 Algorithms and programs   11
  1.4.2 The stored-program computer   15
  1.4.3 Programming languages   18
  1.4.4 What computers can do   21

2 Numbers   23
 2.1 Computing with Integers   23
 2.2 Computing with Real Numbers   29
 2.3 The Relation between Integers and Reals   33

3 Names and Declarations   36

4 Functions   42
 4.1 Functions in General 42
 4.2 Functions in Programming   46
  4.2.1 Procedural and functional abstraction   46
  4.2.2 Functions in ML   48
  4.2.3 Semantics of function applications   52
 4.3 Using Functions to Define Functions   53
 4.4 Type Constraints 55

5 Systematic Program Construction   **59**

5.1   Specifying the Problem 59

5.2   Top-down Design 62

5.3   Program Verification 65

5.4   Running the Program 66

     5.4.1   Error messages 66

     5.4.2   Testing and debugging 68

     5.4.3   Inserting and editing programs 68

6 Truth Values   **70**

6.1   Boolean Values and Expressions 70

     6.1.1   Conditional expressions 71

     6.1.2   Indentation 72

     6.1.3   Boolean functions 73

     6.1.4   Equality operations 74

6.2   Boolean Expressions 76

     6.2.1   Truth tables 78

     6.2.2   Precedences revisited 78

6.3   Lazy Evaluation 79

6.4   Problem Decomposition and Case Analysis 80

7 Characters and Strings   **84**

7.1   The ASCII Code 85

7.2   Escape Sequences 87

7.3   Standard String Functions and Operators 88

8 Pairs and Tuples   **92**

8.1   Pairs 92

     8.1.1   The constructor of pair types 93

     8.1.2   Type completeness 95

     8.1.3   Decomposing pairs 95

     8.1.4   Polymorphic functions 97

     8.1.5   Comparing pairs 99

8.2   Tuples 100

9 Syntax   **104**

9.1   The Lexical Structure 104

9.2   Syntax Charts 105

9.3   BNF Grammars 109

9.4   Context Dependence 111

10 Semantics 112
10.1 Evaluation of ML Programs 114
    10.1.1 Evaluation of expressions 114
    10.1.2 Environments 118
    10.1.3 Evaluation of declarations and programs 121
10.2 Semantics of Functions 123

11 Declarations 127
11.1 Scope Rules 127
11.2 Local Declarations 129
    11.2.1 Local declarations in expressions 129
    11.2.2 Local declarations in declarations 131
    11.2.3 Formal semantics of local declarations 132
11.3 Multiple Bindings 133
11.4 Datatype Declarations 134

12 Pattern Matching and Case Analysis 138
12.1 Pattern Matching 138
    12.1.1 The various pattern forms 139
    12.1.2 Exhaustive and irredundant patterns 144
    12.1.3 Matches 144
    12.1.4 Formal semantics of pattern matching 146
12.2 Case Analysis 147

13 Lists 150
13.1 Construction and Analysis of Lists 150
13.2 Exceptions and Errors 154
13.3 Useful List Handling Functions 155
    13.3.1 Standard list handling functions 155
    13.3.2 Predefined list handling functions 157
13.4 Complexity of Algorithms 160

14 Recursion and Repetitive Computations 164
14.1 General Principles of Recursion 164
    14.1.1 Recursive function definitions 165
    14.1.2 The principle of induction 167
    14.1.3 Recursion over lists 170
    14.1.4 Variations of the basic recursion scheme 172
    14.1.5 Tracing recursive functions 175
    14.1.6 Example: The median of a set of numbers 175
    14.1.7 Semantics of recursive bindings 177
14.2 String Manipulation 179
14.3 Recursion over Natural Numbers 181

15 Higher Order Functions   184

15.1 Partially Applicable Functions 184
15.2 Functional Arguments 189
15.3 Map, a Useful List Handling Function 191
15.4 The Compose Operator 193
15.5 Examples of Higher Order Functions 195
    15.5.1 Curried versions of operators 195
    15.5.2 The standard deviation 195
    15.5.3 Summation of series 197
    15.5.4 Some combinators 199
    15.5.5 Mathematical notation compared with ML 200

16 Operators   202

17 List Handling Functions   209

17.1 List Generating Functions 209
    17.1.1 A general list generator 209
    17.1.2 Random number generators 210
17.2 List Transforming Functions 213
17.3 List Searching Functions 215
17.4 List Reducing Functions 217
17.5 Equations, Algebra, and Efficiency 223
17.6 The Use of Explicit Recursion 224
17.7 Some Data Structures 226
    17.7.1 Sets 226
    17.7.2 Tables 227
    17.7.3 Vectors and matrices 227
    17.7.4 Files 228

18 Classes of Recursive Functions   232

18.1 Primitive Recursive Functions 232
    18.1.1 Course-of-values recursion 232
    18.1.2 Multiple recursion 233
    18.1.3 Mutual recursion 235
    18.1.4 Branching recursion 235
18.2 General Recursion 238
    18.2.1 The Ackermann function 239
    18.2.2 Partial recursive functions 239
18.3 Iteration and Tail Recursion 243
    18.3.1 Number controlled iteration 243
    18.3.2 Tail recursion 245
    18.3.3 Condition controlled iteration 246

19 Concrete Data Types   250
19.1 Types with Structured Objects 253
19.2 Union Types 255
19.3 Named Types 257
19.4 Records 258
19.5 Selectors and Predicates 260
19.6 Non-regular Types 261
19.7 Type Functions 263
19.8 General Properties of Types 264
  19.8.1 Syntax: Type expressions 265
  19.8.2 Semantics: The meaning of a type 265
  19.8.3 Pragmatics: The use of types 266

20 Recursive Data Types   269
20.1 Linearly Recursive Data Types 269
  20.1.1 Lists 269
  20.1.2 Natural numbers 270
  20.1.3 Stacks 272
  20.1.4 Free and non-free types 272
20.2 Binary Trees 275
  20.2.1 Binary branching structures 275
  20.2.2 Labelled binary trees 278
  20.2.3 Binary leaf trees 281
  20.2.4 Full binary trees 284
  20.2.5 General binary trees 286
20.3 Trees and Forests 289
20.4 Abstract Syntax Trees 290

21 Abstract Data Types   298
21.1 Data Abstraction 298
21.2 Linear Structures 302
  21.2.1 Ordered sequences 303
  21.2.2 Sequential files 304
21.3 Sets 307
  21.3.1 Set abstraction 308
  21.3.2 Operations on finite sets 309
  21.3.3 Sets as binary search trees 311
  21.3.4 Infinite sets 312
  21.3.5 Relations 313
  21.3.6 Tables and finite mappings 316
  21.3.7 Graphs 317

22 Input and Output   **320**
22.1 Standard Input and Output Commands 321
22.2 Input and Output of Data Objects 323
22.3 Example: A Vocabulary Examiner 326

23 Programming Methodology   **335**
23.1 Specification 335
    23.1.1 Validation 336
    23.1.2 Rapid prototyping 336
    23.1.3 Automatic programming 337
23.2 Programming 338
    23.2.1 Programming in the large 338
    23.2.2 Top-down design 339
    23.2.3 Bottom-up design 339
    23.2.4 Structured growth 340
    23.2.5 Program derivation 340
23.3 Verification 340
    23.3.1 Bottom-up testing 341
    23.3.2 Debugging 341
    23.3.3 Efficiency and optimization 342
23.4 What is a Good Program? 342

References   **345**

Glossary   **347**

Answers to Exercises   **356**

A The ASCII character set   **376**

B The Standard ML Core Language   **378**

Standard ML Input/Output   **415**

C Syntax Charts for a Subset of Standard ML   **421**

D Predefined Functions   **427**

Index   **439**

Preface

This book has grown out of five years' teaching of functional programming to beginners. To me, a functional language is a major candidate for a good programming language for beginners: it lets you show fundamental programming concepts in a few lines, it supports the teaching of problem solving and good programming techniques, and, not least important, it is fun to use. I believe that functional programming will be used frequently in the future for production programming simply because it can increase program quality, programmer efficiency, and execution speed (by the use of parallel computers). Functional programming languages have nice mathematical properties that support systematic reasoning about programs, which, in turn, contributes to the goal of making programming into an engineering discipline rather than a trial-and-error process. It remains my hope that you will find functional programming as stimulating as I do and have the pleasure of finding nice solutions to various programming problems.

Functional languages

The first "functional programming language" was really invented by the logician A. Church during the 1930s through his lambda calculus; unfortunately, he had no computer to run his programs on. The development of the electronic computer initiated the development of a long series of programming languages suited for this particular computer: FORTRAN, COBOL, Algol, BASIC, Pascal, Ada, and so forth. An increasing discomfort with these languages led to the development of another series of languages: LISP, ISWIM, Scheme (a dialect of LISP), ML, Hope, SASL, and so forth. The driving force behind the development of these languages was conceptual simplicity; no particular machine influenced the design, at least not in the pure forms of the languages.

The name "ML" stands for Meta Language and is the name of the command language in the LCF system, a system for proving the correctness of programs. The language SML, Standard ML, is the result of a standardization effort and a marriage of the languages ML and HOPE. So far, a core of the language has been fixed, but several possible extensions are being tried and experiments with the language are encouraged. The document describing the core of Standard ML (henceforth called ML) is included in Appendix B. ML is not a pure functional language, since it contains features like references and assignments. In this book, mainly the functional part is considered, and the techniques taught are functional rather than imperative; the chapter on input and output is an exception due to the imperative nature of input and output in ML.

ML belongs to the class of functional languages called strict or non-lazy. Later developments have led to the lazy functional languages, for instance, SASL, LML, and Miranda. They allow a nicer treatment of, for instance, interactive programs, conceptually infinite data objects, and networks of parallel processes. On the other hand, there is as yet no accepted standard and also fewer good implementations of lazy languages.

The scope of the book

There is an increasing interest in the theory of programming. A knowledge of the theoretical grounds of programming is, no doubt, useful to a programmer. To understand the theory, however, you need a good intuitive understanding of the underlying concepts. One aim of this book is to make the beginner acquainted with basic concepts without getting deeply involved. In particular, formal methods are avoided when informal methods serve the same purpose. There are two exceptions, though: the syntax and semantics of ML are given both informally and formally, one reason being that these formalisms are useful in the later chapters. Another is that they provide examples of good use of formal methods. Except for some knowledge of grammars, however, you can read the book without looking at these formalisms.

Programming is gradually becoming more mathematical, and a knowledge of some parts of mathematics is a great advantage for a professional programmer. Much development in mathematics has been driven by its use in the natural sciences as well as different engineering disciplines and is mainly concerned with analysis. The type of mathematics needed in computer science, however, is mainly discrete mathematics like set theory, algebra, recursive function theory, logic, and proof theory. The contents of this book should provide a good motivation for courses in discrete mathematics, but does not require them.

The programming methodology advocated in this book is based on the belief that the correctness of a program should be confirmed by reasoning and not by experiment. In consequence, several (informal) proofs of correctness are given, often in the form of an inductive proof. Likewise, useful algebraic properties of programs are derived. Many data structures (data types) are introduced, and the important idea of data abstraction is covered in some depth. In addition, efficiency properties of programs are analysed in an informal way, and the order of the time and space complexity is derived for simple algorithms.

The ability of solving problems cannot really be taught, only learned. Several problem solving techniques are presented, however, and explained by examples. To a beginner, the formal notation provided by a programming language can be difficult to grasp and, for this purpose, program diagrams for functional programs are sometimes used. They provide a visual complement to the real programs and also show the result of the top-down development of programs.

Finally, some words on words. Computer science is a young subject and the terminology has not yet settled. I have made a serious effort to define the words and use them consistently and in a way that I believe is correct and agrees with their use in mathematics. I welcome comments on this issue.

The use of the book

This book is primarily intended for a one-semester course for beginners, but is also suitable as an introduction to functional programming to students who already know some other programming language. The advanced student may wish only to skim through Chapters 1, 5, and 9 as well as parts of Chapters 2, 3, and 4. The beginner, on the other hand, may wish to omit the parts dealing with formal semantics.

The book is primarily meant to be a textbook to be read sequentially and not a reference manual on the ML language. Using the index, however, you can hopefully find a reference to whatever you would like to look up.

Most chapters end with a short summary of their contents. In a glossary, common concepts and pairs of concepts are explained. In the text, important terms and concepts are typed in bold type style when they are introduced or defined, unless that word already appears in the title of the section. The official ML documents for the parts of ML used in the book appear in Appendix B. As a complement, the syntax of ML is given in the form of syntax charts in Appendix C. In the text, many useful functions are defined. They are collected in Appendix D. By providing them as predefined functions in the ML system, students are saved the effort of typing them in. The index contains references to definitions and examples of use of all these functions.

Many examples in the book are given as exercises with answers at the end of the book. They constitute an integral part of the book—to learn to program you have to work through lots of examples and not only look at solutions. In particular, the exercises at the end of each section are selected to support the understanding of the text without taking too much time to carry through. Much of the work with the exercises can be performed without a computer; in fact, the use of pencil and paper stimulates verification by reasoning whereas a terminal stimulates the use of ad hoc methods.

To the student

You are about to learn a most fascinating activity, which can give you many
stimulating experiences. A condition, though, is that you are active. You can
never learn only by looking at what others have done, you must do it yourself. In
the words of Piaget: "We learn most when we invent". If you work with a problem
before you read about its solution, you will get much more out of it. In the book, I
use "??" and "!!" to tell you to put the book aside and try to solve some problem
yourself before continuing. In addition, many important examples and techniques
appear *only* in the exercises. After most sections, a couple of exercises are given.
If you have understood the contents of the section, you should be able to solve
them within a reasonable time. If you cannot solve them, go back and read the
section again, and give yourself the pleasure of finding a solution instead of looking
at the given solution. At the end of each chapter there are more exercises, and also
problems for which no solution or only a hint is given (such exercises are marked
by a star). Some of these problems are quite laborious and intended as suggestions
to the teacher for programming projects and for the interested student.

Before you sit down at the terminal or look at a solution, you should be convinced that your program works correctly. Several techniques are suggested for
acquiring such a conviction. You probably get much more out of discussing your
solutions with your fellow students than "talking" to the computer. I am convinced that there are many nice solutions still to be discovered for the problems
in this book. Please tell me, if you find one, or if you have other comments[1].

Acknowledgements

My interest in and my experience of functional programming mainly come from
the research performed within the Programming Methodology Group at the Department of Computer Sciences at Chalmers University of Technology and the
University of Göteborg. It has been an extremely stimulating environment to
work within, and I want to thank all the current and former members of the group
for their support and help during the work. Special thanks go to Kent Petersson,
Sören Holmström, Kent Karlsson, K.V.S. Prasad, Staffan Truvé, and Mikael Rittri
for many valuable comments and suggestions for improvements.

I sincerely appreciate the encouragement given to me by Professor Hoare as
well as that of the reviewers, who pointed out many errors and suggested several
changes in the style of presentation. A number of people at other departments
have generously given helpful comments and support during the preparation of

---

[1]Please, send any comments on the book to the author at the Department of Computer
Sciences, Chalmers University of Technology, S-412 96, Sweden, or by electronic mail to
"...!mcvax!chalmers!wikstrom", "wikstrom@chalmers.se", or "wikstrom@chalmers.csnet".

the manuscript. I would particularly like to thank Lennart Andersson, Matthew Henessy, Dan Sahlin, Björn von Sydow, and Gavin Wraith. Special thanks also to Lennart Råde for allowing me to use the nice examples in his books on calculator programming.

Needless to say, this book would never have been written, had not a long succession of people developed the field of programming to its current stage. In particular, I would like to acknowledge the authors of numerous articles and books in the field of functional programming and related fields, who have influenced the contents of this book to a large extent. I would also like to thank the ML design group led by Robin Milner for the development of the ML language, a beautiful vehicle for programming, and for allowing me to include the documents describing it.

The financial support for part of this work comes from the Swedish Board for Technical Development, a support that has made much of the work in the Programming Methodology Group possible.

Last, I would like to dedicate this book to my wife and my children. My wife's support and my children's cheerful comments have provided much inspiration during all the years it has taken to write it.

Å. W.
Göteborg, Sweden
June 1987

Chapter 1

Computers, Data, and Programs

Computers influence our lives more and more. The number of computers and the number of application areas are increasing rapidly. Computers have been introduced into a variety of human activities and you cannot avoid computers even if you wish to.

You have most certainly seen a computer and perhaps also used one. A decade ago, computers were mostly used by specialists—today a computer can be used by almost anyone. The personal computers provide easy-to-use programs like games and chess playing programs, word processing systems, database systems, music and speech synthesizers, flexible calculators, book-keeping systems, and so on. Very little training is needed to master many of these systems, and even children can learn to use them.

In sharp contrast to this simplicity is the difficulty of *programming*[1] a computer and instructing it to behave in a certain way. Programming is a *creative* activity that takes time to learn and master. Like any creative activity it is stimulating and challenging. The important part of writing a program is to solve some programming problem. Programming therefore is a kind of *problem solving* and the construction of a nice program can give the same satisfaction as when you solve a difficult problem of some other kind.

In this book you will be introduced to a way of programming called **functional** programming, sometimes also **applicative** programming[2]. Before saying more about computers and programming, we will look at some important concepts and ideas by looking at the history of computing and computers. It is fascinating to realize how many great steps in the development of our civilization were needed before the first computer could be constructed.

---

[1]Emphasized words and names used in programs are italicized. When an important word is introduced it is, as a rule, printed in bold type style, unless it appears in the section heading.

[2]The reason is that *functions* are used extensively and that functions are *applied* to arguments, but much more about this later.

1.1   Symbols and Abstractions

1.1.1   Data

A computer is a machine for processing data, for instance, data about a person, the weather, or a company. Let us look at the meaning of the word "data" more closely. A single item of data is called a *datum*. One way of characterizing a datum is as a *symbol*. We use symbols all the time when we communicate. Even animals use symbols for this purpose: special sounds or movements are used to warn of dangers and others to attract a partner. Advanced use of symbols is a necessary ingredient in the development of a society like ours. We use different sounds when we speak, we write words and sentences, we draw pictures and paint paintings, we use gestures, signal lights, musical notes, and so forth. All the time, physical phenomena or objects are used for their *symbolic* value rather than in their own right; they are used to communicate **information**. Hence, a datum is any physical phenomenon or object that carries information. You might now ask how to define information, but we will not attempt that: whenever you define a concept, you must assume some concept or concepts as known. What it means to receive information is a question you must ask yourself[3]. In summary, you can therefore say that a datum is an *information carrier*.

Examples of symbols (data) conveying information.

Interpretation of data

A symbol or datum is meaningful only if you know how to *interpret* it. If you do not know a foreign language, its words give you no information. Likewise, the bar codes on goods in a store are not meaningful to most people. In addition, many symbols or data can be given different meanings in different contexts. Is some price given with or without value added tax? Is some word an English or a Swedish word? Such questions must be answered before you can interpret a datum. Hence, clear rules about how to interpret data must be given—without such rules you know nothing.

Conversely, the same piece of information may be described by different data: a sentence can be translated into many different languages and still say the same

---

[3]There is a subject called *information theory* in which the concept of information is defined. That definition corresponds essentially to what we call data, however.

thing, and an object or person can have several different names. The number 7, for instance, can by described by many symbols like

$$7 \quad VII \quad seven \quad sju \quad 0111 \quad |||||||| \quad 3+4$$

All the symbols are *names* of the number 7.

1.1.2 Names and concepts

Most machines man uses work with physical objects: a turning-lathe manipulates metal or wood, a washing machine cleans clothes. A computer, on the other hand, manipulates data, which are *descriptions* of real objects. To understand what a computer really does, you have to understand how you use data to describe the real world; otherwise, its work appears as a meaningless manipulation of symbols.

Naming

An important device used to describe real objects is to name them. When you, for instance, christen a child, you associate a name with it: the name is a datum referring to an object in the real world.

This simple idea of naming presupposes that all names are unique, or at least unique within the environment, or context, under consideration. In programs, you also give names to various objects. An association of a name with an object is then called a **binding**, and a set of bindings is called an **environment**. By introducing new names or changing the bindings of old ones, you change the environment you work within. You will find that bindings and environments are of fundamental importance in programs.

Nothing prevents you from naming names. For instance, the name "the Emperor" may be bound to "Napoleon" and "Napoleon" to a particular person. In programming, you sometimes name data objects, and since a data object is a name of something, the name of the data object is a name of a name.

Concepts and classes of objects

Just being able to name individual objects does not carry you far, though. You want to talk about whole collections of objects with similar properties. When you talk about what a tree is, for instance, you do not think of any particular tree, but about trees in general. The word (the symbol) "tree" refers to any object with the properties you expect a tree to have; it is the name of a concept—the concept *tree*. (A symbol surrounded by quotation marks is to be taken literally—as a symbol.) A concept is really a mental structure in your head, an idea. You form concepts by being given examples of objects of the kind. Your brain is then capable of recognizing similarities between the objects—their common properties—and forming the concept. Expressed in another way, you ignore the differences between the objects.

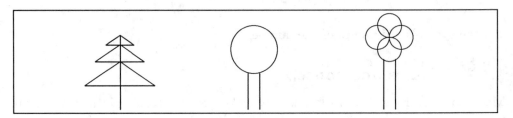

A collection of objects with some properties in common.

The process of ignoring differences and paying special attention to the similarities of objects is called *abstraction*. It is so basic to the way our brain works that we seldom think about it. Since a concept only exists in your head, it is something abstract. The instances of concepts, however, can be concrete objects like trees and cars; for other concepts like shape and number, the instances are abstract objects, too. Abstractions and the formation of concepts are used all the time in programming.

It is not necessary to associate a name with a certain concept. You recognize several shades of colours without being able to tell their names—not all of them even have a name. Naming a concept simplifies communication, though; you can refer to it by its name instead of giving examples of it or describing it each time. When you associate a name with some concept, you extend the "environment" in your brain with a new "binding".

Higher order concepts

The concepts *red*, *blue*, and *green* have something in common—they are all colours. What then is a colour? Answer: it is a concept describing other concepts. If a certain colour is characterized by a collection of objects of that colour, the concept *colour* in itself must be characterized by a collection of collections of objects. You say that the concept *colour* is of a *higher order* than, for instance, the concept *red*, or that the concept colour is *more abstract* than the concept *red*.

Our ability to form concepts of higher order is of utmost importance to our thinking abilities. It allows us to talk about things in very general terms and make general conclusions without having to be concerned about a lot of details. In mathematics, for instance, you work with abstract objects like numbers, functions, sets, and so on. The conclusions are therefore very general and can be applied to a large variety of applications. Programs, in a similar way, describe abstract

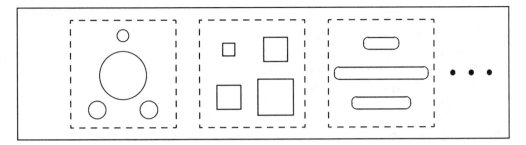

The concept *shape* described by sets of sets of objects of different shape.

objects, and many programs are useful in different contexts. Abstract thinking is a powerful tool, but also something you must get used to: a programmer must be able to think in abstract terms.

Our limited brain

Psychological experiments have shown that our brain can handle 6 or 7 facts simultaneously, perhaps up to 10, but not more. For this reason, abstract thinking really is a key to advanced thinking; without it we would be hopelessly lost in details. Likewise, the only way of mastering the complexity of a large program is to use abstraction and form new concepts. Otherwise, the program will be incomprehensible and possibly incorrect.

By repeatedly collecting concepts into concepts of higher orders, you can build a **hierarchy** of concepts. Simple examples of concept hierarchies are the classification of all living objects, the classification of the books in a library, and the classification of the goods in a store. When programming, you use the idea of abstraction and build programs with a hierarchical structure that reflects the structure of the problem.

Types

A concept describes a collection of objects. Instead of the word "collection", you can use one of the words *class, category*, or *set*. A further alternative is to say that a concept describes a certain *type* of object, for instance, red objects, chairs, or colours. The type of an object is what characterizes the collection of objects of that kind—that is, *a type is a concept*. When programming you work with data objects of different kinds, and you talk about a **data type** as a class of data objects with similar properties. Examples of data types are numbers, characters, and lists of data objects.

Exercises

1.1. Which of the following sentences are false? Explain why!

1. A datum always gives you some information.
2. There can be useful information on a piece of paper.
3. Any set of objects defines a concept.
4. The concept *colour* is more abstract than the concept *circular*.
5. A red object is an example of the concept *colour*.
6. The concept *property* is more abstract than the concept *form*.

1.2   Numbers and Arithmetic

1.2.1   Numbers and numerals

To describe the properties of most objects, numbers are indispensable tools. For instance, properties like length, price, weight, temperature, and salary can be described. Since computers are used to manipulate data about objects, they often manipulate representations of numbers. Let us therefore look at what a number really is and how it can be represented.

The idea of counting is very old in human history. The ability to count objects is usually learned at an early age. Just learning the words one, two, three, four, five, and so on, means nothing, no more than any nursery rhyme; you must also know the meaning of the symbols. How, then, do you describe a number like three? A number is really a concept. To describe a concept you can give examples of objects that have the property characterizing the concept in common. Suitable examples of a number are sets of objects with that many objects in the set.

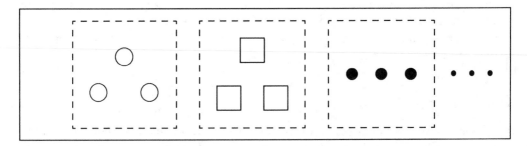

The number 3 can be characterized by all sets with exactly 3 objects.

A *number* like three is an abstract concept, something in your head. As with most other concepts we have given it names, one of which is the word "three". It also has another name, namely the numeral "3". A *numeral* is a special symbol that designates a number. Be sure you understand the difference between the number 3, which is a mental structure in your head, and the numeral "3", which is a name of the number three (henceforth, quotation marks around numerals and expressions will often be omitted, when it is clear from the context what is meant). Numerals are data, but by interpreting them, we get information about a certain number. You say that the numeral 3 *denotes* the number three, or that the *meaning* of the numeral 3 is the number three.

Digits and number systems

The first symbol used for the number three probably was that of showing three fingers. The Latin word for finger is "digitus" and nowadays the word "digit" is used to describe the symbols 0, 1, 2, 3, 4, 5, 6, 7, 8, and 9. Using only fingers for counting soon proved insufficient, however. Several different number systems have instead been devised and used. An important step towards our current number system was the insight that there is a number zero and the introduction of a symbol for it. Thereby the invention of a *positional* number system was possible. As you have ten fingers, ten is the natural choice of a base.

A computer also uses a positional number system, but the base is two instead of ten. Now there are only two digits, 0 and 1, and the binary numerals are 0, 1, 10, 11, 100, 101, 110, 111, 1000, and so forth. The digits 0 and 1 are often called **bits**, an abbreviation of *binary digits*. It is said that the Chinese used this number system more than 4000 years ago. For most users of a computer, however, a knowledge of the binary number system is not required. You work with decimal numbers, and programs in the computer take care of the translation between the two number systems.

1.2.2   Arithmetic and algorithms

When numbers and numerals had been invented, the next natural step was to start manipulating them. Small children often grasp the idea of adding, once they have learned to count. Simple arithmetic is easily done by counting on your fingers. In the early days of our civilization a need for more advanced arithmetic arose. The peasant wanted to calculate the area of his land and the suitable amount of seed for sowing, the merchant wanted to calculate weights and prices, and the sailor wanted to calculate his position and course.

The manipulation of big numbers required a systematic approach. Ability and ease of adding and multiplying numbers were crucially dependent on the number system used. The Hindu-Arabic number system we use today was particularly suitable, and during the ninth century the Arabian mathematician al-Khowarazmi developed methods for doing arithmetic similar to those used today. A method for manipulating data, for example, for multiplying or dividing numbers, is called an *algorithm*. The word is a rewriting of the name "al-Khowarazmi".

$$
\begin{array}{cccc}
\begin{array}{r} 14 \\ +\ \ 28 \\ \hline 42 \end{array}
&
\begin{array}{r} 73 \\ -\ \ 37 \\ \hline 36 \end{array}
&
\begin{array}{r} 23 \\ *\ \ 34 \\ \hline 92 \\ 69 \\ \hline 782 \end{array}
&
\begin{array}{r|l} 169 & 13 \\ \cline{2-2} 13 & 13 \\ \hline 39 \\ 39 \\ \hline 0 \end{array}
\end{array}
$$

The four rules of arithmetic.

To multiply 5678 by 13579, you can use the method you learned in school. You do not really have to understand exactly what you do and why you get the right result; you just manipulate the symbols according to given rules. You will see later that programming amounts to finding suitable methods for manipulating data like numbers, and that programming often requires creativity—creativity of the same kind al-Khowarazmi used when he invented the arithmetic rules.

A **program** is a description of a method for the manipulation of data to get a desired result. When a computer is given a program, it can do calculations by following the program in a slavish manner, exactly as you can multiply numbers without really understanding why you get the right result. A good way of thinking about a computer is as a computing "slave". Once told exactly how to do some manipulation of data, it works both fast and reliably.

1.2.3   Arithmetic expressions

The word "operation" is used in several contexts. You talk about medical operations and military operations. You also talk about operations in a manufacturing process. The idea of the word is that of transforming some starting material or start state into some end product or final state. Similarly, you talk about *arithmetic operations* like addition and multiplication. The starting material is then numbers and so are the results.

As described above, special numerals are used to describe numbers. Some 500 years ago, special symbols were introduced also for the arithmetic operations. For instance, the symbol "+" was used to denote addition. Such a symbol is called an **operator**. It is a *name* of the addition operation. We will in the sequel use "*" to denote multiplication and "/" to denote division, since this is the way it is done in most programming languages. The product of, for instance, 10 and 11 can now be written 10 * 11. The symbols taken together form an *arithmetic expression*. We will talk much more about expressions of this kind, because ML programs are expressions of a similar kind. The expression 10 * 11 is, in fact, a valid program in ML giving 110 as result.

An arithmetic expression is only a sequence of symbols. You cannot know its meaning unless you have carefully defined how it is to be interpreted. Suppose you show the expression 10 * 11 to a person who believes that the binary number system is used. The meaning of the expression is then totally different, as it is if "*" is used to denote addition.

The arithmetic expressions form a tiny language, whose "sentences" are arithmetic expressions. As for any other language, you have to do two things to define it: you have to give its **syntax**, which exactly defines how sentences of the language are formed, and you have to give its **semantics**, which exactly defines the meaning of every possible sentence of the language. You say that the syntax and semantics give the *form* and the *content*, respectively. An alternative syntax for (arithmetic) expressions is to let the operator precede the operands and use special symbols as delimiters. Then, the expression 10 * 11 is written as *(10, 11) instead. The meaning of the constituents can still be the same, but the way they are written is different.

So far we have defined the meaning of the three parts of the expression 10 * 11. The whole idea of forming the expression, however, is to denote the multiplication of 10 and 11. You say that the expression *has the value* 110. You also say that you *calculate* or *compute* the value of the expression, or that you *evaluate* it.

1.2.4 Variables and formulas

Suppose you were asked to transform 72 km/hour into a number of meter/sec. After some thinking you may find that the result is given by the expression 72 * 1000/3600, which has the value 20. Next, suppose you were asked to tell a third person how you, in general, transform a speed given in km/hour into meter/sec. The usual way of doing that is to give a formula, namely the formula *speed* * 1000/3600. For each particular *speed*, for which you want to use the formula, you plug it into the formula instead of the word *speed*. Such a word is called a variable, since it can assume different values at different occasions. A variable is nothing but a *name* whose meaning is not fixed. Conversely, a name with a fixed meaning is usually called a **constant**. For instance, π (3.1415...) is a constant. The invention of variables (during the seventeenth century) was an important step in the development of mathematics, since variables allow you to describe a whole class of *computations* in one single expression. In fact, a formula is an *abstraction* capturing what is common to a class of computations.

When you want to compute the area of a triangle, you can use the formula *base* * *height*/2 and plug in values for the two variables. To compute the area of a square, you can use the formula *side* * *side*, but now you have to be careful to replace both occurrences of the variable *side* by the same value, otherwise the result is meaningless. It is a general rule that a variable must always be replaced by the same value throughout an expression[4].

Exercises

1.2. Which of the following sentences are false? Explain why!
1. A computer is an information processing machine.
2. A program is an algorithm.
3. An algorithm is a method.
4. With a suitable semantics, the value of $2 + 3$ can be 6.
5. A numeral has itself as value.

1.3. Write down the ten first numerals in the unary number system (with the digit 1) and in the ternary number system (with the digits 0, 1, and 2).

1.4. Convert the decimal numbers 9, 32, and 100 into binary numbers and the binary numbers 1111, 101010, and 1000000000 into decimal numbers.

1.3   Modelling the Real World

In striving for a better life, man has tried to control his environment more and more. A prerequisite for such a control is an understanding of the environment and an ability to describe it. There are two important ingredients in this process: the collection of data and facts about the environment and the building of models that connect quantities of various kinds. Using the models and the collected data, you can compute new data and get new facts about the environment. Such models are often expressed in the form of *equations*. For instance, the radius r and the *area* of a circle are connected by the equation $area = \pi r^2$. Given the radius, you can use the formula on the right-hand side to compute the area. To build a strong enough bridge, you use various models and methods for calculating strengths of material. In a company, you want a good picture of what you have in store, which you can get by collecting data about the current situation. Meteorologists try to construct models that predict the coming weather given data about the current weather. The last task is difficult, however, and so far one has only been able to construct models that predict the weather to some extent.

Computers are excellent tools for *collecting*, *storing*, and *manipulating* data. A computer program can describe a model of the real world and by reading suitable data, the computer can compute new data that can give you valuable information. How successful you are in this activity depends on the ease with which you can describe and model the real situation at hand. A good programming language should make it easy to handle data objects of a large variety, and it should make it easy to describe how data are to be manipulated.

---

[4]Still, you can break this rule in many non-functional programming languages.

1.4   Computing Tools and Machines

A prerequisite for our civilization is our ability to use tools. Most tools help us to manipulate concrete objects like metal, wood, and food; they make our hands more efficient. The need to do a lot of mental work like computations suggests similar tools as aids when doing computations. We here define a **computation** as a manipulation of symbols that can be performed as a mechanical process, that is, by a machine. The abacus and other calculating frames have been used for thousands of years as tools for doing simple arithmetic. The discovery of logarithms made possible the invention of the slide rule, which can be used to multiply and divide numbers.

However useful these tools were, they could handle numbers with only a few digits, and each computation required both time and mental effort. Many machines had been constructed for other purposes, and the idea of constructing a computing machine came naturally. During the last centuries, a large variety of them have been constructed. Early trials were made over three hundred years ago. Scientists like Pascal and Leibniz constructed mechanical calculators that could do one or more of the four simple arithmetic operations. Usually, the machines were complicated and did not work very well. However, they had demonstrated the feasibility of a computing machine, and during the nineteenth century, more successful machines were constructed. In the beginning they were hand-driven but, later, electrical machines were constructed.

Of particular interest were the machines constructed by Charles Babbage (1792–1871). His first machine, the difference engine, was constructed to solve a special problem, but his second one, the analytical engine, was a general-purpose computer that could be programmed by placing punched cards into the machine. The way it worked could therefore be changed by feeding the machine with different sets of cards. Early modern computers were based on the same idea. Babbage was never able to complete his machine, but his ideas had proved that a general-purpose computer was feasible. During this century, the development of electronics has made possible the construction of general-purpose computers of the type we have today.

1.4.1   Algorithms and programs

If you want to describe how you perform a particular task, for example, multiply two numbers, bake a cake, or knit a sweater, you must write down the steps you have to go through. Such a description is a form of *program*, because a program is an outline of work to be done, a *plan*. Literally, the word "program" means "before writing" (*pro*, before; *graphein*, to write)—that is, a plan of how you shall write something.

The idea behind a program is an *algorithm*. An algorithm is a *method* for how to act and as such is something abstract, an idea in your head. To be able to communicate it to other people, you have to describe it. Such a description is what we call a program. The relation between an algorithm and a program is about the same as that between information and data. By reading a program, you get information about a method provided you know how to interpret the program. The word program is sometimes also used synonymously with algorithm; you do not differentiate between the program and what it denotes. In fact, the difference between information and data is often blurred in a similar way.

Basic operations

To perform a program, you must know how to perform the *basic operations* of the application area. To multiply two numbers the normal way, you must know how to multiply numbers less than 10. To bake a cake you must know how to stir, how to grease a mould etc., and to knit a sweater you must know how to make plains, purls, and so on. The program only tells in which order and on which material to perform the basic operations.

For any program you talk about the *input* (the starting material) and the *output* (the desired result). When you knit or bake, the input and output are physical objects, but when you do arithmetic, they are numbers.

Combining principles

The basic operations for each application differ to a large extent but, surprisingly, the ways of combining them are very similar. When you execute a program, you perform a **sequence** of operations. A program sometimes prescribes that you shall **repeat** a number of operations a certain number of times or repeat them until some condition is fulfilled. It may also prescribe that you shall **choose** one out of several operations depending on some condition.

The three combining principles sequence, repetition, and choice are basic to all programming languages, but the way they appear differs greatly. It should perhaps also be added that a fourth possibility is to perform several operations concurrently, but we do not consider that possibility.

Imperative programs

The traditional way of programming is called *imperative* programming since your program is a sequence of commands or instructions to be executed by the computer. In ML, you can write imperative programs, but very little is said about that in this book. To see the difference between an imperative and a functional program, let us briefly look at the idea behind imperative programs. A description of how to change a wheel on a car might be:

> lift the car
> take off the wheel
> put on the new wheel
> lower the car

The "program" describes four basic operations to be performed in sequence. To carry out the program, you must know how to lift a car, how to take off wheels, and so forth—the basic operations of the application. To describe how to change all wheels on a car, we assume you know how to change one single wheel:

> take out the four new wheels
> **for each** wheel position: change that wheel
> put away the old wheels

This "program" describes three operations to be performed in sequence. The second of these is a *repetition*, in which the operation of changing one wheel is to be repeated four times. If your car does not start, you might follow this advice:

> **if** the start motor works
> **then** check if there is gas
> **else** check the battery

Here you *choose* between two different operations depending on a condition. When performing this "program", only one of the two operations will be performed.

Functional programs

The imperative style of programming forces the programmer to work with details about how the computer works. To make programming simpler, one tries to relieve the programmer from details about *how* a program is executed and let him concentrate on *what* the program shall do. Ideally, one would like a system that programs itself, but for almost all applications that is unfeasible in practice. A description of what you expect a program to do is usually called a **specification** of a problem. The program contains the details of how it is solved.

A functional program in its simplest form is a set of *equations* of a special form that relate interesting quantities. For instance, you express the fact that the square of x is $x * x$ by the equation $square(x) = x * x$. For example, 49 is the square of 7, since $square(7) = 7 * 7 = 49$.

A computer can do computations. By giving the computer equations of the right form, it can use them to do computations. If you tell an ML system that

$square(x) = x * x$ and then ask it about the value of $square(7)$, it can use the equation as a *computation rule* and compute the value 49.

All equations cannot be used as computation rules, however. The square root of a number, written *sqrt*, can be defined by the equation $sqrt(x) * sqrt(x) = x$. It does not give you much help, if you want the square root of 49, for instance. However, it can be used to check that 7 is the square root of 49, since $7 * 7 = 49$.

To make it possible to compute the square root of numbers, you have to give the computer an equation of the form $sqrt(x) = \ldots$, where the dots have to be replaced by an expression that has the square root of x as value. Such an equation describes an algorithm for computing square roots. In this case it is more difficult to find an equation that can be used for computations, than just specifying what you mean by the square root of some number.

In conclusion, a functional program can be seen both as a set of definitions of properties of objects and as computation rules. As programmers and readers of programs we stress the definitional or *declarative* properties of a program, whereas the computer uses the *operational* properties of it. The equations are used as computation rules, also called *reduction rules* or *rewrite rules*.

Some examples of ML programs

To give you an idea of what an ML program can look like, let us write down some programs. If you do not understand the examples, it does not matter at all. A function for doubling a number is defined by

$$\textbf{fun } double(x) \; = \; 2 * x;$$

If you give this definition to the system and then type in the expression $double(7)$, it will print the result 14.

Let us next define a simple version of a function *change* that given a sum returns a description of how the sum can be exchanged using coins of different values. We assume the values are given in decreasing order in a *coinlist*. The function is defined by two cases. The first says that to exchange the sum 0 you need no coins, and, therefore, the function returns the empty list *nil*. The second case is the general case in which you exchange an amount *sum* using a list of coin values where *coin* is the biggest coin, and *coinlist* is the list of the other coin values in decreasing order. The whole list with *coin* in front of the coins in *coinlist* is denoted by *coin* :: *coinlist*.

$$
\begin{aligned}
&\textbf{fun } \; change \; \; 0 \quad\quad coinlist \quad\quad\quad = \; nil \\
&\quad | \;\; change \;\; sum \;\; (coin :: coinlist) \; = \\
&\quad\quad\quad\quad \textbf{if } sum >= coin \\
&\quad\quad\quad\quad \textbf{then } coin :: change \; (sum - coin) \; (coin :: coinlist) \\
&\quad\quad\quad\quad \textbf{else } change \; sum \; coinlist;
\end{aligned}
$$

If *sum* is greater than or equal to the greatest *coin*, you select that *coin* and exchange the amount *sum − coin* using the same coinlist again. If *sum* is less than *coin*, you exchange *sum* using all but the largest coin. Now, for instance, "*change* 1270 [500, 100, 50, 10]" has the value [500, 500, 100, 100, 50, 10, 10]. The function *change* is *recursive*, since it is defined in terms of itself. In functional languages, recursion is the means for obtaining repetition.

As a final example, let us use ML to define data objects representing arithmetic expressions containing integer constants, an arbitrary number of occurrences of a single variable, and operator expressions with plus and times.

$$\textbf{datatype } EXPR \;=\; Const \textbf{ of } int \;\mid\; Var \;\mid\; Plus \textbf{ of } EXPR * EXPR$$
$$\mid\; Times \textbf{ of } EXPR * EXPR;$$

The expression $x^2 + 3$ is now written $Plus(Times(Var, Var), Const\ 3)$. We can further define a function *eval* that computes the value of an expression given the value of the single variable.

$$
\begin{array}{llcl}
\textbf{fun} & eval\ value\ (Const\ i) & = & i \\
\mid & eval\ value\ Var & = & value \\
\mid & eval\ value\ (Plus(e1, e2)) & = & eval\ value\ e1 + eval\ value\ e2 \\
\mid & eval\ value\ (Times(e1, e2)) & = & eval\ value\ e1 * eval\ value\ e2;
\end{array}
$$

The expression *eval* 3 ($Plus(Times(Var, Var), Const\ 3)$), for instance, has the value 12. You can even define a function for finding the derivative of an expression with respect to the single variable.

$$
\begin{array}{llcl}
\textbf{fun} & diff\ (Const\ i) & = & Const\ 0 \\
\mid & diff\ (Var) & = & Const\ 1 \\
\mid & diff\ (Plus(e1, e2)) & = & Plus(diff(e1), diff(e2)) \\
\mid & diff\ (Times(e1, e2)) & = & Plus(Times(e1, diff(e2)), \\
& & & \quad Times(diff(e1), e2));
\end{array}
$$

For instance, the value of $diff(Plus(Times(Var, Var), Const\ 3))$ is now equal to $Plus(Plus(Times(Var, Const\ 1), Times(Const\ 1, Var)), Const\ 0)$, that is, it is equivalent to $x * 1 + 1 * x + 0$, if x is the variable.

On page 330, you find an example of a big program, a vocabulary examiner, in which many of the "tools" in ML are used.

1.4.2   The stored-program computer

The modern computer was the result of achievements in many different areas. Let us look at why it appeared during the 1940s and not any earlier.

First, man had at this time constructed several advanced and complicated machines, both for manipulation of real objects and for advanced data processing.

Some of them were, in a limited sense of the word, programmable. By making adjustments and settings one could make the machines do different, although similar, tasks. A turning lathe, for instance, could manufacture screwbolts, poles of various sizes, etc. Some machines were programmed using punched cards: the sewing machine could sew different seams depending on the program it was given.

Second, there was a need for advanced computing machines. In special computing factories, large numbers of human computers (in fact, an occupation in previous days) were cooperating to perform time-consuming computations. To make these computations possible, "programs" had to be written for the organization of the work.

Third, mechanical computing machines could store only a few numbers. By having available a machine that could store larger amounts of data, one could foresee the possibility of solving large computation problems. The technology for constructing such a machine was now available through the existence of relays and vacuum tubes. At the same time, the ability to construct advanced electronic devices was sufficiently high.

Fourth, a war speeded up the development and invention of new technology, as many times before in human history. The need to break codes and decipher messages forced the development.

Fifth, the development in mathematics and logic during the first decades of this century was crucial to the development of the modern computer. During the 1930s, a complete theory of computation was developed. Some of the foremost contributors to this theory were also involved in the development of the first computers. In particular, the mathematician John von Neumann developed quite complete principles for a computing machine.

The von Neumann computer

The von Neumann computer consists of three main parts: an input device, an output device, and a central processing unit (CPU). The processing unit consists of three parts: the arithmetic-logical unit (ALU), the control, and the store or the memory. An important property of this computer is that not only data but also programs are stored in the store. This gives it a great flexibility, since the task it performs can easily be changed by storing a new program.

In each bit cell of the store, only two states are possible. Thus, in each cell one bit can be stored. This may seem very limited, but a cell with 8 bits can assume 256 different states and a cell with 16 bits 65536 different states. By the use of various coding schemes, all required data objects can be coded using only zeros and ones. How this is done, a user of a computer seldom has to think about—it is taken care of by a collection of programs permanently stored in the computer, which simplify its use.

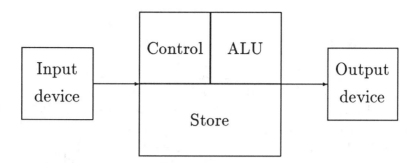

A schematic description of the von Neumann computer.

Each cell in a computer store usually contains 8 bits, a unit most often called a **byte**. Each cell has an address, which is a number from zero and upwards. The number of bytes in a store is normally some power of two. The tenth power of two is 1024, and a store containing 1024 bytes is said to be one kilobyte, written 1 Kbyte or simply 1 K. In most computers, two or more bytes are combined into a **word**, which is the unit that is put into or taken out of the store at a time. In many computers, an address has to fit into one word. If the wordsize is 16 bits, the maximal address is 65536, that is 64 Kbytes. For quite some time, this was a common size of computer stores. Thanks to the rapid development of memory technology, most computers nowadays have much larger stores.

The arithmetic-logical unit contains circuitry that performs simple arithmetic operations on numbers represented by the bits of a word. It can also compare numbers and manipulate the individual bits of a word. The control unit can move data between the memory and a register (a special cell) in the ALU called the *accumulator*. The control contains a *program counter* (another register) holding the address of the cell in the store containing the instruction to be executed. In each working cycle, the instruction referred to by the program counter is fetched from the store to the control and is then interpreted and executed. Normally, the program counter is now incremented to point to the next instruction in sequence, but after the execution of special jump instructions, the sequential execution can be broken.

Let us illustrate how the von Neumann machine works by writing a small program (see next page) that reads a sequence of numbers and then prints their sum. The number of numbers to be summed is input before the numbers themselves. The program is stored in cell 0 and upwards. Each instruction occupies two cells. The instruction address is given in the left column in the figure. The first instruction is an input instruction that reads a number and puts it in cell 100. This cell contains the number of numbers to be added. The accumulated sum is kept in cell 104. All arithmetic is done in the accumulator.

cell	instruction		comment
0:	input	100	input a number and store it in cell 100
2:	zero	104	put a zero in cell 104
4:	load	100	load the number of numbers to accumulator
6:	jmpz	24	jump to cell 24 if accumulator is zero
8:	input	108	input a new number
10:	load	108	load the new number to accumulator
12:	add	104	add the accumulated sum
14:	store	104	store the new accumulated sum
16:	load	100	load the numbers of numbers still to be read
18:	decr		subtract one from this number
20:	store	100	store the decremented number back
22:	jump	4	jump back to read more numbers if any
24:	output	104	output the accumulated sum

A program for adding a number of numbers.

There are several simplifications in this program compared with a real program, but it shows the principles. The programming *level* is very low, since you have to be concerned with many details of the machine.

The first computers used vacuum tubes. They were quite bulky and the average time between failures quite short. The invention of the transistor made computers both more reliable and less bulky. The third generation of computers used large scale integration (LSI) and very large scale integration (VLSI) by which thousands, and nowadays millions, of logical elements can be fitted into a chip of less than one square centimeter. This dramatic technical development in electronics has little counterpart in the function or *architecture* of the computer. On the contrary, the principles developed by John von Neumann are still used in today's computers.

1.4.3   Programming languages

Programming the first computers amounted to the construction of a suitable list of instructions in machine code, a form of binary code. The programming activity was time-consuming, the programs were difficult to read, and a small change in the logic of the program often led to a complete change of the program. As programming costs were still negligible compared with the cost of the computer, this was not considered a problem.

Since the computer store was small, various programming tricks were often used to keep the size of the program and its data down. Such an activity is often called *trick coding*. As a consequence the programs became complex and were difficult both to understand and to change. When computers were later used for non-experimental activity and the stores were cheaper and larger, the need for better ways of using the computer arose. Much time was used for testing and programming costs were no longer negligible.

Some programmers found the work with machine code complicated and invented simpler ways of expressing their programs. The programs were now written in one notation and then translated by hand into machine code. In particular, symbolic names that are easy to remember were used instead of the binary code words. Programs in this way became simpler to read and change. This development led to the idea of making a program that automatically translated the symbolic code into machine code. Such a translating program was called an *assembler*, and the symbolic language an *assembly* language. The use of assembly language simplified the work for the programmer without hiding any machine instructions for him— trick coding could be, and was still, used. Since the programming language now was adapted more to the programmer and less to the computer, the programming level was said to be higher. The programmer efficiency increased and programs were easier to read—the computers could be used in a better way.

High-level languages

The idea of programming in one language and then translating the program into machine code had been fruitful and during the early 1950s work started with the aim of constructing even better languages. In the late 1950s, the programming language FORTRAN was ready for use. It had been developed by a team led by John Backus and the first translator from FORTRAN into machine code was ready around 1957. Such a translator is called a **compiler**. In FORTRAN, ordinary arithmetic expressions can be used and several other programming language constructs simplify the work for the programmer. The introduction of FORTRAN was a great step in the history of programming and resulted in a much improved programmer productivity. It was the first widely used high-level language.

The use of FORTRAN made some trick coding impossible. Programs translated (compiled) into machine code were sometimes both less efficient and more storage consuming than those that experienced assembly programmers could produce. In the beginning, several programmers claimed that FORTRAN would be hopelessly inefficient and never be a substitute for assembly language. Today, we know that assembly language need not be used other than for very special tasks dealing with the more intricate parts of the computer. Even if FORTRAN differs much from assembly language, the underlying principles are much the same: both languages are to a large extent adapted to the von Neumann computer model.

Since the development of FORTRAN, several hundreds of high-level languages

have been designed, few of which have been widely used, however. One that has
found widespread use is BASIC, developed in the mid 1960s. Compared with
FORTRAN, BASIC was to some extent a step backwards. The widespread use of
BASIC is explained by the way you use a BASIC system. A FORTRAN program
is run in **batch mode**. You first write the whole program and then submit it for
compilation. All violations of the rules of the language are reported at the same
time. A BASIC system, on the other hand, is **interactive**, which means that the
system informs you as soon as you type an erroneous statement. It is also easier
to run a program and provide input data to it in an interactive environment. The
interactive mode of work is is probably the most important reason for the success
of BASIC. Another is that the language is quite small and, therefore, easy to learn
and master and suitable also for small computers.

The software crisis

The expectation that the high-level languages would make programming simple
and non-problematic was never met. On the contrary, one started to talk about a
software crisis around 1970. Programs were seldom delivered on time and, when
delivered, they often contained many errors. Programs were difficult to read and
understand, and even more difficult to change and adapt to new requirements.
The increasing use of computers in society made these drawbacks even more acute.
There are several explanations for this crisis. One important reason is that most
high-level languages are not at such a high level as it may seem. They are still
much adapted to the von Neumann computer, and later research has indicated that
this is one of the causes of the problems. Another reason is that programming is
difficult and that you cannot expect to make programming into a trivial activity.

Functional programming languages

The functional languages have their roots in mathematics and logic; they have
not been designed to fit any particular machine model as is the case with most
imperative programming languages. Work by mathematicians and logicians for
more than a hundred years has led to mathematical and logical languages that
support our way of thinking and describing our environment. In particular, the
lambda calculus developed by the logician Alonzo Church during the 1930s has
had great influence on functional languages. It was one of many efforts to capture
the essence of the concept *computability.*

Functional programming languages have several attractive properties. Functional programs can often be viewed as definitions of properties rather than as
computation rules; they are more concerned with *what* than with *how*. Programs
are often 5-10 times shorter than the corresponding FORTRAN programs. The
construction of programs is faster and the programs can be made easier to read

and to change. Functional languages also have properties that make it easier to produce error-free programs and easier to convince yourself that they do what you want.

The first real functional programming language, the language LISP, was designed by J. McCarthy in the late 1950s. Later, LISP was adapted to the von Neumann computer, but much programming could be done in a functional style. In the mid 1960s, P. Landin designed the functional language ISWIM, which has been a base for many other functional languages. It took some ten years more until functional languages began to receive attention and yet another ten years until they became more widely known. One reason was that functional programs were slow to execute. Later developments have shown that they can be executed on conventional computers with almost the same efficiency as conventional programs, even though they are not designed for that type of computer. By the use of new types of computers with many processing units, functional programs can be executed faster than conventional programs, since they do not presuppose a sequential execution. One envisages computers with hundreds or thousands of processing elements all working together on one computation.

1.4.4   What computers can do

As you know, a computer can do quite impressive things. One may wonder how this is possible with a machine that is capable only of performing a small number of operations on sequences of zeros and ones. There are several reasons.

First, the computer can store large amounts of data and also manipulate them at great speed. A typical computer store contains several millions of bytes (8-bit cells) and the processing unit can often perform millions of instructions per second. New computers with a multitude of processors can work at even greater speeds.

Second, even though only zeros and ones can be stored, advanced coding schemes make it possible to represent such complicated data as pictures, sounds, and descriptions of various other phenomena. By emitting a stream of bits to a wave generator, a computer can "talk" in such a way that you hear what it "says". If you consider that using 32 bits, you can represent more than one billion combinations, it may be easier to realize that flexible codings are possible.

Third, most computers contain a large amount of *software* (programs) permanently stored in them. These programs are normally called the *operating system* of the computer. The interface you see as a user is therefore quite different from what you see if you try to use a bare computer without any operating system. Forty years of experience have gone into the development of a modern operating system, which at times requires hundreds of megabytes (1 Mbyte = 1024 Kbytes) of storage.

What computers cannot do

Even though these facts seem impressive as do some uses of computers, it is important to remember that the computer is only a computing slave doing exactly what you tell it to do, no·more and no less. The computer may at times seem to behave in an intelligent manner, but a closer analysis will show that it only mechanically follows a program designed by a human. Today there is little evidence that the computer will be able to do real creative work. That it can do boring work at a great speed has already been demonstrated.

Summary

A *datum* (plural *data*) is any physical phenomenon or object that carries *information*. A *concept* describes a collection of objects with similar properties. It is an abstract object obtained by *abstracting* away irrelevant detail and by paying attention to their common properties. A concept describes a certain *type* of object. In particular, a *data type* is a collection of data objects with similar properties. By *naming* objects and concepts, you can talk about them without describing them. The association between a name and an object is called a *binding*. A set of such bindings constitutes an *environment*.

A *number* is an abstract concept used to describe how many objects there are in a set of objects. The name of a number is called a *numeral*. In the binary number system, numerals are built from two binary digits, the *bits* 0 and 1. An *algorithm* is a systematic way, a method, of manipulating data in order to compute some desired result. *Arithmetic expressions* constitute a small language. The language contains numerals that denote numbers and *operators* that denote arithmetic *operations*. To define a language both the *syntax* (form) and the *semantics* (meaning) must be defined. A *formula* is an arithmetic expression containing *variables*. Such a formula describes a whole class of computations. A *program* is a description of an algorithm (a method). It tells you in which order, and under which conditions, to perform some basic operations. The basic operations are usually combined using the three combining principles *sequence*, *choice*, and *repetition*.

The computer is a computing slave that can work at great speed and store large amounts of data. What it does is controlled by a program written by humans. Programming a computer is a creative activity; executing a program is a mechanical task requiring no creativity. Programming languages have been developed along two lines, one machine-oriented and one human-oriented. The *software crisis* forced the development of better languages. Newer languages like the functional languages have their roots in mathematics and logic. New computer architectures suitable for such languages are currently being developed. They promise greater execution speeds than conventional computers by the use of many processors working in parallel.

Chapter 2

Numbers

The need to evaluate arithmetic expressions appears in many contexts, and since they are simple examples of ML programs, we start with them. In the examples we abstract away from details of the use of numbers like their dimension and unit, trusting that you can imagine specific examples yourself.

In ML, you differentiate between integer numbers and real numbers. An integer never has a fractional part, but a real number may have one. As a consequence, the way numbers are treated is slightly different from the way used in pocket calculators.

A simple definition of an ML *program* is that it is an expression, for instance, an arithmetic expression. The task of the computer is to *compute the value* of this expression. You also say that you run or execute the program. If you run the program $3 + 7$, the computer will compute or *calculate* the value of the expression, and print the result 10.

The examples in this book will be given as seen on a terminal when running an *interactive* system for the programming language ML, an ML *evaluator*. When given an expression, the ML-system will compute and print its value. You say the system uses a read-eval-print loop. The system indicates that it is ready to receive another expression by printing some special symbol called a **prompt** sign (below "–" is used). The user indicates the end of an expression by typing the character ";" followed by a carriage return (not shown below).

2.1 Computing with Integers

We omit details about how to start an ML system and go directly to our first example.

$$- \quad 3 + 7;$$
$$10 \ : \ int$$

The system prints not only the value of the expression, but also its *type*. The type of integers is in ML called *int*. It is an example of a *data type*. The set of all data objects in ML is collected into subsets—data types—containing objects with similar properties. Examples are integers, reals, characters, and lists of objects. You can compare this with the set of all cars which can be divided into subsets of cars of the same type. Different cars have to be handled in different ways and, in the same way, different operations have to be used for data objects of different type. For instance, you can add numbers, you can select the first element out of a pair of data objects, and you can count the elements in a list. We will say that a **type** is a set of data objects and a **data type** is a type together with the operations for manipulating the data objects in the type.

The data type *int* is used to describe integer numbers, which we denote by *integer numerals*. Since there are infinitely many integer numbers we need, potentially, an infinite number of integer numerals.

$$\ldots, \; {}^\sim4, \; {}^\sim3, \; {}^\sim2, \; {}^\sim1, \; 0, \; 1, \; 2, \; 3, \; 4, \; \ldots$$

The three dots means "continue forever". There is only one number "minus two", but it may have many names. In ML its name is ~2 and not the conventional –2.

```
 −  3 − 5;
   ~2 : int
```

Note that the first "−" is the prompt sign, not a minus sign.

Operator expressions

A numeral is the simplest kind of arithmetic expression. When you give a numeral to the ML-system, it will respond with the numeral itself—the value of a numeral is the number it denotes.

```
 −  2345;
   2345 : int
```

We will call expressions that are computed to themselves **canonical expressions**. Usually, you want the computer to perform one or several arithmetic operations.

```
 −  5 + 3;
   8 : int
```

The expression 5 + 3 is an *operator expression*. It consists of three parts: a *left operand* (5), a *right operand* (3), and an *operator* (+). Both operands in 5 + 3 are integer numerals. The operator + is an example of a *binary* operator, since it has two operands. The other binary operators for integer arithmetic in ML are − for subtraction, ∗ for multiplication, *div* for integer division (the remainder is ignored), and *mod*, the modulo operator, yielding the remainder that is left when you perform an integer division.

> — 7 *div* 3 ;
>   2 : *int*

> — 7 *mod* 3 ;
>   1 : *int*

To check if 123 divides 56088 you can use the *mod* operator.

> — 56088 *mod* 123 ;
>   0 : *int*

Obviously, 123 divides 56088, since the remainder is zero.

Division by zero

To divide a number by zero is not a meaningful operation. The result is undefined, and you cannot expect the ML system to give any integer as result. Instead, the computation will be interrupted, and the system will print an error message.

> — 7 *div* 0 ;
> Failure : *div*

You say that the system *raises* the division *exception*. After the failure has occurred, the ML system prints the "ready" prompter indicating that it is willing to accept a new expression. The modulo operator involves a division as well.

> — 7 *mod* 0 ;
> Failure : *mod*

Reducing expressions to their values

An expression describes a computation and most often we are interested in computations involving several basic operations.

> — 2 + 3 + 4 ;
>   9 : *int*

To explain how this computation is performed, we assume that the ML-system all the time tries to *reduce* the expression by replacing subexpressions by their values. The expression $2 + 3$ is reduced in one step to 5 which we write $2 + 3 \longrightarrow 5$. The arrow $\longrightarrow$ is read as "reduces to".

The expression $2 + 3 + 4$ can be reduced in two ways.

$$2 + 3 + 4 \longrightarrow 5 + 4 \longrightarrow 9$$
$$2 + 3 + 4 \longrightarrow 2 + 7 \longrightarrow 9$$

A reduction never changes the value of the expression, only simplifies the expression. A **computation** can be defined as a sequence of reductions, for which the result of the last reduction cannot be reduced further; the result is a *canonical expression*. As you will see later, you can construct expressions leading to *non-terminating* computations; we will say that the value of such an expression is *undefined*.

In the previous example, the result is the same in both cases. Next, let us try the expression $2 + 3 * 4$. Again, there are two possible alternatives.

$$2 + 3 * 4 \longrightarrow 5 * 4 \longrightarrow 20$$
$$2 + 3 * 4 \longrightarrow 2 + 12 \longrightarrow 14$$

This time the results are different, so we have to decide which is the right reduction.

Precedences and order of evaluation

As you might expect, the second alternative is what the ML-system chooses.

```
-   2 + 3 * 4;
    14 : int
```

The reason is that the ML-system uses the same convention as we ordinarily do, namely that $*$ and *div* are performed before $+$ and $-$. You say that $*$ and *div* have higher *precedence* than $+$ and $-$ or that they bind stronger, or more tightly[1].

In ML the idea of precedences is used extensively; there are, in fact, 10 different possible precedences (0 through 9). The operators $*$, *div*, and *mod* all have equal precedence (precedence 7) as have $+$ and $-$ (precedence 6). If you want some other evaluation order than that implied by the precedence rules you have to use parentheses.

```
-   (2 + 3) * 4;
    20 : int
```

The precedences do not tell how to evaluate expressions like $2 + 3 + 4$ with several operators of the same precedence. Normally, operators of equal precedence are evaluated from left to right—you say they *associate to the left*.

```
-   7 div 3 * 5;
    10 : int
```

```
-   7 div (3 * 5);
    0 : int
```

---

[1]There is a list of the precedences on page 411 of the ML Report, Appendix B.

Computing with big integers

In mathematics, you say that addition is **associative**, which means that $x + (y + z) = (x + y) + z$ for any integers x, y, and z. This is not always the case for computer arithmetic, though, since computers always can handle only a finite number of integers, even if the number can be very large. Suppose that 1000 is the largest number that can be represented by your computer. Now, consider evaluation of the expression $2 + 999 + {\tilde{}}900$ both left-to-right and right-to-left.

$$2 + 999 + {\tilde{}}900 \longrightarrow 1001 + {\tilde{}}900 \longrightarrow 101$$
$$2 + 999 + {\tilde{}}900 \longrightarrow 2 + 99 \longrightarrow 101$$

The first computation involves an intermediate result greater than 1000 and should lead to the termination of the program with an error message, whereas the second computation works correctly. Hence, it is important that the evaluation order in a programming language is well defined. The type of error that can occur is called an *overflow* error, since the internal registers of the computer are too small to store the result of the operation.

  — 100000000 * 100000000;
  Failure : *overflow*

Some ML-systems use a special representation for a big integer value, often called a *bigint* or *bignum*.

  — 1000000 * 1000000 * 1000000 * 1000000;
  1000000000000000000000000 : *int*

The problem of overflow is then much less frequent but, since a computer is a finite machine, there are limits even to the number of bigints.

Exponentiation

In ML, there is no operator for exponentiation, but it can easily be defined as will be explained later[2]. It is denoted by the two-character symbol **.

  — 2 ** 3;
  8 : *int*

It is common practice to let exponentiation associate to the right and not to the left as the other arithmetic operators.

  — 2 ** 3 ** 2;
  512 : *int*

---

[2]The exponentiation operator is defined on page 434 in Appendix D.

```
—  (2 ** 3) ** 2 ;
    64 : int
```

The exponentiation operator is defined to have higher precedence (precedence 8) than the other arithmetic operators.

```
—  2 * 3 ** 2 ;
    18 : int
```

Extra spaces and new lines

In any ML program, you can insert spaces and new lines at any place, unless you split symbols like numbers and names. This freedom can be used to make programs more readable, an important aspect when writing a program. Arithmetic expressions are usually written without spaces but you can use them if you want to.

```
—  (3  +  7)  *  5 ;
    50 : int
```

Large expression may be split into several lines.

```
—  1000000000000000000000000*
=  1000000000000000000000000 ;
   1000000000000000000000000000000000000000000000000 : int
```

When you type an expression over several lines, a system usually starts every new line with a prompt like = to indicate that it expects more input before it starts to evaluate the expression. Usually, a semicolon forces it to start the evaluation. We will omit this continuation prompt in the sequel.

Standard functions

The negative number −3 is written ~3 in ML. The symbol ~ is a *unary* operator, that is, an operator with only one operand[3]. A unary operator precedes its operand.

```
—  ~(2 − 5) ;
    3 : int
```

In mathematics, functions are used frequently and also most pocket calculators allow the use of functions. One example is the absolute value function that "removes any minus sign" from an integer numeral.

---

[3]A unary operator is really a function symbol in ML, but more about that later.

    — *abs(˜7)*;
         7 : *int*

    — *abs(7)*;
         7 : *int*

A function symbol followed by an argument such as *abs(7)* is called a *function
application*. The *abs* function is a **standard** function in ML and thus provided by
all ML systems[4]. In most systems many more functions are defined. We will say
that such functions are *predefined*, even if the standard functions, of course, are
predefined, too. The set of predefined functions most certainly differs from system
to system.

Dimensions and units

Suppose you want to compute the area of a rectangle with sides 23 and 37 meters.
You can use the well-known formula *length* * *width* to compute it.

    — 23 * 37;
         851 : *int*

However, you yourself must conclude that the unit of the result is square meters.
If you were to compute the price of 23 objects that cost 37 pounds each, the
result above can also be used. You must keep track of the dimension yourself—the
system does not give you any support in this respect.

Exercises

2.1.   Investigate whether 123 divides 41451 (using an ML system).

2.2.   What is the value of 3 ** 4 ** 4 if ** associates to the left?

2.3.   How many states are possible in cells with 8, 16, and 32 bits?

2.2   Computing with Real Numbers

The idea of counting and the use of natural numbers is very old, but so is probably
the need to talk about parts of whole entities. You start to talk about a half, a
third, a quarter, and so on. Using two integers, you can express any fraction like
1/2, 1/4, 3/2, and 234/53. For a long time it was believed that these *rational*
numbers were sufficient. When Pythagoras discovered that the length of the hypotenuse of a right-angled triangle could not always be expressed as a rational

---

[4]There is a list of the standard functions in ML on page 411 in Appendix B.

number, it was considered such a threat to existing ways of thinking that he had to promise not to tell anybody.

Today, we most often use numerals with a decimal point to express numbers with fractions, for instance, 1.5, 3.14, and 3.3333333. To express *irrational* numbers like *pi* or the square root of 2 in this way, however, an infinite number of digits are needed.

Ideally, you would like to represent every point on the number axis, each point corresponding to one real number. However dense you choose the representable points, however, there are always real numbers in between. Hence, you have to choose a suitable collection of the real numbers to work with and a suitable collection of numerals to represent these real numbers.

The real numerals

To explain the choice of numerals, let us look at the *scientific notation* for real numbers. Starting with the decimal numerals (those with a decimal point) we observe that you can "move" the point by multiplying or dividing by 10.

$$12.34 = 1.234 * 10 = 0.1234 * 100 = 123.4/10 = 1234/100 = \ldots$$

We can rewrite the powers of ten by using exponents.

$$10 = 10^1 \qquad 100 = 10^2 \qquad 1000 = 10^3 \qquad 1/10 = 10^{-1}$$

Using the letter E instead of the notation with 10 raised to a certain number, we can now rewrite the numerals above.

$$12.34 = 12.34E0 = 1.234E1 = 0.1234E2 = 123.4E\tilde{~}1 = 1234E\tilde{~}2 = \ldots$$

These numerals are sometimes called *floating-point* numerals as opposed to the decimal numerals that are called *fixed-point* numerals. Both notations are possible in ML and the exact rule for their form is:

> **Real numeral:** A real numeral consists of an integer numeral followed by a fraction part, by an exponent part, or by both.
> **Fraction part:** A fraction part is a decimal point followed by a positive integer numeral.
> **Exponent part:** An exponent part is the letter E followed by an integer numeral.
> **Integer numeral:** An integer numeral is a sequence of digits possibly preceded by the symbol ~ .

Legal real numerals: 3.14159   ~0.5   3E4   1E~0   ~1E20
Illegal real numerals: 15 .5 5. E3 1E2.0 4.E5 7E + 2 7E − 2

Within the computer, fixed-point and floating point numerals are represented in the same way. The following real numerals all denote the real number 1700.

1.7E3   17E2   017E2   0.17E4   1700.0   1700.0000   170000E~2

Normally, there is a slight difference in their interpretation, however. The number 1700.00 is considered to be more accurate than 1700.0, which in turn is considered to be more accurate than 17E2—the more digits you give, the more accurate the number is. You say that the number has a precision of a certain number of digits. To the ML system, however, they are all the same.

How many digits and how big or small exponents you can use depends on the system and the computer you use. Typically, you can represent numbers in the interval 3.0E~39 to 1.7E38, the corresponding negative numbers, and the number zero, all with an accuracy of sixteen digits. The effect of this representation scheme is that the represented points on the number axis are much closer to each other near zero than near the biggest representable number. This is reasonable because in this way the *relative accuracy* is the same everywhere; the number of digits that can be used is the same.

Computing with real numbers

The data type consisting of all real numerals described above is called *real*. (Remember that it is only a small subset of all the real numbers.)

        − 3.14;
           3.14 : *real*

All integer operators except *div* and *mod* are available for real arithmetic. Let us as an example compute the area of a circle with radius 7 using the formula πr^2.

        − 3.1415927 * 7.0 * 7.0;
           153.9380423 : *real*

Division of two real numbers is denoted by the operator /.

        − 1.0/2.0;
           0.5 : *real*

With real numbers you can perform computations with great precision.

        − 1.0/3.0;
           0.33333333333333333 : *real*

Let us, as another example, compute the volume of the earth using the formula $4\pi r^3/3$ assuming the radius of the earth is 6370000 meters.

        − 4.0 * 3.1415927 * 6370000.0 * 6370000.0 * 6370000.0/3.0;
           1.082696948424497E21 : *real*

The dimension of the result is cubic meters.

Standard functions on real numbers

There are many operations on real numbers that are useful in technical, economical, statistical, and other applications. In ML, some of the most important ones are available as standard functions, and others can easily be defined. (In Appendix D you find some that may be predefined in your system.) The *abs* function described in the section on integers is defined for reals as well.

>   — abs(~3E~3);
>   0.003 : *real*

The square root of a number is that number which multiplied by itself gives the original number. The square root of a number x is usually denoted by $\sqrt{x}$ and defined by the equation $\sqrt{x} * \sqrt{x} = x$ and the condition that $\sqrt{x} \geq 0$. Since the $\sqrt{}$-sign is usually not available on keyboards, you write *sqrt* in ML instead.

>   — sqrt(25.0);
>   5.0 : *real*

There are some other standard functions that often appear in mathematics and in formulas of various kind. Natural logarithms and exponentials are included, but not the common ones (those with base 10).

>   — exp(1.0);
>   2.718281828459045 : *real*

>   — ln(2.71828);
>   0.9999993273472814 : *real*

The trigonometrical functions *sin*, *cos*, and *arctan* are also available.

>   — sin(3.1415927/2.0);
>   0.9999999999999997 : *real*

Real surprises

You have to be careful when working with real numbers.

>   — sqrt(10.0) * sqrt(10.0);
>   10.0 : *real*

>   — sqrt(10.0) * sqrt(10.0) − 10.0;
>   2.220446049250313E~16 : *real*

You are easily misled to believe that what you see of a real numeral is the whole truth. However, some particular system may compute the value of the square root of 4.0 to 2.00000000000000031, but when printed the last and least significant digits are *truncated* (cut off). When performing computations involving many steps, a small error can accumulate and give a result that drastically differs from the correct one. The analysis of such errors is a whole subject in itself, and we will not treat it here; you should be careful when doing computations with reals, though.

The largest and smallest representable numbers

If you try to compute a value that is greater than the largest representable number, the system should stop and print an error message.

>   — 1E20 * 1E20 ;
>   Failure : *

If you use a real numeral that is larger than the greatest representable number, the system should stop and print an error message.

>   — 1E80 ;
>   Failure : Too big numeral

In any system you should be careful when using real numbers, since it is easy to make errors.

2.3   The Relation between Integers and Reals

The type *int* contains the integer numerals and the type *real* the real numerals. The two types are completely disjoint, that is, they have no elements in common. Some elements in the two types denote the same numbers, however. For instance, the two symbols "8" and "8.0" are different as symbols and belong to different data types, but they represent the same number. Some arithmetic operators like + and * apply to both integers and reals, but you are not allowed to have one operand of each type.

>   — 2 * 0.5 ;
>   Type Clash in: 2 * 0.5
>   Looking for a: *int*
>   I have found a: *real*

Conversion between integers and reals

If you want to convert a number from one type to the other you have to use special conversion functions. The function *real* (not the type *real*) converts an integer numeral to a real one in the obvious way.

    — real(2);
       2.0 : real

    — sqrt(real(16 mod 6));
       2.0 : real

In the last example, the use of the *real* function is necessary, since the *mod* operator yields an integer result, and the *sqrt* function expects a *real* argument.

To convert from reals to integers is slightly more complicated. Which integer corresponds to 1.5? There are several ways of converting a real into an integer. One way is to choose the integer closest to the left on the number axis, that is, the largest integer smaller than or equal to the number. Such a conversion function is usually called *floor* and is a standard function in ML.

    — floor(1.5);
       1 : int

    — floor(~1.5);
       ~2 : int

A second alternative is a corresponding *ceiling* function. A third, and often used, choice is a function *round*, which yields the nearest integer. Since there is a choice concerning the treatment of numbers like 1.5 and 2.5, the *floor* function was chosen as the standard one. The *round* function can easily be defined, though (see Appendix D).

Summary

Arithmetic expressions in ML are similar to the conventional ones and use the same *precedences*. We have introduced four types of expression: numeral, operator expression, parentheses expression, and function application. Standard operators with the same precedence *associate to the left*. Real numbers are represented by *fixed* or *floating-point numerals*. Most real numbers have to be represented by approximations. Since the computer works with approximations, small errors may lead to unexpected results. The errors may accumulate and give totally wrong results. The data types *int* and *real* are totally separated, but by using conversion functions you can transform numerals from one type to the other.

Exercises

2.4.   Which number is represented by 1000 in the octal number system, which has the base 8?

2.5.   Compute how much money you will have on your bank account after three years, if you start with 1000 pounds and the interest rate is 7%.

2.6.   A triangle with sides 3, 4, and 5 has one right angle. Compute the area of the triangle using the formulas $base * height/2$ and $\sqrt{p(p-a)(p-b)(p-c)}$, where p is half the sum of the sides a, b, and c.

2.7.   The sine of $\pi/2$ is one. Look up π in some math book and check what happens when you compute $sin(\pi/2)$ with more and more decimals. If your system prints the result 1.0, what is the difference between that result and 1.0?

2.8.   What is the sum of all numbers between 1 and 1000?

2.9.   In ancient Egypt, a clever man asked the king as payment for his services the number of wheat grains you get by putting one grain on the first square of a chess board, two on the second, four on the third, eight on the fourth, sixteen on the fifth, and so on. How many grains would he get?

2.10. To decide which weekday a certain date is, you can use the formula

$$v = A \bmod 7 \qquad \text{where } A = [2.6 * m - 0.2] + d + y + [y/4] + [c/4] - 2 * c$$

The value of $[x]$ is the integer part of x. Here, v is the weekday (with Sunday as day 0), d is the day of the month, m is the month with March as number 1 and February as number 12, y the two last digits of the year, and c the century. Check the formula for some days.

Chapter 3

Names and Declarations

The part of ML described so far constitutes a simple pocket calculator. The programs are arithmetic expressions constructed from numerals, operators, parenthesis, and some standard functions. If you want to compute the area of a circle, you can use the formula πr^2, but you have to replace π by a numerical value. It would be convenient to have the ability to name data objects and, for instance, say that *pi* is a name of 3.1415927. Henceforth, you would not have to remember all the decimals of *pi*.

In everyday life, the use of names simplifies communication, since you can refer to objects and concepts by their name. Instead of a long description, you can use a short name. Furthermore, you use names to indicate the role some object or person plays like the "chief", the "maximum speed", and the "living room". You have the same needs when you write computer programs, because a program is not solely "read" by a computer; it is to be read both by yourself and by others.

Identifiers

A name is called an *identifier* in programming contexts. It has to be some symbol, and were it not for the limited keyboards used today, any variety of symbols could be used. In the future you may well be allowed to use a larger set of symbols.

In ML, an identifier is a string (sequence) of characters. There are two categories of identifiers in ML: *alphanumeric* and *symbolic*. Here we look only at the alphanumeric ones. An **alphanumeric** identifier is any string of letters (a–z, A–Z), digits, primes ('), and underbars (_) starting with a letter[1]. Let us look at some examples

$$A \quad x \quad x' \quad x''' \quad x55 \quad pi \quad Max\_size \quad MaxSize$$

and some non-examples

---
[1]Some very special alphanumeric identifiers can also start with a prime (').

$$7A \quad x" \quad \_max \quad Max-size \quad ident. \quad \AA ke$$

You may recognize the use of primes from mathematics. The underbars are primarily used to form multi-word identifiers, since a space is an illegal character in an identifier. Another way to write multi-word identifiers is to start each new word with a capital letter as in *MaxSize*.

There is one restriction to the given rule. There are some words—the **reserved words**—that are reserved for special use in ML and cannot be used as identifiers. You will soon see examples of them[2].

Value declarations

Your ML-system is interactive which means that you can carry on a "conversation" with it. Primarily, it is your computing slave that evaluates expressions for you, but you can also tell it that you want to name a data object. You then use a value declaration.

$$- \quad \textbf{val} \ pi \ = \ 3.1415927;$$
$$> \quad \textbf{val} \ pi \ = \ 3.1415927 \ : \ real$$

A value declaration starts with the reserved word **val**, an example of a reserved word that cannot be used as an identifier. The value declaration introduces a binding, in this case the name *pi* is bound to the value 3.1415927. The system uses the prompt symbol > to indicate that it has performed the binding. You can now use the name instead of the value.

$$- \quad pi * 7.0 * 7.0;$$
$$153.9380423 \ : \ real$$

$$- \quad sin(pi);$$
$$\tilde{} 4.641020674840618E\tilde{} 08 \ : \ real$$

Since *pi* is used in many contexts, it is predefined in most ML systems.

In a value declaration, an arbitrary expression can occur after the equals sign. Let us introduce the names K and M as abbreviations for the units used for sizes of computer memories.

$$- \quad \textbf{val} \ K \ = \ 2 ** 10;$$
$$> \quad \textbf{val} \ K \ = \ 1024 \ : \ int$$

$$- \quad \textbf{val} \ M \ = \ K * K;$$
$$> \quad \textbf{val} \ M \ = \ 1048576 \ : \ int$$

---

[2]A complete listing is given in Appendix B, page 385.

The effect of executing a value declaration is that the name is bound to the *value* of the expression and not the expression itself. This is the reason for calling it a value declaration. To see the significance of this fact, consider the following example.

$-$ **val** *radius* = 5.0 ;
$>$ **val** *radius* = 5.0 : *real*

$-$ **val** *diameter* = 2.0 ∗ *radius* ;
$>$ **val** *diameter* = 10.0 : *real*

$-$ *pi* ∗ *diameter* ;
    31.415927 : *real*

Now suppose we bind a new value to the name *radius*.

$-$ **val** *radius* = 20.0 ;
$>$ **val** *radius* = 20.0 : *real*

$-$ *pi* ∗ *diameter* ;
    31.415927 : *real*

The value of *pi* ∗ *diameter* is the same as before, since *diameter* still has the value 10.0. Changing *radius* does not change the value of *diameter*, because *diameter* was bound to the value[3] of the expression 2.0 ∗ *radius*, which is 10.0, and not to the expression 2.0 ∗ *radius*.

A binding like *pi* = 3.1415927 is really an equation, which the ML system uses as a rewrite rule: the name is replaced by the value when evaluated. As a reader of a value declaration, you can view it as an equation, a simple *fact*.

A name often introduces an abstraction. There are, for instance, several different numbers you can use to represent the number π. Using the name *pi* you abstract from these differences and think of *pi* as the number π.

The lifetime of a name

In mathematics, some names are called *variables* (often x, y, z, etc.), some names are called *constants* (often a, b, c, etc.), and some are called *parameters*. There is no sharp distinction between the three concepts. They are all used to denote

---

[3]If you are familiar with languages like BASIC and Pascal, you may be misled to believe that a value declaration is a form of assignment statement. This is not the case even though at this stage they look very similar. To avoid problems, try to understand value declarations according to the description given above and not as assignments.

names of objects, and what category you place a name in to some extent depends on the context you consider.

Suppose you write a program handling items of some kind, and the maximal number of items is 1000.

    — **val** *maxnr* = 1000;
    > **val** *maxnr* = 1000 : *int*

During one execution of the program you do not change the value of *maxnr*, so in this sense it is a constant. Later, you may want to change the program to handle 10000 items, so viewed over a longer period, the value of *maxnr* may change and thus it must be considered as a variable. You can also say that you consider *maxnr* as a parameter to the program. As you see, the distinction is not very precise.

An important consequence of introducing a name for a particular value is that to change the value, only one line in the program has to be changed, however many lines the name occurs at; you obtain *modifiability*.

Environments

The value of an expression depends on the values of its variables. The expression $x + 2$ has the value 4 if x is bound to 2, and it has the value 9 if x is bound to 7.

    — **val** x = 2;
    > **val** x = 2 : *int*

    — $x + 2$;
      4 : *int*

    — **val** x = 7;
    > **val** x = 7 : *int*

    — $x + 2$;
      9 : *int*

The part of the program in which a name is known is called the **scope** of the name. Usually, the scope ranges from the place of the declaration to the end of the program. In the example above, however, the scope of the first binding of x is up to the second binding of x and not to the end of the program.

A value declaration introduces a binding. A collection of bindings is called an *environment*. Hence, the value of an expression containing names depends on the environment in which it is evaluated. A requirement is, of course, that all names are bound.

$$- \quad x * y;$$
Unbound identifier: y

When you start an ML session, the environment is not empty; the standard identifiers constitute a standard environment that exists before you start. For instance,
functions like *sqrt* and *abs*, and all the operators (+, *div*, ...) are standard identifiers. Nothing prevents you from binding other values to these names, but that
is not to be recommended. Also note the distinction between a standard name,
which can be rebound to a new value, and a reserved word like **val**, which cannot
be rebound in any way. In your local system, the standard environment is most
probably extended with a set of predefined names like the exponentiation operator **, *pi*, and a lot of functions. You are referred to your local manual to find
out which they are.

That's it

After each evaluation of an expression, the ML system binds the value of the
expression to a special identifier *it*. The expression should occur at the *top-level*,
that is, directly after the prompt and not inside a declaration.

$$- \quad 2 + 3;$$
$$5 \; : \; int$$

$$- \quad it + it;$$
$$10 \; : \; int$$

$$- \quad it;$$
$$10 \; : \; int$$

As a matter of fact, an expression EXPR on the top-level is seen in ML as an
abbreviation of "**val** *it* = EXPR". As a consequence, we can now redefine a *program*
in ML to be a sequence of declarations only, even though for practical purposes
we regard it to be a sequence of declarations *and* expressions.

Choosing identifiers

Large programs can be thousands of lines long. During their lifetime they are read
many times by different persons. You read them when you construct them, when
you look for errors, and when you want to change them. Often, other persons than
the programmer read them. Hence, programs must be as readable as possible: the
programmer is an author conveying a message to the readers.

One way to make programs readable is to choose good identifiers. Suppose you
want to name the maximum number of items in some application. Let us look at
some choices.

```
—   val  m  =  1000;
>   val  m  =  1000  :  int
```

This choice of name does not give the reader of the program much information about the intended use of the name. A name should clearly convey its purpose. Another choice is *max_number_of_items*. This name clearly tells the use of the name. The name is quite long, though, and programs tend to be difficult to read if many identifiers are too long. The name *MaxNrOfItems* is still long, but if you cannot find a good short name, use a longer one. The good choices are not always easy to find, but there are certainly many bad ones.

```
—   val  hundred  =  1000;
>   val  hundred  =  1000  :  int
```

It is tempting to spend too little thought on the choice of identifiers in programs, but that is a bad habit that should be avoided. Those who have written programs with ill-chosen names will bear witness that you cannot read your own program after a couple of weeks or even some days. So, learn good habits from the start!

In mathematics, you often use short names for variables and constants. One reason is that you do not have any particular use of the name in mind. In similar situations, you can also use a shorter name in a program. Usually, such names are used only in very small parts of the program, normally as parameters to functions.

Summary

Any data object in ML can be named in a *value declaration*. The effect of executing a value declaration is to extend the current *value environment* with the *binding* of the name to the value of the expression at the right-hand side (not to the expression itself). The *scope* of a name introduced at the top-level ranges from the point of the declaration to the end of the program, unless the name is redeclared. The names should always be chosen to make the program as readable as possible.

Exercises

3.1. Which of the following sentences are false? Explain why!

1. In a program you can always replace a name by the value it is bound to.
2. In a program, you can always replace all occurrences of a name by the expression in its value declaration. Assume the name is bound only once.
3. If you declare "**val** *two* = 3", the system will complain.

3.2. Introduce the name *e* for the base of the natural logarithms. Use, for example, the standard function *exp*.

Chapter 4

Functions

As the name "functional programming" indicates, functions play an important role in a functional language. You have already seen the functions *abs* and *sqrt*. Functions play a key role in a large part of mathematics. The function concept in mathematics has greatly influenced the design of functional languages. You can define functions in a majority of conventional programming languages as well, but such functions differ slightly from the mathematical functions, and can give rise to unexpected effects when executed. In a pure functional language, functions behave like mathematical functions. ML is not a pure functional language, and you can define peculiar functions in ML also. Essentially, we will consider only a functional subset of ML, though.

4.1 Functions in General

The word "function" is used in everyday sentences like "What function does this machine have?", or "What is his function in the organization?". It is used to designate what a machine or a person really does. Suppose someone presents a machine to you and asks you to tell what it does without investigating its interior. First, you have to find out what you feed into the machine. Suppose it is paper. You can now investigate the machine by inserting different kinds of paper. If the machine now in all cases emits the paper in small, unreadable parts, you might conclude that it is a document shredder; the *function* of the machine is to shred paper. You arrived at this conclusion by investigating what you get out when you insert something, but you never looked at how it was done. The function of the machine is described by the *relation* between the input and the output. Our first conclusion therefore is that "function" has something to do with what someone or something does rather than how it is done. To describe a function, you have to describe *what* effect it has on its input—*how* it performs this effect is of less importance.

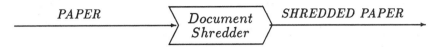

The input and output of a document destroyer.

We described the function of a machine by the relation between its input and output. Not all relations are functional relations in the mathematical sense, however, because for a functional relation the output for some given input must be *unique*. Take, for example, the relation of being the *child of* someone. Since you can have many children, this relation is not functional. The relation *mother-of*, on the other hand, is functional—you have only one mother.

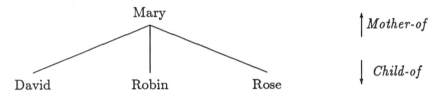

The relations *child-of* and *mother-of*.

The domain and range of a function

All machines as well as all functions are intended to process a certain type of object, called the *argument type*. Similarly, only a certain type of object can be the result of the processing, called the *result type*. The set of allowed inputs to a function is called its *domain* and the set of possible results its *range*. Note that the domain and the argument type need not be the same. For the integer division operation, the second argument is of type *int*, but the domain does not contain the number zero, since division by zero is undefined. Similarly, the result type of the integer *abs* function is *int*, but the range is the non-negative integers. Just knowing the domain and the range of a function seldom tells you much about the function, since you do not know how the output depends on the input; you must also know their relation.

The graph of a function

The relation between the input and output of a function is called the *graph* of the function. The graph is the correspondence between each input and its associated output and is often drawn in a diagram (a graph). Let us draw the graph of a function giving the number of days in a month for a year that is not a leap-year.

The graph shows the domain and the range as well as the relationship between their elements. The range is a subset of the integers.

Domain:	Jan	Feb	Mar	Apr	May	Jun	Jul	Aug	Sep	Oct	Nov	Dec
	↓	↓	↓	↓	↓	↓	↓	↓	↓	↓	↓	↓
Range:	31	28	31	30	31	30	31	31	30	31	30	31

Note that for each element in the domain there corresponds exactly one element in the range. This must be the case, otherwise the relation is not a function. As you see, several elements in the domain can be mapped to the same element in the range.

A problem arises when there are infinitely many elements in the domain. Then, you cannot draw the graph in full. By showing enough points you can often give the observer an idea of which function the graph represents. Can you guess which function this graph represents??[1]

$$1 \quad 2 \quad 3 \quad 4 \quad 5 \quad 6 \quad 7 \quad \cdots$$
$$1 \quad 4 \quad 9 \quad 16 \quad 25 \quad 36 \quad 49 \quad \cdots$$

The graph is intended to represent the squaring function that multiplies the input with itself. You have to be careful, however.

⋯	1987	1988	1989	1990	1991	1992	1993	1994	1995	1996	1997	⋯
⋯	365	366	365	365	365	366	365	365	365	366	365	⋯

From this graph you might be misled to believe that each fourth year is a leap-year, but as you probably know this is not the case: the rule is broken the next time by the year 2100.

Obviously, there are problems describing all functions using only graphs. For functions with an infinite domain you need other means. For instance, you can describe the *square* function by the equation $square(x) = x * x$. There are functions that cannot be described in any finite way whatsoever, but they are of little practical interest.

A child may have many names and the same is true of functions; a function is sometimes said to be a *mapping*, a *transformation*, or an *operation*. The word operation is sometimes also used to denote the application of a function to an argument; you say, for instance, that you perform an addition operation.

What and how

When investigating the paper destroyer, you were only allowed to investigate what it did, not how it worked. Very often, you are also interested in *how* something

---

[1]Double ?? and !! are used to indicate that you should put the book aside and try the problem for yourself before continuing.

is achieved—which *procedure* you use. If you want a hole in a piece of wood, you might use a knife, a hand-driven drill, or perhaps an electric one. You say that you use some *method, procedure, routine,* or *algorithm* to achieve the goal.

Suppose you want to divide several different numbers by 25. You can use the way of dividing numbers you learned in school. Another way is to multiply the number by 4 and then divide the result by 100. A third way is to use a pocket calculator. These methods are three out of many ways of dividing a number by 25; they are different procedures that all perform the same function.

Black boxes and abstraction

The two examples above show that you perform an abstraction when forming the idea of a function. You disregard details about how a function is performed and consider only the relation between the input and the output, that is, what the function achieves. A common way of describing this situation is to talk about a *black box*. You disregard the mechanism inside the box and consider only its input-output relation. When you use the black-box metaphor, you silently assume that you can replace it by another box that achieves the same function. We will often start by describing a function as a box and then fill in the details later.

In computer science, as in mathematics, some concepts like functions are quite abstract and may take time to understand in full. When learning a new concept, try to look at the examples and try also to find your own examples! After a while you are ready to abstract from the details of the individual examples and form the concept in your head. Often, it is a good idea to find non-examples as well. For the function *nr_of_days* above we assumed that the year is not a leap-year. If we abandon that assumption, *nr_of_days* is not a function, since February can be mapped both onto 28 and 29, which violates the uniqueness requirement.

Tables and functions

The domain and the range of functions in programming are always subsets of objects in some data type. A good everyday example of a function relating data objects is a table, for instance, a tax table, the multiplication table, or a nutritional table. In a nutritional table, for instance, you find how many calories there are in an article of food. Another example is the telephone book; it represents a function from a name and an address to a telephone number.

A table is really the graph of a function. However, a function can be represented as a table only if there is a finite number of elements in its domain. Often the domain is, at least conceptually, infinite. Therefore, we need other means than tables to describe functions in programs.

Exercises

4.1. Which of the following sentences are false? Explain why!

1. Different algorithms can compute the same function.
2. You can describe a function by giving a method for it.
3. The relation *wife-of* is a functional relation.

4.2   Functions in Programming

The arithmetic expression $2*3+4$ represents a computation, which we can describe with reductions.

$$2*3+4 \longrightarrow 6+4 \longrightarrow 10$$

The given expression describes one single computation. A formula is an expression containing variables. It represents a whole class of computations, since the variables can assume different values. The formula $n*(n+1)/2$, for instance, yields the sum of all integers from 1 to n. (We will later prove that this really is the case.) If you substitute a number for the variable, you get an expression whose value can be computed.

$$5*(5+1)/2 \longrightarrow 5*6/2 \longrightarrow 30/2 \longrightarrow 15$$
$$10*(10+1)/2 \longrightarrow 10*11/2 \longrightarrow 110/2 \longrightarrow 55$$

The formula describes one computation for each value of n. Since there are an infinite number of positive integers, the formula represents an infinite number of computations.

4.2.1   Procedural and functional abstraction

All the computations described by a formula have something in common. If you perform an abstraction and only consider the *computation pattern*, not the number that is substituted, the result of the abstraction is a computation method, a procedure. Such an abstraction is called a *procedural abstraction*, since the result of the abstraction is a procedure, a method.

Another formula for calculating the same sum is

$$1+2+3+4+\cdots+(n-1)+n$$

It is another method (procedure) for achieving the same goal. In general, there are many possible methods for obtaining a desired result.

The result of a procedural abstraction is a procedure, not a function. To get a function you must perform yet another abstraction which disregards the particular computation method. We have previously described this abstraction by using a black box, in which we hide the particular details of the method used. The result of this abstraction is a function, and the abstraction is therefore called *functional abstraction*. To an external user, the relation between input and output is the important thing; how the computation is performed is less important.

The function associated with the summation formula has an infinite domain. Therefore, we cannot draw a complete graph of it.

$$1 \quad 2 \quad 3 \quad 4 \quad 5 \quad 6 \quad \ldots$$
$$1 \quad 3 \quad 6 \quad 10 \quad 15 \quad 21 \quad \ldots$$

A graph may be meaningful to us because we imagine what the three dots mean; we can never be sure, though. A formula, on the other hand, can describe the result for all arguments in the domain. We will therefore use formulas to describe functions to the computer.

Naming functions

In the previous subsection we talked about the function associated with the formula $n*(n+1)/2$ without giving it a name, but most of the time you also give functions names. A formula does not always describe a function in a unique way, however. The formula

$$amount * (1 + interest/100)^{time}$$

tells how a given *amount* grows with *time* at a certain *interest*. Now suppose you want to investigate how a fixed *amount* of money grows with *time* at a fixed *interest*. To define a suitable function, you must tell what you want to consider *fixed* and what you want to *vary*.

$$capital(time) = amount * (1 + interest/100)^{time}$$

When defining the function *capital*, you indicate that you want to vary the *time* by writing the word *time* within parentheses after the function name *capital*. Indirectly, you then also indicate that the *amount* and the *interest* are fixed—they are considered as constants. The same method is often used in mathematics:

$$f(x) = ax^2 + bx + c$$

The function f is a function of x while a, b, and c are constants.

The formula used to define a function is sometimes called the **body** of the function. The name you use for the quantity that can vary is called the **parameter** of the function. In the examples above, *time* is the parameter of the *capital* function and x is the parameter of f.

To use a mathematical function, you **apply** it to an **argument**. If you want to find out which *capital* you have after 10 years given some fixed *amount* and *interest*, you apply the function *capital* to the argument 10. To compute the value of the function for some argument, you replace the parameter in the body of the function by the argument and compute the value of the expression.

The name you give to a function does not involve the parameter. The name of the second function above is f, not $f(x)$, which is the notation for f *applied* to x. Even in many books on mathematics the difference between f and $f(x)$ is blurred and they talk, for instance, about the function $sin(x)$ instead of the function sin, which is the sine function; $sin(x)$ is the value you get when you apply sin to some particular x.

4.2.2   Functions in ML

Functions in ML can be defined in much the same way as in mathematics. As a first example, let us bind the name *sum1to* to the function that given a positive integer n, returns the sum of the n first non-negative integers.

> ```
> -  fun sum1to (n) = n * (n + 1) div 2;
> >  val sum1to = fn : int -> int
> ```

The reserved word **fun** is used to indicate that you want to name a function. You then give the name followed by the parameter of the function and, after the equals sign, the formula that describes the computation method. In the example, *sum1to* is the name of the function, n is the parameter, and $n*(n+1)$ *div* 2 is the formula, the body, of the function.

The effect of executing this **function declaration** is that the name *sum1to* becomes bound to the function associated with the formula. This function object is denoted by the reserved word **fn** in the system response. One could let the system repeat the the formula, but as argued above we do not want to regard functions as methods or procedures; we want to abstract from that level and view them as black boxes. The system cannot give the graph of the function since it is infinite, so **fn** is chosen instead. As usual, the system responds with the type of the declared object. Both the argument type and the result type of the function are integers, that is, the function is a mapping from integers to integers, which is denoted by $int \rightarrow int$. The system can deduce the type, because the expression contains integer constants. Note that the intended domain is here the non-negative integers only, but the argument type is all the integers.

It is illustrative to compare the form of a function declaration with that of a value declaration.

> ```
> -  val year = 1986;
> >  val year = 1986 : int
> ```

The system response says that *year* has become bound to the value 1986 and that the value has type *int*. In a function declaration a name is bound to an object, too, but that object happens to be a function, a data object as much as an integer.

Using functions

To use a function, you apply it to some argument, which must be in the domain of the function. To compute the sum of the first 100 integers, you can apply the function *sum1to* to the argument 100.

> — *sum1to* (100);
> 5050 : *int*

The result of this function application is obtained by evaluating the body with the argument substituted for the parameter.

> $sum1to\,(100) \longrightarrow 100*(100+1)\ div\ 2 \longrightarrow$
> $100*101\ div\ 2 \longrightarrow 10100\ div\ 2 \longrightarrow 5050$

The operation of applying a function to an argument is denoted in ML simply by letting the argument follow the function. The parentheses are therefore not necessary (as is conventional in mathematics).

> — *sum1to* 100;
> 5050 : *int*

A *function application* is an expression consisting of two parts, the *operator* and the *operand*. Such an application is called a **prefix** application, because the operator precedes the operand. The expression 2+3 is an example of an **infix** application, since the operator is placed between its two operands. Note that we use the words operator and operand when we talk about expressions, that is, symbols, and the words function and argument when we talk about the meaning of these symbols.

Infix application   Prefix application

operator   operator

↓   ↓

2 + 3   *sum1to* 1000

↑ ↑   ↑

operands   operand

The application of a function to an argument is an operation in itself, but no symbol is used for it in ML. If no parentheses are used, then at least one space, or other delimiter, must separate the operator and the operand.

     − *sum1to*100;
Unbound Identifier: *sum1to100*

If you want to apply a function to an operand consisting of several parts, you have to surround the operand by parentheses.

     − *sum1to* (2 + 3);
       15 : *int*

     − *sum1to* 2 + 3;
       6 : *int*

The last expression is interpreted as (*sum1to* 2) + 3, which has the value 6. The reason is that function application binds stronger (has higher precedence) than any other construct in ML.

Let us next define a function *area* that computes the area of a circle with a given radius. We assume that the constant *pi* has been defined in a value declaration. Exactly as parentheses can be omitted in some function applications they can also be omitted in some function declarations.

     − **fun** *area r* = *pi* ∗ *r* ∗ *r*;
  > **val** *area* = **fn** : *real* −> *real*

Since *pi* is bound to a real number, the resulting function is a function from reals to reals. We can now use it to compute the area of a circle.

     − *area* 637.0;
       1274760.9282863 : *real*

Note that the function *area* expects a real number as argument.

     − *area* 637;
Type Clash in: *area* 637
Looking for a: *real*
I have found a: *int*

Parameters and arguments

A parameter is a name used in the function body to refer to the argument.

     − **fun** *double x* = 2 ∗ *x*;
  > **val** *double* = **fn** : *int* −> *int*

The identifier *x* is here used as parameter. Without changing the meaning of the declaration you can replace *x* by some other identifier, if done consistently.

$-$ **fun** *double* $y = 2 * y$;
$>$ **val** *double* $=$ **fn** $:$ *int* $->$ *int*

There are two ways of explaining how a function application is computed. The easiest one is to say that the argument is substituted for the parameter.

$$double(2 + 3) \longrightarrow double(5) \longrightarrow 2 * 5 \longrightarrow 10$$

Note that the argument is the *value* of the operand $2 + 3$, that is, 5, and not the operand itself. You can also explain the evaluation of a function application with environments. When the value of *double* 5 is to be computed, the argument is bound to the parameter y, and the value environment is temporarily extended with this binding during the evaluation of the function body. When the evaluation is completed, the binding is discarded again. We will return to this explanation later.

Function expressions and functions as objects

In a value declaration you introduce a name for an object.

$-$ **val** *max* $= 1000$;
$>$ **val** *max* $= 1000$ $:$ *int*

The name and the value it is bound to can always be used interchangeably.

$-$ *max* $+ 1$;
1001 $:$ *int*

$-$ $1000 + 1$;
1001 $:$ *int*

With a function declaration you introduce a name for a function.

$-$ **fun** *triple* $x = 3 * x$;
$>$ **val** *triple* $=$ **fn** $:$ *int* $->$ *int*

The name *triple* is now bound to the function with parameter x and body $3 * x$. There is, in fact, a special notation for this function in ML.

$-$ **fn** $x => 3 * x$;
fn $:$ *int* $->$ *int*

A *function expression* can be used to describe a function without naming it. It starts with the reserved word **fn** followed by the parameter. After the symbol => the formula describing the computation rule is given. Usually, it contains the parameter.

A function expression like **fn** x => $3 * x$ is an expression denoting a function exactly as 3 is a numeral denoting a number. A function expression is a canonical expression that cannot be further evaluated; you can apply it to an argument, though. In analogy with how you name an arithmetic value in a value declaration, you can name a function value using a value declaration.

$$- \quad \textbf{val } triple = \textbf{fn } x => 3 * x;$$
$$> \quad \textbf{val } triple = \textbf{fn } : int -> int$$

This value declaration is equivalent to the corresponding function declaration.

$$- \quad \textbf{fun } triple \; x = 3 * x;$$
$$> \quad \textbf{val } triple = \textbf{fn } : int -> int$$

In fact, the latter form is only considered as an abbreviation of (a variant of) the former one in ML. The rule when to use **val** and when to use **fun** is simple:

> The reserved word **val** is used when only a single name occurs between **val** and =, otherwise **fun** is used.

The principle that a name can always be replaced by its value allows you to replace a function name in a function application by its associated function expression.

$$- \quad triple \; 5;$$
$$\quad 15 : int$$

$$- \quad (\textbf{fn } x => 3 * x) \; 5;$$
$$\quad 15 : int$$

When changing a name or replacing a name by another expression, you have to ensure that no other name gets rebound, though.

4.2.3   Semantics of function applications

We can now state the rules for the evaluation of a function application F E with operator F and operand E.

1. Evaluate the operator F. The value obtained must be a function object of the form **fn** ID => E′, where ID is the parameter and E′ the body.

2. Evaluate the operand E. The value, which we call V, is the argument to the function.

3. Substitute the value V for all occurrences of the parameter ID in the body E' and evaluate the resulting expression. The obtained value is the value of the function application.

Note that in all examples so far, the operator is either a function expression or a name of a function, so step 1 is trivial. You will later see examples where this is not the case.

Let us define a function f and see how the application $f(2+3)$ is evaluated by the use of substitution.

$$
\begin{aligned}
&- \quad \textbf{val } f \ = \ \textbf{fn } x \ => \ 2 * x * x; \\
&> \quad \textbf{val } f \ = \ \textbf{fn } : \ int \ -> \ int
\end{aligned}
$$

$$
\begin{aligned}
f(2+3) \ &\longrightarrow \ (\textbf{fn } x \ => \ 2 * x * x) \ (2+3) \ \longrightarrow \\
(\textbf{fn } x \ => \ 2 * x * x) \ 5 \ &\longrightarrow \ 2 * 5 * 5 \ \longrightarrow \ 10 * 5 \ \longrightarrow \ 50
\end{aligned}
$$

First, the values of the operator f and the operand (2+3) are evaluated. Note that the value of f is a function expression. Next, the function application is computed by substituting 5 for all occurrences of x in the formula $2 * x * x$, and, finally, the value 50 can be computed.

Exercises

4.2. What are the types of **fn** $x \ => \ pi * x$ and **fn** $x \ => \ real \ x$?

4.3. Reduce by hand $f(f \ 345)$, where f is bound to **fn** $x \ => \ x \ div \ 10$.

4.3 Using Functions to Define Functions

When you define a function, you can use other functions. When you start, you can use the standard functions, but later also the functions you have defined yourself. In fact, ML programs often consist of a number of function declarations, most of which use the other functions.

Rounding real numbers

Given a real number, the *floor* function yields the biggest integer smaller than the number. In most cases you prefer having a function *round* that yields the closest integer instead. We assume that numbers like 1.5 and 2.5 are rounded upwards. Can you define *round*??

We can use the *floor* function simply by first adding 0.5 to the number to be rounded.

>   −   **fun** *round x* = *floor*(*x* + 0.5);
>   >   **val** *round* = **fn** : *real* −> *int*

>   −   *round* 1.6;
>   2 : *int*

>   −   *floor* 1.6;
>   1 : *int*

Note that, in this way, all numbers exactly between two integers will be rounded upwards[2].

Some trigonometrical functions

In ML the sine, cosine, and arcus tangent functions are standard. From some handbook of mathematical formulas you can find suitable definitions of other trigonometric functions, for instance, the cotangent function.

>   −   **fun** *cotan x* = *cos x*/*sin x*;
>   >   **val** *cotan* = **fn** : *real* −> *real*

The sine function has the value zero for some arguments and the cotangent function should therefore raise an exception for such arguments.

>   −   *cotan* 0.0;
>   Failure : /

The arcus sine function can be defined in terms of the arcus tangent function.

>   −   **fun** *arcsin x* = *arctan*(*x*/*sqrt*(1.0 − *x* * *x*));
>   >   **val** *arcsin* = **fn** : *real* −> *real*

The trigonometric functions all work with angles given in radians and not in degrees. Let us a define a version of sine working with degrees instead of radians.

>   −   **fun** *sin360 x* = *sin*(*x* * 2.0 * *pi*/360.0);
>   >   **val** *sin360* = **fn** : *real* −> *real*

>   −   *sin360* 90.0;
>   0.9999999999999998 : *real*

---

[2]Some conventions state that in half of the cases you should round downwards, for instance, for numbers with even integer part.

Logarithms and exponentials

The standard functions *ln* and *exp* both have *e* (2.71828...) as base. Using them you can define functions having 10 as base.

> — **fun** *ln10* *x* = *ln* *x*/*ln* 10.0;
> > **val** *ln10* = **fn** : *real* —> *real*

> — **fun** *exp10* *x* = *exp*(*x* ∗ *ln* 10.0);
> > **val** *exp10* = **fn** : *real* —> *real*

As you see, you can use functions to define other functions and in that way get a useful collection of functions. Those you suspect may be of frequent use can be included in a library of functions for later use.

Composing functions

In ML, the predefined functions and operators constitute our tool box. Normally, you use several of them to get a result. To *compose* two functions, you apply one of them to the result of applying the other to some argument.

$$abs(cube(\tilde{\ }3)) \longrightarrow abs(\tilde{\ }27) \longrightarrow 27$$

The operators in an expression containing more than one operator are similarly computed in sequence.

$$2 ∗ 3 ∗ 4 \ div \ 6 \longrightarrow 6 ∗ 4 \ div \ 6 \longrightarrow 24 \ div \ 6 \longrightarrow 4$$

Now, suppose you want to compute the area of a circle and then round the result. We have already defined a function *area* for computing the area of a circle and *round* for rounding real numbers. We can now compose them.

> — **fun** *rounded_area* *r* = *round*(*area* *r*);
> > **val** *rounded_area* = **fn** : *real* —> *int*

> — *rounded_area* 2.0;
> > 13 : *int*

The normal way of executing a program is to perform operations sequentially, which you do by composing functions and operators in ML. For most computations, however, you also need means for expressing choices and repetitions.

4.4 Type Constraints

Types play an important role in ML. Much more will be said about them later, but you need some knowledge of types to be able to continue.

Type checking

Before evaluating an expression, the system checks that the types of its subparts fit together.

        — $2 * 1.5$;
        Type Clash in: $(2 * 1.5)$
        Looking for a: int
        I have found a: $real$

To perform the type checking, the system deduces the types of all subparts starting with atomic parts like numerals, standard operators, functions, and other names, whose types are already known. It then derives the types of bigger and bigger subexpressions, until the type of the whole expression is derived. This activity is called *type deduction*. In ML, the user therefore seldom has to inform the system about the intended types of new objects; the system can still perform a complete type check. If subparts have conflicting types, the expression contains a type error, and an error message is printed. The type checker in the ML-system is a valuable help for the programmer, since it catches many programming errors.

Type constraints

For some legal expressions, the type checker cannot deduce the type, however. Instead, the user must provide some type information. Suppose you want to define a function that squares its argument. Your first suggestion is probably

        —   **fun** sq $x = x * x$;
        Unresolvable overloaded identifier: x
        Definition cannot be found for the type: $('a * 'a) \rightarrow 'a$

The problem is that the type checker cannot tell if the argument is to be of integer or real type. The solution is to tell the system about your intention.

        —   **fun** sq $x : int = x * x$;
        >   **val** $sq = $ **fn** $: int \rightarrow int$

The meaning of the type constraint $: int$ is that the *result* of the function is to be an integer. If you want to tell the system that the *argument* is to be an integer, you have to indicate this with parentheses.

        —   **fun** sq $(x : int) = x * x$;
        >   **val** $sq = $ **fn** $: int \rightarrow int$

Note that the type checker can deduce the type also of the function. You can, in fact, inform the system about the type of the argument by replacing one of the x's on the right-hand side by $(x : int)$.

```
  —  fun sq x = x * (x : int);
  >  val sq = fn : int -> int
```

A further alternative is to constrain the type of the whole right-hand side.

```
  —  fun sq x = x * x : int;
  >  val sq = fn : int -> int
```

The rule is that you can replace any expression by the expression followed by a colon and its type. Since type constraints bind very weakly, you usually have to surround them by parentheses.

Most often you do not have to think about type constraints. In the beginning, you may wait until the system complains and then insert a type constraint at some appropriate place. However, it is good programming practice to derive by hand the type of each function you define, before you give the definition to the system.

Integer and real versions of functions

If, in addition to the function squaring integers, you also want a function for squaring reals, you cannot use the same name—a name can only mean one thing at a time. To make it easier to remember names, we introduce a *naming convention* and add the suffix $'i$ (for *int*) and $'r$ (for *real*) after the function name.

```
  —  fun sq'i x : int = x * x;
  >  val sq'i = fn : int -> int
```

```
  —  fun sq'r x : real = x * x;
  >  val sq'r = fn : real -> real
```

Normally, we also define the name without the suffix for the case we expect to occur most frequently (cf. Appendix D).

```
  —  val sq = sq'i;
  >  val sq = fn : int -> int
```

There is one exception to the rule that functions cannot be used both for reals and integers: the standard function *abs*. Similarly, most operators can be used both for integers and reals[3].

---

[3]Some functional languages use the type *num* containing both integers and reals, which simplifies matters a great deal.

Summary

A *function* is a mapping (transformation) from a set of objects, its *domain*, to another set of objects, its *range*. The *graph* of a function is the set of individual input-output pairs. A requirement on a function is that for each input there is a *unique* output. A formula describes a whole class of computations. With *procedural abstraction*, you abstract from the individual computations and look only at the method (the algorithm) itself. A function can be *implemented* (realized) using different computation methods (algorithms, procedures, routines). With *functional abstraction*, you abstract from details about how to compute function values. Functions can be described by (*canonical*) *function expressions* of form **fn** ID => EXPR, where ID is the parameter and EXPR an expression (formula). Functions can be named in value or *function declarations*. Functions are used by *applying* them to arguments. Most computations are the result of *composing* several functions.

Exercises

4.4.   Define a function *double* that calculates the number of years it takes for an amount of money to double at a certain interest. For instance, *double* 100 should give the result 1. Use, for example, the *ln* function. (You need some knowledge of mathematics to solve this problem.)

Chapter 5

Systematic Program Construction

To become a good programmer you must not only learn a programming language; you must learn how to use it to write good programs for a variety of programming tasks. Experience has shown that except for small problems, programming is an intellectually challenging activity that requires both talent, knowledge, and carefulness. By learning good methods you can improve your programming capability, but, since programming is a form of problem solving, there will always be an important part of the programming activity that depends on the skill of the programmer.

If you have little programming experience, parts of this chapter may be difficult to grasp in full detail on your first reading, and it may be advisable to read it once more when you have more experience. Try, however, to work systematically from the beginning.

5.1   Specifying the Problem

Let us look at a typical problem, a puzzle.

> Given twelve marbles, one of which differs in weight, find in three weighings with a common balance which of the marbles that differs and whether it is lighter or heavier than the others!!

A solution to this problem is a *method* for deciding which marble differs and how it differs from the others. What you need is an *algorithm* for performing the weighings.

> A problem is a description of *what* you want, and a solution is a description of *how* to achieve it.

Programming problems

A programming problem is similar to other problems. Its solution is a program, an algorithm. Hence, programming is a form of problem solving.

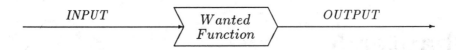

Some programming problems are easy, and you never really think of them as problems. Most programming problems, however, require thought—often much thought. There are two primary sources of difficulty. One is that it may be difficult to find a suitable method for the problem or some subproblem. The other is to master the complexity of a large problem: each subproblem may be simple, but putting the solutions together in a good way can be difficult.

Problem solving versus computation

Suppose you want to add all numbers between 1 and 1000. One method is to add all the thousand numbers, a method that is very time-consuming. Another method is to evaluate the expression $1000 * (1000 + 1)/2$, which gives the desired sum. To find the last solution takes some time; you have to solve a problem. Once found, however, the computation is simple.

Problem solving and computation are very different activities. Problem solving is a creative activity for which it is difficult to give precise rules. A computation is mechanical in character: it follows a given set of rules in a slavish manner. This is the reason why computers are excellent for doing computations, but bad at solving problems. Now, you can say, adding all numbers from 1 to 10000000 using the first method is really a problem for a person. This is true in one sense, but the problem is of a different character—had you only patience and time you would be able to do it without any really creative thinking.

Specifications

Before you start solving a problem, you have to to describe it in a precise way. There are several reasons. The obvious one is that you have to know what to solve—it is easy to forget some aspects of the problem. Another is that in this way you get a good knowledge of the problem, which you need when you solve it. A third is that the description can serve as a documentation of what your program is supposed to solve.

A precise description of a problem is usually called a *specification*. You can write it in a natural language, but it is difficult to make such specifications both precise and readable. Therefore, you often use some mathematical notation. It is beyond the scope of this book to show a complete specification language. However, we can use equations to capture many requirements on the program. In addition, such equations may start you on the way to a solution. After all, equations of a particular form are used to define functions in ML.

A specification must contain three parts: the domain, the range, and the condition relating the input and output. For instance, the domain for the square root function is the non-negative reals, and so is the range. It is specified by the equation $sqrt(x) * sqrt(x) = x$, which relates the argument x to the result $sqrt(x)$.

The domain of the absolute value function abs is the real numbers and its range the non-negative reals. To relate the input and output, you use two *conditional* equations.

$$abs(x) = \begin{cases} x & \text{if } x \geq 0 \\ -x & \text{if } x < 0 \end{cases}$$

The specification is split into two *cases*.

The factorial of a positive integer n is the product of all numbers between 1 and n. The factorial of 0 is usually defined to be 1. It is undefined for negative integers. We can specify *fac* by two equations

$$fac\,(0) = 1$$
$$fac\,(n) = 1 * 2 * \cdots * n \qquad \text{for all } n > 0$$

We here use the three dots to indicate the multiplication of a sequence of numbers. The dots are a helpful tool when you want to specify the *repetition* of some operation. Another, slightly more difficult, way to describe repetition is to use *recursion*.

$$fac\,(0) = 1$$
$$fac\,(n) = n * fac\,(n-1) \qquad \text{for all } n > 0$$

The function is now defined in terms of itself; it is recursive.

It is important to work with the specification so much that you are convinced that it specifies what you want, that all aspects are specified, and that no parts of it are contradictory. In this way you are much better prepared for the construction of a program satisfying the specification. If you start programming too early, you may solve the wrong problem or solve the problem in the wrong way. To convince yourself that a specification expresses your intention is usually called **validation**. Validation is by necessity an informal activity, since you check your specification against ideas in your head.

5.2   Top-down Design

Having completed the specification, the next step is to find a function that solves the specified problem. You can then use a method called top-down design.

For most problems, there is no predefined function that solves your problem directly; you have to define a new function. When defining this function, you can use all predefined functions. Most of the time, however, you also need some auxiliary functions that solve subproblems. A good way to work is to *assume* that these auxiliary functions are already defined and define your main function under this assumption. When the main function is completed, you continue to define the auxiliary functions. Again, you may need new auxiliary functions, and again you assume that these are already defined. Proceeding in this manner, you must finally reach a stage at which all functions are defined in terms of the predefined ones. This way of working is sometimes also called *step-wise refinement*.

Example: The volume of a sphere computed to two decimals

Let us define a function that computes the volume of a sphere with a given radius such that the result is given with two, correctly rounded, decimals. We can visualize the problem in a diagram.

A first version of a program diagram for the volume program.

The diagram is a short description of the problem, a *partial specification*. Our task is now to specify the three named entities in the diagram. The *RADIUS* of a sphere is any non-negative real number and so is its volume. The volume of a sphere is given by the formula $vol = \frac{4}{3}\pi r^3$, which can be found in a mathematics book. According to the informal description, the result is to be rounded to two correct decimals. If the third decimal is less than five, you truncate the result to two decimals. If it is greater than or equal to five, you add 0.01 before truncation.

A good habit is to pay extra attention to the special cases. To avoid overflow, the radius must be such that the corresponding volume does not exceed the largest real number that can be represented; the exact limit depends on the ML-system you use. Hence, the radius r must satisfy the condition $\frac{4}{3}\pi r^3 \leq maxreal$. It should also be noted that for large spheres, the integer part of the volume will be so big, that the computer cannot keep track of the decimals; the computer may, for instance, compute only with sixteen significant digits.

Refinement of input and output

In the diagram, the input and output are described in everyday terms. Our next step is to choose a suitable representation for them. The domain and the range are the non-negative reals, so we choose the type *real* both as argument and result type.

After each refinement in a top-down design you have to investigate if the goal is reached. If there were a suitable function *vol_2dec* in ML you could stop here. There is no such function, however, so you have to continue. Can you think of any way of splitting the problem of defining *vol_2dec* into some simpler problems??

Sequential decomposition

Looking at the condition in the specification, there seem to be two subproblems to the given problem: to compute the volume and to do the correct rounding. It is also clear that you should compute the volume before rounding. Let us therefore *assume* that there exists a function *vol* for computing the volume of a sphere and a function *round2* that performs the correct rounding. We can show the refinement in a diagram.

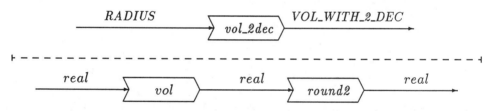

The first refinement of *vol_2dec* and the input and output.

The dotted line indicates that the lower part of the diagram is a *refinement* of the upper part. Since the refinement consists of two functions to be executed sequentially, we call this refinement a *sequential decomposition*. It is a very common problem solving technique, which we will use many times. We can now define *vol_2dec*.

```
-  fun vol_2dec r = round2(vol r);
>  val vol_2dec = fn : real -> real
```

Now, both *vol* and *round2* have to be defined. The specification of *vol*, which is a formula, is executable, so we can use it directly.

```
-  fun vol r = 4.0 * pi * r * r * r/3.0;
>  val vol = fn : real -> real
```

Now, we have arrived at a function that is completely defined—only predefined operators and constants are used. Next, we have to refine *round2*. One method for rounding to two decimals is to multiply by 100, truncate the decimals, and divide by 100.

>   − **fun** *round2 x* = *real*(*round*(*x* ∗ 100.0))/100.0 ;
>   > **val** *round2* = **fn** : *real* −> *real*

Now, all function definitions are elaborated.

Is the solution correct?

One way of checking a program is to act as a computer and *execute* the program *by hand* for some inputs. At the same time you examine each part of the program to see if it works for all possible combinations of input data. The primary purpose of execution by hand is not to check that you get the right result—you can use the computer for that—but to think about each part of the program and check that it works correctly. Another way to understand a program better is to leave it for a while and then look at it again. Many times, you will find that you understand the problem and its suggested solution better: your brain has put things in place in the meantime. Let us go back to *round2*.

>   − **fun** *round2 x* = *real*(*round*(*x* ∗ 100.0))/100.0 ;
>   > **val** *round2* = **fn** : *real* −> *real*

The first computation is described by the expression $x \ast 100.0$. You have to ask yourself questions like "Does it work for all x's?", "Can overflow occur?", "Does it work for zero and for negative numbers?", "Are there any numbers it does not work for?", and so on. Act as if someone else had written the program and you can bet that you can find an error.

The specification of our problem allows any radius giving a result less than *maxreal*. Since the result is multiplied by 100 by *round2*, our solution is not satisfactory; we must look for a better realization. Can you find one??

You can split a real number x into its integer part with the expression $floor(x)$ and its decimal part with $x - real(floor\ x)$. You can then use the previous method on the decimal part, and afterwards add the integer part to the rounded decimal part.

>   − **fun** *round2 x* =
>   *real*(*floor x*) + *real*(*round*(100.0 ∗ (x − *real*(*floor x*))))/100.0 ;
>   > **val** *round2* = **fn** : *real* −> *real*

For large volumes, you need a system with bigints, since *floor* converts a real number into an integer.

A complete program

Finally, we can write down the complete program. The program consists of four declarations.

> **val** pi = 3.1415927;
> **fun** $vol\ r$ = $4.0 * pi * r * r * r/3.0$;
> **fun** $round2\ x$ =
> $real(floor\ x) + real(round(100.0 * (x - real(floor\ x))))/100.0$;
> **fun** $vol\_2dec\ r$ = $round2(vol\ r)$;

Note that you always have to define a constant or a function before it is used. Also note that an ML program is a sequence of declarations. If you give this program to your ML-system, the four new names will become bound and, henceforth, you can work in an extended environment.

> $-$ vol_2dec 2.0 ;
>   33.51 : $real$

5.3 Program Verification

A **correct** program is a program that satisfies its specification. A correct program does not necessarily do what you want, since the specification might express something other than what you intend. If the specification is validated, however, there is good hope that the program solves the problem. To know that a program is correct, you have to *verify its correctness* in some way. The more rigorous proof you give, the more certain you can be of its correctness. A program that satisfies its specification is often said to be an **implementation** of the specification.

Let us return to the *sum1to* function. It can be specified by the equation $sum1to(n) = 1 + 2 + \cdots + n$. The traditional way of verifying a program is to test it. Suppose, you define an implementation by $sum1to(n) = n\ div\ 2 * (n + 1)$. By testing you find that it gives the same result as the specification for 0, for 2, for 10, and for 1000. Is it correct??

Testing can only show the presence of errors, never their absence. In fact, the given solution works for even, but not for odd, numbers. Testing is therefore not a sufficient method for verification unless you can test all cases, but that is seldom possible, since there are too many cases.

The alternative to test a program is to *prove* that it works for all possible inputs. A simple proof of the correctness of the formula can be derived from the following table, where the third line is obtained by adding the elements above.

$$
\begin{array}{ccccccccc}
1 & + & 2 & + & \ldots & + & (n-1) & + & n \\
n & + & (n-1) & + & \ldots & + & 2 & + & 1 \\
(n+1) & + & (n+1) & + & \ldots & + & (n+1) & + & (n+1)
\end{array}
$$

If S is the sum, then, obviously, $2 * S = n * (n + 1)$, since there are n terms on the last row. Hence, $S = n * (n + 1)$ *div* 2. We can use integer division, since either n or $n + 1$ must be even. If n is zero, the formula yields zero, which is also the sum of all numbers from one to zero. This completes the proof that the formula satisfies the specification for all non-negative numbers n.

Proving programs correct

When proving a theorem in mathematics, the proof usually deals with one single fact only—all unnecessary details have been eliminated. A program often contains a lot of non-controversial details. Correctness proofs of programs therefore tend to be long and boring, and it is unlikely that programmers will have the patience to perform such proofs. The boring details of the proof can probably be taken over by the computer, and many researchers try to construct proof systems in which the programmer performs the crucial parts only; they are often just a minor part of the whole proof. More research is still needed to make such systems practically useful, though.

A reasonable approach today is to prove the crucial parts of the program using informal methods. There is good evidence that this will make the total time spent on the program shorter. A programmer who knows how to prove a program correct has good help of this knowledge when writing a program, even if he does not prove it. For some programs in this book, informal proofs will be given.

Exercises

5.1. Which of the following sentences are false? Explain why!

1. Some programs can be proved by testing.
2. A correct program can be trusted.
3. A program that meets its specification does what you expect it to do.

5.4   Running the Program

The next step in the program development is to run the program on the computer. It is tempting to type a program in before you have examined it carefully and tried to verify it in various ways. Try to avoid that!

5.4.1   Error messages

You are not completely without a safety net when you test your program; the ML system can find errors for you. Most of them may be of a clerical nature, but bad thinking sometimes results in a program that breaks the language rules. In particular, the type system of ML helps you to find some logical errors. By and large, however, the system cannot correct logical errors. If the method you have invented does not solve your problem, the system can do nothing about it.

The ML-system reports about three types of error: *syntactical* errors, *type* errors, and *run-time (execution)* errors. The error messages you get may vary from system to system.

Syntax errors

If you break the syntax rules, which give the allowed forms of programs, you get a syntax error. One example is that you write − instead of ˜.

    −   −3 + 4;
    Parse error:
         Was expecting   ";"
    In: ... <? > −

Another common example is the presence of an unmatched parenthesis.

    −   round(sqrt(100.0)));
    Parse error:
         Was expecting   ";"
    In: ... round (sqrt (100.0)) < ? >)

The question mark shows the point where the error was detected.

If there is a missing parenthesis in your program, the system prints an equal sign telling that the program is not complete. If you type another semicolon, you will get the error message.

    −   round(sqrt(100.0);
    =   ;
    Parse error:
         Insufficient repetition
    In: ... round (sqrt (100.0) ; < ? > ;

Sometimes the cause of an error is not at the same place as where the error is detected. If you cannot detect the error where the system claims it should be, look at the earlier parts of your program to see if the cause can be found there. Very rarely, an error depends on an error in the system.

Type errors

A typical example of a type error is that you mix integers and reals.

```
–   2 + 3.5;
Type Clash in:      2 + 3.5
Looking for a:      int
I have found a:     real
```

Sometimes, type error messages can be difficult to interpret. By simulating how the system itself deduces types, you can be guided in your search for the error. A good habit is to derive the type of every expression, before you type it in. It is a good complement to other methods of verifying programs.

Run-time errors

When you work in an interactive environment, you cannot see any sharp border-line between translation and checking on the one hand and execution on the other. However, a program is not run if there are syntax and type errors in it. The cause of a run-time error is that you try to execute an operation with an illegal argument.

```
–   3 div 0;
Failure : div
```

Overflow and an attempt to take the square root of a negative number are other examples that cause execution errors.

5.4.2   Testing and debugging

When you test your program, you may get a result that is not what you want—there is a logical error in your program. Such errors are often called *bugs*, and the search for them *debugging*. To find all errors, try to select test cases that test all situations that can occur. In particular, do not forget the special cases!

Random debugging

When you find an error it is tempting to give way to the first thought for removing the bug that comes to your mind. That is a dangerous working habit. You then skip all the previous steps in the program development. In this way you may correct some symptom of the error and not its cause. Of course, if you had planned to write, for instance, 8.6 and wrote 6.8, you can correct it immediately. Most of the time, however, you will save time by leaving the terminal and repeat the steps described above.

5.4.3   Inserting and editing programs

In some ML systems there is an editor to be used for changing programs. In other systems, you keep your program in a file and use a separate text editor to change it. With the *use* command, you can read a number of files containing declarations and expressions.

$$use[\text{"pgm1.ml"}, \text{"pgm2.ml"}];$$

Now suppose you discover an error in the file *pgm1.ml*, change it with your text editor, and read the file with the *use* command again. To your surprise you may find that the error is still there. The reason is that the declarations in *pgm2.ml* still uses the old definitions; you have to read *pgm2.ml* as well again.

Summary

Let us list the main steps you go through in a systematic program construction.

Specification: Specify the domain, the range, and the condition between the input and output. Make use of equations.

Validation: Investigate every part of the specification to see that it is complete, that it is free from contradictions, and that it agrees with what you intend.

Refinement of input and output: For every function, decide how to represent the input and output using the data types available in ML.

Top-down design: Work top-down and assume that required auxiliary functions are available when you solve the main problem. Later, define the auxiliary functions, perhaps with the aid of further auxiliary functions.

Verification: Try to convince yourself in various ways that your program meets the specification by using program proving, hand execution, type deduction, and similar methods.

Testing: Test your program systematically. Run it on inputs representing all typical cases that can occur. Do not forget the special cases!

Chapter 6

Truth Values

To split a problem into several cases is a common problem solving technique. It is called *decomposition into cases* or *case analysis*. The corresponding action in the solution to the problem is a *choice* between two actions. To handle choices in programs, we need data objects that can describe the outcome of a test, that is, that can be true or false.

Choices in mathematics

Many problems are best specified by a set of conditional equations, that is, equations that must be true only if some condition holds. Most often, the corresponding function contains tests, after which one of several computations is chosen. The *abs* function is defined with two equations:

$$abs(x) = \begin{cases} x & \text{if } x \geq 0 \\ \tilde{}x & \text{if } x < 0 \end{cases}$$

Another example of case analysis is present in the *signum* function:

$$signum(x) = \begin{cases} 1 & \text{if } x > 0 \\ 0 & \text{if } x = 0 \\ \tilde{}1 & \text{if } x < 0 \end{cases}$$

This function yields the result 1 for positive arguments, 0 for the argument 0, and ~1 for negative arguments; function evaluation is split into three cases.

6.1 Boolean Values and Expressions

Comparison operators

To implement the *abs* or *signum* function specified above, you need operators for comparing numbers. In ML, there are six *comparison* operators, also called

70

relational operators:

=	equal	<	less than	<=	less than or equal to
<>	not equal	>	greater than	>=	greater than or equal to

Some of them like <= use two characters; in mathematics it is usually written as
≤. These operators are defined both for integers and reals (and, in fact, also for
strings of characters). They are all binary operators. The question now is what
the result of a comparison like $2 < 3$ is in ML.

True and false

A statement like $x < y$ can be either true or false. In ML, there are two data objects
true and *false*, and their type is called *bool* after the mathematician George Boole
(1815-1864). The data objects are also said to be *boolean* values or *truth* values.

> − $3 + 4 = 4 + 3$;
> *true* : *bool*

> − $1.2 > 2.1$;
> *false* : *bool*

The words *true* and *false* are data objects—symbols—which can be used to represent real situations that can be in one of two states: married or not married, man
or woman, negative or non-negative, and so on. Compare this with the usage of
numbers, which represent properties like length and weight.

6.1.1   Conditional expressions

To implement the given specification of *abs*, we use a conditional expression.

> − **fun** *abs* x = **if** $x >= 0$ **then** x **else** ~x ;
> > **val** *abs* = **fn** : *int* −> *int*

The conditional expression is written using the three reserved words **if, then,** and
else, each followed by an expression. The value of the first expression must be a
truth value, a boolean value. The other two expressions can have any type, but
they must have the *same* type. Note that the system is able to deduce the type of
abs by using the fact that 0 is an integer numeral. We can now use *abs*.

> − $abs(3 - 7)$;
> 4 : *int*

The function *abs* is standard in ML. If you redefine it in this way, you can no
longer get the old definition back without restarting the system.

    — *abs*(~3.0);

Type Clash in:	*abs*(~3.0)
Looking for a:	*int*
I have found a:	*real*

The standard function *abs* is defined for both reals and integers, but our version is not, and there is no way in ML for the user to define such functions.

Reduction of conditional expressions

To make clear how a conditional expression is computed, let us follow a computation in detail. We assume that x is bound to ~3.

        if x >= 0 **then** x **else** ~x $\longrightarrow$
        if ~3 >= 0 **then** x **else** ~x $\longrightarrow$
        if *false* **then** x **else** ~x $\longrightarrow$
        ~x $\longrightarrow$ ~(~3) $\longrightarrow$ 3

The general rule for reducing a conditional expression **if** B **then** E$_1$ **else** E$_2$ is:

1. Evaluate B.
2. If the value of B is *true*, the value of the conditional expression is the value of E$_1$, otherwise it is the value of E$_2$.

Note that only one of E$_1$ and E$_2$ is evaluated.

6.1.2 Indentation

A program should always be written to be as readable as possible. The definition of *abs* is small and readable the way it is. In most programs, however, conditional expressions are best written on several lines. The splitting can be done in several ways. We will often use a version where the three expressions appear on lines of their own.

    — **fun** *abs* x = **if** x >= 0
                      then x
                      else ~x;
   > **val** .*abs* = **fn** : *int* $\rightarrow$ *int*

The reserved words **then** and **else** are written aligned under **if**. To let the lines start to the right of the left margin is called indentation. An alternative indentation is to combine the two first lines.

    — **fun** *abs* x = **if** x >= 0 **then** x
                         else ~x;
   > **val** *abs* = **fn** : *int* $\rightarrow$ *int*

The idea of indentation is to make clear the structure of an expression, thereby producing a more readable program. It is common practice to use indentation in all programs.

Encapsulated expressions

The function *signum* is defined with three cases, but conditional expressions allow only two alternatives. A train switch also allows only two outgoing tracks, but using two consecutive switches you get three outgoing tracks. We use the same idea for *signum*.

> ```
> -   fun signum x  =  if x > 0
>                      then 1
>                      else  if x = 0
>                            then 0
>                            else ~1;
> > val signum  =  fn  :  int -> int
> ```

An expression that occurs within another expression is said to be encapsulated or *nested*. You have, in fact, encountered encapsulated expressions several times: the expression $2 + 3$ is encapsulated in $7 * (2 + 3)$, for instance. An alternative indentation is

> ```
> -   fun signum x  =  if x > 0 then 1
>                      else if x = 0 then 0
>                      else ~1;
> > val signum  =  fn  :  int -> int
> ```

Indentation is nothing that is described in a programming language definition—it is just a convention or agreement. The form of indentation should be chosen to optimize readability. It is also important that one consequent choice is made.

6.1.3   Boolean functions

A function can yield a truth value as result. Such a function is sometimes called a *predicate*. Let us define a predicate *negative* that checks if a number is negative.

> ```
> -   fun negative x  =  x < 0;
> > val negative  =  fn  :  int -> bool
> ```

The body of the function is a relational expression, and the result of the function is therefore of type *bool*; the function is a boolean function.

> ```
> -   negative(~3);
>     true : bool
> ```

Many beginners define functions like *negative* using a conditional expression.

> — **fun** *negative x* = **if** *x* < 0
>   **then** *true*
>   **else** *false*;
> > **val** *negative* = **fn** : *int* −> *bool*

It is not an error, but it is saying the same thing twice. In fact, you can always write a boolean function without a conditional expression at the top-level, as you will soon see.

Let us next define a function *even* testing if an integer is even, that is, divisible by 2. The value of *n mod* 2 is the remainder you get when you divide *n* by 2. If the remainder is zero the number is even, otherwise it is odd.

> — **fun** *even n* = *n mod* 2 = 0;
> > **val** *even* = **fn** : *int* −> *bool*

Note how the equals sign is used for two different purposes.

6.1.4   Equality operations

The equality operator = and the inequality operator <> are defined for almost all types of data objects in ML, functions being an important exception. You have to be cautious when you use an equality operator on real numbers, however, as the following example shows.

> — *sqrt* 10.0 ∗ *sqrt* 10.0;
> 10.0 : *real*

The square root of a number multiplied with itself should give the original number as a result. We therefore expect the following equality to be *true*.

> — *sqrt* 10.0 ∗ *sqrt* 10.0 = 10.0;
> *false* : *bool*

Surprisingly, the result is *false* and the reason can be seen if you subtract the right-hand side from the left-hand side.

> — *sqrt* 10.0 ∗ *sqrt* 10.0 − 10.0;
> 2.220446049250313E~16 : *real*

The ML system can compute only an approximation to the square root of ten. The value of *sqrt* 10.0 ∗ *sqrt* 10.0 is therefore not exactly 10.0, even though the system prints 10.0; the least significant digits are ignored by the print routine in the system.

An equality operator for real numbers

The equality operator $=$ is therefore unsuitable for real numbers. Usually, you want to consider two real numbers as equal if they are sufficiently close each other. You cannot just test if their difference is less than a small number, because when comparing two very small numbers, you want the difference to be smaller than when comparing two big numbers. You may want to consider 10000000000000.1 and 10000000000000.2 as equal but not 1.1 and 1.2—their difference is the same, though. You want to compare the *relative* magnitude of the numbers, not their *absolute* magnitude. In ML you can define a suitable operator for testing equality of real numbers and in Appendix D the operator $==$ is defined for this purpose.

> — $sqrt\ 10.0 * sqrt\ 10.0 == 10.0$;
> $true : bool$

Let us now define a function *integer* that tests if a real number is a close approximation to an integer. Can you define it??

The function *round* gives the nearest integer of a real number. If x is close to *round* x we consider x as an "integer".

> — **fun** $integer\ x = x == real(round\ x)$;
> \> **val** $integer =$ **fn** $:\ real\ ->\ bool$
>
> — $integer(sqrt\ 25.0)$;
> $true : bool$

Equality of functions

You may wonder why you cannot test if two functions are equal. Consider, however, the two function expressions **fn** $x => 2 * x$ and **fn** $x => x + x$. They obviously define the same function, but they use different methods. In general, there are many, very different, ways of defining the same function. An important result from the theory of computability states that you cannot define a function that decides if two function definitions describe the same function. Hence, there is no possibility to let the ML system decide if two functions are equal.

Exercises

6.1. Define a function *odd* that tests if an integer is odd (not even).

6.2. Define a function *invert* that given a real number x gives the result $1/x$. If the argument is 0, the result of the function shall be *maxreal*.

6.3. Define a function *anniversary* that tests if 10 is a factor of a given age.

6.4. Define a function *issquare* that tests if a positive integer is equal to the square of some integer.

6.2   Boolean Expressions

In an arithmetic expression like $2 + 3$ both the operands and the result are arithmetic. In a relational expression like $2 < 3$ the operands are arithmetic and the result is boolean. In a boolean expression, both the operands and the result are boolean.

Conjunctions

Suppose you want a function *digit* that tests if an integer is one of the ten numbers 0 through 9. Thus, an integer n is a digit if $0 \leq n$ *and* $n < 10$, which is expressed by the *conjunction* expression in ML.

```
–   fun  digit n  =  0 <= n andalso n < 10;
>   val  digit  =  fn  :  int –> bool

–   digit(~7);
    false : bool
```

A conjunction expression consists of two boolean expressions separated by the reserved word **andalso**. It is true if both its subexpressions are true. In mathematics, the *digit* condition is often written $0 \leq n < 10$, but in ML you have to split the condition into its two parts. The meaning of the mathematical form is, of course, exactly the same—it is just a shorthand notation.

A conjunction can contain more than two subexpressions. Suppose you need a function *div345* that tests if a given number is divisible by 3, 4, and 5.

```
–   fun  div345 n  =  n mod 3 = 0 andalso
                      n mod 4 = 0 andalso
                      n mod 5 = 0;
>   val  div345  =  fn  :  int –> bool

–   div345 60;
    true : bool
```

Disjunctions

In Exercise 6.3 you defined a function *anniversary* that tests if 10 is a factor of a given number. Suppose you want to consider multiples of 25 to be particular events, too. You can do that with the *disjunction* expression in ML.

```
–   fun  anniversary age  =  age mod 10 = 0 orelse age mod 25 = 0;
>   val  anniversary  =  fn  :  int –> bool
```

A disjunction expression consists of two boolean expressions separated by the
reserved word **orelse**. It is true if *at least one* of the subexpressions is true.

> — *anniversary* 75;   One condition is true
> *true* : *bool*

> — *anniversary* 50;   Both conditions are true
> *true* : *bool*

A conjunction or disjunction can be used also in a conditional expression. Suppose
you want the function *anniversary* to return the age if the condition is satisfied
and −1 otherwise.

> — **fun** *anniversary' age* = **if** *age mod* 10 = 0 **orelse** *age mod* 25 = 0
>   **then** *age*
>   **else** ˜1;
> > **val** *anniversary'* = **fn** : *int* −> *int*

> — *anniversary'* 35;
> ˜1 : *int*

Note that the first version of *anniversary* yields a boolean result and, therefore,
can be defined without a conditional expression. Conversely, a conjunction and
disjunction can always be rewritten using a conditional expression but, as a rule,
you should not do that.

Negations

The two functions *even* and *odd* decide whether an integer is even or odd. Since
an integer is odd if it is not even, you should be able to define *odd* using *even*. In
ML, you use the standard function *not* to negate a truth value.

> — **fun** *odd n* = *not*(*even n*);
> > **val** *odd* = **fn** : *int* −> *bool*

A negation is *true* if its argument is *false* and vice versa. Let us reduce *odd* 3.

> *odd* 3 ⟶ *not*(*even* 3) ⟶ *not*(3 *mod* 2 = 0) ⟶
> *not*(1 = 0) ⟶ *not*(*false*) ⟶ *true*

6.2.1   Truth tables

To describe boolean operations, truth tables are often used. In a truth table you give the value of an operation for all possible arguments. This is possible only when there is a finite number of possible arguments—a corresponding table for an arithmetic operation is infinite since there are infinitely many numbers.

$b1$	$b2$	$b1$ and $b2$	$b1$ or $b2$	not $b2$
false	*false*	*false*	*false*	*true*
false	*true*	*false*	*true*	*false*
true	*false*	*false*	*true*	
true	*true*	*true*	*true*	

A useful result about these operations is de Morgan's laws:

$$b1 \ \ and \ \ b2 = not(not \ \ b1 \ \ or \ \ not \ \ b2)$$
$$b1 \ \ or \ \ b2 = not(not \ \ b1 \ \ and \ \ not \ \ b2)$$

It is common that facts about boolean operations come in pairs; you talk about the *duality* principle.

Exercises

6.5.   Define *anniversary* without a disjunction expression.

6.6.   Verify de Morgan's laws using truth tables.

6.2.2   Precedences revisited

In arithmetic, $*$ has higher precedence than $+$. Similarly, a conjunction expression (with **andalso**) has higher precedence than a disjunction (with **orelse**). In fact, a conjunction is a "multiplicative" operation and disjunction an "additive" operation. Let us summarize the precedences of all operators you have seen so far.

```
~     not
*   /   div   mod
+   −
=   <>   <   >   <=   >=
andalso
orelse
```

The precedences are chosen so as to minimize the use of parentheses. For instance, no parentheses are needed in the expression $x + y < 10$ **andalso** $x <> y$. In the expression $(x + y) * z$ the parentheses cannot be omitted without changing the meaning of the expression. In a similar way, parentheses are sometimes needed in a boolean expression. Suppose you want *anniversary* to yield *false* also for the age zero. Thus, *anniversary* yields *true* when *age* is not zero and when *age* at the same time is divisible by 10 or 25. To define the function you can almost literally translate the preceding sentence!!

$$
\begin{aligned}
- \quad & \textbf{fun } anniversary'' \; age \; = \; age <> 0 \textbf{ andalso} \\
& \qquad\qquad (age \; mod \; 10 = 0 \textbf{ orelse} \\
& \qquad\qquad \; age \; mod \; 25 = 0); \\
> \quad & \textbf{val } anniversary'' \; = \; \textbf{fn} \; : \; int \; \text{--> } bool
\end{aligned}
$$

If you omit the parentheses the meaning of the function is changed, since **andalso** binds stronger than **orelse**.

Exercises

6.7. What is the meaning of *anniversary''* without parentheses?

6.8. Define a function *is_leapyear* that tests if a year is a multiple of 4. Then extend the definition to handle the fact that only centuries divisible by 4 are leap-years so, for instance, the year 2000 is a leap-year but 1900 and 2100 are not.

6.3 Lazy Evaluation

Let us return to the function *digit*.

$$
\begin{aligned}
- \quad & \textbf{fun } digit \; n \; = \; n >= 0 \textbf{ andalso } n < 10; \\
> \quad & \textbf{val } digit \; = \; \textbf{fn} \; : \; int \; \text{--> } bool
\end{aligned}
$$

Let us first look at how *digit* applied to 3 is computed.

$digit \; 3 \longrightarrow 3 >= 0 \textbf{ andalso } 3 < 10 \longrightarrow true \textbf{ andalso } 3 < 10 \longrightarrow$
$true \textbf{ andalso } true \longrightarrow true$

First, the left operand of **andalso** is computed and after that the right operand is computed. Next, let us look at how *digit* applied to ~3 is computed.

$digit \; \tilde{}3 \longrightarrow \tilde{}3 >= 0 \textbf{ andalso } \tilde{}3 < 10 \longrightarrow false \textbf{ andalso } \tilde{}3 < 10$

Let us stop at this stage. Do you have to compute the right operand?? Not really, since it does not matter if the right operand yields *true* or *false*, the result will still be *false*. An economical system could skip, or *short-circuit*, the evaluation of the right operand of **andalso**, if the value of the left operand is *false*. This computation strategy is a special case of a general strategy called *lazy evaluation*, in which you compute operands to functions and operators only if they are really needed. You also say that a *normal* evaluation order is used. In ML, the operands are normally computed whether you need them or not, which is called *strict* or *applicative* evaluation order; the exceptions are the boolean and conditional expressions.

Lazy evaluation is used not only to save computation time: in some cases strict and lazy evaluation give different results. Let us define *is_square* that tests if an integer is the square of some integer. Suppose that *sq* squares an integer.

> $-$ **fun** *is_square i* $=$ *sq(round(sqrt(real i)))* $= i$;
> $>$ **val** *is_square* $=$ **fn** : *int* $->$ *bool*

Note that *i* must be converted into a real number before *sqrt* can be used. Does this definition of *is_square* work for all integers??

If you try to apply *is_square* to a negative integer, the *sqrt* function will give a run-time error and the computation will stop. This is not in agreement with our specification: a negative integer is not the square of any integer, and the function should therefore give *false* as a result. To solve this problem, we have to assure that the argument is non-negative before we take the square root of it.

> $-$ **fun** *is_square i* $=$ $i >= 0$ **andalso** *sq(round(sqrt(real i)))* $= i$;
> $>$ **val** *is_square* $=$ **fn** : *int* $->$ *bool*

If *i* is less than zero, the left operand of the conjunction will have the value *false*. Since ML uses lazy evaluation for boolean expressions, the right operand will never be computed, and the result will be *false* as required. With strict evaluation, the right operand is always computed, and the computation will stop erroneously with a run-time error.

The conditional expression is also computed lazily. The condition is first evaluated and then one of the branches—the other is never evaluated. You can therefore define *is_square* with a conditional expression instead of a conjunction.

> $-$ **fun** *is_square i* $=$ **if** $i < 0$
>   **then** *false*
>   **else** *sq(round(sqrt(real i)))* $= i$;
> $>$ **val** *is_square* $=$ **fn** : *int* $->$ *bool*

6.4   Problem Decomposition and Case Analysis

Sequential decomposition is one way of decomposing a problem. The problem is then split into subproblems, whose solutions are composed sequentially. Some problems, however, cannot be decomposed in this way. The problem with marbles, for instance (page 59), requires an analysis of two cases: balance and unbalance. You have decomposed the problem into two subproblems. In each particular examination of marbles, only the solution to one of them will be used. The choice is based on the outcome of a test, a case analysis. When you solve each subproblem, you are allowed to use the knowledge of the outcome of the test. For instance, if you get balance in the first weighing, you know that one of the remaining marbles must be the one that differs. This problem solving method is called **decomposition into cases**: you split your original problem into a number of subproblems that can be treated separately. It reduces the complexity of the original problem, provided you decompose the problem in a useful way. Often, you discover that you can use decomposition into cases when you specify the problem; the use of conditional equations comes naturally for may problems.

Example: Summation of integers

The function *sum1to* sums all integers from 1 to a given number n. Now suppose you want a function *semisum* that sums every other non-negative number less than or equal to n. If $n = 9$, for instance, it shall compute the sum 1+3+5+7+9 and if $n = 10$ the sum 2+4+6+8+10. We assume that the argument to *semisum* is positive. Before you continue, try to sketch a solution!!

A reasonable approach for solving this problem is to split it into two cases, one for even arguments and one for odd arguments. Let us start with the even case. Let i be an integer such that $n = 2 * i$. We then have

$$S = 2 + 4 + 6 + ... + 2 * i = 2 * (1 + 2 + 3 + ... + i)$$

The sum of all numbers from 1 to i is given by $i * (i + 1) \ div \ 2$. Hence, $S = 2 * i * (i + 1) \ div \ 2$. Replacing i by $n \ div \ 2$ yields

$$S = 2 * n \ div \ 2 * (n \ div \ 2 + 1) \ div \ 2 = n * (n + 2) \ div \ 4$$

A similar method can be used for the odd case, but an even simpler solution is possible. Let us look at the accumulated sum for some of the first numbers.

Argument	1	3	5	7	9	11	...
Accumulated sum	1	4	9	16	25	36	...

A sum is simply the square of the order number of the column in the table, and since this number is given by $(n + 1) \ div \ 2$, we get

$$S = sq(n + 1) \ div \ 4$$

We have now solved the two cases and can compose them into a final solution.

```
- fun semisum n = if even n
                  then n * (n + 2) div 4
                  else sq(n + 1) div 4;
> val semisum = fn : int -> int

- semisum 9;
  25 : int
```

Example: Reversing digits

Suppose you want a function *reverse* that reverses the digits in a given integer numeral. For instance, *reverse*(375) yields 573. We assume that the arguments are non-negative integers less than 1000. Can you solve the problem??

If the number is less than 10 the solution is, trivially, the number itself. Our first step is therefore to split the problem into two subproblems, one for numbers less than ten and one for numbers greater than or equal to 10. We continue to split also the second subproblem into two problems, one for two-digit numbers and one for three-digit numbers. Working top-down, we assume the existence of two auxiliary functions *rev2* and *rev3*.

$$
\begin{aligned}
\textbf{fun } \textit{reverse } n \ = \ & \textbf{if } n < 10 \textbf{ then } n \\
& \textbf{else if } n < 100 \textbf{ then } \textit{rev2 } n \\
& \textbf{else } \textit{rev3 } n\,;
\end{aligned}
$$

> **val** *reverse* = **fn** : *int −> int*

Note that you do not have to check that $n \geq 10$ in the second test. The defined function is the result of decomposing the problem into three subproblems, two of which remain to be described in more detail. If n is a two-digit integer, $n \ div \ 10$ gives the first digit and $n \ mod \ 10$ the last one.

> − **fun** *rev2* n = $10 * (n \ mod \ 10) + n \ div \ 10$;
> > **val** *rev2* = **fn** : *int −> int*

Similar reasoning leads to the solution of the *rev3* problem.

> − **fun** *rev3* n =
> > $100 * (n \ mod \ 10) + 10 * (n \ div \ 10 \ mod \ 10) + n \ div \ 100$;
> > **val** *rev3* = **fn** : *int −> int*

Summary

Many programming problems are solved by decomposition into two or more subproblems, which can be solved separately. In the resulting program, a test is made to decide which case is at hand. The simplest kind of test can have two outcomes, in ML represented by the data objects *true* and *false* of type *bool*. Using the *conditional expression* (**if**— **then**— **else**) a choice between two computations can be made. Using *indentation*, you can show the structure of a conditional expression. There are six relational operators in ML: =, <>, <, <=, >, >=. Several conditions can be combined in an expression. A *conjunction* using **andalso** is true if both its operands are true. A *disjunction* using **orelse** is true if at least one of its operands is true. These boolean expressions are evaluated *lazily*: the second operand is evaluated only if it is needed. A *negation* using the function *not* is true if its argument is false and vice versa. Arithmetic operators have higher precedence than relational operators. A conjunction has higher precedence than a disjunction, but lower than a relational expression.

Exercises

6.9. In a game for children several persons count in order from 1 and upwards. You must say "peep" for each number that is divisible by seven and for each numeral that contains the digit 7. Define a function *peep* that gives the value *true* if at least one of the two conditions is satisfied. Define one version of *peep* for numbers less than 100 and one for numbers less than 1000.

6.10. Define *semisum* without a conditional expression by combining the two formulas. Which solution do you prefer and why?

6.11. Define a function *ceiling* similar to *floor*, but "truncating" in the other direction.

Chapter 7

Characters and Strings

In the early days of computers numerical computations dominated. Today, computers are used for many other types of computations, for instance, text processing. To be able to work with texts, you need data objects that represent characters and texts[1]. In ML, there is a predefined data type *string*, whose objects are sequences of characters. To mark a string, you surround it by double quotes. A character can, for instance, be a letter, a digit, or some special sign.

- ”This is a string” ;
  ”This is a string” : *string*

- ”abc...xyz ABC...XYZ 123...90 <>!’&/()=?+*-:.;, . . .” ;
  ”abc...xyz ABC...XYZ 123...90 <>!’&/()=?+*-:.;, . . .” : *string*

The double quotes around the strings are necessary; they tell the system that the characters shall be taken literally. Without quotes, the system will try to interpret the string as a name, an expression, or something similar.

- ”pi” ;
  ”pi” : *string*

- *pi* ;
  3.1415927 : *real*

- ”3+5” ;
  ”3+5” : *string*

- 3 + 5 ;
  8 : *int*

---

[1]Certain parts of this chapter are very special, and are included mainly for reference purposes.

>   − *hello*;
> Unbound identifier : *hello*

A string like "pi" is thus taken *literally*; no meaning is assigned to it. The size of a string can be both one and zero.

>   − "a";
> "a" : *string*

>   − "";
> "" : *string*

The empty string should not be confused with the space character.

>   − " ";
> " " : *string*

The string " " is of size one, whereas the empty string is of size zero.

In most programming languages, the data type *character* is predefined in the language, not *string*. In ML, a *character* is represented by a string of size one.

String valued functions

Strings are data objects as much as numbers and truth values and can be the argument to or the result of a function.

>   − **fun** *is_zero* n = **if** $n = 0$ **then** "yes" **else** "no";
> > **val** *is_zero* = **fn** : *int* $->$ *string*

>   − *is_zero*(403 *mod* 13);
> "yes" : *string*

7.1   The ASCII Code

To do more advanced string processing, you must know which characters are allowed in a string and how these characters are represented within the computer. A representation of characters is usually called a **code**. The most commonly occurring character code is the ASCII code—the American Standard Code for Information Interchange. The ASCII code is the code used in ML[2].

---

[2]If you run ML on a machine using a code other than ASCII, that code might be used by your ML system. The language ML is, however, based on the ASCII code and to get full portability of programs between systems, all implementations should use the ASCII code.

In the standard ASCII code there are 128 characters. They are represented internally by the numbers 0 through 127. Using seven bits, you can represent exactly 128 different characters. Most computers use 8-bit bytes, and each *code word* is stored in a one-byte memory cell. The 8th bit is sometimes used as a check bit when transferring characters over a medium that is not completely reliable.

In the ASCII code, described in Appendix A, there are four groups of characters: letters, digits, special characters, and control characters. The code words are: for capital letters 65 through 90, for lower-case letters 97 through 122, for digits 48 through 57, and for control characters 0 through 32 and 127. The remaining code words are used for the special characters.

Transfer functions

In ML, there are two functions for transferring a character (a string of size one) to its code word and vice versa. The function *ord* (for *ordinal*) yields the code word of a character as an integer between 0 and 127.

> — *ord* "a" ;
> 97 : *int*

The function *chr* is the inverse of *ord* and yields the character corresponding to a given code word. The space character, for instance, has code word 32.

> — *chr* 32 ;
> " " : *string*

> — *chr* 51 ;
> "3" : *string*

The digits correspond to the code words 48 through 57, not 0 through 9. All the control characters are non-printable characters and are used to control peripheral devices in different ways. Code word 7 usually makes the bell ring, for instance.

> — *chr* 7 ;   The bell rings
> "" : *string*

The system prints the string "" as result. It is a string of size one, but the character is invisible, since it is a control character. Some of the control characters affect the position of the next character to be printed, namely *backspace* (BS), *horizontal tabulation* (HT), *line feed* (LF), *form feed* (FF), and *carriage return* (CR). The *space* (SP) is usually considered as a control character, too.

> — *chr* 10 ;   The line feed character
> "
> " : *string*

National characters

In some natural languages, special national characters are used. In Swedish, for instance, the letters å, ä, and ö are used. For national characters, you must use the code word of some other character and give it a special meaning. For instance, the Swedish characters are usually given by the following special characters:

Normal character	National character	Code word
}	å	125
{	ä	123
|	ö	124
]	Å	093
[	Ä	091
\	Ö	092

The order of the code words does not correspond to the order of the letters in the Swedish alphabet, which leads to problems when you want to sort strings in alphabetical order. Furthermore, problems arise when you want to use the normal interpretation of the character and not the national one. Similar problems occur in other languages having national characters not included in the ASCII code.

Exercises

7.1. Define *digitval* giving the numerical value of a digit character.

7.2. Define *to_capital* that transforms a small letter into the corresponding capital letter.

7.2   Escape Sequences

Using the *chr* function to get the control characters is slightly laborious. In ML, you can sometimes use an escape sequence to include a control character in a string. An escape sequence always starts with the character \, the *backslash*, and is then followed by one or several printable or non-printable characters. The escape sequence \n corresponds to *line feed* (LF) and \t to horizontal tabulation (HT).

> — "a tab\tand a line feed\nfollowed by a tab\tstop" ;
> "a tab   and a line feed
> followed by a tab   stop" : *string*

Since the backslash is used as an escape character, you cannot include it directly in a string. Instead, you write \\ to get the effect of a single backslash. Also, the *double quote* must be treated specially, since it is used as string delimiter. By preceding it by a backslash, you can include it in a string.

– "A backslash surrounded by double quotes: \"\\\" " ;
"A backslash surrounded by double quotes: "\" " : *string*

Another way of including a character in a string is to put a backslash followed by the ASCII code word of the character. The code word must always contain three decimal digits—leading zeros must often be used.

– "\077\076" ;
"ML" : *string*

On a keyboard, there is usually a special key called "control". It is to be pressed at the same time as you press some other key in order to give that key a special meaning. Many control characters can be inserted from the keyboard in this way. For instance, "control h" may give a back space. You can include any control character "control c" in a string by preceding the character c by a backslash and a circumflex: \^c.

A very special use of escape sequences is the possibility of ignoring a sequence of formatting characters by surrounding them by two backslashes. This allows you, for example, to type long strings on more than one line; you write a backslash at the end of one line and another at the start of the next line.

– "This string is not very long,\
\ but it is typed in on two lines" ;
"This string is not very long, but it is typed in on two lines" : *string*

Many terminals have a graphical or semi-graphical mode in which you can draw pictures. You then need special characters that set the terminal in graphical mode etc. Which function each character has depends on the kind of terminal.

7.3   Standard String Functions and Operators

The function *size* yields the size (length) of the string.

– *size* "What is the size of me?" ;
23 : *int*

– *size* "" ;
0 : *int*

The binary operator ^ *concatenates* two strings, that is, puts them together.

– "tog" ^ "ether" ;
"together" : *string*

— "new" ^ *chr* 10 ^ "line" ;
"new
line" : *string*

The concatenation operator is an additive operator and has the same precedence as plus and minus (precedence 6).

Lexicographic order

In ML, there are six standard, relational operators ($=, <>, <, <=, >, >=$). They are defined not only for numbers, but also for strings. The comparison is based on the ASCII code representation of the string. If the string is of size one, a character with a smaller code word is less than one with a greater code word.

— "a" $<$ "b" ;
true : *bool*

— "A" $<$ "a" ;
true : *bool*

— " " $=$ "\032" ;
true : *bool*

For strings of size greater than one, the comparison is based on the first character pair that differs in the two strings. Such an order is sometimes called a *lexicographic order*.

— "a13" $>$ "a12" ;
true : *bool*

The strings can even be of different sizes.

— "a131" $>$ "a12" ;
true : *bool*

If one of the strings to be compared is equal to an initial segment of the other, the longer string is considered to be greatest.

— "milne" $<$ "milner" ;
true : *bool*

Let us define a function *is_empty* that tests if a given string is empty.

— **fun** *is_empty* s = s = "" ;
> **val** *is_empty* = **fn** : *string* $->$ *bool*

— *is_empty* " " ;   The space character
false : *bool*

The non-printable characters can, of course, not be seen on a screen, but they are still characters.

— *is_empty* "\007" ;
false : *bool*

Two multi-typed functions

The standard function *makestring* can sometimes be useful. Given an argument of some type, it returns the string that the system would print when given the same argument.

— *makestring*(55 + 55) ;
"110" : *string*

— *makestring* "what" ;
"what" : *string*

Exactly which types of argument are allowed to *makestring* is left open to the implementor (the person constructing the ML system), and you have to consult the manual for your system to find out what your system allows. Therefore, you should not use *makestring* in a program that may be ported to some other computer. Programs that are difficult to port cause enormous problems in the use of computers, and, ideally, no part of a language should be left undefined in this way unless absolutely necessary. In the rest of the book we assume that *makestring* is defined for integers, however.

The function *print* is a function that gives its argument as result, that is, it is the *identity* function. As a *side-effect*, however, its argument is printed as it would have been printed by the system.

— *print*(2 + 3) ;
5 5 : *int*

— *print* "hello" ;
"hello" "hello" : *string*

The first "hello" is the side-effect, and the second one is the result of the function. Side-effects have no place in a pure functional language. The function *print* is included as an aid for finding errors in a program and should not be a part of a real program. Since *print* and *makestring* are not fully specified in the language, they should be avoided as far as possible.

Summary

A data object of type *string* is a sequence of characters. In ML, you surround it by double quotes. A *character* in ML is treated as a string of size one. There are four classes of characters: letters, digits, special characters, and control characters. The control characters are usually non-printable and can be included in a string using an *escape sequence* (starting with a backslash). Characters are represented by code words according to the ASCII code; they are numbers in the range 0 through 127. The function *ord* gives the code word of a character and *chr* the character corresponding to a code word. The six ordinary relational operators can be used to compare strings in *lexicographic* order. The function *size* gives the size of a string. The operator ˆ can be used to concatenate two strings. The function *print* is a function with a side-effect and should primarily be used for debugging.

Exercises

7.3. Define the predicates *digit*, *lowercase*, *uppercase*, and *letter* with their obvious meanings. Ignore any national characters.

Chapter 8

Pairs and Tuples

Most objects around us are constructed by putting other objects together. Similarly, you can construct *structured* or *compound* data objects by putting together other data objects. Examples of compound objects in ML are pairs, tuples, records, and lists. Such objects are sometimes called **data structures**.

When you construct composite data objects, you start with *atomic* objects like numbers, truth values, and strings. The constructed objects can then be used as components in objects with a more complicated structure. This process can be repeated as many times as you like. The resulting objects get a *hierarchical* structure.

Data objects are used to describe aspects of the real world. Numbers, for instance, can describe quantities like lengths and prices. Boolean values can describe conditions and strings of characters names, addresses, articles, etc. These atomic data objects describe only one single aspect of the real world. To describe a person, for instance, you want to collect several pieces of information about the person into one single data object, a *record* about the person. When you write programs dealing with such information, you want to treat such a record as one unit; this helps you to master the complexity of a big program.

When you put data objects together into composite objects, you do it because they have something in common. Just putting things together at random does not help you. In a good program, data objects are combined in such a way that those data objects that have most in common are most closely connected. To *model the real world* in this way is an important part of the programming task. In ML, you have several tools at your help.

8.1 Pairs

To put data objects together you also need some "glue" to unite the objects. Suppose you want to combine 3 and *true* into a new, composite data object—a *pair*. You then have to tell the system that you want to unite them.

   — $(3, true)$;
   $(3, true)$: $int * bool$

The comma and parentheses constitute a **pair constructor**, which constructs a pair data object out of two other data objects. This pair expression cannot be reduced any further; it is a canonical expression. In general, a pair expression has the form (E_1, E_2), where E_1 and E_2 are arbitrary expressions.

   — $(5 - 2, \ not \ false)$;
   $(3, true)$: $int * bool$

The system evaluates the components of the pair expression. The pair constructor itself (the comma and the parentheses) cannot be "computed away", however; the idea of a constructor is that it constructs a new data object. In fact, *true* and *false* are the constructors of boolean values, and the numerals can be considered as the constructors of integers and reals. Whenever you give the system an expression consisting only of constructors, it will respond with the expression itself; canonical expressions have themselves as values.

8.1.1   The constructor of pair types

The types of the components of the pair $(3, true)$ are *int* and *bool*, respectively. The type of the pair itself is denoted by *int * bool*, which is the type of all pairs whose first component is an integer and second component is a truth value.

$$(7, false) \quad (0, true) \quad (\tilde{}6, false) \quad (123456789, true)$$

Let us look at pairs of type *bool * bool*. There are four possible pairs of this type:

$$(false, false) \quad (false, true) \quad (true, false) \quad (true, true)$$

The number of boolean values is two, and the number of pairs in *bool * bool* is therefore two times two. If there are *n1* objects of some type *T1* and *n2* objects of some type *T2*, there are *n1 * n2* objects of type *T1 * T2*. The two stars in the previous sentence are different; the first denotes arithmetic multiplication and the second the formation of pairs of two types of objects. The reason for chosing the same symbol is that a pair type is the product of two sets, often called the **cartesian product** of the sets. No confusion can occur since the operands of the multiplication operator are arithmetic expressions, and the operands of the type product are type expressions, and they can never be mixed in ML.

   The type operator * is often called a **type constructor**, since it constructs a new type given two other types. Do not confuse the pair type constructor * with the pair constructor denoted by a comma and parentheses. The type constructor constructs a new type, and the pair constructor a new data object that belongs to a pair type.

A type is really a set of data objects. A system response like 3 : *int* can be read as "3 belongs to the type *int*" or "3 is a member of the type *int*". In the same way (3, *true*) : *int* ∗ *bool* can be read as "the pair (3, *true*) is a member of the type *int* ∗ *bool*".

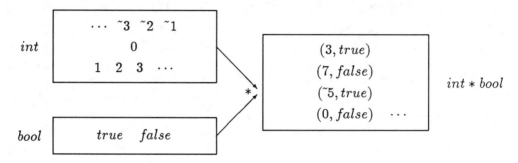

The formation of the data type *int* ∗ *bool*.

Pairs of pairs

A component of a pair can be of any type.

    — (3.0, "three");
      (3.0, "three") : *real* ∗ *string*

If pairs are a type of data object in ML and the components of a pair can be of any type, you should be able to construct pairs whose components are pairs.

    — (3, (*true*, 1.5));
      (3, (*true*, 1.5)) : *int* ∗ (*bool* ∗ *real*)

The second component of this pair is another pair of boolean and real values. A function is also a data object in ML and can therefore be a component of a pair.

    — (*sqrt*, *true*);
      (**fn**, *true*) : (*real* −> *real*) ∗ *bool*

Remember that the system always prints the word **fn** for all function objects. If a pair is to be a data object with the same rights as other data objects, you should be able to name a pair, too.

    — **val** *origin* = (0.0, 0.0);
  > **val** *origin* = (0.0, 0.0) : *real* ∗ *real*

- **val** *person* = ("Smith", 37);
> **val** *person* = ("Smith", 37) : *string ∗ int*

- (*origin, person*);
  ((0.0, 0.0), ("Smith", 37)) : (*real ∗ real*) ∗ (*string ∗ int*)

8.1.2 Type completeness

Having seen how you can use compound objects like functions and pairs in the same ways as any other data objects, you might ask if there are any restrictions or exceptions to the use of data objects of some type. A pleasing fact about most functional programming languages, including ML, is that the answer is no. What you can do with objects of one type, you can do with objects of any other type. Data objects of all types are first class citizens of the language or, in other words, all types are *complete*. This does not mean that you, for instance, can negate pairs or multiply functions, but it means that any data object can be

- the argument to a function
- the result from a function application
- named in a definition
- a part of a structured data object, etc.

A pair can, for instance, be the the value of a conditional expression and the result from a function.

- **fun** *test13 i* = **if** *i mod* 13 = 0
                    then (*i*, "divisible by 13")
                    else (*i*, "not divisible by 13");
> **val** *test13* = **fn** : *int* −> *int ∗ string*

- *test13* 351;
  (351, "divisible by 13") : *int ∗ string*

Type completeness makes a language easy to use; you do not have to think about peculiar restrictions.

8.1.3 Decomposing pairs

To do any meaningful computations with pairs, you have to be able to extract the components out of it. Suppose you want a function *max* that selects the greatest number out of a pair of numbers. A first effort of defining *max* might be

- **fun** *max p* = **if** ???

The problem is that we have no means of selecting the components out of the pair p. The solution is **pattern matching**. A pattern like (x, y) can be matched against a pair with the effect that the components become named x and y.

> — **fun** $max\,(x, y) : int\ =\ $ **if** $x > y$ **then** x **else** y;
> \> **val** $max\ =$ **fn** $:\ int * int\ ->\ int$

> — $max(3, 5)$;
> $5\ :\ int$

When max is applied to the pair (3,5), the pair is matched against the pattern (x, y) in the function definition. The pair and the pattern have the same form, so the match *succeeds*. At the same time, the name x becomes bound to 3 and y to 5. Let us reduce $max(3, 5)$.

$$max(3, 5) \longrightarrow \textbf{if } 3 > 5 \textbf{ then } 3 \textbf{ else } 5 \longrightarrow$$
$$\textbf{if } false \textbf{ then } 3 \textbf{ else } 5 \longrightarrow 5$$

You may be familiar with expressions like $max(3, 5)$ from mathematics. In mathematics you say that the function max has two arguments, but in ML you say it has one argument, which is a pair. A function in ML *always* has only one argument.

If you try to apply max to something that is not a pair, the system will report a type error.

> — $max(3, 5, 7)$;
> Type Clash in: $(max\ (3, 5, 7))$
> Looking for a: $int * int$
> I have found a: $int * int * int$

We can also define max using a function expression.

> — **val** $max\ =$ **fn** $(x : int, y)\ =>$ **if** $x > y$ **then** x **else** y;
> \> **val** $max\ =$ **fn** $:\ int * int\ ->\ int$

To inform the system that max has integer arguments, we constrain the type of x to int; the system can then deduce the other types.

Let us now look at a function taking a pair as argument and also giving a pair as result. When dividing two integers you get both a quotient and a remainder.

> — **fun** $divide\,(i, j)\ =\ (i\ div\ j, i\ mod\ j)$;
> \> **val** $divide\ =$ **fn** $:\ int * int\ ->\ int * int$

> — $divide(100, 3)$;
> $(33, 1)\ :\ int * int$

Selectors

Pattern matching is a nice way of selecting the components of a pair. Another possibility is to introduce two functions *fst* and *snd* that select the first and second component of a pair (they are defined below).

>   — *snd* (**3**, *true*) ;
>   *true* : *bool*

>   — *fst person* ;
>   "Smith" : *string*

Equipped with these *selectors*, we can define *max* in the way we first tried.

>   — **fun** *max p* : *int* = **if** *fst p* > *snd p* **then** *fst p* **else** *snd p* ;
>   > **val** *max* = **fn** : *int* ∗ *int* −> *int*

This definition is more complicated than the version using pattern matching. As a rule, we will therefore use pattern matching. Matching against a pair is really the *inverse* operation of constructing it, which we can express by saying that *pair*(*fst p*, *snd p*) = *p* for all pairs *p*. This nice symmetry between construction of data objects and their analysis through pattern matching you find for many data types in ML.

The functions *fst* and *snd* are standard functions in ML and have the special names *#1* and *#2*.

>   — *#2* (**7**, **9**) ;
>   **9** : *int*

Before you continue, try to figure out the types of *fst* and *snd*!!

8.1.4   Polymorphic functions

If you apply *fst* to (**3**, *true*), its type is *int* ∗ *bool* −> *int*. If you apply it to ("Smith", **37**), its type is *string* ∗ *int* −> *string*. Obviously, the type of *fst* depends on the type of its argument. If *'a* and *'b* are arbitrary types, you can describe the general appearance of the type of *fst* as *'a* ∗ *'b* −> *'a*. The important fact about this type is that the type of the first component and the type of the result are the same. Let us now define *fst*.

>   — **fun** *fst* (*x*, *y*) = *x* ;
>   > **val** *fst* = **fn** : *'a* ∗ *'b* −> *'a*

The names $'a$ and $'b$ are examples of **type variables** denoted by names starting with a $'$. A type variable can denote any type in ML. If a type variable occurs several times in a type expression, it must be substituted by the same type at all its occurrences. Let us look at instances of the type of *fst* remembering that $*$ has higher precedence than $->$ in type expressions.

$$real * bool -> real$$
$$(bool * int) * (real * bool) -> bool * int$$
$$(real -> int) * bool -> (real -> int)$$

In fact, there is an unlimited number of possible instantiations of the type of *fst*, since there is an unlimited number of different types in ML.

A function that is assigned a type expression with one or several type variables is said to be *polymorphic*, which means that it can have several, different types—you say it has a **polytype**. The function *snd* is polymorphic, too.

$$-\quad \textbf{fun}\ \ snd\ (x,y)\ =\ y\,;$$
$$>\quad \textbf{val}\ \ snd\ =\ \textbf{fn}\ :\ 'a *' b\ ->\ 'b$$

Polymorphic functions are extremely useful. In one function definition, you define a number of functions that are computationally similar. Without polymorphism you have to give one definition for each case.

A polymorphic function is an abstraction in which you have abstracted away from the particular type of the argument to the function. A function is assigned a polytype if no information about the type of its argument is needed. In the definition of *fst*, for instance, the types of the components are not important; the only important fact is that the argument is a pair. Polymorphism makes programming simpler, since you can define functions that are useful in a variety of applications; you do not have to specialize them more than necessary.

Overloading

A concept related to polymorphism is overloading. In ML, operators like $+$, $*$, $<$, and also the function *abs* are overloaded, which means that they handle arguments of more than one type, usually both *int* and *real*, but sometimes also *string*. A polymorphic function is defined in a single definition, but for an overloaded function one definition must be given for each type. The comparison of numbers and the comparison of strings are certainly not performed in the same way, for instance. You can say that overloading is the use of one function symbol for many different, but usually related, functions. The ML programmer cannot define overloaded functions; those that can be used are standard functions built into the system.

Wild cards

In the definition of *fst*, both arguments were named, but only the first argument name was really used on the right-hand side.

$$- \quad \textbf{fun } \mathit{fst} \ (x, y) \ = \ x \,;$$
$$> \quad \textbf{val } \mathit{fst} \ = \ \textbf{fn} \ : \ 'a * 'b \ -> \ 'a$$

The work of writing the *y* is not great, but in a larger function definition, it can be an advantage to stress that some part of the argument is not needed. In ML, you use the wild card _ to show this fact.

$$- \quad \textbf{fun } \mathit{fst} \ (x, \ \_) \ = \ x \,;$$
$$> \quad \textbf{val } \mathit{fst} \ = \ \textbf{fn} \ : \ 'a * 'b \ -> \ 'a$$

The wild card matches anything, but no name is given to the matched object, so you can never access it.

8.1.5 Comparing pairs

The equality operators $=$ and $<>$ are defined for almost all types of data objects in ML.

$$- \quad (2 * 3, not \ false) <> (round(sqrt(36.0)), true) \,;$$
$$false \ : \ bool$$

Relational operators like $<$ and $>$ are not defined for pairs, however. If you want to order pairs in some application, you must define a comparison function. Suppose you work with pairs of integers. A reasonable ordering is obtained by comparing the first components of the pairs and, if they are equal, comparing the second components, that is, a form of lexicographic order.

$$- \quad \textbf{fun } \mathit{lt} \ ((i1 : int, j1 : int), (i2, j2)) \ = \ i1 < i2 \ \textbf{orelse}$$
$$i1 = i2 \ \textbf{andalso} \ j1 < j2 \,;$$
$$> \quad \textbf{val } \mathit{lt} \ = \ \textbf{fn} \ : \ (int * int) * (int * int) \ -> \ bool$$

$$- \quad \mathit{lt} \ ((2, 3), (2, 4)) \,;$$
$$true \ : \ bool$$

Unfortunately, if you want a similar function for real numbers, you have to define a new version of the function; you cannot define overloaded functions as a user.

Exercises

8.1. What is the type of $(sin, (3, true))$?

8.2. What types are assigned to **fn** $x \implies x$, to **fn** $(\_, (x, \_)) \implies x$, and to **fn** $(x, y) \implies (y, x)$? Give one instantiation of each type.

8.2   Tuples

A tuple is a collection of data objects. A pair, for instance, is a 2-tuple, since it contains two components. In ML you can work with tuples of any **arity**: triples, quadruples, 5-tuples, etc.

    − $(1, 2, 3)$;
       $(1, 2, 3)$: $int * int * int$

This triple is quite different from a pair in which one component is a pair.

    − $(1, (2, 3))$;
       $(1, (2, 3))$: $int * (int * int)$

Our functions *fst* and *snd* are defined for pairs, but not for triples.

    − *fst* $(1, (2, 3))$;
       1 : int

    − *fst* $(1, 2, 3)$;
    Type Clash in: $(fst (1, 2, 3))$
    Looking for a: $'a * 'b$
    I have found a: $int * int * int$

The best way to select the components out of a triple is to use pattern matching, but there are predefined selectors in ML of the form #*n* that selects the *n*th component out of a tuple.

    − *#3* $(1, 3, 5)$;
       5 : int

The #-selectors are overloaded and not polymorphic, since you have to give different definitions for tuples of different arity. For instance, *#2* can be used for pairs, triples, quadruples, and so forth.

Let us now define a function *radius* that, given the x, y, and z coordinates of a point in a 3-dimensional space, computes its distance from origin, the point $(0, 0, 0)$. The radius is given by a formula that is a generalization of the theorem of Pythagoras to 3 dimensions.

    − **fun** *radius* (x, y, z) = $sqrt(x * x + y * y + z * z)$;
    > **val** *radius* = **fn** : $real * real * real \rightarrow real$

    − *radius* $(1.0, 1.0, 1.0)$;
       1.7320508075689 : $real$

Example: Capital growth

Let us define a function for computing capital growth.

$$\underline{\hspace{1cm} CAPITAL * INTEREST * YEARS \hspace{1cm}} \rangle\!\!\!\! growth \rangle \hspace{1cm} CAPITAL \longrightarrow$$

A *capital* grows every year with a factor $(1 + interest/100)$. If the money is saved *time* years, the final capital is given by the formula

$$capital * (1 + interest/100)^{time}$$

To translate this formula into ML, you need an exponentiation operation for real numbers. Working top-down, we assume the availability of a function *power* that satisfies the equation

$$power(a, b) = a^b$$

For instance, $power(2.0, 3.0) = 8.0$ and $power(3.0, 0.0) = 1.0$. We can now define *growth*.

```
 —  fun  growth (capital, interest, time) =
              capital * power(1.0 + interest/100.0, time);
 >  val  growth = fn  :  real * real * real —> real
```

A function like *power* is probably predefined in your ML system, but with some knowledge of mathematics you can define it yourself. You want to find a y such that $y = a^b$, where we assume that a and b are not negative. Taking the logarithm of both sides yields

$$ln(y) = ln(a^b)$$

From mathematics it is known that $ln(a^b) = b * ln(a)$. Hence, $ln(y) = b * ln(a)$. Now, applying the exponential function to both sides gives

$$exp(ln(y)) = exp(b * ln(a))$$

Using the fact that $exp(ln(y)) = y$, we get $y = exp(b * ln(a))$. We can now define the *power* function.

```
 —  fun  power (a, b) = exp(b * ln a);
 >  val  power = fn  :  real * real —> real
```

This completes our problem solving, but we have to convince ourselves that the solution is correct. We have derived all formulas, so we have already given some arguments for the solution. To be more sure, we test it. When testing, you should first test the function *power*, since it does not use any other user-defined function (often called *bottom-up testing*).

 − $power(2.0, 3.0)$;
   8.000000000000001 : $real$

 − $power(3.0, 0.0)$;
   1.0 : $real$

The last test is an important one, since it tests a very special case; special cases are very easily forgotten when you design and test your programs.

Next, we test the function $growth$. One test is to see that we get the capital itself after zero years and another one is to see that the amount doubles after one year at 100 % interest.

 − $growth(100.0, 5.0, 0.0)$;
   100.0 : $real$

 − $growth(100.0, 100.0, 1.0)$;
   200.0 : $real$

These are very special cases and we should also try some general case. We check that the capital grows with a factor 1.331 in 3 years at 10 % interest, a fact you can calculate by hand.

 − $growth(100.0, 10.0, 3.0)$;
   133.1 : $real$

Example: Second degree equations

The equation $ax^2 + bx + c$ has two solutions given by the formulas

$$x_1 = \frac{-b + \sqrt{b^2 - 4ac}}{2a} \qquad x_2 = \frac{-b - \sqrt{b^2 - 4ac}}{2a}$$

For some values of the constants a, b, and c, the solutions are complex numbers. We assume here that we deal only with equations having real roots, but in a real program that fact should be checked. We define a function $roots$ that given the constants a, b, and c gives the pair of roots as result.

 − **fun** $roots$ (a, b, c) = $((\tilde{}b + sqrt(b * b − 4.0 * a * c))/(2.0 * a),$
                          $(\tilde{}b − sqrt(b * b − 4.0 * a * c))/(2.0 * a))$;
 > **val** $roots$ = **fn** : $real * real * real −> real * real$

 − $roots(2.0, \tilde{}13.0, 15.0)$;
   $(5.0, 1.5)$: $real * real$

An effort to find imaginary roots will lead to a negative argument to the $sqrt$ function, and the computation will raise an exception.

 − $roots(1.0, 1.0, 1.0)$;
   Failure : $sqrt$

Later, you will see how you can generate a failure if some condition is not satisfied.

Summary

A *pair* contains two components, which can be of different types. The *pair constructor* is denoted by parentheses and a comma. The *type constructor* for pairs is denoted by *. A *tuple* can contain arbitrarily many components. A *polymorphic* function is a function that can assume several different, but structurally similar, types. A *type variable* is a variable ranging over types. The name of a type variable always starts with a prime. An *overloaded* function can likewise assume different types, but one definition must be given for each instance. In ML, the user cannot define overloaded functions; only some standard functions are overloaded. For any tuple, there are standard *selectors* #n that select the nth component out of a tuple.

Exercises

8.3. Testing never proves the absence of errors and, in fact, *power* is not properly defined. Can you complete it?

8.4. Define *max3* that gives the greatest integer in a triple of integers.

8.5. What are the types of the functions

1) **fn** (x, y) => $(x + y)/2.0$ 2) **fn** (x, y, z) => **if** x **then** y **else** z
3) **fn** $(x, (y, z))$ => $((x, y), z)$ 4) **fn** (x, y) => **if** $x < y$ **then** x **else** y

8.6. Define functions for complex addition and multiplication. Represent a complex number by a pair of real numbers. Then, redefine *roots* so that the result is a pair of complex numbers.

8.7. The factorial of a number n, denoted $n!$, is in mathematics defined by the formula $1 * 2 * 3 * \cdots * n$. Define a function *fak* that computes an approximation to the factorial of a given integer using Stirling's formula:

$$n! \approx \sqrt{2 * \pi} * n^{n + \frac{1}{2}} * e^{-n}$$

Compare it with the predefined function *fac* for some arguments.

Chapter 9

Syntax

A complete description of a language contains three parts: the syntax, the semantics, and the pragmatics. The **syntax** describes the form of the language, that is, which sentences are well-formed sentences of the language and which structure they have. The **semantics** describes the meaning of well-formed sentences, that is, how they are to be understood. The **pragmatics** is concerned with how a language is used, with conventions and the most practical way of using it.

You can talk to someone that does not fully master the language you talk, because a person has a great capability of filling in missing details. Efforts to make computers fill in details have largely failed so far. It is therefore of great importance that a programming language is well-defined, so it is clear which sequences of characters constitute well-formed programs and what the exact meanings of these programs are. To ease the use of a language, indentation and layout rules help; they are examples of the pragmatics of the language.

9.1   The Lexical Structure

To describe a natural language, you have to describe its sentences. A sentence is formed by putting together words and punctuation marks according to given rules. The words are sometimes called the *lexical* items; a *lexicon* is a listing of all words of a language. The *grammar* of a language gives the rules for forming the sentences, but is not concerned with individual words. In the same way, we divide the description of a programming language into two parts: the lexical part and the program structure part. Examples of lexical items are constants (numerals, truth values, etc.), identifiers, reserved words, terminators, separators, and so on. When describing the structure of a programming language, these lexical items are treated as atomic items, which are not further divided.

In a program, some symbols are used for *formatting*: space characters, new lines, and tabulation characters can usually be inserted freely between the lexical items. They are sometimes necessary to separate lexical items, but are otherwise ignored by the compiler. A **comment** is a sequence of characters surrounded by (∗ and ∗), and is normally treated in the same way. It can be inserted wherever some other formatting character can be inserted.

The program structure of a language can be described in several ways. Let us look at syntax charts and BNF grammars.

9.2 Syntax Charts

A syntax chart is one way of describing the structure of programs and their parts. For instance, the simplest form of value declaration is given by the syntax chart

VALUE DECLARATION

A description of a computation uses three combining principles: sequence, choice, and repetition. The same principles are used when describing the sentences of a language, even though they are used in a different way. Let us give a chart for describing an INTEGER NUMERAL. We first draw a chart for digits. To the left of the chart we write the kind of syntactic entity the diagram describes, in this case DIGIT.

DIGIT

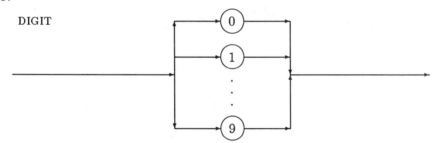

A digit is one of ten alternatives. To mark a *choice* in a syntax chart, you split a line into several lines. To investigate if a character is a digit, you follow the different tracks and investigate if you can go from the start to the end with matches only. The DIGIT chart matches the ten digits and nothing else.

We can now describe an INTEGER NUMERAL, which is a sequence of digits, possibly preceded by a minus sign (˜).

INTEGER NUMERAL

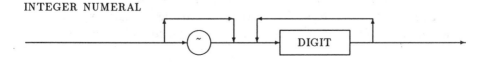

A square box like the one containing the word DIGIT designates that you should temporarily use another diagram, here the diagram for DIGIT. The numeral ˜37 , for instance, is matched by the chart: you choose the lower branch of the first choice and match ˜, then match the digit 3, and finally go one turn around and match 7.

The chart for an integer numeral uses all three combining principles. A numeral is a sign followed by an unsigned numeral, which is an example of a sequence. A numeral can contain a sign or not, which is a choice. Finally, an unsigned numeral is a sequence of digits, which is described by repeating the DIGIT chart as many times as needed; in the chart drawn as a "loop". Note that a repetition must be followed by a choice; otherwise, you would never be able to stop the repetition. A chart containing repetition describes an infinite number of possibilities. For any given string, however, only a finite number of matches have to be made.

In a chart, circular and oval boxes always describe **terminal symbols**, which are symbols occurring in the programs to be described. A rectangular box always contains the name of another chart indicating that it should be matched before continuing. If you want, you can substitute the diagram itself for a rectangular box. For instance, the DIGIT chart can be inserted into the chart for an INTEGER NUMERAL.

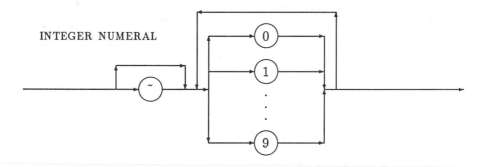

Consequently, there is no unique way of constructing a syntax chart. Usually, you use one chart for each distinguishable class of syntactic entities, like NUMERAL, DECLARATION, EXPRESSION, etc, which eases the use of the grammar.

Iteration and recursion

Suppose you want a syntax chart for arithmetic expressions containing numerals and the four arithmetic operators. Such an expression always starts with a numeral and is then possibly followed by one or several instances of an operator and a numeral.

OPERATOR

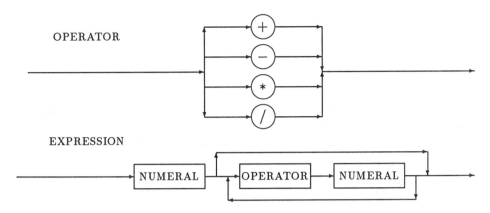

EXPRESSION

A repetition described by a loop, that is, a possibility of going around in the chart, is called *iteration*. Now, suppose you want parentheses in your expressions. If you try, you will find that you cannot describe such expressions using only iteration. A parentheses expression like $(2 + 3)$ consists of the parentheses and another expression $2 + 3$. To define expressions, you must use the definition of expression itself. In the chart below, three kinds of expression are described: numerals, parentheses expressions, and operator expressions.

EXPRESSION

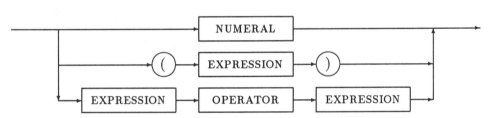

A chart containing a reference to itself is said to be *recursive*. The given chart matches expressions like $(2 + 3)/(4 * (5 - 6))$. Try to match this expression using the chart!!

Precedences

The given diagram does not describe the precedences of the operators. An expression like $2+3*4$ can be interpreted in two ways: as an addition with a multiplication as right operand or as a multiplication with an addition as left operand. The first alternative is the one we want, because multiplication has higher precedence than addition. The traditional way of showing precedences in syntax charts is to split a syntactic entity into several entities and charts. EXPRESSION, for instance, is then split into EXPRESSION (with + and −), TERM (with * and /), and FACTOR (with numerals and parentheses expressions). Such an approach is suitable when there are few precedence levels. In ML there are many levels, and we will therefore use another method.

The fact that one kind of syntactic construction has higher precedence than another means that you should try one specific choice before the other, when matching a part of a program. To designate the preferred choice, we use a *double* arrow. Usually, this choice is higher up in the chart—the way you read the chart anyway. In the EXPRESSION diagram below, multiplicative operators have higher precedence than additive ones. Now, matching $2 + 3 * 4$, you will match multiplication before the addition.

EXPRESSION

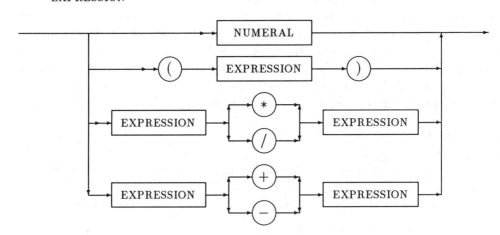

In Appendix C, you find syntax charts for ML. They are handy when you are uncertain about what is allowed in ML. They give you a good picture of the language, too.

Acceptors and generators

Syntax charts are used as *accepting* devices. You match a string against a chart to see if it is an instance of the entity described. You can turn the whole procedure around, however, and use the chart as a *generator*. It generates one sentence for each possible walk-through. In this way you can use the chart to generate all sentences of the kind under consideration. The set of these sentences is the **language** described by that chart. For instance, the language of arithmetic expressions is the set of expressions generated by the syntax chart EXPRESSION.

9.3 BNF Grammars

Another way of describing the syntax of a programming language is to use a BNF grammar. BNF is short for Backus-Naur Form, which was the form of syntax used to describe the programming language Algol; John Backus and Peter Naur were two of the group of people defining Algol. A BNF grammar describes the same thing as a syntax chart, but in another way. We will use charts in the text, but since the official ML Report (Appendix B) uses a BNF grammar, a short description is given here. Later, when talking more about data types, we will make comparisons with BNF grammars so, if you wish, you can postpone the reading of this section until then. The kind of BNF grammar used in the ML Report is not the one ordinarily used, so if you have seen a BNF grammar before, you will find some differences.

Let us describe the grammar for digits. The symbol ::= is read as "is defined by" or simply "is". Traditionally, the symbol | is used to mark a choice, but we use a new line to represent a choice.

$$
\begin{array}{lll}
\text{DIGIT} & ::= & 0 \\
& & 1 \\
& & \vdots \\
& & 9
\end{array}
$$

Compare this **production** with the chart for DIGIT above!!

To describe repetition you can use both iteration and recursion. Let us start describing an expression using recursion.

$$
\begin{array}{lll}
\text{EXPRESSION} & ::= & \text{NUMERAL} \\
& & (\text{ EXPRESSION }) \\
& & \text{EXPRESSION OPERATOR EXPRESSION}
\end{array}
$$

Note that you can take the grammar and, by filling in boxes and lines, end up with the corresponding chart; charts are just a graphical way of giving a grammar.

Precedences

In the form of BNF grammar we describe, a construction with high precedence appears above one with lower precedence. Another method of assigning precedences is also used in the ML Report: each operator is assigned a precedence between 0 and 9. For instance, multiplicative operators have precedence 7, additive operators 6, and relational operators 4. A complete listing is given on page 411 in the ML Report. The precedences of all constructions but the binary operators are, however, shown by placing constructions with high precedence above those with low precedence.

Iteration

A special notation is used in the ML Report to describe iteration. A tuple is a sequence of at least two expressions separated by commas and surrounded by ordinary parentheses. A tuple can also contain zero expressions, but never only one. The texts within parentheses to the right of the productions are comments.

$$\text{TUPLE} \quad ::= \quad () \qquad\qquad\qquad\qquad\qquad\qquad (\text{0-tuple})$$
$$(\text{EXPRESSION}_1, \_ , \text{EXPRESSION}_n) \qquad (\text{n-tuple, } n > 1)$$

Iteration is denoted by writing the construct to be repeated twice. To the first occurrence, the digit 1 is appended and to the second occurrence, the letter n.

In a tuple, the comma is used as a *separator*: it occurs between expressions. In a program, on the other hand, a semicolon is used as a *terminator* after each declaration in the program. In the grammar, you now place a semicolon after, but not before, the second occurrence of DECLARATION.

$$\text{PROGRAM} \quad ::= \quad \text{DECLARATION}_1 ; \_ \text{DECLARATION}_n ; \qquad (n \geq 0)$$

Optional parts

In a grammar, you sometimes want to mark some parts as optional. A numeral can be described as an unsigned numeral, optionally preceded by a minus sign. Optional parts are surrounded by double angles.

$$\text{NUMERAL} \quad ::= \quad <<\,\tilde{}\,>> \quad \text{UNSIGNED\_NUMERAL}$$

Left and right associativity

An expression containing several occurrences of the same entity in sequence can be interpreted in several ways. For instance, you can interpret the expression $5 - 4 - 3$ as $(5 - 4) - 3$ or $5 - (4 - 3)$. In the first case you say that the minus associates to the left and in the second case to the right. In the grammar, the associativity is marked by placing an L or R after the alternative, but before the comment. The function type operator $->$ associates to the right, for instance.

$$\text{TYPE} \quad ::= \quad \text{TYPE}_1 \;->\; \text{TYPE}_2 \qquad \text{R(function type)}$$

As a consequence, the type $int -> real -> bool$ is to be interpreted as the type $int -> (real -> bool)$ and not as $(int -> real) -> bool$.

All standard binary operators associate to the left. In ML, you can define new operators and have then the choice of making them right or left associative.

9.4 Context Dependence

Syntax charts and BNF grammars cannot describe all aspects of the syntax of a programming language. For instance, they can never describe that a name must be declared before it is used. The ML grammar generates expressions like $3 + true$ and $x > 3$ **orelse** x, since no types rules are expressed in the BNF grammar. We therefore have to describe which sentences generated by the grammar do not belong to the language. Such restrictions are normally described by text in natural language, even if there are formal methods for doing it.

The reason that a BNF grammar is not sufficient is that it cannot express *context dependencies*. In the last expression above, the name x has to be both a number and a truth value, which is not possible. Other types of context dependencies, which cannot be described by a BNF grammar, are that identifiers have to be defined before they are used and that they cannot be bound to two different values.

Summary

The syntax of a programming language can be described by a *syntax chart* or by a *BNF grammar*; they are only different ways of saying the same thing. A grammar describes a *language*, that is, the set of possible sequences of characters (sentences, programs) of the language. The three combining principles sequence, choice, and repetition are used in a grammar. Repetition can be described by *iteration* or *recursion*. Iteration can describe only some forms of recursion. Precedences can be described by ordering choices in decreasing precedence. BNF grammars and charts cannot describe *context dependent* properties of a language.

Exercises

9.1. Which of the following sentences are false? Explain why!

1. Syntax charts and BNF grammars have the same descriptive power.
2. If you have iteration in a BNF grammar, you do not need recursion.
3. Since context dependent properties of a language cannot be described by a BNF grammar, they are not part of the syntax of a language.
4. A method for describing syntax must contain possibilities for expressing sequence, choice, and repetition.

9.2. Give the grammar of a BNF grammar, in which only sequence, choice, and recursion can be used. To describe it, you can use all devices described above, though.

Chapter 10

Semantics

The most difficult, but also the most important, part of the definition of a language is its semantics. It gives the meaning of the language. Without a semantics, you can say nothing whatsoever about how to interpret a sentence. You may claim that by merely looking at the syntax charts for expressions, you know what $2 + 3$ is without looking at a semantics. This is the case because you suppose that 2, 3, and + mean what they usually mean. How can you be sure that this is the case? Suppose that + denotes multiplication so that $2 + 3$ is 6 and not 5. Of course, it would be a stupid idea to define a language that does not conform to common practice, but without a semantics you cannot be sure.

The value of $2 + 3$ is almost certainly 5 in all ML systems, but what is the value of 1000000000 * 1000000000? In some systems you get the number 1000000000000000000, but some systems raise an error since they cannot handle such large numbers. Similarly, what is the value of $3 > 0$ **orelse** $1 \, div \, 0 = 0$? If **orelse** is evaluated lazily, it is *true*, otherwise a failure occurs. These simple examples show that there are good reasons for having a precise semantical description, which you can consult when in doubt about some language construct. The semantics of ML is given in the ML Report in Appendix B.

A well-defined semantics is important for other reasons too. To be able to move programs from one ML system to another, the ML systems must implement (realize) the same language. Without a clear semantics, there is a risk that different implementors interpret the meaning of the language in different ways with the result that a program can give different results on different computers.

A third motivation for a good semantical description is that it can be the base for a theory about the language and, in particular, a theory about how you prove that programs are correct. Using such theories, you can develop systems that check that your proofs are correct and possibly also help you with parts of the proofs. Much research is currently going on concerning these questions, but they are outside the scope of this book.

How to define a semantics

There are several ways of defining the semantics of a programming language, each with their advantages and disadvantages. For a beginner, a description in natural language is the easiest to read without any training. Unfortunately, natural language descriptions tend to be long and sometimes not as precise as you think. For instance, the word "or" can mean "one of but not both" or "one or both". Such problems can often be avoided by the use of a formal notation.

We will describe the semantics primarily using natural language, but some parts will be given also in a formal way. The formal description is not difficult to understand, once you have grasped the idea behind it and it will, most likely, increase your understanding of ML. If you find it difficult, however, you can skip it on your first reading—all of the semantics is described informally, too. Another purpose of the introduction of a formal notation is to ease your reading of the ML Report, which otherwise can be quite difficult to grasp. Since the Report is the ultimate description of the language, you should be able to read it and consult it when in doubt.

Operational semantics and abstract machines

To define the semantics of ML, you can describe exactly *how* programs are executed, that is, which operations are performed and in which order they are executed. We will give such a description by describing a hypothetical machine that executes ML programs. Such a machine is often called an *abstract machine*, since only the most important aspects of how it works are described—you abstract from the details of a real computer. It can also be viewed as an abstract *interpreter* for ML, that is, an evaluator of ML programs. We have, in fact, already made small steps towards this goal. To describe the evaluation of expressions, we use reductions.

$$2 + 3 * 4 \longrightarrow 2 + 12 \longrightarrow 14$$

Now, suppose you have a machine that can perform reductions. It reduces expressions until no more reductions are possible and then prints the result. By defining precisely how this **reduction machine** works, you get an *operational* semantics of ML.

The *program store* of the reduction machine contains the program to be executed. First, we consider only expressions as programs. The machine works by making reductions directly on the program according to rules stored in the *control* of the machine. It stops when no more reductions are possible. The program $2 + 3 * 4$ is first reduced to $2 + 12$ and then to 14. No further reductions are now possible, and the machine stops.

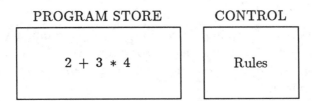

A simple reduction machine.

In contrast to most other computers, the reduction machine manipulates the program itself. When the machine starts, the program store contains the program to be executed, and when the machine stops, the program store contains the result of the program. The reduction machine also contains an *environment store* for keeping track of names and their bindings, but for the time being we investigate reduction of expressions without names.

10.1   Evaluation of ML Programs

Syntactically, an ML program is a sequence of declarations. It can, indeed, also be a single expression, but such an expression is considered only as an implicit declaration of the name *it* (cf. page 40).

10.1.1   Evaluation of expressions

To give the semantics of expressions, you have to describe how each form of expression is evaluated—how it is reduced to its value. The arrow $\longrightarrow$ is used to designate one single reduction step. We now have to define rules that in a *unique* way describe how all reducible expressions are to be reduced, and that describe which expressions cannot be further reduced. These rules give all pairs E_1 and E_2 such that $E_1 \longrightarrow E_2$ and no other pairs.

When you evaluate an expression you get a *canonical expression* as result. This canonical expression is a *description* of the value of the expression, but we will often say that it *is* the value. There are only a few forms of canonical expression, and they constitute the possible results of ML programs, results we interpret as values.

Evaluation of canonical expressions

Here is a list of some canonical expressions:

numeral:	3	3.14	tuple value:	$(3, true)$
truth value:	*true*	*false*	unit value:	$\{\}$
string:	"abc"	"123"	function value:	**fn** $x \Rightarrow x + 1$

A canonical expression cannot be further reduced. You also say that it is an expression that has itself as value.

— $(3, true)$;
$(3, true) : int * bool$

Note that in a canonical tuple expression all components must be canonical. This is not the case for canonical function expressions (often simply called function expressions), since the expression to the right of $=>$ can be any expression.

— **fn** x $=>$ $3 + 3$;
fn $: 'a \rightarrow int$

The expression 3+3 is not evaluated.

There are no semantic rules for the reduction of canonical expressions. On the contrary, the absence of such rules is a way of saying that they cannot be reduced.

Evaluation of parentheses expressions

Parentheses are often used to mark which subexpression of an expression is to be evaluated first.

$$2 * (3 + 4) \longrightarrow 2 * (7) \longrightarrow 2 * 7 \longrightarrow 14$$

The second reduction amounts to removing the parentheses. They cannot be removed in the first reduction, since that would change the meaning of the expression. The reason they can be removed in the second step is that, at that stage, they surround a canonical expression[1].

The general rule for reducing a parentheses expression is that the parentheses can be removed once the contained expression has been reduced to canonical form. We shall later describe this fact in a precise way, but we do it informally first.

1. An expression within parentheses can be reduced without changing the meaning of a program.
2. Parentheses can be removed when surrounding a canonical expression[2].

To make these rules precise, suppose that e is any expression and that e can be reduced to e'. Formally, we write $e \longrightarrow e'$, where we assume that e and e' range over arbitrary expressions. We can now make statement 1 a bit more precise.

1. If e is an expression and e is reducible to e', that is $e \longrightarrow e'$, then the expression (e) can be reduced to (e'), that is, $(e) \longrightarrow (e')$.

---

[1] In a real machine or ML system, an expression is normally translated into a form without parentheses. The rules for parentheses are then not needed.

[2] Function expressions are, in fact, an exception to this rule, but we ignore that here. Consider, for instance, **fn** x $=>$ x 3 and (**fn** x $=>$ x) 3, which have different meanings.

This statement consists of a *premise* $e \longrightarrow e'$ and a *conclusion* $(e) \longrightarrow (e')$, which is true if the premise is true. It is common practice to write such rules in a uniform way using a solid line with all premises above the line and the conclusion below.

1. $$\frac{e \longrightarrow e'}{(e) \longrightarrow (e')}$$

Such a rule is called a **derivation rule**, since you derive a fact from other facts.

Imagine that several derivation rules are stored in the reduction machine and that the machine tries to find a suitable rule when reducing a program. The rule to use is the one in which the expression to the left of the arrow in the conclusion (the reduction below the line) has the same form as the expression to be reduced. Rule 1 can therefore be used for any expression within parentheses. Let us give some examples of instances of the rule.

$$\frac{2 * (3 + 4) \longrightarrow 2 * (7)}{(2 * (3 + 4)) \longrightarrow (2 * (7))}$$

$$\frac{2 + 3 \longrightarrow 5}{(2 + 3) \longrightarrow (5)}$$

$$\frac{(2 + 3) \longrightarrow (5)}{((2 + 3)) \longrightarrow ((5))}$$

Combining the last two examples you get

$$\frac{\dfrac{2 + 3 \longrightarrow 5}{(2 + 3) \longrightarrow (5)}}{((2 + 3)) \longrightarrow ((5))}$$

To reduce $2 + 3$, however, a rule for addition is needed.

Rule 1 can be used repeatedly until the contained expression is canonical. Now, the second rule for removing parentheses can be used. Suppose that v is a canonical expression. Then, (v) can be reduced to v. Formally, we have

2. $$\frac{}{(v) \longrightarrow v}$$

where v is a variable ranging over canonical expressions. In this rule there is no premise, only a conclusion. Such rules are sometimes called **axioms** and are usually written without the line.

In conclusion, when trying to reduce an expression, you must find a rule in which the left part of the conclusion matches the expression. You must now go on and look at the premises of this rule and try to find rules that allow the reductions in the premises. These rules may lead to new premises but, finally, you must end up with axioms, which never have premises, so that the search stops. You can now work backwards and perform the reductions until the expression is reduced.

Evaluation of operator expressions

In ML, there are several standard operators like $+$, $*$, and $\char94$. An operator expression consists of an operator surrounded by two operands, both of which are expressions themselves. In ML, such an expression is evaluated by first evaluating the left operand, then the right operand, and finally performing the operation associated with the operator. Let us first state this for addition; the rules for the other operators look the same. Informally, we have

1. If e_1 and e_2 are expressions and e_1 is reducible to e_1', that is, $e_1 \longrightarrow e_1'$, then $e_1 + e_2 \longrightarrow e_1' + e_2$.
2. If n is a numeral and $e_2 \longrightarrow e_2'$, then $n + e_2 \longrightarrow n + e_2'$.
3. If n_1 and n_2 are numerals, then $n_1 + n_2 \longrightarrow n_3$, where n_3 is the sum of n_1 and n_2.

In the third rule, the sum of two numbers is mentioned, so we have to describe what summation means in this context. Usually, the summation operation is dependent on the computer you use. For small integers it agrees with what you learn in school, but for large enough numbers, a summation leads to an overflow error. In the rules below, we will use the symbol $\oplus$ to denote the summation you get on a particular machine. We can now rewrite the rules in a formal way.

$$1. \quad \frac{e_1 \longrightarrow e_1'}{e_1 + e_2 \longrightarrow e_1' + e_2}$$

$$2. \quad \frac{e_2 \longrightarrow e_2'}{n_1 + e_2 \longrightarrow n_1 + e_2'}$$

$$3. \quad n_1 + n_2 \longrightarrow n_3 \qquad \text{where } n_3 = n_1 \oplus n_2$$

Let us reduce $2 * 3 + 4 * 5$ using the rules. We omit the rules used for the reduction of the multiplications.

$$2 * 3 + 4 * 5 \longrightarrow 6 + 4 * 5 \longrightarrow 6 + 20 \longrightarrow 26$$
$$\text{Rule:} \qquad 1 \qquad\qquad 2 \qquad\qquad 3$$

By introducing a very special integer *error*, you can explain an overflow by saying that if $n_1 \oplus n_2$ leads to an overflow, n_3 is this special *error* value. The condition that an overflow occurs is that the true sum of n_1 and n_2 cannot be represented by the system.

Evaluation of conditional expressions

Suppose that b is a boolean expression and that e_1 and e_2 are two expressions of the same type. To evaluate the conditional expression **if** b **then** e_1 **else** e_2, the machine must first evaluate the boolean expression b. If it is *true*, the conditional expression can be reduced to e_1, and if it is *false* it can be reduced to e_2. Formally,

1.
$$\frac{b \longrightarrow b'}{\textbf{if } b \textbf{ then } e_1 \textbf{ else } e_2 \longrightarrow \textbf{if } b' \textbf{ then } e_1 \textbf{ else } e_2}$$

2.   **if** *true* **then** e_1 **else** $e_2 \longrightarrow e_1$

3.   **if** *false* **then** e_1 **else** $e_2 \longrightarrow e_2$

Note that a conditional expression is evaluated lazily. Only one of the expressions e_1 and e_2 is evaluated.

if $2 < 3$ **then** $2 + 3$ **else** 1 *div* $0 \longrightarrow$
if *true* **then** $2 + 3$ **else** 1 *div* $0 \longrightarrow 2 + 3 \longrightarrow 5$

The expression 1 *div* 0 is never reduced.

Non-terminating computations

In ML, you can construct expressions that can be reduced forever, that is, the chain of reductions does not reach a canonical expression. The symptom for the user either is that nothing happens or that the system runs out of memory space. We will later look at expressions that can give rise to non-terminating computations.

10.1.2   Environments

The value of an expression containing a variable is dependent on the value of the variable. In ML, you can bind a value to a name using a value declaration.

```
—   val x = 3;
>   val x = 3 : int
```

The reduction machine must in some way keep track of what bindings are introduced. For this purpose we extend it with a special **environment store**. Each cell in this store contains a pair, the first element of which is a name and the second the value bound to that name. After binding x to 3, the machine will have the binding $x = 3$ in its environment store.

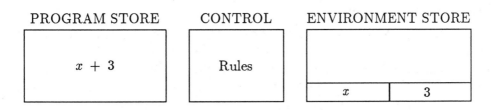

| PROGRAM STORE | CONTROL | ENVIRONMENT STORE |

When reducing $x + 3$, the first reduction is to replace x by its value, which is found by looking in the environment store.

$$x + 3 \longrightarrow 3 + 3 \longrightarrow 6$$

For each declaration, a new binding is introduced into the environment store.

    − **val** y = 5;
    > **val** y = 5 : *int*

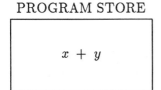
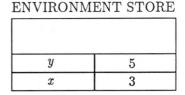

When the reduction machine tries to reduce a name, it searches the environment to find its value. In ML, you can rebind a name to a new value.

    − **val** x = 7;
    > **val** x = 7 : *int*

The old binding to x is now removed, and the new binding is inserted instead.

$$x + y \longrightarrow 7 + y \longrightarrow 7 + 5 \longrightarrow 12$$

Note that the old binding can never be used again. Later, you will see how temporary bindings can be introduced.

Environments and variables

To describe bindings and environments in a precise way, we need a suitable notation for them. Suppose that id is an identifier (a name) and that v is a value. Then, $id = v$ is the binding of the identifier id to the value v. For instance, the declaration **val** $x = 3$ yields the binding $x = 3$.

An environment usually contains several bindings. Suppose that id_1 through id_n are identifiers and that v_1 through v_n are values. We then denote the environment consisting of the bindings $id_i = v_i$ for $i = 1, 2, \ldots , n$ by

$$\{id_1 = v_1,\ id_2 = v_2,\ \ldots ,\ id_n = v_n\}$$

For instance, if you bind x to 3 and then y to 5, you get the environment $\{x = 3,\ y = 5\}$. We consider an environment as a *set* of bindings, where a name can occur at most once. The order of the bindings is therefore not essential.

We also need a notation for adding new bindings to an environment. Suppose that Env_1 and Env_2 are environments. Then $Env_1 + Env_2$ is the environment in which the bindings of Env_2 supersede those of Env_1. For instance,

$$\{x = 3,\ y = 5\} + \{x = 7\}\ \longrightarrow\ \{x = 7,\ y = 5\}$$

We further need a notation for looking up a value in an environment. If id is a name and Env an environment, the value associated with id in Env is denoted by $Env(id)$. For instance, the value associated with y in $\{x = 3,\ y = 5\}$ is denoted by $\{x = 3,\ y = 5\}(y)$ and is 5. The notation $Env(id)$ much resembles a function application, which is no coincidence: an environment is, in fact, a mapping from identifiers to values, that is, a function.

Environments and expressions

An expression containing a name must be evaluated in an environment in which the name is bound. If e is an expression and Env is an environment, we write $\langle e \mid Env \rangle$ to denote that e shall be evaluated in the environment Env. For instance, $\langle x + y \mid \{x = 3, y = 5\} \rangle$ means that the expression $x + y$ shall be evaluated in the environment $\{x = 3, y = 5\}$. Do not confuse $\langle e \mid Env \rangle$ (evaluating an *expression* in an environment) and $Env(id)$ (looking up a *name* in an environment).

$$\langle x + y \mid \{x = 3, y = 5\} \rangle\ \longrightarrow\ \langle 3 + y \mid \{x = 3, y = 5\} \rangle\ \longrightarrow$$
$$\langle 3 + 5 \mid \{x = 3, y = 5\} \rangle\ \longrightarrow\ \langle 8 \mid \{x = 3, y = 5\} \rangle$$

A pair of an expression and an environment is often called a *closure*. A closure is a description of the current *state* of the reduction machine, where the expression is the contents of the program store and the environment the contents of the environment store. The effect of evaluating declarations is that the environment store is changed. Therefore, from now on we let the reductions work on closures and not on expressions, so that we describe how the whole state of the machine is transformed by the reductions.

Evaluation of variables

The simplest form of expression containing a name is a single name. Suppose that id is a name and that Env is an environment. To evaluate the expression id simply amounts to looking the name up in the environment.

$$\frac{Env(id) = v}{\langle id \mid Env \rangle \longrightarrow \langle v \mid Env \rangle}$$

The rule says that if the *name id* is bound to v in the environment Env, then the value of the *expression id* evaluated in the environment Env is v.

Any expression can contain variables, and we have to extend all the previous rules to handle environments. For instance, the rules for a conditional expression now become

1. $$\frac{\langle b \mid Env \rangle \longrightarrow \langle b' \mid Env \rangle}{\langle \textbf{if } b \textbf{ then } e_1 \textbf{ else } e_2 \mid Env \rangle \longrightarrow \langle \textbf{if } b' \textbf{ then } e_1 \textbf{ else } e_2 \mid Env \rangle}$$

2. $\langle \textbf{if } true \textbf{ then } e_1 \textbf{ else } e_2 \mid Env \rangle \longrightarrow \langle e_1 \mid Env \rangle$

3. $\langle \textbf{if } false \textbf{ then } e_1 \textbf{ else } e_2 \mid Env \rangle \longrightarrow \langle e_2 \mid Env \rangle$

10.1.3 Evaluation of declarations and programs

So far, we have described how to evaluate expressions in environments, but not how environments are created in the first place. When a value declaration is evaluated, the result is an environment, not a value. We therefore extend the class of objects that can occur in the program store with environments, in addition to programs. The "value" of a value declaration is an environment containing the bindings introduced by the declaration, but not any previous bindings; they are already stored in the environment store. For instance, when you evaluate the declaration **val** $x = 3$ you get the environment $\{x = 3\}$ as result. In general, the right-hand side of a declaration is an expression, which must be evaluated. We now formalize this fact in a rule, assuming that e is an expression and id a name. Env is the environment that exists *before* evaluation of the declaration, that is, the result of previous declarations.

1. $$\frac{\langle e \mid Env \rangle \longrightarrow \langle e' \mid Env \rangle}{\langle \textbf{val } id = e \mid Env \rangle \longrightarrow \langle \textbf{val } id = e' \mid Env \rangle}$$

When the expression has been evaluated, the resulting environment can be created. We assume that v is a value.

$$2. \quad \langle \mathbf{val}\ id\ =\ v \mid Env \rangle \ \longrightarrow\ \langle \{id = v\} \mid Env \rangle$$

Note that we also allow an environment to be the result of an evaluation. We do this only to show how the machine works; in a real ML system, you will never get an environment as a result. After the evaluation of a declaration, the resulting environment must be combined with the previous environment Env—the combined environment is the one in which the next declaration is to be evaluated. In terms of the reduction machine, you have to add the computed environment to the environment store. Suppose that $decl$ is a declaration, that $decls$ is a sequence of declarations, and that Env is an environment.

$\vdots$	Current environment here is Env
$decl;$	Yields the environment Env'
$decls$	To be evaluated in the environment $Env + Env'$

Note how the bindings in $decl$ are accumulated to the old environment. We can now formalize the evaluation of a program, which is a sequence of declarations.

$$1. \quad \frac{\langle decl \mid Env \rangle \ \longrightarrow\ \langle decl' \mid Env \rangle}{\langle decl;\ decls \mid Env \rangle \ \longrightarrow\ \langle decl';\ decls \mid Env \rangle}$$

$$2. \quad \frac{\langle decl \mid Env \rangle \ \longrightarrow\ \langle Env' \mid Env \rangle}{\langle decl;\ decls \mid Env \rangle \ \longrightarrow\ \langle decls \mid Env + Env' \rangle}$$

A declaration can introduce several bindings, for example, when matching a tuple. The semantics of pattern matching is given in Chapter 12.

The standard environment

The ML language really consists of two parts, a kernel and a set of standard bindings. These standard bindings together form what is called the standard environment containing, for instance, *true* and *false*, the arithmetic operators, and functions like *abs*, *not*, and *sqrt*. When the reduction machine starts the evaluation of a program, the environment store contains these standard bindings. In most systems, the initial environment also contains some more predefined functions, but they are not part of the ML language.

10.2   Semantics of Functions

Functions, of course, play a central role in a functional language. The important property of a function is that it can be applied to different arguments at different times. To give the semantics of functions you have to describe both how functions are defined and how they are applied to arguments. The semantics of functions in the general case raises some obstacles and, to ease your understanding, the semantics will be developed in three steps, two of which are described in this chapter and the last one in Chapter 14. Each new step will subsume the earlier ones, and only the last description will handle functions in their full generality.

Functions as objects

Normally, you define a function in a function declaration.

$$- \quad \textbf{fun } f \ x \ = \ x + 3 \, ;$$
$$> \quad \textbf{val } f \ = \ \textbf{fn} \ : \ int \ -> int$$

This way of defining a function supports the belief that a function only occurs together with an argument in a program. As mentioned several times before, a function declaration is only a derived form of a particular kind of value declaration.

$$- \quad \textbf{val } f \ = \ \textbf{fn } x \ => x + 3 \, ;$$
$$> \quad \textbf{val } f \ = \ \textbf{fn} \ : \ int \ -> int$$

This declaration has the same effect as the previous one but stresses the fact that a function is an object in itself. In our first effort to formalize the semantics of functions, we treat a function declaration by considering the corresponding value declaration and use the machinery developed for value declarations. The two previous declarations then both yield the environment $\{f = \textbf{fn } x \ => \ x + 3\}$.

Function applications

We must now define how functions are applied. The general form of a function application is one expression followed by another expression, for instance $f \ 5$. Both the operator (the first expression) and the operand (the second expression) can be complicated expressions, for instance, as in $(\textbf{if } x > 0 \textbf{ then } f \textbf{ else } g)(x+1, x-1)$. To perform the application, you must therefore first evaluate the operator and the operand. Again, an expression is evaluated from left to right.

1. $$\frac{\langle e_1 \mid Env \rangle \ \longrightarrow \ \langle e_1' \mid Env \rangle}{\langle e_1 \ e_2 \mid Env \rangle \ \longrightarrow \ \langle e_1' \ e_2 \mid Env \rangle}$$

2. $$\frac{\langle e_2 \mid Env \rangle \ \longrightarrow \ \langle e_2' \mid Env \rangle}{\langle (\textbf{fn } id \ => \ e) \ e_2 \mid Env \rangle \ \longrightarrow \ \langle (\textbf{fn } id \ => \ e) \ e_2' \mid Env \rangle}$$

Note that **fn** *id* => *e* is a canonical expression. These two rules take care of evaluating the individual expressions in a function application. We now have to describe how a function is applied to its argument. We have previously performed applications by substituting the argument for the parameter. Let us now instead use environments.

An erroneous attempt

One idea is to bind the argument to the parameter and add this binding to the current environment. Let us look at why this is incorrect.

$$\langle (\textbf{fn } id \Rightarrow e)\, v \mid Env \rangle \longrightarrow \langle e \mid Env + \{id = v\} \rangle$$

Now, the application $f\,5$ yields the correct result 8, and everything looks fine.

Bound and free variables

If a function contains a name, which is not a parameter, that name is said to be **free** in the function, whereas a parameter is said to be **bound**. The given rule does not work correctly for functions containing free variables.

```
  -  val y = 3;
  >  val y = 3  :  int

  -  fun f x = x + y;
  >  val f = fn  :  int -> int

  -  f 5;
     8 : int
```

Now let *Env* be the environment $\{y = 3, f = \textbf{fn } x \Rightarrow x + y\}$. Then,

$$\langle f\,5 \mid Env \rangle \longrightarrow \langle (\textbf{fn } x \Rightarrow x + y)\,5 \mid Env \rangle \longrightarrow$$
$$\langle x + y \mid Env + \{x = 5\} \rangle \longrightarrow \langle 5 + y \mid Env + \{x = 5\} \rangle \longrightarrow$$
$$\langle 5 + 3 \mid Env + \{x = 5\} \rangle \longrightarrow \langle 8 \mid Env + \{x = 5\} \rangle$$

So far everything looks fine. Suppose, however, that we continue the example by binding a new value to *y*.

```
  -  val y = 7;
  >  val y = 7  :  int

  -  f 5;
     8 : int
```

The system tells us that the result of $f\ 5$ still is 8, but if we try to reduce $f\ 5$ using our rule above, we will get the result 12, since y is now bound to 7 in Env. The reason is that we have to use the environment valid at the declaration of the function, not the one valid when the function is applied to its argument. Hence, we have to change our application rule.

Closures

When evaluating a function application, we have to start with the environment valid when declaring the function and extend it with the bindings to the parameters. Hence, for any function declaration, we have to remember not only the function expression, but also the environment valid at the time of declaration, that is, we have to bind the name of the function to a closure. The reason it is called a closure is that an expression containing free variables is called an *open* expression, and by associating to it the bindings of its free variables, you close it. For example, the function f will be bound to the closure $\langle \mathbf{fn}\ x\ =>\ x + y \mid \{y = 3\}\rangle$, since the environment just before the function declaration is $\{y = 3\}$. The environment valid after the function declaration now is

$$\{f = \langle \mathbf{fn}\ x\ =>\ x + y \mid \{y = 3\}\rangle,\ y = 3\}$$

since two declarations have been evaluated. If you now bind y to 7 in a new declaration, the new environment will be

$$\{f = \langle \mathbf{fn}\ x\ =>\ x + y \mid \{y = 3\}\rangle, y = 7\}$$

Looking up y in this environment gives the result 7, but $f\ 5$ will give the result 8, since the old binding of y will be used when evaluating the application.

The rule for defining a function must now include the formation of a closure containing the current environment.

3. $\langle \mathbf{val}\ f\ =\ \mathbf{fn}\ id\ =>\ e \mid Env\rangle\ \longrightarrow\ \langle\{f = \langle \mathbf{fn}\ id\ =>\ e \mid Env\rangle\} \mid Env\rangle$

The evaluation of the two subexpressions of a function application is essentially the same as before, only that the value of a function name is a closure, not a function expression.

$$f\ 5\ \longrightarrow\ \langle \mathbf{fn}\ x\ =>\ x + y \mid \{y = 3\}\rangle\ 5$$

When performing the application, you must reinstall the old environment from the closure and extend it with the binding to the parameter.

4. $\langle\langle \mathbf{fn}\ id\ =>\ e \mid Env\rangle\ v \mid Env'\rangle\ \longrightarrow\ \langle\langle e \mid Env + \{id = v\}\rangle \mid Env'\rangle$

The body is now evaluated in the new environment.

5. $$\frac{\langle e \mid Env\rangle \;\longrightarrow\; \langle e' \mid Env\rangle}{\langle\langle e \mid Env\rangle \mid Env'\rangle \;\longrightarrow\; \langle\langle e' \mid Env\rangle \mid Env'\rangle}$$

When the body is reduced to a canonical expression, the temporary environment is thrown away.

6. $\quad \langle\langle v \mid Env\rangle \mid Env'\rangle \;\longrightarrow\; \langle v \mid Env'\rangle$

We can now complete the evaluation of f 5.

$$\langle f\ 5 \mid Env\rangle \;\longrightarrow\; \langle\langle \textbf{fn}\ x \;=>\; x+y \mid \{y=3\}\rangle\ 5 \mid Env\rangle \;\longrightarrow\;$$
$$\langle\langle x+y \mid \{x=5, y=3\}\rangle \mid Env\rangle \;\longrightarrow\; \cdots \;\longrightarrow\;$$
$$\langle\langle 8 \mid \{x=5, y=3\}\rangle \mid Env\rangle \;\longrightarrow\; \langle 8 \mid Env\rangle$$

Since the evaluation of one function application can lead to the evaluation of many other applications, the machine must be able to save environments. Usually, a so-called stack is used for this purpose (cf. page 167).

The way of handling free variables described above is called **static binding**. The word static means that you can see directly from the definition of a function what it does. This is an important property and greatly simplifies the under-standing of a program. Another alternative for handling free variables is to use **dynamic binding**, where the application environment is used in a function application instead of the declaration environment. The meaning of a function now depends on which bindings are in effect when you apply the function to some argument—the meaning is not fixed, but can vary from application to application, which is not desirable.

To describe the semantics of recursive functions, we need yet another extension to the rules for functions. This extension is described in Chapter 14.

Summary

One way of defining the semantics of a programming language is to define an *abstract machine* that evaluates programs. For ML, we define a *reduction* machine that reduces expressions to *canonical* expressions. To handle variables, the machine contains an *environment store* with bindings, in which variables can be looked up. The machine works according to special *axioms* and *derivation rules* that describe how expressions shall be reduced. To handle free variables, the rules manipulate *closures*, that is, pairs of an expression and an environment. To evaluate functions, function names are bound to closures containing the environment valid at the point of declaration, a scheme called *static binding*.

Chapter 11

Declarations

We have looked at value declarations and at function declarations, which are only a special kind of value declaration. With both, you give a name to a data object. You can also introduce new data types with new data objects in special data type declarations. Again, you name objects.

By naming an object, you usually perform an abstraction. When a function has been named, for instance, you do not have to remember exactly how it is computed. By using expressive names you increase the readability of the program. Moreover, you often increase the modifiability, since, even though the name is used at several places in the program, its meaning is defined at only one place.

When defining a programming language you want to make it as general as possible without making it big and complicated. An *extensible* language has a small kernel and powerful extension mechanisms. Such a language can easily be adapted to many different applications. In ML, there are various kinds of declarations by which you can extend the language in different directions, starting with a small kernel only.

11.1 Scope Rules

When using a name in a large program developed by many programmers, there is always a risk that someone does not know what the name stands for, that the name has several meanings, or that the meaning of the name has been changed without the knowledge of everybody. By delimiting the **scope** of a name, you avoid some such problems. Let us look at the *scope rules*, which tell in which part of a program a declared name is known.

A program is a sequence of declarations. These declarations are said to occur at the *top-level*. We can now formulate the first scope rule.

> A name declared at top-level is known from the point of its declara-
> tion to the next declaration of the same name or, if the name is not
> redeclared, to the end of the program.

Thus, a name is not known before it is declared, and if it is redeclared, the old
meaning is hidden. Note that a declared name is known only in the declaration
after the one in which it is declared. However, in a recursive declaration, to be
described later, the name is also known in the declaration itself.

Temporary bindings and local scopes

In a large program, you sometimes want to use the same name for several different
objects in different parts of the program. You then need a way of letting it be
known only within a certain program fragment. Such a scope is called a **local**
scope. For instance, the parameter in a function definition is known only in the
function body and does not interfere with the surrounding program.

```
    -   val  n  =  5;
    >   val  n  =  5  :  int


    -   fun  sum1to n  =  n * (n + 1)  div  2;
    >   val  sum1to  =  fn  :  int −> int


    -   sum1to 100;
        5050 : int
```

There are two different uses of the identifier n. In the first declaration, n is bound
to 5. In the declaration of the function $sum1to$, n is used as a parameter. This use
of n is valid only in the function body—it has a local scope. The name n declared
at the top-level is therefore inaccessible in the body. When the function is applied
to the argument 100, the parameter n becomes bound to 100, and the function
body is evaluated with this binding to n. During the function application, the
former binding of n to 5 is *temporarily* hidden, but becomes visible again after the
application.

```
    -   sum1to n;
        15 : int
```

Note that $sum1to$ is applied to the value of n, that is, 5; no confusion with the
parameter n therefore occurs.

11.2 Local Declarations

In some programs you need auxiliary declarations, which are valid only locally. There are two types of local declaration: declarations local to expressions and declarations local to other declarations.

11.2.1 Local declarations in expressions

In your geometry book, you might find the Heron formula for calculating the area of a triangle with sides a, b, and c.

$$\sqrt{p*(p-a)*(p-b)*(p-c)} \qquad \text{where} \quad p = \frac{a+b+c}{2}$$

In the formula, p is half of the perimeter. Now, suppose you want to define a function *area* with parameters a, b, and c. Then, you want to evaluate p and use the computed value when calculating the area; otherwise, you have to calculate p four times. A *local declaration* comes to rescue here.

$$-\quad \textbf{fun } area\ (a,b,c)\ =\ \textbf{let val } p\ =\ (a+b+c)/2.0$$
$$\textbf{in } sqrt(p*(p-a)*(p-b)*(p-c))$$
$$\textbf{end};$$
$$>\quad \textbf{val } area\ =\ \textbf{fn}\ :\ real*real*real\ ->\ real$$

The value of p is calculated in a local value declaration, which is valid only in the expression between the reserved words **in** and **end**. As a rule, it should be indented as in the Heron example. Thanks to the local declaration, we can use the Heron formula as it is and avoid duplicate calculations. We can now use the function *area*.

$$-\quad area\ (3.0, 4.0, 5.0);$$
$$6.0\ :\ real$$

The syntax of a local declaration is

LOCAL DECLARATION

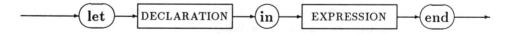

We must also define the semantics of an expression with a local declaration. The value of a local declaration is the value of the expression after the reserved word **in** evaluated in the current environment extended with the environment returned by the declarations occurring between **let** and **in**. These declarations are valid only locally in the expression.

A particular kind of declaration is a declaration sequence and, consequently, there can be several declarations after **let**. Further, since a local declaration is an expression, you can give it to the ML system to be evaluated.

> $-$ **let val** $x = 3$
>   **val** $y = x * x$
>   **in** $x * y$
>   **end** ;
> $27 : int$

Note that you do not need a semicolon between declarations in a declaration sequence. You can insert them if you want to, however. After the evaluation of the local declaration expression, the bindings have vanished.

> $-$ $x * y$;
> Unbound identifier : x

Example: Discount calculation

A carpet company gives 5 % discount if a customer buys a wall-to-wall carpet for 100 pounds or more. The cost of a carpet is calculated from the *length*, *width*, and square meter *price* before value added tax, which is 20 %. We want a function *cost* that yields the cost given the *length*, *width*, and *price* of the carpet.

Before investigating if the customer will get a discount, the nominal *amount* must be calculated. We use a local declaration, since the name *amount* has to be used several times.

> $-$ **fun** *cost* $(length, width, price) =$
>   **let**   **val** $amount = length * width * price * 1.2$
>   **in**   **if** $amount < 100.0$
>   **then** *amount*
>   **else** $amount * 0.95$
>   **end** ;
> $>$ **val** *cost* $=$ **fn** $: real * real * real -> real$

11.2.2 Local declarations in declarations

When defining a function, you often need auxiliary functions and other declarations. Some or all of the names introduced in these declarations may be particular to the defined function and should therefore have a restricted scope. Others may be names you want to use in other parts of the program.

In Chapter 5, a function *vol2* was defined. In the program, the auxiliary names *pi*, *vol*, and *round2* were introduced. The constant *pi* is of general interest, but we hide the two functions.

>   − **val** *pi* = 3.1415927;
>   > **val** *pi* = 3.1415927 : *real*

>   − **local fun** *vol r* = 4.0 ∗ *pi* ∗ *r* ∗ *r* ∗ *r*/3.0
>   **fun** *round2 x* = *real*(*floor x*)+
>   *real*(*round*(100.0 ∗ (*x* − *real*(*floor x*))))/100.0
>   **in fun** *vol2 r* = *round2*(*vol r*)
>   **end**;
>   > **val** *vol2* : *real* −> *real*

Using a local declaration you limit the scope of the declarations between **local** and **in** to the declaration(s) between **in** and **end**. Note that the system responds with the type of the exported name only.

Hiding names

Consider the following definition of *anniversary*.

>   − **local fun** *divides*(*x, y*) = *y mod x* = 0
>   **in fun** *anniversary age* = *divides*(10, *age*) **orelse** *divides*(25, *age*)
>   **end**;
>   > **val** *anniversary* : *int* −> *bool*

Suppose you are writing a big program and that several programmers are involved in the work. If the function *divides* is defined at some other place in the program with a different meaning, you have to make it local; otherwise, other occurrences of *divides* may use the wrong definition.

Another risk of not making *divides* local is that someone else might find use for it. This is not dangerous in itself, but suppose you do not know about this and change your definition of it, for example, by switching the arguments. Then, some other programmer will find that a function that was working correctly before, now works incorrectly.

> If possible, make declarations local in order to avoid name clashes
> and programs that are difficult to modify.

If you define a function that is generally known and there is no risk of misinter-
pretations, you can make it generally available. Such a function should, however,
be accompanied by a precise specification and, preferably, be put in a library of
function definitions.

11.2.3   Formal semantics of local declarations

A local declaration expression is evaluated by first evaluating the declaration in
the current environment, here called Env.

$$1. \quad \frac{\langle decl \mid Env \rangle \longrightarrow \langle decl' \mid Env \rangle}{\langle \textbf{let } decl \textbf{ in } e \textbf{ end} \mid Env \rangle \longrightarrow \langle \textbf{let } decl' \textbf{ in } e \textbf{ end} \mid Env \rangle}$$

Suppose that Env' is the environment you get by evaluating $decl$. The evaluation
of the expression then takes place in the extended environment $Env + Env'$.

$$2. \quad \langle \textbf{let } Env' \textbf{ in } e \textbf{ end} \mid Env \rangle \longrightarrow \langle \langle e \mid Env + Env' \rangle \mid Env \rangle$$

The result of evaluating a local declaration is a closure. The evaluation of closures
is described on page 125. The semantics of a declaration with a local declaration
is similar.

$$1. \quad \frac{\langle decl \mid Env \rangle \longrightarrow \langle decl' \mid Env \rangle}{\langle \textbf{local } decl \textbf{ in } decl'' \textbf{ end} \mid Env \rangle \longrightarrow \langle \textbf{local } decl' \textbf{ in } decl'' \textbf{ end} \mid Env \rangle}$$

$$2. \quad \langle \textbf{local } Env' \textbf{ in } decl'' \textbf{ end} \mid Env \rangle \longrightarrow \langle \langle decl'' \mid Env + Env' \rangle \mid Env \rangle$$

As an example, suppose that there is only one value declaration after **let**.

$$\langle \textbf{let val } id = v \textbf{ in } e \textbf{ end} \mid Env \rangle \longrightarrow$$
$$\langle \textbf{let } \{id = v\} \textbf{ in } e \textbf{ end} \mid Env \rangle \longrightarrow$$
$$\langle \langle e \mid Env + \{id = v\} \rangle \mid Env \rangle$$

The current environment Env is extended with the new binding.

A closer examination reveals that a local declaration expression and a function
application have much in common. In fact, you really do not need the local
declarations, but can do with only functions. Can you see how the Heron function
can be defined without a local declaration??

By creating a function that has p as parameter and then applying this function
to half the perimeter, you can achieve the same effect.

- **fun** $area\ (a, b, c) =$
  $(\textbf{fn}\ p\ =>\ sqrt(p * (p - a) * (p - b) * (p - c)))((a + b + c)/2.0)\,;$
> **val** $area = \textbf{fn}\ :\ real * real * real\ ->\ real$

After the declaration, *area* will be bound to the function expression

$$\textbf{fn}\ (a, b, c)\ =>\ (\textbf{fn}\ p\ =>\ sqrt(p * (p - a) * (p - b) * (p - c)))\ ((a + b + c)/2.0)$$

11.3   Multiple Bindings

In mathematics, the *tanh* (hyperbolic tangent) function is defined by

$$tanh(x) = \frac{e^x - e^{-x}}{e^x + e^{-x}}$$

You can define it in the same way in ML.

- **fun** $tanh\ x\ =\ (exp\ x - exp(\tilde{}x))/(exp\ x + exp(\tilde{}x))\,;$
> **val** $tanh = \textbf{fn}\ :\ real\ ->\ real$

However, the computations of the exponentials are duplicated, and if *tanh* is often used a more efficient version may be needed. Since both $exp\ x$ and $exp(\tilde{}x)$ are duplicated, you need two local names. A *multiple binding* is one way of defining several names in a declaration.

- **fun** $tanh\ x\ =\ \textbf{let}\ \textbf{val}\ \ e1\ =\ exp\ x$
  $\qquad\qquad\qquad \textbf{and}\ e2\ =\ exp(\tilde{}x)$
  $\qquad\quad \textbf{in}\ (e1 - e2)/(e1 + e2)$
  $\qquad\quad \textbf{end}\,;$
> **val** $tanh = \textbf{fn}\ :\ real\ ->\ real$

A multiple binding is a variant of a value binding. The syntax of a value binding is (omitting recursive bindings)

VALUE BINDING

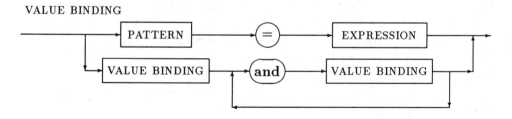

A multiple value binding is evaluated by evaluating all constituent bindings in the current environment. The result is an environment containing all new bindings. Note that names declared within the multiple binding are accessible only after the binding, not within itself.

```
−  val  x  =  5
   and  y  =  x * x ;
Unbound identifier : x
```

Multiple bindings are really needed only in so-called mutually recursive function declarations; in the examples above you can do with sequences of declarations.

Formal semantics of multiple bindings

We show here multiple bindings with only two bindings, but the rules can easily be generalized. All the bindings are to be evaluated from left to right within the old environment, facts captured by the first two rules. Each binding yields an environment as result. The combination of these environments is then returned as the result from the multiple binding, a fact described by the third rule.

$$1. \quad \frac{\langle bind_1 \mid Env \rangle \longrightarrow \langle bind_1' \mid Env \rangle}{\langle \textbf{val } bind_1 \textbf{ and } bind_2 \mid Env \rangle \longrightarrow \langle \textbf{val } bind_1' \textbf{ and } bind_2 \mid Env \rangle}$$

$$2. \quad \frac{\langle bind_2 \mid Env \rangle \longrightarrow \langle bind_2' \mid Env \rangle}{\langle \textbf{val } Env_1 \textbf{ and } bind_2 \mid Env \rangle \longrightarrow \langle \textbf{val } Env_1 \textbf{ and } bind_2' \mid Env \rangle}$$

$$3. \quad \langle \textbf{val } Env_1 \textbf{ and } Env_2 \mid Env \rangle \longrightarrow \langle Env_1 + Env_2 \mid Env \rangle$$

Exercises

11.1. Define the *tanh* function using a declaration sequence instead of a multiple binding.

11.4   Datatype Declarations

In a value or function declaration, you give a name to a data object. You can also introduce new data types with new data objects in special datatype declarations. A data type is a set of data objects and a collection of operations suitable for dealing with these data objects. The type *bool*, for instance, contains the two data objects *true* and *false*, and the type *int* contains a finite set of numerals, namely *minint*, ..., ~1, 0, 1, ..., *maxint*.

Modelling the real world

A program together with its input data usually constitute a model of some application area. For each new area, objects or phenomena in the real world have to be described by data objects. In a language with a fixed number of data types and data objects, you have to invent more or less ingenious codings when describing objects. In an extensible language, you are provided with facilities that let you adapt your language to each new area. By defining new data types, you can avoid codings, and in this way increase the readability of your program. Another advantage of introducing new types is that the ML system can check your program for errors in a much better way.

Introducing new data objects

Suppose you want to represent the seven days of the week in a program. You may, for instance, use the numbers 1 through 7 or the strings "mon", "tue", ..., "sun". In both cases, you use another type of data object to represent days. A better way, however, is to define a data type *DAY* containing seven *new* data objects. A new data object must be an identifier, and we here choose the three first letters of each day. Since these names construct new data objects, they are the *constructors* of the data type.

$$\begin{aligned}
&- \ \textbf{datatype } DAY \ = \ Mon \mid Tue \mid Wed \mid Thu \mid Fri \mid Sat \mid Sun; \\
&> \ \textbf{datatype } DAY \ = \ Mon \mid Tue \mid Wed \mid Thu \mid Fri \mid Sat \mid Sun \\
&\quad \ \ \textbf{con } Mon \ = \ Mon \ : \ DAY \\
&\quad \ \ \textbf{con } Tue \ \ = \ Tue \ : \ DAY \\
&\quad \quad \ \ \ldots \\
&\quad \ \ \textbf{con } Sun \ \ = \ Sun \ : \ DAY
\end{aligned}$$

In this datatype declaration, eight new identifiers are introduced: one type name and seven new constructors, each indicated by the word **con**. Since this kind of data type is declared by enumerating its elements, it is sometimes called an **enumeration** type. As a convention, we always use capital letters in type names, but that is nothing that is enforced by the ML system. In the same way, we let all new constructors start with a capital letter. This convention helps us to differentiate between three categories of object: types, data objects (constructors), and names of values. In particular, since the system differentiates between lower and upper case letters, identifiers like *PERSON*, *Person*, and *person* are different and can be used in the same program to name different things.

After the declaration of the type *DAY*, the ML system knows about the new data objects.

$$\begin{aligned}
&- \ Wed; \\
&\quad \ Wed \ : \ DAY
\end{aligned}$$

The data objects are all canonical expressions and therefore evaluate to themselves; the value of *Wed* is *Wed* in the same way as the value of *true* is *true*. Also note that the ML system now knows about the type *DAY* and can decide correctly the type of *Wed*.

According to the type completeness principle, you can use a data object of type *DAY* as any other data object.

> — (*Wed*, 11.30);
>   (*Wed*, 11.3) : *DAY* ∗ *real*

> — **fun** *is_workday day* = *day* <> *Sat* **andalso** *day* <> *Sun*;
> > **val** *is_workday* = **fn** : *DAY* −> *bool*

As mentioned, a data type is a set of data objects together with a collection of operations for dealing with these data objects. For enumeration types, the only operations available in ML are tests for equality (=) and inequality (<>). By defining functions like, for instance, *is_workday*, you extend the repertoire of operations for dealing with *DAY*. The primary way of investigating new data objects, however, is pattern matching, which is treated further in the next chapter.

The possibility of introducing new types and data objects considerably increases the modelling power of a language, as the following examples try to show.

> **datatype** *COLOUR*   = *White* | *Yellow* | *Red* | *Green* | *Blue* | *Black*;
> **datatype** *DIRECTION* = *West* | *South* | *East* | *North*;
> **datatype** *SUIT*   = *Spades* | *Hearts* | *Diamonds* | *Clubs*;
> **datatype** *OPERATOR* = *Plus* | *Minus* | *Times* | *Divide*;

Some standard data types

In ML, the type *bool* is considered as an extension to the kernel of the language and in the ML Report it is defined in a datatype declaration.

> — **datatype** *bool* = *true* | *false*;
> > **datatype** *bool* = *true* | *false*
> > **con** *true* = *true* : *bool*
> > **con** *false* = *false* : *bool*

If our naming convention had been used in ML, the constructor names would have been *True* and *False* and the type name *BOOL*.

A very special standard type in ML is the *unit* type[1]. It contains only one data object, sometimes called the *hermit*, and in ML denoted by {} or ().

> — **datatype** *unit* = {};
> > **datatype** *unit* = {}
> > **con** {} = {} : *unit*

---

[1]The *unit* type is defined in a slightly different manner in ML.

$-$ {};
      {} : *unit*

$-$ ();
      {} : *unit*

The *unit* type might seem useless but is, in fact, often used in (strict) functional programs as you will see later.

Semantics of data types

In a datatype declaration you introduce names both for a new type and for new data objects. We will here consider only the treatment of data objects. When the reduction machine encounters constants like 3 or *true*, it recognizes them as constants and, therefore, does not try to evaluate them further. A data object like *Wed* is a constant, too, and the reduction machine must therefore store this fact. We ignore the details of how this is done in the machine, however.

Summary

The *scope* of a name is the part of the program in which it is known. A parameter to a function has a *local* scope being the whole body of the function, unless the name is rebound in the body. Declarations can be made local to expressions and to other declarations using *local declarations*. By making names local, you avoid name clashes and the use of a definition by mistake. With a *datatype* declaration, you can define a new data type and *constructors* for the type. Datatype declarations make it easier to model the real world in a faithful way.

Exercises

11.2. Define suitable data types for describing some makes of cars, some shapes of objects, the two sexes, the pieces you use in chess, or some other types of your own choice.

11.3. Redefine the function *complroots* from Exercise 8.6 by using local declarations.

Chapter 12

Pattern Matching and Case Analysis

As humans we analyse data all the time. Coming to a cross-road, you analyse
the lights to see if they are red or green and then act accordingly. In your brain,
the signals are matched against acquired *patterns*. In the same way, arguments
to functions can be matched against different forms of patterns in order to be
analysed, and the computation can then proceed accordingly.

Certainly, the form of pattern matching to be performed is dependent on the
type of data object to be analysed. In ML, pattern matching is the opposite process
of constructing a data object. For each way of constructing a data object, there is
a corresponding type of pattern. Understanding this *duality* is an important step
in your understanding of ML, and of programming in general.

12.1   Pattern Matching

Pattern matching occurs in several contexts in ML. The left-hand side of a value
declaration is a pattern and so is the part of a function declaration that is to be
matched against the argument.

$$- \quad \textbf{val } (x, y) = (2, false);$$
$$> \quad \textbf{val } x = 2 \; : \; int$$
$$\textbf{val } y = false \; : \; bool$$

$$- \quad \textbf{fun } f(x, y, z) = (x + y + z)/3.0\,;$$
$$> \quad \textbf{val } f = \textbf{fn} \; : \; real * real * real \; -> \; real$$

The result of matching against a pattern is an environment, that is, a set of
bindings.

12.1.1 The various pattern forms

Variable patterns

A pattern which consists of only a variable (a name) matches anything. The result of the match is an environment in which the name is bound to the matched data object. Pattern matching against a variable therefore results in the *naming* a data object or a part of it.

```
-  fun ident x = x ;
>  val ident = fn : 'a -> 'a
```

When applying *ident* to 3, for instance, 3 is matched against the pattern x, and the environment $\{x = 3\}$ is returned. In matching against a variable, no analysis takes place. Matching against a variable therefore always succeeds. You will later see that most other types of pattern match only a subset of all data objects of the type.

Wild cards

In the definition of the function *fst*, a wild card is used as second pattern, because we are not interested in the second element.

```
-  fun fst (x, _ ) = x ;
>  val fst = fn : 'a * 'b -> 'a
```

The wild card pattern is like a variable in that it matches any data object. No naming takes place, however, so the empty environment is returned.

Constant patterns

By a constant, we here mean an atomic canonical expression like 3, *true*, and *Wed*. Let us, as a simple example, write a function taking the hermit {} as argument.

```
-  fun hello {} = "hello" ;
>  val hello = fn : unit -> string

-  hello {} ;
   "hello" : string
```

The argument {} is matched against the *constant* pattern {}. Matching against a constant pattern succeeds only if the argument and the pattern are identical. When matching against a constant pattern, no naming takes place, and the empty environment is therefore returned as a result.

Example: Delayed evaluation

A typical use of the *unit* type and the element {} is to delay an action. Division by zero always leads to an exception, which halts the execution.

> — **val** *halt* = 1 *div* 0 ;
> Failure : *div*

The right-hand side of a value declaration is always evaluated directly, but that is not the case in a function declaration.

> — **fun** *halt* {} = 1 *div* 0 ;
> > **val** *halt* = **fn** : *unit* −> *int*

The division is not performed, and the declaration is executed in a normal way. A function is a data object, so we can give it to the system.

> — *halt* ;
> **fn** : *unit* −> *int*

A function expression has itself as value, so the division is not performed. If *halt* is applied to {}, however, the function body will be evaluated.

> — *halt* {} ;
> Failure : *div*

By creating a function expression of an expression with a unit type argument, its evaluation is delayed until that function is applied to {}. In this way, you can get the effect of lazy or delayed evaluation of any expressions in ML. Many functional languages use lazy evaluation as a standard evaluation strategy, and tricks like the one described here need not be used.

Constructor patterns

Pairs like $(2, 3)$ and (*true*, "hello") are constructed using the pair constructor (..., ...). When analysing a pair, a pattern resembling the pair constructor is used. Instead of the data objects, *patterns* are used.

PAIR PATTERN

A pair pattern is matched by a pair only if the elements of the pair are matched. You have seen pair matching several times before.

    — **fun** *divides* $(x, y) = y \bmod x = 0$;
    > **val** *divides* = **fn** : *int* * *int* $->$ *bool*

Since the subpatterns are variables in this case, a non-empty environment is returned, but that is not necessary.

    — **fun** *nonsense* $(\{\}, \{\}) = \{\}$;
    > **val** *nonsense* = **fn** : *unit* * *unit* $->$ *unit*

The pair constructor and the pair pattern are good examples of the principle that pattern matching is the inverse of construction. The pair constructor puts two data objects together, and the pair pattern splits a pair into its parts, usually giving them names at the same time.

Alternative patterns

A pair can be constructed in only one way, but for most data types there are several ways of constructing their objects. There are two boolean constructors, *true* and *false*, and when writing a function taking a *bool* as argument, you want to split the computation into two cases. This is done by the use of alternative patterns.

    — **fun** *not true* = *false*
       | *not false* = *true*;
    > **val** *not* = **fn** : *bool* $->$ *bool*

When matching against alternative patterns, the patterns are tried one after the other until one that matches is found. For many alternative patterns, the order of matching against patterns is essential. For the *not* function, however, the order is not essential.

In the previous chapter the type *DIRECTION* was defined[1].

    datatype *DIRECTION* = *North* | *East* | *South* | *West*

Let us define a function *bearing* giving the bearing of the four directions in degrees.

    — **fun** *bearing North* = 0
       | *bearing East* = 90
       | *bearing South* = 180
       | *bearing West* = 270;
    > **val** *bearing* = **fn** : *DIRECTION* $->$ *int*

---

[1]From now on, some system responses for data types will be omitted.

Since there are four members in the type, there are four alternative patterns. Again, you can list the alternatives in any order. Note that the symbol | is used both in the pattern and in the type declaration, which stresses the correspondence between the construction of data objects of some type and their analysis by pattern matching.

The function *is_workday* (page 136) can also be defined using alternative patterns.

```
—  fun  is_workday Sat  =  false
    |  is_workday Sun  =  false
    |  is_workday _    =  true;
>  val  is_workday  =  fn  :  DAY -> bool
```

Here the last five alternatives are taken care of by the wild card pattern. In contrast to the two previous declarations, the order of the patterns is now essential; the wild card must be tried last. The price you pay for the convenience of reducing seven patterns into three is that you cannot view the alternatives as a set of equations; you have to read them in the right order. As a rule, it is easier to read definitions, if the order is not essential. On the other hand, the reduction of the number of alternatives improves readability. Which is best must be decided from case to case.

The suits of a deck of cards can be defined by an enumeration type.

datatype *SUIT* = *Spades* | *Hearts* | *Diamonds* | *Clubs*

A card can now be represented by a pair of type *SUIT* $*$ *int*. One example is the pair (*Spades*, 12). Suppose that for a card-playing program you need a function *gt_card* that decides if one card is higher than another assuming that the suits in *SUIT* are given in decreasing order and that the values of the cards have their arithmetic order. Before defining *gt_card*, we define an auxiliary function *gt_suit* deciding if one *SUIT* is greater than another according to the given order. There are sixteen pairs to be matched, but many can be combined using wild cards.

```
—  fun  gt_suit ( _ , Spades)  =  false
    |  gt_suit (Spades, _ )  =  true
    |  gt_suit (Clubs, _ )   =  false
    |  gt_suit ( _ , Clubs)   =  true
    |  gt_suit (s1, s2)       =  s1 = Hearts andalso s2 = Diamonds;
>  val  gt_suit  =  fn  :  SUIT * SUIT -> bool
```

The function *gt_card* can now be defined, observing that if two cards have the same value, the order of their suits is considered.

```
—  fun  gt_card ((s1, v1 : int), (s2, v2)) =
           v1 > v2 orelse (v1 = v2 andalso gt_suit(s1, s2));
>  val  gt_card  =  fn  :  (SUIT * int) * (SUIT * int) -> bool
```

Patterns with type constraints

Any pattern can be combined with a type constraint, which consists of a colon and a type. A type constraint restricts the type of the arguments that can be matched against the pattern to the one specified in the constraint. Type constraint patterns have low precedence and usually have to be surrounded by parentheses. Their primary usage is to inform the system about the type in such cases where the system cannot deduce the type itself.

Type constraints can also be used to constrain the type of an argument to a polymorphic function. Suppose you want a function *get_suit* that selects the suit out of a card object. You can use the *fst* function but a better name would be an advantage.

```
-   fun get_suit (s, _) = s;
>   val get_suit = fn : 'a * 'b -> 'a
```

The problem with *get_suit* is that it can be applied to any type of pair. With type constraints you can solve this problem.

```
-   fun get_suit (s : SUIT, _ : int) = s;
>   val get_suit = fn : SUIT * int -> SUIT
```

Note that we restrict the type of the second element without using that value in order to restrict *get_suit* as much as possible. Type constraints can be used to decrease the risk of using the wrong function by mistake.

Layered patterns

When you match against a pattern with several parts, you sometimes also want to name the whole object. A layered pattern allows you both to name a data object and to match it against a structured pattern. The two patterns are separated by the reserved word **as**.

```
-   fun mirror (p as (x, y)) = (p, (y, x));
>   val mirror = fn : 'a * 'b -> ('a * 'b) * ('b * 'a)
```

```
-   mirror (3, 7);
    ((3, 7), (7, 3)) : (int * int) * (int * int)
```

When matching against a layered pattern, the resulting environment contains bindings both to the whole object and to those parts matched by variables.

12.1.2   Exhaustive and irredundant patterns

Suppose you forget some case in the definition of *gt_suit* (page 142).

$$
\begin{aligned}
- \quad &\textbf{fun} \;\; gt\_suit \;(\_ , Spades) \; = \; false \\
&\mid \;\; gt\_suit \;(Spades, \_) \; = \; true \\
&\mid \;\; gt\_suit \;(Clubs, \_) \;\;\; = \; false \\
&\mid \;\; gt\_suit \;(\_ , Clubs) \;\;\; = \; true \\
&\mid \;\; gt\_suit \;(Diamonds, Diamonds) \; = \; false\,;
\end{aligned}
$$

Warning: Patterns not exhaustive

> **val** *gt_suit* = **fn** : *SUIT* ∗ *SUIT* −> *bool*

The ML system now complains that the patterns are not *exhaustive*; you have
forgotten some case. The advantage of this capability of the ML system cannot be
exaggerated. It is a common programming error to forget some case when defining
a function, usually some very special case. By using pattern matching extensively,
you take advantage of the system and avoid many annoying errors.

The ML system gives a warning also if a pattern is *redundant*, that is, if the
pattern will never be used, because the preceding patterns match all that the
redundant pattern can match. This is a clear indication that you have made some
mistake. Again, this might help you to catch errors in your program at an early
stage.

If a pattern matches both something that is matched by earlier patterns and
something new, the order of the patterns is essential. If the patterns, on the
other hand, are *disjoint*, the equations can be read in any order, a property that
simplifies the reasoning about the function.

Measurements of the cost of errors in professional programming has shown that
the cost of finding and correcting an error increases with an order of magnitude
for each phase of the development for which it remains undetected. It is extremely
expensive to correct an error in a program in production, but if the error is detected
when the program is checked for the first time, the cost is negligible. The type
system of ML can detect an astonishing number of errors and is often of great
help.

12.1.3   Matches

Alternative patterns can be used also in function expressions.

$$
\begin{aligned}
- \quad &\textbf{val} \; is\_workday \; = \; \textbf{fn} \;\; Sat \; => \; false \\
&\mid \;\; Sun \; => \; false \\
&\mid \;\; \_ \;\;\;\; => \; true\,;
\end{aligned}
$$

> **val** *is_workday* = **fn** : *DAY* −> *bool*

The kind of function declaration you have seen previously is just a derived form of a value declaration similar to the one above. The construction occurring after **fn** is called a *match*, which consists of a sequence of **rules** separated by a | symbols.

MATCH

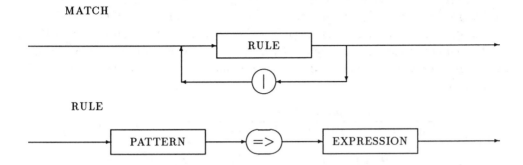

RULE

In the diagrams below, patterns are split into two kinds: PATTERN and ATOMIC PATTERN.

PATTERN

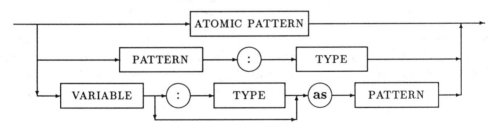

ATOMIC PATTERN

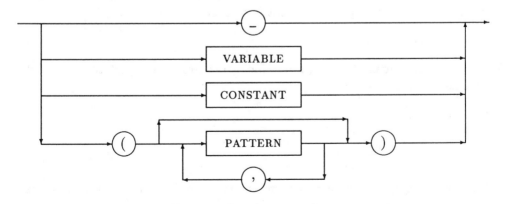

12.1.4   Formal semantics of pattern matching

Crucial to the semantics of pattern matching is that the application of a pattern to a value can succeed or fail. In our rules, we will mark a failure by letting the application return a special failure environment *Failure*. According to the syntax, a match is a sequence of rules (not to be confused with our semantic rules). Pattern matching is tried from left to right (top to bottom) until a match is found. Let us give the semantic rules for the case with two rules; it can easily be generalized. To denote that a pattern is matched against a value, we simply write the value after the pattern.

1. $$\frac{\langle pat\ v \mid Env \rangle \longrightarrow \langle Env' \mid Env \rangle}{\langle (pat\ \Rightarrow\ e \mid rule_2)\ v \mid Env \rangle \longrightarrow \langle \langle e \mid Env + Env' \rangle \mid Env \rangle}$$

2. $$\frac{\langle pat\ v \mid Env \rangle \longrightarrow \langle Failure \mid Env \rangle}{\langle (pat\ \Rightarrow\ e \mid rule_2)\ v \mid Env \rangle \longrightarrow \langle rule_2\ v \mid Env \rangle}$$

3. $$\frac{\langle pat\ v \mid Env \rangle \longrightarrow \langle Env' \mid Env \rangle}{\langle (pat\ \Rightarrow\ e)\ v \mid Env \rangle \longrightarrow \langle \langle e \mid Env + Env' \rangle \mid Env \rangle}$$

4. $$\frac{\langle pat\ v \mid Env \rangle \longrightarrow \langle Failure \mid Env \rangle}{\langle (pat\ \Rightarrow\ e)\ v \mid Env \rangle \longrightarrow \langle match\_error \mid Env \rangle}$$

If both matches fail, a match exception is generated, and the computation stops.

We must now describe which environments the different forms of pattern yield when matched against a value. We omit the current environment of the closures, since that is never changed. Matching against a variable creates a binding to the matched value.

5. $id\ v \longrightarrow \{id = v\}$

Matching against a variable can never give a failure. This is also the case for the wild card, but the empty environment is returned instead.

6. $\_\ v \longrightarrow \{\}$

When matching against a constant, the value must be equal to the constant, otherwise a failure results.

7. $con\ con \longrightarrow \{\}$

8. $$\frac{con \neq v}{con\ v \longrightarrow Failure}$$

When matching against a pair pattern, the two constituent patterns must match. The result is the sum of the two resulting environments.

9. $$\frac{pat_1\ v_1\ \longrightarrow\ Env_1 \qquad pat_2\ v_2\ \longrightarrow\ Env_2}{(pat_1, pat_2)\,(v_1, v_2)\ \longrightarrow\ Env_1 + Env_2}$$

10. $$\frac{pat_1\ v_1\ \longrightarrow\ Failure}{(pat_1, pat_2)\,(v_1, v_2)\ \longrightarrow\ Failure}$$

11. $$\frac{pat_2\ v_2\ \longrightarrow\ Failure}{(pat_1, pat_2)\,(v_1, v_2)\ \longrightarrow\ Failure}$$

When matching against a layered pattern, the match succeeds if the parts match. The whole value always matches the variable pattern.

12. $$\frac{pat\ v\ \longrightarrow\ Env}{(id\ \textbf{as}\ pat)\ v\ \longrightarrow\ Env + \{id = v\}}$$

13. $$\frac{pat\ v\ \longrightarrow\ Failure}{(id\ \textbf{as}\ pat)\ v\ \longrightarrow\ Failure}$$

The handling of type constraints is done by the type system, and we will not describe it here.

As a general rule, a pattern can never contain the same name twice. We refrain from formalizing this fact, though.

12.2   Case Analysis

Programming is a form of problem solving. One common problem solving method is to decompose a problem into several cases, where the subproblem for each case is to be solved under some condition. Thanks to the condition, the subproblem is easier to solve than the whole problem.

Case expressions

In a conditional expression a computation is split into two cases, and by the use of repeated conditional expressions several cases can be analysed. Sometimes, you want a generalization of conditional expressions, which can handle many alternatives. Suppose you want a function day_of_year that given the $year$, the $month$, and the $date$ gives the ordinal number of the day; the first day of a year is counted as day number one. The year is needed because of leap-years. How can this problem be split into cases??

A reasonable method is to find out how many days there are in the months before the given month, then add the date, and finally adjust for a possible leap-year. This method requires that you split the problem into 12 subproblems. For that purpose we use a case expression, which contains the expression to be tested and a match (page 145) against which the value of the expression is to be matched. We assume that the function *is_leapyear* is already defined (cf. Exercise 6.8).

> **datatype** *MONTH* = *Jan* | *Feb* | *Mar* | *Apr* | *May* | *Jun* |
> *Jul* | *Aug* | *Sep* | *Oct* | *Nov* | *Dec*;

> — **fun** *day_of_year* (*year*, *month*, *day*) =
>   **let val** *leapdays* = **if** *is_leapyear year* **then** 1 **else** 0
>   **in case** *month* **of** *Jan* => *day*
> | *Feb* => 31 + *day*
> | *Mar* => 59 + *day* + *leapdays*
> | *Apr* => 90 + *day* + *leapdays*
> | *May* => 120 + *day* + *leapdays*
> | *Jun* => 151 + *day* + *leapdays*
> | *Jul* => 181 + *day* + *leapdays*
> | *Aug* => 212 + *day* + *leapdays*
> | *Sep* => 243 + *day* + *leapdays*
> | *Oct* => 273 + *day* + *leapdays*
> | *Nov* => 304 + *day* + *leapdays*
> | *Dec* => 334 + *day* + *leapdays*
>   **end**;
> > **val** *day_of_year* = **fn** : *int* * *MONTH* * *int* —> *int*

The syntax of a case expression uses the syntax of a match.

CASE EXPRESSION

The semantics of a case expression is also very simple to give, once you have defined the semantics of pattern matching; a case expression is simply a derived form of a function application.

> **case** EXPR **of** MATCH == (**fn** MATCH) EXPR

Let us as an example write an expression that translates a *DIRECTION* (page 141) into a bearing using both a case expression and a function application.

> **case** *dir* **of** *North* => 0   (**fn** *North* => 0
> | *East* => 90 | *East* => 90
> | *South* => 180 | *South* => 180
> | *West* => 270 | *West* => 270) *dir*

The two expressions are equivalent. The reason for introducing the case expression is that it is more readable, but it does not add any new power to the language. Even the conditional expression is introduced only as a convenience; it can be rewritten using a case expression and, thus, also using a function application.

$$\textbf{if } \text{BEXP } \textbf{then } E_1 \textbf{ else } E_2 \ == \ \textbf{case } \text{BEXP } \textbf{of} \quad \begin{aligned} &\textit{true} \ => \ E_1 \\ | \ &\textit{false} \ => \ E_2 \end{aligned}$$

Summary

The constructors of a data type decide in which ways you can construct the data objects of the type. Through *pattern matching* you perform the inverse of construction and analyse all data objects. A *match* is a sequence of alternatives or *rules* of the form PAT => EXP. The order of alternative patterns is essential if there are overlapping patterns. A match can be used both in a function expression and in a *case expression*. A pattern can be one of the following kinds: *variable pattern, wild card, constant pattern, constructor pattern, alternative pattern, type constraint pattern,* and *layered pattern*. Patterns are used also in value and function declarations.

Exercises

12.1. Define a function f with the following specification. The function takes a pair (x, y) as argument, where x and y are real numbers. If both x and y are non-zero, the result is given by the formula $x/y + y/x$. If both x and y are zero, the result is 2. Otherwise, the result is 1E30.

a) Define the function using a function declaration with pattern matching.

b) Define the function using a value declaration and a function expression with pattern matching.

c) Define the function using a function declaration and a case expression. Compare the three definitions, and make sure you understand the similarities and differences.

Chapter 13

Lists

Many descriptions of reality have the form of a sequence of data objects. A telephone book is a list of names and numbers. A library has a file of cards describing books. Physical experiments often result in long lists of numbers. The employees in a company and the products in a store are described by files of records, where each record describes a single person or product. Characteristic of all these examples is that you have a large number of data objects, all of the same type.

13.1 Construction and Analysis of Lists

A list is an ordered sequence of data objects, all of which are of the same type. Let us look at the list of the three numbers 4, 2, and 3.

> — [4, 2, 3];
> [4, 2, 3] : *int list*

The elements are separated by commas and surrounded by square brackets. The type of a list is written as the type of the elements followed by the list type constructor *list*. A list of strings, for instance, has the type *string list*.

> — ["string", "list"];
> ["string", "list"] : *string list*

These two lists are canonical list expressions, that is, they are fully reduced. In a list *expression*, the components may be expressions.

> — [2.0/4.0, *sqrt* 25.0];
> [0.5, 5.0] : *real list*

Suppose you want to describe some persons, where each person is described by *name*, *weight*, and *age*. You can then use a list of triples.

- ["anderson", 73, 58), ("jones", 86, 37), ("smith", 67, 40)];
  [("anderson", 73, 58), ("jones", 86, 37), ("smith", 67, 40)]
    : (*string* * *int* * *int*) *list*

Lists versus tuples

Characteristic of lists is that they can contain a varying number of elements, but that the type of element is fixed. Characteristic of tuples, on the other hand, is that they contain a fixed number of elements, but that the types of the elements can be different. A tuple is surrounded by parentheses and a list by square brackets.

- [2, 3];
  [2, 3] : *int list*

- [(2, 3)];
  [(2, 3)] : (*int* * *int*) *list*

The first list contains two elements, the second list only one. Note also that the lists [2, 3] and [2, 3, 4] have the same type, but that the tuples (2, 3) and (2, 3, 4) do not.

Lists of lists

The type completeness principle says that what you can do with objects of one type you can do with objects of all other types. Consequently, you should be able to create lists of lists, lists of functions, etc.

- [[2, 3], [3, 2, 1]];
  [[2, 3], [3, 2, 1]] : *int list list*

- [*sin, sqrt, abs*];
  [**fn, fn, fn**] : (*real* −> *real*) *list*

Note that the functions must have the same type.

The empty list

A list can also be empty and contain no elements.

- [];
  [] : *'a list*

Since the ML system cannot deduce the type of the elements in an empty list, the list is given a **polytype**, which is described by a type expression with the type variable *'a*. The empty list can also be called *nil*, but the system always uses [].

$$- \quad nil;$$
$$[] : \text{'}a\ list$$

We will use them interchangeably.

The list constructors

We have now looked at list expressions, but for any data type you also need suitable operations to manipulate its data objects. Let us first look at how you construct new lists. The operator ::, which is called *cons* (from *construct*), creates a new list from an element and a list.

$$- \quad 3 :: [5, 7];$$
$$[3, 5, 7] : int\ list$$

The precedence of :: (precedence 5) is between that of additive and relational operators.

$$- \quad 6 - 5 :: [5 - 6];$$
$$[1, \tilde{\ }1] : int\ list$$

$$- \quad (6 > 5) :: [5 > 6];$$
$$[true, false] : bool\ list$$

The parentheses are necessary because :: binds stronger than >.

For each data type, it is important to know the minimal collection of operations needed to construct all objects of the type. For lists, *nil* and :: are sufficient, since every list can be constructed by starting with the empty list and then inserting the elements in the right order. Let us construct the list [1,3,5] using *nil* and *cons*.

$$- \quad 1 :: 3 :: 5 :: nil;$$
$$[1, 3, 5] : int\ list$$

The list notation with square brackets is introduced only as a convenience. Note that :: associates to the right; otherwise, parentheses would be needed.

Pattern matching and analysis of lists

We have earlier stated the principle that the analysis of data objects is the inverse of their construction. The basic way of analysing objects is pattern matching. Since lists can be constructed in two ways, you can expect that two alternative patterns are needed. The empty list *nil* is a constant and to match it we use the constant pattern *nil*. To match a list that has been constructed with *cons*, you need a kind of pattern called **infixed construction**. It consists of a constructor surrounded by two patterns. As an example, we define a function *null* testing whether a list is empty or not.

```
   —  fun null nil  =  true
       |  null (x :: xs)  =  false;
   >  val null  =  fn  :  'a list −> bool
```

In the second pattern, the variable x matches the first element of the list and the variable xs the list obtained when the first element is removed. We here use a convention that if the first element is given some name, the remaining part of the list is given the name obtained by appending the suffix "s" to the name of the first element. In this way, you can decide from the name if an object is a list or not. By suffixing another "s" as in xss, you tell that an object is a list of lists.

In the definition of *null*, x and xs are never used. The second alternative pattern can therefore be replaced by a wild card.

```
   —  fun null nil  =  true
       |  null _  =  false;
   >  val null  =  fn  :  'a list −> bool
```

The *null* function is a polymorphic function, which can handle all types of list; the type of the elements is not important for the emptiness of a list. Polymorphism allows you to define general functions applicable to many types of object. Without it, one version of *null* would be needed for each type of element.

```
   —  null [];
       true : bool
```

```
   —  null [[]];
       false : bool
```

Note that [[]] is not empty, since it contains one element, which is the empty list.

Constructors, selectors, and predicates

Instead of using pattern matching to analyse lists, you can define and use special *selectors*, by which you can pick out parts of lists, and a *predicate* that informs you if a list is on *nil*-form or *cons*-form. As predicate we use the function *null* and as selectors the operations *hd* (head) and *tl* (tail). The first element of a list is selected with *hd*, and the list that remains when you remove the first element is selected with *tl*.

```
   —  hd [1, 2, 3];
       1 : int
```

```
   —  tl [1, 2, 3];
       [2, 3] : int list
```

The constructors *nil* and *cons*, the selectors *hd* and *tl*, and the predicate *null* are what you need for handling lists if you do not use pattern matching.

The functions *hd* and *tl* have some special properties. First of all they are polymorphic.

> — *hd*;
> **fn** : *'a list −> 'a*

> — *tl*;
> **fn** : *'a list −> 'a list*

Note that *hd* and *tl* have different types—*hd* yields an element and *tl* a list of elements. Second, they are both **partial**, meaning that they are not defined for all lists: they are undefined for the empty list.

> — *hd nil*;
> Failure : *hd*

> — *tl nil*;
> Failure : *tl*

Other partial operations are *div* and *mod*, which are not defined when the second operand is zero. A function that is well-defined for all arguments of its argument type is said to be **total**; it gives meaningful results for all arguments.

To summarize, we can say that for any non-empty list *xs*, the operations are related by the equation $hd\ xs :: tl\ xs = xs$. Compare that equation with the equation $(fst\ p, snd\ p) = p$ for pairs.

Exercises

13.1. What are the types of the expressions [[true]], [[]], *tl*[3], and *tl*[3, []]?

13.2   Exceptions and Errors

To define the functions *hd* and *tl*, you are faced with a problem: what is the result if the argument is *nil*? What you want is that the system stops with an error message. In ML, exceptions solve this problem. In an exception declaration you can declare one or several exceptions and then use the **raise** construct to force a computation to stop.

> — **exception** *hd* **and** *tl*;
> > **exception** *hd* : *unit*
> > **exception** *tl* : *unit*

```
—  fun  hd  nil  =  raise hd
    |  hd (x :: _)  =  x ;
>  val  hd  =  fn  :  'a list –> 'a

—  fun  tl  nil  =  raise tl
    |  tl ( _ :: xs)  =  xs ;
>  val  tl  =  fn  :  'a list –> 'a list

—  hd nil ;
Failure : hd
```

The simplest kind of exception has the type *unit,* but other types are possible. For most applications, the *unit* type is sufficient. Note that the same name can be used both for a function and an exception.

Exercises

13.2. Define a function *second* that gives the second element of a list.

13.3   Useful List Handling Functions

A general list handling function must handle lists of all lengths. The general method for achieving this is recursion, a way of repeating a computation many times. You can define many functions without recursion, however, simply by using standard and predefined list handling functions, which are defined with recursion.

13.3.1   Standard list handling functions

There are only a few standard functions for handling lists in ML.

The append operator

The *cons* operator allows you to insert an element into a list, but very often you want to concatenate two lists, that is, put two lists together. This can be done with the *append* operator @. The lists must, of course, be of the same type.

```
—  [1, 3, 5] @ [2, 4, 6] ;
   [1, 3, 5, 2, 4, 6] : int list
```

Either or both operands can be *nil.*

```
—  [true, false] @ nil ;
   [true, false] : bool list
```

> — [] @ [];
>   [] : *'a list*

The *append* operator has the same precedence as the *cons* operator.

> — [3] @ (1 :: *nil*);
>   [3, 1] : *int list*

Parentheses are necessary since left associative operators of equal precedence are applied from left to right.

To some extent, the append operator plays the same role for lists as addition does for numbers. It is associative, since xs @ (ys @ zs) = (xs @ ys) @ zs. The empty list corresponds to zero, since xs @ nil = xs and nil @ xs = xs. You say that nil is the *identity element* of lists with respect to @. The append operator is not commutative as addition is, though, since xs @ ys is not equal to ys @ xs.

The reverse and last functions

The *rev* function reverses all elements of a list.

> — *rev* [3, 4, 5];
>   [5, 4, 3] : *int list*

> — *rev nil*;
>   [] : *'a list*

Now let us define a function *last* that gives the last element of a list. A simple solution is to reverse the elements of the list and then use *hd* to select the first element.

> — **fun** *last xs* = *hd* (*rev xs*);
> > **val** *last* = **fn** : *'a list* –> *'a*

> — *last* [1, 5, 9];
>   9 : *int*

It seems to work, but the definition is in fact incomplete. Can you see why??

> — *last nil*;
> Failure : *hd*

The computation stops which is okay—you cannot select an element out of an empty list—but the error message says *hd*. This does not give you as much information as if it had said *last* instead[1].

---
[1]From now on we omit the system responses for exception declarations.

exception *last* ;

```
—  fun  last  nil  =  raise  last
      |  last  xs  =  hd(rev  xs);
>  val  last  =  fn  :  'a  list  —>  'a
```

In a small program it may not be important if the error message is *hd* or *last*, but when trying to find an error in a large program it can be very helpful.

The list function template

An important lesson can be learned from the way we have defined functions working with lists. Lists can be constructed in two ways and we therefore, as a rule, use two alternative patterns, one for *nil* and one for *cons*. Hence, when defining a list handling function, we can start with the *template*

```
fun  f  nil      =  ?
   |  f  (x :: xs)  =  ??
```

Since the patterns are exhaustive, you avoid many errors if you use this template. For some functions, however, the template may have to be changed slightly, as for *last* above.

13.3.2 Predefined list handling functions

In this book, many useful functions are defined, and they could all be included as predefined functions in an ML system. There is a conflict here, however. On the one hand, you want your system to be as small as possible so it is easy to learn. On the other hand, you want all useful functions predefined to avoid the need for declaring them. The choice of which functions to predefine is delicate. Appendix D contains many functions, and you should not feel that you have to master them all from the beginning. When you become more experienced, a larger subset of them will be useful working tools for you. Most certainly you also want to add some more functions that are useful in your application or perhaps change the definition of the existing ones. Let us now look at some useful list handling functions. We collect them into groups of similar functions.

List reducing functions

A list reducing function takes a list as argument and gives a non-list result. A simple example is the *len* function giving the length of a list.

```
—  len  [0, 1, 2, 3];
   4 : int
```

— *len nil*;
   0 : *int*

Given a list of lists, *len* only counts the number of lists, that is, the number of elements on the top level of the list.

— *len* [[1, 3], [], [2, 4, 6]];
   3 : *int*

— *len* [[[[]]]];
   1 : *int*

Another useful list reducer is *sum* that sums all integers in a list of integers.

— *sum* [1, 3, 5, 7, 9];
   25 : *int*

When introducing a predefined function, it should be accompanied by a precise specification, so no doubt about its meaning can arise. You can express that *sum* adds all numbers in the list by using the "..." notation often used in mathematics.

$$sum\ [x_1, x_2, \ldots, x_n] = x_1 + x_2 + \cdots + x_n$$

For a specification as well as for a function definition you must ask yourselves if it is correct and complete. Since a list can be empty, you must define *sum* for the empty list as well. A reasonable choice is that it is zero, since adding zero to any number gives the number itself as result. Another explanation is that if you look at summing as an accumulation, you can start with zero, and add successive numbers. For a mathematician the choice is evident, since such a definition has pleasing algebraic properties: zero is the *identity element* of addition, because $x + 0 = x$ and $0 + x = x$.

$$sum\ [] = 0$$
$$sum\ [x_1, x_2, \ldots, x_n] = x_1 + x_2 + \cdots + x_n$$

A function similar to *sum* is *prod* that multiplies all numbers in a list. The natural choice for the product of all numbers in an empty list is 1, since $x * 1 = x$ and $1 * x = x$.

$$prod\ [] = 1$$
$$prod\ [x_1, x_2, \ldots, x_n] = x_1 * x_2 * \cdots * x_n$$

Here are some examples.

— *prod* [1, 2, 3, 4, 5, 6];
   720 : *int*

— *prod* (*tl* [4]);
   1 : *int*

Example: The average value of a list of numbers

The average value of a list of integers is the sum of all integers divided by the number of them. Can you see how to define a function *average*??

The *sum* function can add the integers for us and their number can be computed by the *len* function. Since the argument to *average* is a list, we start with the list template.

$$
\begin{aligned}
\textbf{fun} \quad &average\ nil &= \quad ? \\
| \quad &average\ (x :: xs) &= \quad ??
\end{aligned}
$$

The average value of an empty list is not meaningful, and we raise an exception for that case. For the second case there is no need to select the parts of the list, since *sum* can sum a whole list. The list contains integers, but since the average value can be a real number, we transform the sum and the length into real numbers.

> **exception** *average*;

> — **fun** *average nil* = **raise** *average*
> | *average xs* = *real(sum xs)/real(len xs)*;
> > **val** *average* = **fn** : *int list* —> *real*

> — *average* $[1, 2, 3, 4, 5, 6]$;
> $3.5 : real$

A list generator

A reducer takes a list and produces a non-list. A *generator* produces a list from non-list arguments. A very useful generator is the *fromto* operator —— producing a list of successive numbers.

> — $1 -- 10$;
> $[1, 2, 3, 4, 5, 6, 7, 8, 9, 10] : int\ list$

Note that both limits are included in the list. We must now specify what happens if the left operand is greater than the right operand. One choice is to give a list with the numbers in decreasing order. However, by defining *fromto* as below, several functions definitions using it become simpler.

$$
i -- j = \begin{cases} [i, i+1, i+2, \ldots, j] & i < j \\ [i] & i = j \\ [\,] & i = j + 1 \\ \text{undefined} & \text{otherwise} \end{cases}
$$

The factorial of a number n (often written $n!$) is the product of all numbers from 1 to n. The factorial of zero is defined to be one. The function is undefined for negative arguments. Can you define *fac*??

The *fromto* operator can produce a list of all numbers from one to n and *prod* can multiply them. The factorial of zero should be one. Thanks to our definition of *fromto*, we do not have to treat this case in a special way. The list of numbers from one to zero is defined to be the empty list and the product of all numbers in the empty list is one. This is no coincidence, but a consequence of chosing definitions with nice mathematical properties. The lesson is that you can often simplify your programs by being careful in defining your functions for the special cases. If n is negative, *fromto* raises an exception, but to get the right error message, we introduce the exception *fac*.

```
exception fac;

- fun fac n = if n < 0
                then raise fac
                else prod (1 - -n);
> val fac = fn : int -> int

- fac 6;
  720 : int

- fac 0;
  1 : int

- fac (~7);
Failure : fac
```

Exercises

13.3. Define a function *remlast* that removes the last element of a list.

13.4. Define a function *palindrome* that given a list checks if it equals itself read backwards.

13.4 Complexity of Algorithms

We have previously defined a function *sum1to* that sums all numbers from one up to a given number n. The verbal description of the function directly suggests the use of *sum* and *fromto* in a similar way as in the definition of *fac*.

```
exception sum1to;
```

```
–   fun sum1to n  =  if n < 0
                     then raise sum1to
                     else sum(1 − −n);
>   val sum1to  =  fn  :  int −> int
```

This definition should be contrasted to the previous definition of *sum1to*.

```
–   fun sum1to n  =  if n < 0
                     then raise sum1to
                     else n ∗ (n + 1) div 2;
>   val sum1to  =  fn  :  int −> int
```

A first question is if the functions do the same thing. In fact, they do not, because for some numbers, the first definition will give a correct value, but the second will raise an overflow exception. The reason is that in the second case you compute a product and then divide it by two. The risk is that the product is greater than *maxint*. In the first case no number larger than the sum is computed.

Ignoring the problem with large numbers, are the definitions equal? In fact, they will compute the same result, but a computation using the first definition will take longer time for all but very small n. The reason is that in the second case you always perform exactly three arithmetic operations, but in the first case the number of arithmetic operations grows proportionally with n. Similarly, you need a memory space proportional to n in the second case to store the list with n numbers, but in the first case you need very little space.

The situation is typical. From a given specification you can often find some quite simple way of computing the specified function, but it may be inefficient or space consuming. By devoting some thought to the problem, you may come up with a better, but more complicated, algorithm. To convince yourself that the first definition is correct is often trivial. In our case, the first definition can even be regarded as a specification of *sum1to*. To prove that the second definition is correct may require a more complicated argument; in our case a small mathematical proof (page 65). Often, it is a good idea to use the simplest definition you can find in the first place, and then try to find a more efficient version if that is necessary.

Measuring the complexity

For *sum1to*, it is quite clear that the second solution is superior to the first one in terms of both time and space requirements. This is not always the case. Suppose that you want a function f taking a natural number n as argument and that you define three versions of f, whose time consumptions are $5n$, $10n$, and n^2. Which is the best one??

For very small n, the term n^2 is smallest. For $n = 5$, $5n = n^2$ and for $n = 10$, $10n = n^2$. For $n > 10$, the n^2 version behaves worse than the other two. Unless you are interested in using f only for small n, the $5n$ version is best and the n^2 is worst. To simplify comparisons, you would like a simple way of characterizing the complexity of an algorithm, be it the time or space complexity. It is common practice to use the **order** concept for this purpose. It tells how an algorithm grossly behaves for large ns. For instance, both the $5n$ version and the $10n$ version grow linearly with n. You say they are of order n and ignore the difference in the constant factor. Similarly, algorithms with time consumption n^2, $n^2 + n$, and $100n^2$ are all of order n^2. You select the term that dominates when n is large and then remove possible constant factors. An algorithm with time consumption $n * log(n)$ behaves worse than one with n, however; you can only remove constant factors, never a factor depending on n. An algorithm whose time consumption does not depend on n is said to use constant time.

For the function f, the argument was a number. If the argument is a list, you most often describe the complexity of the algorithm in terms of the length of the list. For each particular algorithm, you have to select a suitable measure of the complexity. It may, for instance, be the sum of a number and the length of a list.

Some algorithms have an exponential behaviour, for instance, 2^n or 10^n. Such a behaviour is usually so bad that the algorithm can be used practically only for very small arguments. For some problems, it is known that no algorithm with polynomial time behaviour exists. Such problems are said to be *intractable*. For other problems, one has so far only been able to find algorithms with exponential behaviour, and there is little hope that algorithms with polynomial behaviour will be found. Nobody has been able to prove that only exponential algorithms exist for these problems, though. In this book, we will mainly consider algorithms of order $log(n)$, n, $n * log(n)$, and n^2. In the answer to Exercise 15.19 on page 362, there is a table showing how these quantities vary with n.

Summary

A *list* is a sequence of objects, all of the same type. It can be constructed using only the two constructors *nil* and :: (*cons*) and analysed using pattern matching with two alternatives. Without pattern matching, the selectors *hd* (head) and *tl* (tail) and the predicate *null* are needed. These functions are polymorphic. The selectors are also *partial*, since they cannot handle empty lists. A function that is not partial is said to be *total*. When defining functions on lists, you should start with the template

$$
\begin{aligned}
\textbf{fun}\ \ f\ nil\ \ \ \ &=\ ? \\
|\ \ f\ (x :: xs)\ &=\ ??
\end{aligned}
$$

Often, you can make functions very useful, if you define the *nil* case in a proper way.

Exercises

13.5. Which of the following sentences are false? Explain why!

1. A list can be arbitrarily long.
2. The function *null* is partial, since it cannot handle integers.
3. The *sum* function is polymorphic, since it can handle lists of various lengths.
4. The operators :: and @ both put two lists together.
5. All elements in a list must have the same type, but in a list of lists, the elements of the sublists can have various types.

13.6. The binomial coefficients are given by the formula

$$\binom{n}{m} = \frac{n!}{(n-m)! * m!}$$

where $0 \leq m \leq n$. First define a function *bin* using the *fac* function and the formula above. Then, define a more efficient version that makes no unnecessary multiplications.

Chapter 14

Recursion and Repetitive Computations

As mentioned, a description of a computation, is, in general, based on the combining principles sequence, choice, and repetition. Sequential computations are achieved by composing functions and operators and choices by conditional expressions and alternative patterns. With recursion you can express repetitive computations.

Functions like *len* and *sum* take lists as arguments. Since a list can be of any length, you need some way of handling lists that are arbitrarily large. The solution in a functional language is a *recursive* definition, which is a form of circular or self-referential definition. There is nothing magical about such a definition, but it may take some time to get used to the idea. Since recursion is absolutely fundamental in functional programming, make sure you grasp the idea before continuing to the next chapter.

14.1 General Principles of Recursion

The word *recur* means "to return to" or "to reappear". In a recursive definition, you define something in terms of itself. Some recursive definitions are truly circular and therefore, in some sense, meaningless. Consider the following conversation:

> – How many days are there in a fortnight?
> – As many as in two weeks.
> – How many days are there in two weeks?
> – As many as in a fortnight.

The interrogator is probably not much helped by the answer. Many self-referential definitions, however, are well behaved and completely meaningful. In fact, we have used a recursive definition to define arithmetic expressions:

An arithmetic expression is a constant, a variable, an operator expression, or a parentheses expression. Each operand of an operator expression is an expression, and a parentheses expression contains an expression.

Hence, an expression is defined in terms of expressions, and you probably still think the definition is meaningful. Can you see why??

An expression can be a constant or a variable, which is easy to understand. A parentheses or operator expression is an expression that contains other expressions as parts. The reason we are allowed to use recursion is that the subexpressions are *parts* of the original expression and, therefore, smaller than the original expression. Using the definition once more we arrive at even smaller expressions and, finally, we get atomic expressions like constants and variables.

14.1.1 Recursive function definitions

A naive way of defining the function *len* would be to use alternative patterns, one for each possible length of a list.

$$\begin{aligned}
\textbf{fun} \ \ &len \ nil \ = \ 0 \\
| \ &len \ (\ \_ :: nil) \ = \ 1 \\
| \ &len \ (\ \_ :: \ \_ :: nil) \ = \ 2 \\
| \ &len \ (\ \_ :: \ \_ :: \ \_ :: nil) \ = \ 3 \\
&\ldots
\end{aligned}$$

Obviously, this method is not sufficient, since we can define *len* only for lists of a finite number of lengths, and we want a definition for lists of *all* lengths. What we need is some *finite* way of describing all possible lists.

We have observed that all lists can be constructed using only two constructors: *nil* and *cons*. A list is constructed by inserting an element into another list using *cons*. The given description is recursive: to get a list you insert an element into a list. Exactly as with expressions, however, the list you insert the element into is shorter than the resulting list, and the description is therefore meaningful.

A good way of defining a function over a list is to use a *template* with two alternative patterns, one for *nil* and one for *cons*.

$$\begin{aligned}
\textbf{fun} \ \ &len \ nil \ \ \ \ \ = \ ? \\
| \ &len \ (x :: xs) \ = \ ??
\end{aligned}$$

Try to fill in the question marks before you read further!!

The length of the empty list is zero. In the second case, you want to find the length of the list $x :: xs$, which has been constructed by inserting the element x into the list xs. The length of $x :: xs$ must therefore be one more than the length of xs. The question now is how to get the length of the list xs. It seems we are back where we started. However, we were able to define what a list is using the concept of a list recursively. In the same way we are allowed to use the definition of *len* recursively. The length of xs is given by the expression *len xs*, and since xs is shorter than $x :: xs$, the definition is meaningful.

```
–  fun len nil  =  0
    | len ( _ :: xs)  =  1 + len xs;
>  val  len  =  fn  :  'a list –> int

–  len [1, 3, 5, 7];
    4 : int
```

Since the element x is not used, it has been replaced by a wild card.

Problem solving by recursive decomposition

Let us look closer at how we solved the problem of defining *len*. First, we divided the problem into two subproblems, which is a form of decomposition into cases. In the function definition this corresponds to the use of alternative patterns. To solve the second case, we assumed that we could use *len* itself to compute the length of the sublist xs—it uses (or calls) itself recursively. We call this problem solving technique recursive decomposition: you split a problem into two subproblems and at the same time assume that you have already solved the problem for some arguments. We will motivate our right to do so in a moment.

Recursive computations

Recursive definitions can be explained in several ways. The important one is based on what is called induction, but let us first look at how recursive functions are computed. The reason is to show that there is nothing magical with recursive definitions. Once you believe this, try to avoid understanding them in terms of computations. Let us now look at how the length of the list [1,3,5] is computed. Parentheses are used to show in which order the operations are performed.

$$len\ [1, 3, 5] \longrightarrow$$
$$1 + len\ [3, 5] \longrightarrow$$
$$1 + (1 + len\ [5]) \longrightarrow$$
$$1 + (1 + (1 + len\ nil)) \longrightarrow$$
$$1 + (1 + (1 + 0)) \longrightarrow$$
$$1 + (1 + 1) \longrightarrow$$
$$1 + 2 \longrightarrow$$
$$3$$

To find the length of the list [1,3,5] you have to compute the length of the list [3,5]. On the next last line you see that this subcomputation yields the result 2 and the length of the whole list therefore is 3. You can imagine having computer slaves to do computations for you. The first slave is given the whole list. He asks another slave to compute the length of the tail of this list. This slave, in turn, asks a third slave to compute the length of the tail of his list, and so on, until some slave is asked to compute the length of *nil*. He can now report back the result zero to his master, who can report the result one, and so on, until the first slave can report the result for the whole list.

$$
\begin{array}{lccccccc}
\text{Task:} & len\ [1,3,5] & \longrightarrow & len\ [3,5] & \longrightarrow & len\ [5] & \longrightarrow & len\ nil \\
\text{Result:} & 3 & \longleftarrow & 2 & \longleftarrow & 1 & \longleftarrow & 0
\end{array}
$$

To compute the length of the list $x :: xs$, the length of xs must first be computed. The original computation must therefore be postponed until the subcomputation is completed. The number of postponed subcomputations before the first addition can take place is equal to the length of the list. In the computer, the administration of postponed computations is usually organized on a **stack**, which is a list of objects used according to the LIFO principle, that is, Last In First Out. This is exactly what is needed, since the last suspended subcomputation is the one that must be resumed first. The size of this stack must be large enough to handle the maximum number of recursive applications you want to perform. In most ML-systems, the size of the stack is a limiting factor. Some recursive functions, however, may be transformed by the system into a form that requires only a constant amount of space. Which definitions are optimized in this way is very system dependent, though.

Exercises

14.1. Define *sum* (*prod*) that sums (multiplies) all integers in a list of integers.

14.2. Reduce the expression *sum* $[1, 2, 3]$ by hand.

14.1.2 The principle of induction

You have now seen how recursive functions are computed, and may believe that recursive definitions are meaningful. There is a more convincing way of explaining recursive functions, though, which is very important to understand when you define your own recursive functions. The idea of induction (sometimes called mathematical induction) is used over and over again in mathematical proofs. To prove that a recursive function performs its task, you also use a form of induction. Let us, however, look at an inductive proof before we consider recursion.

The non-negative integers are usually called the *natural* numbers, since they occur when you perform the very fundamental action of counting. As mentioned earlier, the invention of a symbol for zero had a great influence on the development of mathematics, so let us accept the idea to start counting from zero. Counting means to go through the natural numbers one after the other in a predefined order; each natural number has exactly one *successor*. You can go on counting forever, and, in consequence, there is an infinite number of natural numbers.

If you want to prove that *all* natural numbers have some property, you have to give a proof for an infinite number of numbers. The situation is, in fact, similar to the problem of defining *len* for lists of all lengths. Let us, as an example, prove that the function *sum1to* really computes the sum of all numbers from 1 to n for any n.

> ```
> −  fun sum1to n = n * (n + 1) div 2;
> >  val sum1to = fn : int −> int
> ```

A proof by induction is performed in three steps. First you prove the **base case**, which for natural number amounts to proving that the claim is true for zero. Hence, we have to prove that *sum1to* applied to zero gives the sum of all number from 1 to zero. There are no such numbers, so the sum should be zero. Since $0 * (0 + 1) \ div \ 2 = 0$ we have proved the base case.

> ```
> −  sum1to 0;
>    0 : int
> ```

The next step in an induction proof is the crucial one. You make an **induction hypothesis**, which amounts to assuming that what you want to prove is true for some natural number k. For our example we assume that

$$sum1to \ k = k * (k + 1) \ div \ 2 \qquad \text{(Induction hypothesis)}$$

We now have to to prove that the property we are considering is true for $k + 1$ under the assumption that it is true for k. This step is called the **inductive step**. Hence, we have to prove that

$$sum1to \ (k + 1) = (k + 1) * (k + 2) \ div \ 2$$

You may ask what we achieve by such a proof. A little thought should convince you that it is all we need. First, we prove the property for zero. Next, we prove that if the property is true for some natural number k, then it is also true for $k+1$. Now we know it is true for zero. Using the inductive step we therefore know it is true also for one. If it is true for one, however, then by the inductive step it must be true also for two, and if it is true for two, it must be true for three, and so on, forever. Thus, the property holds for all natural numbers.

Let us now prove the inductive step. The sum of all numbers from 1 to $k + 1$ must be the same as adding $k + 1$ to the sum of all numbers from 1 to k, that is,

$$sum1to\,(k+1) = sum1to\ k + (k+1)$$

The next step in the proof is the important one. We use the induction hypothesis that tells us that $sum1to\ k = k * (k+1)\ div\ 2$. Thus,

$$sum1to\,(k+1) = k * (k+1)\ div\ 2 + (k+1)$$

Next, we multiply and divide the last term by two, which cannot change its value.

$$sum1to\,(k+1) = k * (k+1)\ div\ 2 + 2 * (k+1)\ div\ 2$$

If we multiply both sides by two we get

$$2 * sum1to\,(k+1) = k * (k+1) + 2 * (k+1)$$

The right-hand side is equal to $(k+1) * (k+2)$. Since both sides must be even numbers ($k+1$ or $k+2$ must be even), we can integer divide them by two and get

$$sum1to\,(k+1) = (k+1) * (k+2)\ div\ 2$$

which is what we want to prove.

Having proved the base case and the inductive step, we are allowed to conclude that $sum1to$ gives the right result for all natural numbers by a principle called the induction principle or mathematical induction. The word "induction" means to draw a general conclusion from some more specific facts; here we draw the conclusion that a property holds for *all* natural numbers, once we have proved the base case and the inductive step.

An incorrect induction proof

You have to be careful when you use induction, though. Consider the statement[1]:

If, in a set of blondes, at least one is blue-eyed, then all are.

In a set with only one blonde, all are blue-eyed if she is, so the base case is okay. Now assume that the property is true for all sets with k blondes. We now have to prove that it is true for all sets with $k + 1$ blondes. Remove one blonde out of the group. If there is at least one blue-eyed among the remaining k blondes, all are according to the inductive hypothesis. This does not prove anything about the single blonde, but since you can exchange her for any other blonde in the group, the property must be true for all blondes. Obviously there must be something wrong with the argument and you are urged to find the error before continuing!!

You may believe the error is the way you exchange blondes. It is perfectly okay, however. The error is the special case when you go from sets with one blonde to sets with two: there is no one to exchange with.

---

[1] The example is due to G. Polya, Stanford University.

Exercises

14.3. Prove by induction that $x^m * x^n = x^{m+n}$. By definition, $x^0 = 1$ and $x^{m+1} = x * x^m$.

14.4. Let $S_n = 1 + r + r^2 + \cdots + r^n$. Prove by induction that $S_n = \frac{r^{n+1}-1}{r-1}$, assuming $r \neq 1$.

14.1.3   Recursion over lists

There is a great similarity between lists and natural numbers. The empty list *nil* corresponds to zero and the *cons* operation to the successor operation. Instead of assuming that a property holds for the natural number k and proving that it also holds for $k + 1$, we now assume that some property holds for a list xs and prove that it also holds for the list $x :: xs$, where x is any element of the right type. Since this induction is based on the structure of the list, it is often called *structural* induction. Let us prove that *len* really computes the length of its argument.

```
 -  fun len nil  =  0
     |  len ( _ :: xs)  =  1 + len xs;
 >  val len  =  fn  :  'a list -> int
```

Our first task is to prove that *len* computes the right length of the empty list—our base case. This length is zero, and since *len nil* $\longrightarrow$ 0 the base case is proved. The next step is the induction step. We assume that the length of a list xs is given by the expression *len xs*. Under this assumption we have to prove that *len* computes the right length of the list $x :: xs$. Inserting an element into a list must yield a list which is one unit longer. Since the length of xs is given by *len xs*, the length of $x :: xs$ must be given by $1 + len\ xs$. Since $len(x :: xs) \longrightarrow 1 + len\ xs$ we can, by induction, conclude that *len* really computes the length of any list.

Recursion assumptions

The idea of structural induction over lists gives us a powerful problem solving technique. To define a function f taking a list as argument, you start with the usual template.

```
 fun  f nil     = ?
     |  f (x :: xs)  = ??
```

The problem is now split into two subproblems, one for the empty list and one for non-empty lists. To define the result for the empty list is often simple. The problem is usually the second case. By using the induction principle you get great help: you can assume that the function you are about to define is *already* defined and works for the list xs in the pattern. That is, you are allowed to use the expression $f\ xs$ in the second alternative and assume that it gives the right answer. We call this assumption the recursion assumption. Let us as an example define rev for reversal of a list. We start with the template.

$$\textbf{fun}\ \ rev\ nil\quad\quad =\ ?$$
$$|\ \ \ rev\ (x::xs)\ \ =\ ??$$

The reversal of an empty list must be the empty list. The next step is to find the reversal of the list $x::xs$. The recursion assumption allows us to assume that the reversal of xs is given by $rev\ xs$. Appending x at the end of $rev\ xs$, we get the required reversal.

$$-\ \ \textbf{fun}\ rev\ nil\ =\ nil$$
$$|\ \ \ rev\ (x::xs)\ =\ rev\ xs\ @\ [x]\ ;$$
$$>\ \textbf{val}\ \ rev\ =\ \textbf{fn}\ :\ 'a\ list\ ->\ 'a\ list$$

Note that rev as well as len is polymorphic and works for all types of lists.

$$-\ \ rev\ [[2,3],[4,5]]\ ;$$
$$[[4,5],[2,3]]\ :\ int\ list\ list$$

Only the elements at the top level are reversed; the sublists are unchanged.

A procedure for defining recursive functions

At first, you may find it difficult to define recursive functions. Most certainly, you will be able to do it, once you have enough practice. Using the method suggested above simplifies your task considerably. It is performed in four steps:

Template: Start with the template for the function.

$$\textbf{fun}\ \ f\ nil\quad\quad =\ ?$$
$$|\ \ \ f\ (x::xs)\ =\ ??$$

Base case: Find the result of applying f to nil.

Recursion assumption: Assume that $f\ xs$ computes the right result for xs.

Inductive step: Using the recursion assumption, find how to compute $f(x::xs)$.

You will meet variations of this basic scheme, but the idea will be the same. An important observation is that the way a list is constructed and the way it is analysed are closely connected. There are two ways of constructing lists, and we use two alternative patterns. A list is a recursive structure, since we build a list by inserting an element into another list. When we define a recursive function having a list as argument, we use a recursive call to manipulate another list.

You will find the same regularity for other data types. Many programming problems can therefore be solved by looking at how the data objects are constructed and then using this knowledge to analyse them. Often, the constructors suggest the patterns to be used, and the ML system can help you to check that all cases are taken care of.

Exercises

14.5. Define a function *sql* that squares all elements in a list of integers. Use the four steps above, and make sure you understand all details.

14.6. Define a function *flat* that, given a list of lists, appends all the sublists in order. For instance, *flat* $[[1, 2], [3, 4]] \longrightarrow [1, 2, 3, 4]$. Derive the type of *flat*.

14.1.4 Variations of the basic recursion scheme

Handling several arguments

The append operator @ concatenates two lists. Let us define a corresponding function *append* that takes a pair of lists as argument. Our basic scheme does not work any longer, because the argument is a pair, not a list.

What we have: $([a_1, a_2, \ldots, a_n], [b_1, b_2, \ldots, b_m])$ $n \geq 0, m \geq 0$
What we want: $[a_1, a_2, \ldots, a_n, b_1, b_2, \ldots, b_m]$

When you build a list, you insert the elements one after the other at the front of the list. We can therefore get the required list by breaking the first list into pieces and inserting its elements into the front of the second list. Thus, we do the recursion over the first list and keep the second list as it is. Our template is

```
fun  append (nil, ys)   = ?
  |  append (x :: xs, ys)  = ??
```

The result of putting *nil* in front of *ys* is *ys*. The recursion assumption tells us that *append* (*xs, ys*) really appends the two lists *xs* and *ys*. To append *x :: xs* and *ys*, we simply insert *x* in front of *append* (*xs, ys*).

```
-  fun append (nil, ys)  = ys
     |  append (x :: xs, ys)  = x :: append (xs, ys);
>  val  append  =  fn  :  'a list * 'a list -> 'a list
```

```
-  append ([true, false], [false, true, true]);
   [true, false, false, true, true]  :  bool list
```

The importance of formulating the recursion assumption cannot be overstressed: it helps you to decompose a problem into much simpler problems.

Let us define a function for checking if some object is a member of a list or not. An object can never be a member of an empty list, so the result for the empty list must be *false*. The recursion assumption says that $mem(xs, a)$ has the value *true* only if a is a member of xs. Now, a is a member of $x :: xs$ if it is equal to x or a member of xs.

```
—  fun  mem  (nil, a)  =  false
    |  mem  (x :: xs, a)  =  a = x  orelse  mem(xs, a);
>  val  mem  =  fn  :  "a list * "a —> bool
```

Note that, thanks to the laziness of **orelse**, the list is searched only until an a is found. Type variables with two primes are used to denote all types that allow tests for equality, but not, for instance, functions. Hence, *mem* uses a restricted form of polymorphism.

Handling special cases

The function *last* defined by $last\ xs = hd(rev\ xs)$ selects the last element of a list. Using recursion, we can define a more efficient version of *last*. Now, the empty list cannot be used as a base case, since an exception should be raised for *nil*. Instead, we use the one-element list as base case; the empty list is treated as an erroneous argument. Our template is

```
fun  last nil  =  raise last
  |  last (x :: nil)  =  ?
  |  last (x :: xs)  =  ??
```

Since, according the recursion assumption, *last xs* gives the last element of xs, it must also give the last element of $x :: xs$.

```
exception last;
```

```
—  fun last nil  =  raise last
    |  last (x :: nil)  =  x
    |  last ( _ :: xs)  =  last xs;
>  val  last  =  fn  :  'a list —> 'a
```

Now suppose you want a function *maxl* that gives the greatest integer of a list of integers. There is no natural choice of a greatest element of the empty list, so we raise an error for that case and use the one-element list as base case.

```
exception maxl;
```

```
  - fun maxl nil  = raise maxl
    | maxl (x :: nil)  = x
    | maxl (x :: xs)  = max(x, maxl xs);
  > val maxl  = fn   : int list -> int
```

Multiple recursion

Let us define a function *addlists* that adds two lists element-wise. The lists must be of equal length. For instance, $addlists\ ([1, 3, 5], [2, 4, 6]) \longrightarrow [3, 7, 11]$. Can you define *addlists*??

We have to add elements in corresponding positions, which suggests that we traverse the two lists in a synchronous fashion. If the lists are of different length, one list will be exhausted before the other, and we then raise an error. In our template we get four cases for all combinations of empty and non-empty lists.

```
fun  addlists (nil, nil)      = ?
   | addlists (nil, y :: ys)   = raise addlists
   | addlists (x :: xs, nil)   = raise addlists
   | addlists (x :: xs, y :: ys) = ??
```

The way the template is given, the order of the four equations is not essential. You can use *ys* instead of *y* :: *ys* in the second alternative and *xs* instead of *x* :: *xs* in the third, but then the order of the alternatives is essential. The first choice shows most clearly the four cases, but the second is often chosen because it is simpler to write.

In the first alternative in the template, there are no elements to add, so the result must be *nil*. For the last case, we can assume that $addlists(xs, ys)$ adds *xs* and *ys*. We get the required list by inserting $x + y$ into this list. Since the second and third case yield the same result, we can merge them and place them after the two correct alternatives.

```
exception addlists;

  - fun addlists (nil, nil) : int list  = nil
    | addlists (x :: xs, y :: ys)  = x + y :: addlists(xs, ys)
    | addlists ( _ , _ )  = raise addlists;
  > val addlists  = fn   : int list * int list -> int list
```

Exercises

14.7. Define *count* that counts how many times an object occurs in a list.

14.8. A vector can be represented by a list of numbers. Define *scalprod* for computing the scalar product of two vectors, which is the sum of the pair-wise products of their elements. Derive its type.

14.1.5   Tracing recursive functions

Even if you try to convince yourself with various techniques that your program is correct, there may still be errors in it, which you discover when you test it. One useful technique for finding errors is to have the arguments printed for some crucial functions each time they are called; you *trace* the execution. The special function *print* prints the values of expressions of some types, the exact choice of types being system dependent.

As a simple example, let us print the arguments to *addlists* for the case when both lists are non-empty. The printing is not really part of the function; it is performed only as a *side-effect*. The **sequence** construct allows you to evaluate a sequence of expressions. The expressions are separated by semicolons and surrounded by parentheses. The value of a sequence expression is the value of its last expression; the other expressions are meaningful only if they give rise to side-effects when evaluated. By definition, a pure functional language cannot contain constructs leading to side-effects. The side-effects we use here, however, are not part of the computation, but an aid for finding errors.

$$
\begin{array}{ll}
- & \textbf{fun } addlists\ (nil, nil)\ :\ int\ list\ =\ nil \\
  & |\quad addlists\ (nil, ys)\ =\ \textbf{raise } addlists \\
  & |\quad addlists\ (xs, nil)\ =\ \textbf{raise } addlists \\
  & |\quad addlists\ (x :: xs, y :: ys)\ =\quad (print\ x;\ \ print\ "\,+\,"; \\
  & \qquad\qquad\qquad\qquad\qquad\qquad print\ y;\ \ print\ "\,=\,"; \\
  & \qquad\qquad\qquad\qquad\qquad\qquad print(x + y);\ \ print\ "\backslash n"; \\
  & \qquad\qquad\qquad\qquad\qquad\qquad x + y :: addlists(xs, ys))\,;
\end{array}
$$

$>$ **val** $addlists\ =\ $**fn**$\ :\ int\ list * int\ list\ ->\ int\ list$

$-\ \ addlists\ ([7, 3, 9], [2, 8, \tilde{\ }3])\,;$
  $7 + 2 = 9$
  $3 + 8 = 11$
  $9 + \tilde{\ }3 = 6$
  $[9, 11, 6]\ :\ int\ list$

The function gives the same result as our previous version, since the value of the sequence expression is the value of its last expression.

In passing, it can be observed that a parentheses expression in ML is considered as a sequence expression with exactly one expression.

14.1.6   Example: The median of a set of numbers

The median of a set of numbers is the number with the property that there are equally many numbers smaller than and bigger than itself. For instance, the median of $[5, 2, 4, 3, 1]$ is 3. For lists with an even number of elements, we chose the smaller of the two "medians". For instance, the median of $[5, 3, 4, 2]$ is 3. The median of an empty set of numbers is not defined.

One way to solve this problem is to order the numbers in increasing order and then select the number in the "middle". The solution is an example of *sequential decomposition*. Can you solve the two subproblems??

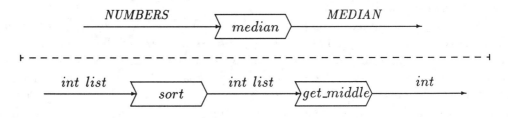

Let us first define *median* under the assumption that we already have defined *sort* and *get_middle*. We have to raise an exception for the empty list.

> **exception** *median* ;

```
− fun median nil  =  raise median
   | median xs    =  get_middle(sort xs);
> val median = fn : int list −> int
```

The first subproblem is to sort a list of numbers. Let us start with a template.

```
fun  sort nil       =  ?
   | sort (x :: xs) =  ??
```

Given a list $x :: xs$, we are entitled to assume that *sort xs* yields a sorted list. To sort $x :: xs$ amounts to inserting x at the right place in *sort xs*. We therefore need an auxiliary function *insert* that inserts a number into a sorted list so that the result is sorted. Working top-down, we assume that *insert* is already defined.

```
− fun sort nil = nil
   | sort (x :: xs)  =  insert(x, sort xs);
> val sort = fn : int list −> int list
```

We now have to define *insert*. To insert x into $y :: ys$, we have to compare x and y. If x is less than or equal to y, x must be inserted in front of the whole list. If x is greater than y, x has to be inserted into ys at its right place and y in front of the obtained result. In the second pattern, we need both the whole list and its parts, which we can get with a layered pattern (page 143). We use the name yys to denote a list whose head is y and whose tail is ys.

```
  — fun insert (x : int, nil)  =  x :: nil
    | insert (x, yys as y :: ys)  =  if x <= y
                                     then x :: yys
                                     else y :: insert(x, ys);
  > val insert  =  fn : int * int list -> int list
```

Note how the recursion assumptions lead us towards the goal for both functions.

The second part of the *median* problem is to select the "middle" element out of a sorted list. We use the function *index* (page 182) that selects an element at a given position in a list. Convince yourself that $(len\ xs + 1)\ div\ 2$ gives the required position for all lists!!

```
  — fun get_middle xs  =  index((len xs + 1) div 2, xs);
  > val get_middle  =  fn : 'a list -> 'a
```

With a local declaration, you can make one or both of the auxiliary functions local and export only *median*.

Exercises

14.9. Define *merge* that merges two sorted lists of integers into a sorted list. Use a layered pattern to simplify the definition.

14.10. Define a function *initsegment* that checks if one list is an initial segment of another list. A list is an initial segment of itself, and nil is an initial segment of every list. Derive the type of *initsegment*.

14.1.7   Semantics of recursive bindings

An ordinary value declaration cannot be recursive.

```
  — val ys  =  1 :: ys;
  Type checking error in: ys
  Unbound value identifier: ys
```

If *ys* is defined previously, however, the given declaration is meaningful.

```
  — val ys  =  [2];
  > val ys  =  [2] : int

  — val ys  =  1 :: ys;
  > val ys  =  [1,2] : int
```

The expression 1 :: *ys* is evaluated in the environment valid right before the declaration, that is, in the environment $\{ys = [2]\}$. Now, let us construct the corresponding situation using functions.

```
—  fun  len xs  =  7 ;
>  val  len  =  fn  :  'a  ->  int

—  fun  len nil  =  0
    |  len ( _ :: xs)  =  1 + len xs ;
>  val  len  =  fn  :  'a list  ->  int

—  len [3, 4] ;
   2 :  int
```

In the last declaration, *len* is used recursively in contrast to *ys* above, which uses the previous binding.

An non-recursive function declaration can be transformed into an equivalent value declaration. Now, suppose we try the same thing with the *len* function.

```
—  val  len  =  fn nil  =>  0
    |  ( _ :: xs)  =>  1 + len xs ;
Type checking error in:  len
Unbound value identifier:  len
```

The rewriting is no longer possible, because *len* is recursive. To inform the system of this fact, the reserved word **rec** must follow **val**.

```
—  val rec  len  =  fn nil  =>  0
    |  ( _ :: xs)  =>  1 + len xs ;
>  val  len  =  fn  :  'a list  ->  int
```

When using a function declaration with **fun**, the system automatically assumes that the declaration may be recursive.

Formal semantics of recursive bindings

Recursion is a very powerful tool, but also slightly complicated. This complication is reflected in the formal semantics. Previously, we said that functions are evaluated in the environment valid before the declaration; we constructed a closure consisting of the function and the current environment in order to handle free variables. The closure was denoted by $\langle \textbf{fn}\ id\ =>\ e \mid Env \rangle$ (we ignore more complicated patterns) and a declaration was reduced as

$$\langle \textbf{val}\ f\ =\ \textbf{fn}\ id\ =>\ e \mid Env \rangle \longrightarrow \langle \{f = \langle \textbf{fn}\ id\ =>\ e \mid Env \rangle \} \mid Env \rangle$$

In a recursive function declaration, the name of the function must be known in the declaration itself. We therefore have to extend the environment in the closure with a binding to the function name itself. This binding is the self-referential one and refers to the closure itself. We draw an arrow to show this reference.

$$\langle \mathbf{val\ rec\ } f \ =\ \mathbf{fn\ } id \ =>\ e \mid Env \rangle \ \longrightarrow$$

$$\langle \{ f = \langle \mathbf{fn\ } id \ =>\ e \mid Env + \{ f = * \} \rangle \} \mid Env \rangle$$

The effect of the self-reference is that you can use the function itself in its definition. We will below show only the star, but think of it as a reference—an arrow.

Let us look at how the declaration of *len* is evaluated. The first reduction is to transform the function declaration to the corresponding value declaration and the second reduction to form the closure with the self-reference.

$$\langle\ \mathbf{fun\ }\ len\ nil\ =\ 0$$
$$\mid\ len\ (\ \_ :: xs)\ =\ 1 + len\ xs \mid Env \rangle \ \longrightarrow$$

$$\langle \mathbf{val\ rec\ } len\ =\ \mathbf{fn\ } nil\ =>\ 0$$
$$\mid\ (\ \_ :: xs)\ =>\ 1 + len\ xs \mid Env \rangle \ \longrightarrow$$

$$\langle \{ len = \langle \mathbf{fn\ } nil\ =>\ 0$$
$$\mid\ (\ \_ :: xs)\ =>\ 1 + len\ xs \mid Env + \{ len = * \} \rangle \} \mid Env \rangle$$

Notice the two uses of the |. A fully formal treatment of recursive bindings is outside the scope of this book; the description above should, however, give you an idea of how an interpreter for ML can treat recursive functions.

Exercises

14.11. What is the type, if any, of *selfapply* defined by *selfapply f = f f*?

14.2 String Manipulation

A string can contain an arbitrary number of characters. Therefore, you need recursion in some form for much string manipulation. A string is, however, similar to a list.

> — "string" ;
>   "string" : *string*

> — ["s","t","r","i","n","g"];
>   ["s","t","r","i","n","g"] : *string list*

In most languages, the type of character is the basic type; a string is considered as a list of characters only. To manipulate a string in ML, you normally transform it into a list of characters, perform the manipulation, and then transform the result back into a string again. The standard function *explode* transforms a string into a list of strings of size one, and the function *implode* does the reverse. In fact, *implode* accepts any list of strings.

      — *implode* ["a","bc","def"];
      "abcdef" : *string*

Let us define a function *palindrome* that checks if a string is the same read forwards and backwards. We first define a function for reversing a string.

      — **fun** *revstring* s = *implode*(*rev*(*explode* s));
      > **val** *revstring* = **fn** : *string* $->$ *string*

      — **fun** *palindrome* s = s = *revstring* s;
      > **val** *palindrome* = **fn** : *string* $->$ *bool*

By exploding a string, you can often use some predefined list manipulation function. If this is not possible, you have to use explicit recursion, but the recursion will be over a list, not a string. Let us define a function *remove* that removes all occurrences of a given character from a string. Can you define it??

    Since the argument to *remove* is a string, we have to define an auxiliary function that manipulates the corresponding list of characters.

      — **local fun** $rem(c, nil)$ = nil
           | $rem(c, x :: xs)$ = **if** $x = c$
                       then $rem(c, xs)$
                       else $x :: rem(c, xs)$
      in fun $remove(c, s)$ = *implode*($rem(c, (explode\ s))$)
      end;
      > **val** *remove* = **fn** : *string* $*$ *string* $->$ *string*

Note the use of the recursion assumption $rem(c, xs)$.

Exercises

14.12. Define a function *to_dec* that takes a string containing a binary number as argument and gives the corresponding decimal number. For instance, we have *to_dec* "110" $\longrightarrow$ 6.

14.13. Define a function *position* that gives the position of a substring within another string. For instance, *position*("end","extend") is 4. If the string does not occur, an exception shall be raised. What is the reasonable position of the substring ""?

14.3   Recursion over Natural Numbers

When defining functions whose domain is the natural numbers, you usually use the integers as argument type and raise an error if the argument is negative.

> ```
>   −   fun  fac n  =  if n < 0
>                      then raise fac
>                      else prod (1 −− n) ;
>   >   val  fac  =  fn  :  int −> int
> ```

We have been able to define functions like *fac* over natural numbers without recursion, since predefined functions like *prod* and *fromto* are defined using recursion. Let us now define *fac* without first building a list of the numbers to be multiplied.

Natural numbers are similar to lists. The constructors of lists are *nil* and *cons*. The corresponding constructors of natural numbers are *zero* and *succ*, the successor operation. In the template for lists, you do pattern matching against the *cons* operator (::). We cannot do the corresponding pattern matching against the *succ* operator, since we use integers, and they are not defined using *succ* in ML. Instead, we have to match against a name and subtract one from it to get the next smaller number.

> ```
>   fun  fac 0  =  ?
>    |   fac n  =  ??
> ```

The recursion assumption tells us that $fac(n − 1)$ gives the factorial of $n − 1$.

> ```
>   −   fun  fac 0  =  1
>        |   fac n  =  n * fac (n − 1) ;
>   >   val  fac  =  fn  :  int −> int
> ```

You cannot select the negative numbers by pattern matching, so we use a conditional expression to take care of them.

> ```
>   −   fun  fac n  =  if n < 0
>                      then raise fac
>                      else case n of 0  =>  1
>                                 |   n  =>  n * fac (n − 1) ;
>   >   val  fac  =  fn  :  int −> int
> ```

In an ML system, there is a check that the pattern matching is exhaustive. Why, then, is there no warning in the first definition of *fac* above??

The answer is that negative numbers are matched by the second alternative, so the matching is exhaustive. Using the first definition we get

$-\ fac\ (\tilde{} 1)\,;$
Failure : Stack overflow

The recursion will, in principle, go on forever but, since a computer is a finite machine, some type of overflow will finally occur.

A *partial* function is a function that is not defined for all its arguments. The function *fac* is partial since the argument type is *int*, but the domain only the natural numbers. In such cases, you should always raise an exception for negative arguments.

Multiple recursion over natural numbers and lists

Some useful functions for handling lists also take a natural number as argument, and a multiple recursion over a natural number and a list is needed. Let us define a function *index* that selects an element at a given position in a list. The first element has position one. Can you define *index*??

One solution is to step through the list and at the same time decrease the position number until it has reached one. There are six combinations of empty and non-empty lists and of non-positive numbers, the number one, and numbers greater than one. By picking out the meaningful combinations first, we can merge the error cases into one alternative at the end. Given arguments n and $x :: xs$ we know that $index(n-1, xs)$ selects the correct element by the recursion assumption.

> **exception** *index*;
>
> $-\ $**fun** $index\ (1, x :: xs)\ =\ x$
> $\ \ \ \ |\ index\ (n, x :: xs)\ =\ index\ (n-1, xs)$
> $\ \ \ \ |\ index\ (\ _,\ _\ )\ =\ $**raise** $index\,;$
> $>\ $**val** $index\ =\ $**fn**$\ \ \ :\ int * 'a\ list\ \rightarrow\ 'a$

If *index* is given a non-positive number and a non-empty list, the second pattern will match. When the list has been traversed to the end, however, the error alternative will be chosen. Note that *index* like many other list handling functions is polymorphic and can handle lists of all types.

Exercises

14.14. Define a function *power2* that raises the number two to a given number.

14.15. Define a function *duplicate* that duplicates an object a number of times and yields a list of the objects. For instance, $duplicate("la", 3) \longrightarrow ["la", "la", "la"]$. Also, derive its type.

14.16. Define a function *take* that selects the n first elements of a list. Then, define *drop* that drops the n first elements of a list.

14.17. Define a function *substring* that selects a substring of a given size and at a given position out of a string. It shall raise an exception if the selection cannot be made.

Summary

A *recursive* function is defined in terms of itself. An application is meaningful only if the chain of recursive calls terminates. By breaking down an argument in the opposite way of its construction, the recursion always stops. For a list $x :: xs$, the function is defined recursively with the argument xs and for a natural number n with the argument $n - 1$. This simple type of recursion is often called *primitive recursion* over lists and natural numbers. On page 171, a procedure for defining recursive functions is described. It is based on the principle of *mathematical induction*, for lists usually called *structural* induction. In an *inductive proof*, you prove that a property holds for some *base* case, and, if the property holds for a certain value, it also holds for the "successor" of this value. The last step is called the *inductive step*.

Exercises

14.18. Prove by induction that the sum of all squares of the numbers 1 through n is $n*(n+1)*(2*n+1)/6$. Then, define two versions for computing the mentioned sum and compare their complexity (cf. Exercise 14.5).

14.19. In statistics, the standard deviation of a list of numbers $x_1, x_2, \ldots, x_n$ is given by the formula

$$\sqrt{\frac{(\sum_{i=1}^{n} x_i^2) - n\bar{x}^2}{n - 1}}$$

where $\bar{x}$ is the average value of the numbers. Define a function for computing the standard deviation of a list of real numbers.

Chapter 15

Higher Order Functions

Much of the power of a functional language comes from advanced use of functions. In particular, a function can be an argument to another function as well as the result of a function application. Functions with one or both of these properties are said to be higher order functions. They make it possible to define very general functions that are useful in a variety of applications. Usually, higher order functions are also polymorphic, another possibility of capturing a whole set of particular functions in one definition. These functions are often quite abstract, but they are an essential part of functional programming and are used over and over again. (If you feel uncertain about what a function really is, you may do well to read the two first sections of Chapter 4 again.)

15.1 Partially Applicable Functions

A function in ML always takes one argument. There are no exceptions to this rule, but as readers of programs we can view some functions in a different way. Let us define a function *plus* adding two numbers. It takes a pair as argument.

```
-   fun plus (x, y) : int  =  x + y ;
>   val plus  =  fn  :  int * int  ->  int
```

Often, you say that *plus* takes two arguments, knowing that it really takes only one argument, which is a pair. Both arguments to *plus* must be given at the same time. You can, however, define a function that takes one argument after the other. You then omit the comma and the parentheses. (Do not bother about the type of *add* now!)

```
-   fun add x  y : int  =  x + y ;
>   val add  =  fn  :  int  ->  int  ->  int
```

184

$$- \quad add \ 3 \ 4;$$
$$7 \ : \ int$$

For the time being we view *add* as if it first takes one argument and then the next one; later will be explained why *add* really takes only one argument. Functions like *add* are said to be partially applicable, and are drawn as function boxes with several input arrows.

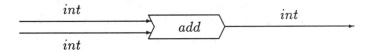

The diagram for *add* should be contrasted to the one for *plus*.

$$int * int \qquad \overline{\hspace{1cm}} \big\rangle \quad plus \quad \big\rangle \qquad int \qquad \overline{\hspace{1cm}}$$

Some "partially applicable" devices

A TV-set can be viewed as a partially applicable function. Its main function is to transform electromagnetic waves into light and sound waves, but before watching you select the channel you want (we ignore other adjustments). Hence, the TV first takes a channel as argument and then the waves to be transformed. In itself, the TV is quite a general function with many channels. Once you select a channel, you specialize its function to transforming the waves for this channel. But the TV is still a function! It is a function from waves to waves. In conclusion, a partially applicable function is a function that given its first argument returns a new, more specialized, function. If you supply this function with an argument, you get the final result.

CHANNEL ⟩ *TV-set* ⟩ *WAVES*
WAVES

A computer is used to calculate some output from a given input, but before performing the calculation, you provide it with a program—its first "argument". Thereby, you specialize it to perform some particular function. Hence, a computer can be viewed as a partially applicable function which, when given first a program and then an input, computes the output.

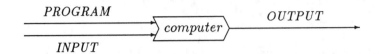

Curried functions

A partially applicable function is often called a curried function after the logician
H. B. Curry. The use of partially applicable functions was really invented by the
logician M. Schönfinkel, though. Let us return to the *add* function, which is a
curried version of *plus*. We have concluded that a partially applicable function is
really a function that, when given its first argument, returns a more specialized
function as result. Let us look at the type of *add*.

>   − **fun** *add x y : int = x + y*;
>   > **val** *add* = **fn** : *int −> int −> int*

The arrow −> associates to the right, so the type of *add* is interpreted as the
type *int −> (int −> int)*. Hence, *add* takes an integer as argument and returns
a function from integers to integers as result. This can be made more clear by
rewriting the declaration using a function expression.

>   − **fun** *add x = **fn** y : int => x + y*;
>   > **val** *add* = **fn** : *int −> int −> int*

The function *add* takes one (and only one) argument and returns a function as
result—the type of the right-hand side is a function. We can even go one step
further and use the **fn**-notation for the first argument, too.

>   − **val** *add* = **fn** *x =>* **fn** *y : int => x + y*;
>   > **val** *add* = **fn** : *int −> int −> int*

Obviously, *add* is a function yielding a function as result. Let us now use the fact
that *add* is partially applicable and define the successor function.

>   − **val** *succ* = *add* 1;
>   > **val** *succ* = **fn** : *int −> int*

The result of applying *add* to 1 is a function, which increases its argument by 1.

>   − *succ* 10;
>   11 : *int*

You can also define the predecessor function and a function adding 10 to its argument.

    — **val** *pred* = *add* (˜1);
    > **val** *pred* = **fn** : *int* −> *int*

    — **val** *add10* = *add* 10;
    > **val** *add10* = **fn** : *int* −> *int*

    — *add10* (*pred* 5);
      14 : *int*

It is not necessary to introduce a name for the function that results when you apply *add* to its first argument—you can use the application directly.

    — (*add* 10) 5;
      15 : *int*

Since function application associates to the left (in contrast to the arrow −> in the function type), the parentheses are not necessary.

    — *add* 10 5;
      15 : *int*

Compare the diagrams for *add*, *add* 10, and *add* 10 5! The first one describes a curried function, the second one an ordinary function, and the third one a saturated expression.

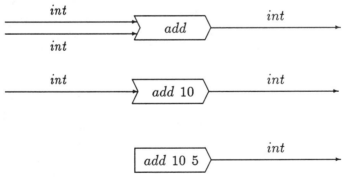

Many times, we will use functions like *add* 10 that are the result of applying a curried function to one of its arguments only.

Why curried functions?

Partially applicable functions are convenient to use, but you can always get the same effect without them. Using them, there is less to write, and the programs are often more readable. More important, however, is that the possibility of defining curried functions supports the search for powerful functions useful in a variety of applications—they help you to abstract.

From now on, most functions having "several" arguments will be defined as partially applicable functions. For instance, the predefined function *max* is curried, in contrast to our previous definition.

    − **fun** *max x y* : *int* = **if** *x > y* **then** *x* **else** *y*;
    > **val** *max* = **fn** : *int −> int −> int*

Most of the time we will not take advantage of the partial applicability, but it is seldom a disadvantage: you get less to write and the possibility of applying it to its first argument only.

Functions with many arguments

It is also possible to define partially applicable functions with many arguments. The function *max3*, for instance, selects the greatest of three numbers.

    − **fun** *max3 x y z* = *max x* (*max y z*);
    > **val** *max3* = **fn** : *int −> int −> int −> int*

Conversion between curried and uncurried functions

At times, you want to convert an uncurried function into its curried version or vice versa. Let us define two functions *curry* and *uncurry* performing these conversions for functions with two arguments. Suppose that *f* is a function taking a pair as argument. The function, which is the result of *curry f*, is then a partially applicable function taking the components of the pair one at a time.

    − **fun** *curry f* = **fn** *x* => **fn** *y* => *f*(*x, y*);
    > **val** *curry* = **fn** : (*'a * 'b −> 'c*) −> *'a −> 'b −> 'c*

For instance, *curry plus* is the curried version of *plus*.

    − *curry plus* 2 3;
      5 : *int*

To *uncurry* a function, you do the reverse.

    − **fun** *uncurry f* = **fn** (*x, y*) => *f x y*;
    > **val** *uncurry* = **fn** : (*'a −> 'b −> 'c*) −> *'a * 'b −> 'c*

Now, *uncurry add* is a function taking a pair as argument.

    − *uncurry add* (2, 3);
      5 : *int*

Make sure you understand the types of *curry* and *uncurry*. Further note that *curry* is the inverse of *uncurry* and vice versa. Hence, for all functions f and g of the right type, we have

$$curry(uncurry\ f) = f$$
$$uncurry(curry\ g) = g$$

For instance, f can be the function *add* and g can be *plus*.

Exercises

15.1. Define a partially applicable function *times* that multiplies its two arguments. Define it with no, one, and two uses of **fn**. Use it to define *double* for doubling a number using both a function and value declaration, the last one both with and without **fn**-notation.

15.2. What is the type of f defined by **fun** $f\ (x, y)\ xs = (x + y) * len\ xs$?

15.3. Consider the definition **fun** *what* $x\ y\ z$ = **if** x **then** y **else** z. Describe the type and the properties of *what*!

15.4. Define two functions *curry3* and *uncurry3* for converting between curried functions and functions taking triples as arguments. Then, derive their types.

15.2 Functional Arguments

A curried function yields a function as result. The real power of higher order functions, though, comes from functions taking other functions as arguments. Such functions can capture computational patterns that appear in many contexts.

Let us compare with an everyday example. An electric drilling-machine can be viewed as a "higher order function", which is both curried and takes a function as argument. The machine itself has the capability of revolving. To use it, you first provide it with some tool, for instance, a drill, a saw, a grinder, or a lathe. Each of these tools perform some "function". Its first "argument" is therefore a "function".

$$electric\_drilling\_machine : TOOL \rightarrow ITEM \rightarrow PRODUCT$$

The general applicability of the machine stems from the possibility of using it with such a variety of tools. It has the typical property of a function with a function as argument: it can be used in drastically different applications.

If we look only at the main behaviour of a computer, its "type" can be given as $PROGRAM \rightarrow INPUT \rightarrow OUTPUT$. A program is usually a function from some input to some output. Hence, the computer can be seen as a function, whose first argument is a function.

Let us now define a function *twice* that given a function and some object, applies the function to the object twice.

$$\begin{array}{c} 'a \rightarrow 'a \\ \xrightarrow{\hspace{3cm}} \\ 'a \end{array} \rangle\; twice\; \rangle \xrightarrow{\hspace{2cm}} 'a$$

```
–  fun twice f x = f(f x);
>  val twice = fn : ('a –> 'a) –> 'a –> 'a

–  twice square 5;
   625 : int
```

Let us follow the details of the reduction of the last expression.

$$twice\; square\; 5 \longrightarrow square(square\; 5) \longrightarrow square(25) \longrightarrow 625$$

To understand the type of *twice*, remember that a partially applicable function with two arguments has a type of the form $'a \rightarrow 'b \rightarrow 'c$. The first argument to *twice* is a function, and the type of a function is always of the form $'a \rightarrow 'b$. Since you apply the argument function to the result of an application to itself, its argument and result types must be the same, which you can also see from the system response.

It is not necessary to name the *square* function—you can use a function expression instead.

```
–  twice (fn x => x * x) 5;
   625 : int
```

Note that no type constraint is needed for the *square* function; the constant 5 informs the system about the type.

Since *twice* is partially applicable, you can apply it to its first argument only. Suppose you want a function *power4* that raises its argument to the fourth power. This is exactly to *square twice*, however.

```
–  val power4 = twice square;
>  val power4 = fn : int –> int
```

Now, you have to use **val** and not **fun**, since there is a single name on the left-hand side; the fact that the result is a function does not have any effect. If you want you can make the argument to *power4* explicit.

```
–  fun power4 x = twice square x;
>  val power4 = fn : int –> int
```

The effect is the same as the previous definition. In general, the definition with all arguments written out is easier to read, which is a more important aspect than the number of symbols you have to write. In the sequel, some function definitions will be given in the shorter form in order to show the possibility, even if the longer version is more readable. As an exercise, you can always fill in the extra arguments.

The order of the arguments to curried functions

When defining *power4* with a value declaration we use the fact that the function is the first argument to *twice* and not the second—a curried function must be applied to its arguments in the right order. Most of the time, there is a best choice of the order of the arguments to a curried function. The first argument should be the one that will vary least or, expressed in another way, the argument you most often want to specialize the function with. In general, functional arguments should be given before non-functional arguments. If you place the arguments in the right order, you can sometimes use the function very neatly.

Exercises

15.5. Define *thrice* that applies its first argument three times to its second argument. Derive its type and also reduce *thrice double* 3 by hand.

15.6. Derive the types of the functions specified by

$$f1 \ x = x \ 1 \ 1 \qquad\qquad f2 \ x \ y \ z = x(y \ \hat{} \ z)$$
$$f3 \ x \ y \ z = x \ y \ z \qquad\qquad f4 \ x \ y = \textbf{fn} \ z \ => \ x :: y$$

15.3 Map, a Useful List Handling Function

Lists are used frequently in functional programming. Fortunately, you can define a collection of functions that capture most of what you want to do with lists. Most of them are higher order functions, and we will now look at what is perhaps the most important one.

Let us compare with an everyday situation. In a factory with an assembly line, you process a sequence of objects. At each station you do the same thing to the objects, for instance, you draw a nut. Thus, you perform the same operation to all objects in the line.

The function *map* takes a function and a list as arguments and applies the function to all elements in the list; for instance, it squares all numbers in a list.

> — *map square* $[1, 3, 5]$;
> $[1, 9, 25]$: *int list*

We can specify *map* by the equations:

$$map \ f \ nil \ = \ nil$$
$$map \ f \ [x_1, x_2, \ldots, x_n] \ = \ [f \ x_1, f \ x_2, \ldots, f \ x_n]$$

The argument f is a function so its type has the form $'a \ -> \ 'b$. Since the function is to be applied to the elements in the list, the argument list must have the type $'a \ list$ and the result list type $'b \ list$. The type of map is, therefore

$$('a \ -> \ 'b) \ -> \ 'a \ list \ -> \ 'b \ list$$

The type of the map function can be described in a diagram.

To define map, you have to use recursion over the list. To map f to all elements in a list $x :: xs$, you are allowed to assume that $map \ f \ xs$ performs the task for the list xs.

```
-  fun  map f nil  =  nil
   |  map f (x :: xs)  =  f x :: map f xs;
>  val  map  =  fn  :  ('a -> 'b) -> 'a list -> 'b list
```

Let us look at the details of reducing the expression $map \ square \ [1, 3, 5]$.

$$map \ square[1, 3, 5] \ \longrightarrow$$
$$square \ 1 :: map \ square[3, 5] \ \longrightarrow \ \ldots \ \longrightarrow$$
$$1 :: (square \ 3 :: map \ square \ [5]) \ \longrightarrow \ \ldots \ \longrightarrow$$
$$1 :: 9 :: (square \ 5 :: map \ square \ nil) \ \longrightarrow \ \ldots \ \longrightarrow$$
$$1 :: 9 :: 25 :: nil \ \longrightarrow \ 1 :: 9 :: [25] \ \longrightarrow \ 1 :: [9, 25] \ \longrightarrow \ [1, 9, 25]$$

Since map is partially applicable, you can use it with only one argument.

```
-  val  square_list  =  map square;
>  val  square_list  =  fn  :  int list -> int list
```

Exercises

15.7. The length of a list can be computed by mapping a function transforming all elements to the number 1 and then summing them. Define len in this way and compare its time complexity with the recursive version.

15.8. Define a function $swapl$ that takes a list of pairs as argument and returns a list of pairs in which the elements are swapped. Derive its type.

15.9. Define $map2$ that applies a function to all elements in all lists in a list of lists. Derive its type.

15.4 The Compose Operator

One of the main problem solving methods is sequential decomposition: the problem of defining a function is decomposed into the problem of defining two simpler functions. Suppose that the function f is the result of composing g and h. Then

fun $f\ x\ =\ g\,(h\ x)$

In the definition, you name the argument to the function f, but that is not necessary. The compose operator, denoted by a lower-case o, has the effect of composing two functions. It captures the essential idea behind sequential composition.

val $f\ =\ g\ o\ h$

The compose operator takes two functions as operands and yields a new function as result. Thus, it is a higher order operator in both senses of the word. The type of the result of h must equal the type of the argument to g, since g will be applied to this result. The compose operator is a standard operator in ML and has lower precedence than any other standard operator (precedence 3). Formally, you can specify it by the equation $(f\ o\ g)\ x = f\,(g\ x)$. Note that the right operand to *compose* is the function that is applied first. In some mathematics books, the compose operator is defined with the operands reversed. We have defined several functions that are the composition of other functions, for instance, *twice* (page 190) and *last* (page 156).

      $-$ **fun** *twice* $f\ =\ f\ o\ f$;
      $>$ **val** *twice* $=$ **fn** $:\ ('a\ ->\ 'a)\ ->\ 'a\ ->\ 'a$

      $-$ **val** *last* $=\ hd\ o\ rev$;
      $>$ **val** *last* $=$ **fn** $:\ 'a\ list\ ->\ 'a$

Let us reduce *twice square* 5 using the new definition of *twice*.

      $twice\ square\ 5\ \longrightarrow\ (square\ o\ square)5\ \longrightarrow$
      $square(square\ 5)\ \longrightarrow\ square\ 25\ \longrightarrow\ 625$

As further examples, we can define functions *second* and *third* that give the second and third element of a list. We omit the cases with too short lists.

      $-$ **val** *second* $=\ hd\ o\ tl$;
      $>$ **val** *second* $=$ **fn** $:\ 'a\ list\ ->\ 'a$

      $-$ **val** *third* $=\ hd\ o\ tl\ o\ tl$;
      $>$ **val** *third* $=$ **fn** $:\ 'a\ list\ ->\ 'a$

Note the order of the operands. First you apply *tl* until the required element is first in the list, and then you apply *hd* to this list.

      $third\ [1,3,5]\ \longrightarrow\ (hd\ o\ tl\ o\ tl)\ [1,3,5]\ \longrightarrow\ (hd\ o\ tl)(tl\ [1,3,5])\ \longrightarrow$
      $(hd\ o\ tl)\ [3,5]\ \longrightarrow\ hd(tl\ [3,5])\ \longrightarrow\ hd\ [5]\ \longrightarrow\ 5$

Composing curried functions

Using the compose operator, you can rewrite the declaration **fun** $f\ x\ =\ g(h\ x)$ to **fun** $f\ x\ =\ (g\ o\ h)\ x$. Now, the parameter x occurs only at the end of both sides, and you can therefore rewrite the declaration to **val** $f = g\ o\ h$. You cannot always "abbreviate" parameters in this way, however. Let us define a function *subfac* with the specification

$$subfac\ i\ j\ =\ \begin{cases} i * (i+1) * (i+2) * \ldots * j & i \leq j \\ 1 & i = j+1 \\ \text{undefined} & \text{otherwise} \end{cases}$$

Now, let *fromto* be the curried function corresponding to the *fromto* operator.

>   – **fun** *subfac n m* = *prod* (*fromto n m*);
>   > **val** *subfac* = **fn** : *int* –> *int* –> *int*

The expression *fromto n m* denotes the application of the function *fromto n* to *m*. The right-hand side can therefore be rewritten.

     fun *subfac n m* = (*prod o fromto n*) *m*

No parentheses are needed around *fromto n*, since function application binds stronger than composition. We are now allowed to remove the parameter *m*.

     fun *subfac n* = *prod o fromto n*

It is tempting to repeat the trick and remove also the parameter *n*. That would be possible if the right-hand side were (*prod o fromto*) *n*, but the right reading is *prod o* (*fromto n*). What we need is a compose operator, whose second operand is a curried function. This function shall consume both its arguments before the first operand is applied to the result. Now, let *oo* be an operator specified by (*g oo h*) $x\ y = g(h\ x\ y)$. Using *oo*, you can give a very short definition of *subfac*.

     val *subfac* = *prod oo fromto*

Exercises

15.10. Define a curried function *compose* that does the same thing as the compose operator. Also derive its type. Do the same thing for the operator *oo*.

15.11. Define the function *map2* from Exercise 15.9 using a value declaration and a compose operator.

15.12. If *xs* is a list, the evaluation of *map f* (*map g xs*) requires two traversals of *xs*. Simplify the expression so that only one traversal is needed.

15.13. What is the type of *curry o curry*?

15.5   Examples of Higher Order Functions

15.5.1   Curried versions of operators

Often, you need a curried function corresponding to an operator, since you want to apply it to only one argument and use the resulting function as an argument to some other function. The functions *add*, *subtract*, *times*, and *over* correspond to the arithmetic operators[1]. Note that *subtract* and *over* take their arguments in reverse order.

> — **fun** *over x y* = *y/x* ;
> > **val** *over* = **fn** : *real* −> *real* −> *real*

Here are the specifications of some other functions, which we will use in the sequel without defining them again.

invert x	=	$1.0/x$	*pair x y*	=	(x, y)
divides n i	=	*n mod i* = 0	*cons x xs*	=	*x* :: *xs*
hasfactor n i	=	*i mod n* = 0	*append xs ys*	=	*xs* @ *ys*
conj b1 b2	=	*b1* **andalso** *b2*	*postfix x xs*	=	*append xs* [*x*]
disj b1 b2	=	*b1* **orelse** *b2*	*eq x y*	=	*x* = *y*
fromto i j	=	*i* −− *j*	*neq x y*	=	*x* <> *y*

The functions *conj* and *disj* are *strict* (not lazy), and therefore evaluate both their arguments even though this is not always necessary. They are useful when explaining some other functions, though.

Exercises

15.14. Derive the types of the functions just specified.

15.5.2   The standard deviation

The mean value of a set of numbers is the sum of the numbers divided by the number of numbers. Sometimes, you want to know also how scattered the numbers are relative to their mean value. The standard deviation gives such a measure. If all numbers are equal, for instance, the standard deviation is zero. For a sequence of numbers $x_1, x_2, \ldots, x_n$, $n > 1$, the standard deviation is defined by

$$\sqrt{\frac{\sum_{i=1}^{n}(x_i - \overline{x})^2}{n - 1}} \qquad \text{where} \qquad \overline{x} = \frac{\sum_{i=1}^{n} x_i}{n}$$

---

[1]We sometimes use suffix $'i$ and $'r$ to differentiate between integer and real versions. See also Appendix D.

In ML, we can represent the sequence by a list of real numbers. We get the number n from the length of the list and the mean value x_mean by dividing the sum of the numbers by n. Since we work with real numbers, we transform n into a real number from the beginning. We can now write down the main structure of $stand\_dev$.

$$\textbf{fun } stand\_dev\ xs\ =\ \textbf{let}\ \ \textbf{val } n\ =\ real(len\ xs)$$
$$\textbf{in}\ \ \textbf{let val } x\_mean\ =\ sum'r\ xs/n$$
$$\textbf{in}\ \ ???\ \ xs$$
$$\textbf{end}$$
$$\textbf{end}$$

The formula itself can be derived by translating a verbal description of the computation into ML in quite a straightforward manner. First you subtract the mean value from all numbers. Then, you square the resulting differences. Next, you sum all the squares, divide the sum by $n - 1$ and, finally, take the square root of the obtained quotient. The computation is a sequential composition of five actions. The first two actions are to do the same thing to all elements of a list, for which *map* is ideally suited. We do these two actions in one traversal.

$$-\ \ \textbf{fun } stand\_dev\ xs\ =$$
$$\textbf{let}\ \ \textbf{val } n\ =\ real(len\ xs)$$
$$\textbf{in}\ \ \textbf{let val } x\_mean\ =\ sum'r\ xs/n$$
$$\textbf{in}\ (sqrt\ o\ over\ (n-1.0)\ o\ sum'r\ o$$
$$map\ (sq'r\ o\ subtract'r\ \ x\_mean))\ xs$$
$$\textbf{end}$$
$$\textbf{end};$$
$$>\ \ \textbf{val } stand\_dev\ =\ \textbf{fn}\ :\ real\ list\ ->\ real$$

$$-\ \ stand\_dev\ [3.0, 4.0, 5.0, 6.0]\,;$$
$$1.290994448735806\ :\ real$$

Note the use of curried functions applied to one of their arguments only. The use of the compose operator shows how the problem has been split into subproblems. You can also write the main expression of the function without the compose operator.

$$sqrt(sum'r(map\ (sq'r\ o\ subtract'r\ \ x\_mean)\ xs)/(n-1.0))$$

What you prefer is largely a matter of taste. You may, as a third possibility, improve readability by introducing a local name also for the sum.

15.5.3 Summation of series

The summation of a series of numbers commonly occurs in mathematics and, for this reason, a special notation has been introduced.

$$\sum_{i=n}^{m} x_i = x_n + x_{n+1} + \cdots + x_m$$

The sum of the squares of the first 100 integers, for instance, is written $\sum_{i=1}^{100} i^2$ and is in ML computed by

>   —   *sum(map sq (fromto 1 100))*;
>   338350 : *int*

Many a time, you use series with an infinite number of terms. The base e of the natural logarithms, for instance, is given by the infinite sum $\sum_{i=0}^{\infty} \frac{1}{i!}$. Some infinite sums converge, and you get a good approximation to them by taking only a suitable number of the initial terms.

>   —   *sum'r (map (invert o real o fac)(fromto 0 15))*;
>   2.718281828459 : *real*

Note how each term is computed by applying a function to an index.

Looking for abstractions

In programming, you can avoid much extra labour by defining the right functions, usually general functions which are both higher order and polymorphic. As a programmer you should all the time try to abstract and find what is common to similar expressions. The two summations above, for instance, are similar. So, what is the essence of summation of series??

There are three things that vary in the examples: the lower limit, the upper limit, and the form of the terms. The limits are simply integers. A term can be described by a function which, when applied to some index, gives the corresponding term. This is the function we map to the list of integers produced by *fromto*.

>   —   **fun** *sigma term lower upper* =
>   *sum(map term (fromto lower upper))*;
>   >   **val**   *sigma* = **fn** : *(int –> int) –> int –> int –> int*

You can define *sigma'r* in a similar way. Using the summation functions, we can now redo the two examples above.

>   —   *sigma sq 1 100*;
>   338350 : *int*

- $sigma'r$ $(invert \ o \ real \ o \ fac)$ 0 15;
  2.718281828459 : $real$

A closer examination of the definition of $sigma$ reveals that you can shorten it using the oo operator (cf. page 194).

- **fun** $sigma \ term$ = $sum \ o \ map \ term \ oo \ fromto$;
- > **val** $sigma$ = **fn** : $(int -> int) -> int -> int -> int$

Once $sigma$ is defined, you can use it for all summation—you have captured the essence of summation. If you always try to abstract and introduce functions for common situations, you can simplify your work considerably.

Numeric integration

To understand this example you need some knowledge of mathematics. The definite integral $\int_a^b f(x)dx$ can be computed by computing the size of the area between the curve of f and the x-axis between the points a and b. One way of computing an approximation to this area is to split it into n thin rectangles. The approximation to the integral is then given by the formula

$$h * \left(\frac{f(a) + f(b)}{2} + \sum_{i=1}^{n-1} f(a + i*h) \right) \qquad \text{where} \quad h = \frac{b-a}{n}$$

Summation and integration have much in common, and the function $integrate$ also takes a function and two limits as arguments. In addition, the number of rectangles must be given.

- **fun** $integrate \ f \ a \ b \ n$ =
        let val h = $(b - a)/real \ n$
        in $h * ((f \ a + f \ b)/2.0+$
            $sigma'r \ (\textbf{fn} \ i \ => \ f(a + real \ i*h))$ 1 $(n-1))$
        end;
- > **val** $integrate$ = **fn** :
        $(real -> real) -> real -> real -> int -> real$

To test $integrate$, we compute the integral of the function $f(x) = x^3$ between 0 and 2, which should yield 4 as a result. We expect to get a better and better approximation as the number of rectangles increases.

- $integrate$ (**fn** x => $x * x * x$) 0.0 2.0 10;
  4.04 : $real$

- $integrate$ (**fn** x => $x * x * x$) 0.0 2.0 1000;
  4.000004 : $real$

Exercises

15.15. The exponential function can be defined by $e^x = \sum_{i=0}^{\infty} \frac{x^i}{i!}$. Define $expn$ with arguments x and n, the upper limit in the sum. Compare $expn$ with the exp for some values of x and n.

15.16. A good way of computing the integral $\int_{x_0}^{x_n} f(x)dx$ is to use the Simpson formula

$$\frac{h}{3}(f(x_0) + 4f(x_1) + 2f(x_2) + 4f(x_3) + \cdots + 2f(x_{n-2}) + 4f(x_{n-1}) + f(x_n))$$

where $h = \frac{x_n - x_0}{n}$ and n even. Define a function for integration using this formula and compare it with $integrate$ above.

15.5.4 Some combinators

Some, very general, polymorphic functions are sometimes called combinators. They have their origin in a branch of logic called combinatory logic. The purpose of combinators is to rewrite functions without any variables. Lately, combinators have been used as a basis for the construction of reduction machines for functional languages; they are, in fact, used as machine instructions. (For the use of combinators for the implementation of functional languages, see Turner 79.) The combinator I stands for the identity function.

```
-   fun I x = x;
>   val I = fn : 'a -> 'a
```

As an example of its use we define the function $sum1to$ using the sum $\sum_{i=1}^{n} i$. The terms in this sum equal the index.

```
-   fun sum1to n = sigma I 1 n;
>   val sum1to = fn : int -> int
```

Another combinator is the K combinator which takes two arguments and returns the first one regardless of what the second one is.

```
-   fun K x y = x;
>   val K = fn : 'a -> 'b -> 'a
```

If you want to define len by transforming all elements of the list to 1 and then summing them, you can use the function K 1 for the transformation.

```
-   val len = sum o map (K 1);
>   val len = fn : 'a list -> int
```

Exercises

15.17. The S combinator is specified by the equation $S\ f\ g\ x = f\ x\ (g\ x)$. Prove that $I = S\ K\ K$ and that $succ = S(S(K\ add)(K\ 1))\ I$.

15.5.5 Mathematical notation compared with ML

The notation used in mathematics has been developed over several hundred years. Concise and readable symbols are used for common concepts such as summation, integration, indexing, and exponentiation. In ML, you have to translate the mathematical notation into the corresponding expressions. This translation is often straightforward, however, since the two notations are nothing but different ways of saying the same thing.

Mathematical notation regularly uses two dimensions, for instance, for indices and limits in summations. It also uses special symbols not available on keyboards. In programming languages you have to use ASCII characters in one dimension, that is, line after line. With the growing use of work stations and graphical terminals, you are no longer limited to one dimension, and it would be quite possible to allow much more flexible symbols as names for functions and other objects in a programming language. In this way it would be possible to have programs that look like ordinary mathematical formulas. At present, you have to do the translation into ML. Thanks to the use of polymorphic and higher order functions, there is a close correspondence between the two, though.

Summary

A *partially applicable* or *curried function* is a function taking several arguments, one after the other. It is said to be *higher order* as are functions taking functions as arguments. Higher order functions allow the definition of very general functions useful in many contexts, since they are more abstract and capture very general computation patterns.

Exercises

15.18. The semifactorial of an odd (even) positive integer is the product of all odd (even) integers between 1 and the integer. Define *semifac* without explicit recursion.

15.19. Use the computer to compute how the terms $log_2(n)$, n, $n * log_2(n)$, n^2, n^3, and 2^n grow with n. Choose $n = 1$, 10, 100, 1000, and 10000.

15.20. In Section 17.1, Pascal's triangle is described. It can be generated using the binomial coefficients defined in Exercise 13.6. Use *map*, *fromto*, *pair*, and *map2* (Exercise 15.9) to define *Pascal*.

15.21. The equation

$$\sum_{i=1}^{\infty} \frac{1}{i^2} = \frac{\pi^2}{6}$$

can be used to compute an approximation to π. Define a function *pii* taking the upper limit n as argument. Find out how many terms you need to get 2 correct decimals (3.14).

15.22. Define *sine* using the series $sin(x) = x - \frac{x^3}{3!} + \frac{x^5}{5!} - \frac{x^7}{7!} + \cdots$.

15.23. What is the type of the function defined by $f = map\ map$?

15.24. Define a curried function *stop* that given a function and an integer raises an exception if the number is less than zero and otherwise applies the function to the number. Then use *stop* to define *fac*. Use a function expression in the definition of *fac*.

15.25. A peculiar function is the Y-combinator, which allows you to define recursive functions with ordinary value declarations, that is, without the word **rec**.

```
fun Y f x  =  f (Y f) x;
val len  =  Y (fn len' => fn nil => 0
                        |  _ :: l => 1 + len' l);
```

Examine the properties of the Y-combinator by hand execution or by tracing, and try to explain why it can handle recursion.

Chapter 16

Operators

There are several objectives behind the design of a programming language. Most important is, of course, that you can use it to express computations. In fact, very little is needed to achieve this goal. ML is based on the lambda calculus which was developed during the 1930s, that is, before the advent of real computers. The pure lambda calculus contains only variables, function expressions, and function applications. It has been proved that you can still express all computations that you can describe in any other formalism. A consequence of using such a small language, however, is that you have to use intricate codings and your programs then become unreadable.

Symbolic identifiers

One way of increasing readability is to name objects with identifiers. In ML, there are two kinds of identifiers: *alphanumeric* and *symbolic*. An alphanumeric identifier is any sequence of letters, digits, primes, and underbars starting with a letter or, in the case of a type variable, with a prime. A symbolic identifier is any sequence of the following *symbols*:

$$! \ \% \ \& \ \$ \ + \ - \ / \ : \ < \ = \ > \ ? \ @ \ \backslash \ \tilde{} \ ` \ \hat{} \ | \ *$$

Note that the single quote is `, not '. An exception to both these rules is the use of an identifier, which is a reserved word like **val** or |.

The type variables, which always start with a prime, form a class for themselves. All the other kinds of identifier can be used for any purpose in ML, for instance, as value names, as function names (which are really value names), as type names, as exception names, or as names of data objects.

```
-   val  |||||||||| = 10 ;
>   val  |||||||||| = 10 :  int
```

```
-   datatype + - * /  =  + + +  |  - - -  |  * * *  |  /// ;
>   datatype + - * /  =  + + +  |  - - -  |  * * *  |  ///
    con + + +  =  + + +  :  + - * /
    ...
```

An identifier is always taken to be the longest possible sequence of characters that can be interpreted as an identifier. Often, you therefore have to surround it by spaces or other characters that cannot be used in an identifier.

```
-   val |||= 3;
Parse Error In:   val |||= 3
```

The equals sign must be separated from the identifier, since an equals sign is an allowed character in a symbolic identifier.

Let us now introduce a short name for the *curry* function (page 188).

```
-   val $ = curry;
>   val $ = fn : ('a * 'b -> 'c) -> 'a -> 'b -> 'c

-   $ plus 2 3;
    5 : int
```

The *uncurry* function is much more seldom used, but let us for reasons of symmetry introduce a short name for it, too.

```
-   val ~$ = uncurry;
>   val ~$ = fn : ('a -> 'b -> 'c) -> 'a * 'b -> 'c

-   ~$ ($ plus) (2,3);
    5 : int
```

Prefix and infix notation

A prefix operator is placed before its operand, whereas an infix operator is placed between its two operands. Normally, alphanumeric identifiers are used for prefix operators and symbolic identifiers for infix operators. This is nothing prescribed by the language, however, only a convention. Most standard identifiers obey this convention. Exceptions are *div* and *mod* which are used in infix position and ~ which is used in prefix position. When you choose a name for some object, readability and ease of use should guide your choice. If the object you name is used in some other discipline, for instance, in mathematics or physics, you should adhere to common practice, if possible.

The relation between functions and operators

A function is usually given a name.

- **fun** *plus* (x, y) : *int* = $x + y$;
- > **val** *plus* = **fn** : *int* * *int* −> *int*

The *plus* function performs the same operation as +, but is used in prefix position. A function name can be the operand to some other function, but that is not the case for an infix operator.

- *map plus* [(1, 2), (3, 4)] ;
  [3, 7] : *int list*

- *map* + [(1, 2), (3, 4)] ;
  Type Clash in: *map* + [(1, 2), (3, 4)]
  Looking for a: ($'a$ −> $'b$) −> $'a$ *list* −> $'b$ *list*
  I have found a: (*int* * *int*) *list*

The function of an infix operator

In ML, you can obtain the function associated with an infix operator by preceding it with the reserved word **op**.

- *map* (**op** +) [(1, 2), (3, 4)] ;
  [3, 7] : *int list*

The expression **op** + denotes a function from a pair of integers to an integer. The **op** construction is a form of *atomic* expression and therefore binds more strongly than any other expression in ML, even stronger than a function application. Parentheses are therefore never needed around it.

- *map* **op** + [(1, 2), (3, 4)] ;
  [3, 7] : *int list*

If you want to stress that the word **op** is associated with the +, you can omit the space between them.

- *map* **op**+ [(1, 2), (3, 4)] ;
  [3, 7] : *int list*

This is only possible for symbolic identifiers, since **op** followed by an alphanumeric identifier, like *opdiv*, would be treated as a single identifier.

Curried versions of operators

Suppose you want a function *succl* that adds 1 to all elements in a list of integers. You can now use the curried version of the function associated with $+$.

  –   **val** *succl* $=$ *map* ($ (**op**+) 1);
  $>$ **val** *succl* $=$ **fn** : *int list* $\rightarrow$ *int list*

Using $ and **op**, you do not have to remember the name of the curried version of $+$. If you consider the $ operator too cryptic, you can use *curry* instead.

  –   **val** *succl* $=$ *map* (*curry* (**op**+) 1);
  $>$ **val** *succl* $=$ **fn** : *int list* $\rightarrow$ *int list*

In most situations, however, *map succ* or *map* (*add* 1) is to be preferred, since they are more readable.

Non-commutative operators

A commutative operator is such that you can swap its operands with unchanged result. The inequality operator, for instance, is commutative since $x <> y = y <> x$.

Now, suppose you want a function *predl* that subtracts 1 from all elements in a list of integers. You cannot replace the $+$ by a $-$ in the definition of *succl*, since for an element i in the list, you get $1 - i$ and not $i - 1$ as you want. You need a way of swapping the "arguments" to a function taking a pair as argument.

  –   **fun** $><$ f $=$ **fn** (x, y) $=>$ $f(y, x)$;
  $>$ **val** $>< =$ **fn** : $('a * 'b \rightarrow 'c) \rightarrow 'b * 'a \rightarrow 'c$

  –   **val** *predl* $=$ *map* ($ ($><$ (**op** $-$)) 1);
  $>$ **val** *predl* $=$ **fn** : *int list* $\rightarrow$ *int list*

Using only $ and $><$, you do not need predefined curried versions of operators at all. However, programs soon become difficult to read if they contain unfamiliar operators, and almost always it is better to spell out your intention.

  –   **val** *predl* $=$ *map* (*subtract* 1);
  $>$ **val** *predl* $=$ **fn** : *int list* $\rightarrow$ *int list*

Defining your own infix operators

To define an infix operator, you must do two things: define a function that takes a pair as argument and tell the system that you want to use the function name as an infix operator. How you do these actions depends on the order you perform them.

We have previously used the == operator, which tests if two real numbers are almost equal. Let us now define it. If the two numbers are exactly equal, the result is, of course, *true*. In Sect 6.1, it was explained that you should test the relative magnitude of the numbers, not their absolute magnitude. You can do this by dividing the difference between the numbers by their sum. To avoid division by zero, you have to check that the sum is not zero. If the sum is zero we consider the numbers as unequal.

$$
\begin{aligned}
- \quad &\textbf{fun } == \ (x, y) \ = \ x = y \textbf{ orelse} \\
&\qquad\qquad x + y <> 0.0 \textbf{ andalso } abs((x - y)/(x + y)) < 1E\tilde{\ }16\,; \\
> \quad &\textbf{val } === \ \textbf{fn} \ : \ real * real \ -> \ bool
\end{aligned}
$$

Now you have to tell the system that you want to use the name == as an infix operator, which you do with the **infix directive**.

$$- \quad \textbf{infix } == \ ;$$

The system does not reply anything to a directive, but henceforth you can use == in infix position.

$$
\begin{aligned}
- \quad &0.0 == 0.0\,; \\
&true \ : \ bool
\end{aligned}
$$

If, on the other hand, you give the infix directive before defining the function, the system expects the name == to appear in infix position in the definition.

$$\textbf{fun } x == y \ = \ x = y \textbf{ orelse } \ldots$$

An alternative is to transform == to a prefix operator by the use of **op**.

$$\textbf{fun op } == \ (x, y) \ = \ x = y \textbf{ orelse } \ldots$$

The last definition is analogous to how you can use **op** to transform an infix operator to a prefix one.

$$
\begin{aligned}
- \quad &\textbf{op } == \ (0.0, 0.0)\,; \\
&true \ : \ bool
\end{aligned}
$$

With the **nonfix** directive, the effect of the infixing can be undone.

− **nonfix** == ;

− == $(0.0, 0.0)$;
$true\ :\ bool$

Any identifier may be infixed, not only symbolic ones. Suppose you want an operator *rep* such that x *rep* n yields a list of length n containing only the element x.

− **infix** *rep* ;

− **fun** x *rep* $0\ =\ nil$
    | x *rep* $n\ =\ x :: (x\ rep\ (n-1))$;
> **val** $rep = $ **fn** $:\ 'a * int\ \text{--}> 'a\ list$

− "no" *rep* 3;
["no", "no", "no"] $:\ string\ list$

Associativity of operators

An associative operator like + satisfies the equation $a + (b + c) = (a + b) + c$, if we disregard the possibility of overflow. Other examples of associative operators are $*$, $\hat{\ }$, and @. Subtraction and division are not associative since, for instance, $4 - (3 - 2)$ does not equal to $(4 - 3) - 2$.

For a non-associative operator it is important that the operands are evaluated in the right order. An identifier that is made infix using the infix directive becomes left associative: several occurrences of the operator in a row are evaluated from left to right. Usually, you want operators to be left-associative, but some operators like the exponentiation operator $**$ are normally right-associative. To make it right-associative you use the **infixr** directive.

− **infixr** $**$;

− **fun** $i ** 0\ =\ 1$
    | $i ** j\ =\ i * (i ** (j-1))$;
> **val** $** = $ **fn** $:\ int * int\ \text{--}> int$

− $2 ** 2 ** 3$;
$256\ :\ int$

− **infix** $**$;

− $2 ** 2 ** 3$;
$64\ :\ int$

Precedence of user-defined operators

By default, the precedence of an infix operator is as low as possible, that is, it has precedence 0.

```
  -  2 + 3 ** 4;
     625 : int
```

The + binds stronger than **, contrary to what you want. You can set the precedence of an operator to one of the precedences 0 through 9 when you give an **infix** directive. Since we want exponentiation to have higher precedence than the other arithmetic operators, we give it precedence 8.

```
  -  infixr 8 ** ;
```

```
  -  2 + 3 ** 4;
     83 : int
```

On page 411 in the ML Report, the precedences of the standard operators are given. When you define an operator of your own, you should choose a precedence that makes it easy to use and such that it conforms to normal usage. If you give it too high or too low precedence, you may be forced to use extra parentheses. If, for instance, you define a relational operator on some type of object, you should choose precedence 4, since that is the normal precedence for relational operators.

Summary

An identifier can be *alphanumeric* or *symbolic*. Both types can be used for naming all kinds of object except type variables, which must be named by alphanumeric identifiers starting with a prime. A function name can be placed in *prefix* or *infix* position; the choice is made through *directives*. An infix function identifier is often called an *operator*. With directives you can prescribe the *precedence* and *associativity* of an operator.

Exercises

16.1. Define the compose operators *o* and *oo* with suitable precedence and associativity.

16.2. Define the operators >| and |> to mean *take* and *drop*, which are defined in Exercise 14.16. Select a suitable precedence.

Chapter 17

List Handling Functions

To manipulate a list, you usually use recursion. Most manipulations follow one of a few, very common, patterns. For each of these patterns you can, once and for all, define a function which takes care of it. To do the same thing to all elements in a list, for instance, you use the *map* function. By using a predefined function, you avoid, so to speak, to reinvent the wheel. Further, you improve the readability of your program, since other programmers recognize these functions and know what they do. Without them, a reader of your program must investigate which kind of recursive pattern you use.

17.1   List Generating Functions

17.1.1   A general list generator

The most common generator is the *fromto* generator. Let us here define a more general list generator, which also shows the principle of *iteration* (cf. Section 18.3). Given a *start* element, you can generate a list by applying a function *next* a number of times to the start element. The elements of the list will be *start, next start, next(next start)*, etc.

> − **fun** *genlist start next* 0 = *nil*
> | *genlist start next n* =
>   *start* :: *genlist (next start) next* $(n-1)$;
> > **val** *genlist* = **fn** : $'a \rightarrow ('a \rightarrow 'a) \rightarrow int \rightarrow 'a\ list$

Using *genlist* you can, for instance, define *fromto*.

> − **fun** *fromto n m* = **if** $n > m + 1$
>   **then raise** *fromto*
>   **else** *genlist n succ* $(m - n + 1)$;
> > **val** *fromto* = **fn** : $int \rightarrow int \rightarrow int\ list$

In Pascal's triangle, you get the next row by adding the two elements closest above and by surrounding the sums by ones.

$$
\begin{array}{ccccccccccc}
 & & & & & 1 & & & & & \\
 & & & & 1 & & 1 & & & & \\
 & & & 1 & & 2 & & 1 & & & \\
 & & 1 & & 3 & & 3 & & 1 & & \\
 & 1 & & 4 & & 6 & & 4 & & 1 & \\
1 & & 5 & & 10 & & 10 & & 5 & & 1 \\
\end{array}
$$

The numbers in row $n + 1$ are the coefficients of the polynomial $(x + y)^n$. They are often called the binomial coefficients. We use an auxiliary function *addpairs* that given one line computes the sums on the next line. It produces the last, but not the first 1. Starting with the list $[1]$, *Pascal* uses *addpairs* to compute the successive rows. The result is a list of lists.

> — **local fun** *addpairs nil = nil*
>   *addpairs* $[x : int] = [x]$
>   *addpairs* $(x :: y :: xs) = x + y :: addpairs \ (y :: xs)$
>   **in fun** *Pascal n = genlist* $[1]$ $(cons \ 1 \ o \ addpairs) \ n$
>   **end**;
> > **val** *Pascal* = **fn** : *int* $->$ *int list list*

> — *Pascal* 6;
> $[[1], [1, 1], [1, 2, 1], [1, 3, 3, 1], [1, 4, 6, 4, 1], [1, 5, 10, 10, 5, 1]]$: *int list list*

17.1.2   Random number generators

In some programs, you want to generate numbers at random, for instance, to generate a line on a pools coupon or random events in some simulation program. Ideally, you would like the program to generate different numbers each time it is run, but that is not possible in ML: an expression yields the same result each time it is evaluated[1]. By supplying your program with different start values, however, you can get different numbers at different runs. Such a start value is often called a *seed*.

A simple random number generator is the 147 generator. You start with a decimal number between 0 and 1 having many decimals. The sine function can yield such a number, so here we use $sin(0.1)$ as start seed.

> — **val** *seed* = *sin* 0.1;
> > **val** *seed* = 0.09983341664682815 : *real*

---

[1] In a language in which you can access the clock of the computer, you can use the time to compute "random" numbers.

You now multiply the seed by 147 and consider the fraction of the result. Let us introduce a function *random* computing the next seed given the current one.

- **fun** *random seed* = **let val** x = *seed* $* 147.0$
                              in $x - real(floor\ x)$
                              end ;
> **val** *random* = **fn** : *real* $->$ *real*

- **val** *seed* = *random seed* ;
> **val** *seed* = 0.6755122470837387 : *real*

Continuing in this way, you can generate *pseudo-random* numbers. The question of what to consider as truly random numbers is difficult and will not be dealt with here.

Example: Throwing a dice

With a random number generator you can *simulate* a dice. Let us investigate how many times each face comes up when you throw a dice. Since our generator is not altogether random, our experiment is as much a test of the random number generator as of a dice. Let us to do a series of 10 experiments with 600 throws in each experiment and see how many times each face comes up. They should appear approximately 100 times each in each experiment, so let us compute the standard deviation from the expected number 100 in each experiment. Let us also for each experiment compute the average value of the faces, which should be approximately 3.5 and, in addition, compute the average value of the average face values of the experiments as well as their standard deviation.

When you solve a problem, you should try to abstract from the particular details of the problem. The most important way to do this is to introduce a function with one or several parameters. Part of the problem solving is to select suitable functions. Most problems can be decomposed into largely independent subproblems. If you do the decomposition in the right way, you often end up with functions that are useful also for similar problems.

Let us first provide functions for generating a list of random integers. We then need a function for generating a list of random real numbers.

- **fun** *randlist n seed* = *genlist seed random n* ;
> **val** *randlist* = **fn** : *int* $->$ *real* $->$ *real list*

To get a random integer in the interval n to m given some random real number, we use the auxiliary function *randint*.

- **fun** *randint i j x* = $floor(x * real(j - i + 1)) + i$;
> **val** *randint* = **fn** : *int* $->$ *int* $->$ *real* $->$ *int*

We can now get a list of random integers by mapping *randint* onto a list of random real numbers.

```
-  fun randintlist i j n seed = map (randint i j) (randlist n seed);
>  val randintlist = fn : int -> int -> int -> real -> int list

-  randintlist 1 6 10 (sin 0.1);
   [1, 5, 2, 1, 2, 6, 6, 6, 2, 1] : int list
```

If you use another seed, you get another list of random numbers.

```
-  randintlist 1 6 10 (sin 0.2);
   [2, 2, 1, 5, 5, 3, 5, 1, 1, 5] : int list
```

Next, we have to provide a tool for performing a series of experiments. To make the tests independent of each other, we want them to be based on different seeds.

```
-  fun genseeds n = map (abs o sin o real) (1 -- n);
>  val genseeds = fn : int -> real list
```

Higher order functions can capture very general situations. Let us define a function *experiments* that takes some function *experiment* as argument. This argument function generates an experiment result given a seed.

```
-  fun experiments experiment n = map experiment (genseeds n);
>  val experiments = fn : (real -> 'a) -> int -> 'a list
```

Now, let *dicetest* be a function generating a number of throws with a dice.

```
-  fun dicetest n seed = randintlist 1 6 n seed;
>  val dicetest = fn : int -> real -> int list
```

We also need a function counting faces.

```
-  fun countfaces throws =
           map (count throws) (1 -- 6);
>  val countfaces = fn : int list -> int list

-  experiments (countfaces o dicetest 600) 3;
   [[96, 92, 92, 92, 111, 117], [92, 112, 99, 105, 95, 97],
    [113, 113, 101, 95, 91, 87]] : int list list
```

Finally, we have to define functions for gathering the statistics. We assume that *result* is bound to the value of *experiments* (*dicetest* 600) 10 and that the functions *average*, *stand_dev*, and *round2* are already defined.

  — **fun** *deviation_of_throws experiments* =
         map (*round2 o stand_dev o map real*)
          (*map countfaces experiments*);
> **val** *deviation_of_throws* = **fn** : *int list list −> real list*

  — *deviation_of_throws result*;
     [11.12, 7.32, 11.08, 10.37, 11.1, 10.56, 6.54, 13.45, 6.48, 15.63] : *real list*

  — **fun** *face_averages experiments* =
         map (*round2 o average*) *experiments*;
> **val** *face_averages* = **fn** : *int list list −> real list*

  — *face_averages result*;
     [3.64, 3.48, 3.33, 3.37, 3.6, 3.46, 3.53, 3.44, 3.45, 3.49] : *real list*

  — *round2(sum'r it/real(len it))*;
     3.48 : *real*

  — **fun** *face_deviation experiments* =
         round2 (*stand_dev*(*face_averages experiments*));
> **val** *face_deviation* = **fn** : *int list list −> real*

  — *face_deviation result*;
     0.09 : *real*

A functional program is often a set of functions, each of which can be used by itself. If you search for generality you often get both a nice program and a set of functions useful in other applications like, for instance, *random, randlist, randintlist,* and *experiments*.

Exercises

17.1. Investigate how probable it is that at least two persons in a group of people are born on the same day of the year. Try to find out by simulation how large a group you need to get a probability greater than a half.

17.2. In a one-dimensional random walk you start at zero and with equal probability add or subtract one to your "position" repeatedly. Define a function that generates a random walk of a given length as a list of numbers.

17.2 List Transforming Functions

The main list transformers are *map, rev, flat,* and @. Let us look at a common use of *map* and also at some other transformers.

Double use of map

The function *allpairs* computes all possible pairs you get by combining elements out of two lists. For instance, $allpairs([1,2],[3,4]) = [(1,3),(1,4),(2,3),(2,4)]$. If the argument lists are ordered, the order of the resulting pairs is called the *lexicographic* order of pairs, since it is similar to how you order words in a lexicon. Let us now define *allpairs*. Using *map* you can go through the elements of the first list. For each of these elements you must pair it with all elements in the second list. Using *map* again, you can go through the second list and form the pairs. The result is a list of lists, one list for each element of the first list. With *flat* this list of lists is transformed into a list as required.

> — **fun** *allpairs xs ys* = *flat* (*map* (**fn** *x* => *map* (*pair x*) *ys*) *xs*);
> > **val** *allpairs* = **fn** : $'a\ list * 'b\ list \to ('a * 'b)\ list$

> — *allpairs* $[1,2,3]\ [1,2]$;
> $[(1,1),(1,2),(2,1),(2,2),(3,1),(3,2)] : (int * int)\ list$

Pairs of lists and lists of pairs

Suppose you want to add two lists of numbers element-wise. You can use explicit recursion, but the need to pair elements of two lists is common enough to render a predefined function *combine* that transforms a pair of lists of equal length into a list of pairs.

$$combine([x_1, x_2, \ldots, x_n], [y_1, y_2, \ldots, y_n]) = [(x_1, y_1), (x_2, y_2), \ldots, (x_n, y_n)]$$

Using *map*, we can now add two lists of numbers.

> — *map* (**op**+) (*combine*$([1,2,3,4],[2,3,4,5])$);
> $[3,5,7,9] : int\ list$

A nice use of *combine* is to define a variant of *addpairs* used to generate Pascal's triangle in the previous section.

> — **fun** *addpairs' xs* = *map* (**op** +) (*combine* $([0]$ @ *xs*, *xs* @ $[0])$);
> > **val** *addpairs'* = **fn** : $int\ list \to int\ list$

Now, *Pascal* is simply defined by *Pascal n = genlist* $[1]$ *addpairs' n*.

In this section, we have used *combine* without defining it: its specification tells you all you need to know about it. Make it a habit to specify functions as abstractly as possible before you implement them.

Exercises

17.3. Define a function *sigma2* that generalizes *sigma* to two indices. It shall compute the sum $\sum_{i=n}^{m} \sum_{j=k}^{l} term(i,j)$.

17.4. Define *combine*. Then specify and define *split*, the inverse of *combine*. Finally, try to capture the relation between the two functions using equations.

17.5. Define a predicate *conjl* giving the conjunction of a list of truth values. Then, define a predicate *sorted* checking that a list of integers is sorted. Use a technique similar to the one used when defining *addpairs'*.

17.6. Define *pairwise* that applies a function element-wise to the elements of two lists. For instance, *pairwise times* $[1, 2]\ [3, 4] = [3, 8]$.

17.7. Define a function *diagonals* with argument n that generates all pairs of natural numbers, whose sum is at most n. The pairs shall be generated so that the sum of the components increases. For instance, the expression *diagonals* 2 will yield the result $[(0, 0), (0, 1), (1, 0), (0, 2), (1, 1), (2, 0)]$.

17.3 List Searching Functions

A list *searching* function searches a list for elements with some special property. The function *filter*, for instance, selects all elements out of a list that have some property. Since there may be many such elements, the result is a list. One argument to *filter* must be a data object which represents a property. We use a boolean function, which gives the value *true* if and only if the argument has the property. The property of being an even number, for instance, is represented by the function *even*.

> — *filter even* $[1, 2, 3, 4, 5]$;
> $[2, 4]$: *int list*

Let us derive the type of *filter*. Its first argument is a boolean function. Hence, its type is $'a \rightarrow bool$. Since this function is to be applied to the elements of a list, the list must have type $'a\ list$. The elements of the result list are taken from the original list, so the type of *filter* is $('a \rightarrow bool) \rightarrow 'a\ list \rightarrow 'a\ list$. We use recursion to define *filter*. When applying *filter* to a non-empty list $x :: xs$ with a property p, you can assume that *filter* p xs works correctly for the list xs.

> — **fun** *filter p nil* = *nil*
> | *filter p* $(x :: xs)$ = **if** *p x*
>   **then** x :: *filter p xs*
>   **else** *filter p xs*;
>   > **val** *filter* = **fn** : $('a \rightarrow bool) \rightarrow 'a\ list \rightarrow 'a\ list$

Example: Prime numbers

A prime number is a number greater than 1 having no other factors than 1 and itself. A non-trivial factor of a number n must be one of the numbers 2 through $n-1$, so we have to check if any of these numbers divides n. Using *fromto* we can generate the possible factors and then filter out the real factors.

>   − **fun** *factors* n = *filter* (*divides* n) $(2 -- (n-1))$;
>   > **val** *factors* = **fn** : *int* −> *int list*

>   − *factors* 36;
> $[2, 3, 4, 6, 9, 12, 18]$: *int list*

>   − *factors* 37;
>   [] : *int list*

To check if a number is prime, you check if the list of factors is empty.

>   − **val** *prime* = *null* o *factors*;
>   > **val** *prime* = **fn** : *int* −> *bool*

>   − *filter prime* $(2 -- 50)$;
> $[2, 3, 5, 7, 11, 13, 17, 19, 23, 29, 31, 37, 41, 43, 47]$: *int list*

Note that if you apply prime to a number less than 2, an exception will be raised by *fromto*, an indication of the adequacy of the definition of *fromto* (Section 13.3.2).

Finding only one element with some property

Sometimes, you want to *find* the first element of a list having some property. You can filter out all elements with that property using *filter* and then pick out the first element of the list. If the list is empty, an exception should be raised.

>   **exception** *find*;

>   − **fun** *find* p xs = **case** *filter* p xs **of** *nil* => **raise** *find*
> | x :: _ => x;
>   > **val** *find* = **fn** : $('a -> bool) -> 'a list -> 'a$

This definition is inefficient, since you search for all elements with the property, but need only one[2]. With explicit recursion, you can define a more efficient version. Let us, however, define a function *findl* instead. It yields a list with the required element if there is any and an empty list otherwise.

---

[2]Using a language with lazy evaluation, the search stops as soon as one element with the property is found.

```
   —  fun findl p nil  =  nil
      |  findl p (x :: xs)  =  if p x then [x] else findl p xs;
   >  val findl  =  fn  :  ('a -> bool) -> 'a list -> 'a list
```

In the definition of *factors* above, all factors are generated, but to define *prime* it is sufficient to know if there is a factor or not. Using *findl*, you can define a more efficient version of *prime* (cf. Exercise 17.9).

```
   —  fun prime n  =  null(findl (divides n) (2 -- (n - 1)));
   >  val prime  =  fn  :  int -> bool
```

Exercises

17.8. Define *count* with (Exercise 14.7) and without recursion. Compare the efficiency of the two definitions.

17.9. Change the definition of *prime* so only as many numbers as are really needed to decide if a number is prime are tested.

17.10. Find all numbers less than 1000 such that the sum of the cubes of their digits equals the number.

17.4   List Reducing Functions

A list reducing function is a function taking a list argument and producing a non-list result. Examples are *sum*, *prod*, *len*, and *maxl*. An interesting fact is that all these functions are instances of a very general computation pattern called *list reduction*. If you want to compute the sum of the numbers $[7, 3, 13]$ by hand, you evaluate the expression $7 + 3 + 13$ and to compute the product, you evaluate $7 * 3 * 13$. The expressions are similar. Suppose that $xs = [x_1, x_2, \ldots, x_n]$. Then, you can specify *sum* and *prod* by

$$sum\ nil = 0 \qquad\qquad prod\ nil = 1$$
$$sum\ xs\ = x_1 + x_2 + \cdots + x_n \qquad prod\ xs\ = x_1 * x_2 * \cdots * x_n$$

The specifications are similar. The function *flat* can be specified similarly by the equations *flat nil* = *nil* and *flat xs* = x_1 @ x_2 @ $\cdots$ @ x_n.

To abstract is to look for similarities and to disregard differences, which you do by introducing parameters to a function. There are two differences between the equations: the result for the empty list and the operator used. If f is the function to be defined, u the result for the empty list, and $\star$ the binary operator, then the common properties of the equations are captured by the equations

$$f\ nil\ = u$$
$$f\ [x_1, x_2, \cdots, x_n]\ = x_1 \star x_2 \star \cdots \star x_n$$

If, for instance, $u = 1$ and $\star$ stands for $*$, the defined function f equals *prod*. The aim of this section is to define a function *reduce*, which captures the essence of reduction, and by which you can define the other functions. For instance, we will find that $prod = reduce\ times\ 1$. There are some more preliminaries, though.

Reducing non-associative operators

The given equations do not fully specify the function f, since the evaluation order for the operators must be specified, too. If the operator is associative, that is, if $x \star (y \star z) = (x \star y) \star z$ for all x, y, and z, then the order is immaterial. For instance, @ is associative. We will later define two reduction functions: one working left-to-right and one right-to-left. Let us as an example rewrite the expression $7 + 3 + 13$ using *add*. The first expression uses right-to-left evaluation and the other left-to-right evaluation.

$$add\ 7\ (add\ 3\ (add\ 13\ 0)) \qquad\qquad add\ (add\ (add\ 0\ 7)\ 3)\ 13$$

Identity elements

An element u is said to be a left identity to $\star$ if $u \star x = x$ for all x and a right identity if $x \star u = x$. If both equations are true, u is an identity element of $\star$. For instance, the identity elements of $+$, $*$, and @ are 0, 1, and *nil*, respectively. When defining a function using *reduce*, the second argument should be an identity element to the first argument (the operator). In this way, the defined function will have nice mathematical properties, which simplify many uses of the function. If an operator has only a right or left identity element, only one of the two implementations below is applicable.

A straightforward implementation of reduction

Let us start to define *reduce* using the list template and the recursion assumption.

```
fun  reduce f u nil      = ?
   |  reduce f u (x :: xs) = ??
```

Reduction of an empty list yields the identity element u. We can now assume that *reduce f u xs* reduces the list xs, and our task is to reduce $x :: xs$, which is done by applying f to x and the reduced list.

```
  –  fun reduce f u nil = u
       |  reduce f u (x :: xs)  =  f x (reduce f u xs);
  >  val reduce  =  fn : ('a –> 'b –> 'b) –> 'b –> 'a list –> 'b
```

We can now easily define the reducers above.

    — **fun** *sum xs = reduce add* 0 *xs*;
    > **val** *sum =* **fn** : *int list −> int*

    — **fun** *flat xss = reduce append nil xss*;
    > **val** *flat =* **fn** : *'a list list −> 'a list*

We use the name *xss* to emphasize that the argument is a list of lists. Note that
the accumulation starts with the last element in the list and continues towards the
front, that is, right-to-left evaluation is used.

$$add\ 7\ (add\ 3\ (add\ 13\ 0)) \longrightarrow add\ 7\ (add\ 3\ 13) \longrightarrow add\ 7\ 16 \longrightarrow 23$$

Operationally, you can describe this reduction as a *successive accumulation*: you
start with 0 and successively add the numbers. More abstractly, however, *sum*
computes the sum of all numbers in a list—the order of summation is not important
on the abstract level (provided no overflow occurs).

The power of reduce

The function *reduce* is very general, and you can use it to define almost any list
handling function without using explicit recursion. Let us, for instance, define
append. The normal recursive definition is

    — **fun** *append nil ys = ys*
      | *append* (*x* :: *xs*) *ys = cons x* (*append xs ys*);
    > **val** *append =* **fn** : *'a list −> 'a list −> 'a list*

We can now make the reduction over the first list and use the second one as start
value.

    — **fun** *append xs ys = reduce cons ys xs*;
    > **val** *append =* **fn** : *'a list −> 'a list −> 'a list*

The accumulation consists of the insertion the elements of the first list to the front
of the accumulation list. The elements of the first list are consumed backwards.
Note that the first and second argument to *cons* have different types, and still
it can be an argument to *reduce*—the type of the first argument to *reduce* is
'a −> 'b −> 'b.

In Section 14.1.6, a function *sort* was defined using the auxiliary function *insert*.
This sorting method is called insertion sort and can be described as a successive
accumulation. You start with the empty list and then insert each element of the
list to be sorted into the accumulation list at the right place using *insert*.

    — **val** *sort = reduce insert nil*;
    > **val** *sort =* **fn** : *int list −> int list*

Indeed, a concise definition of a sorting algorithm, which shows the power of *reduce*.

Another way of understanding reduction

The effect of *reduce* can be illustrated nicely by showing how *reduce* transforms its argument list. Before you continue, you are urged to find out which function is defined by *reduce cons nil* !!

To simplify matters, we look at what happens when you reduce the list [7, 3, 13]. Using *cons* and *nil*, you can rewrite the list as

> *cons* 7 (*cons* 3 (*cons* 13 *nil*))

Let us also write down the effect of *sum* and *sort* on this list.

> *add* 7 (*add* 3 (*add* 13 0))
> *insert* 7 (*insert* 3 (*insert* 13 *nil*))

In each case you have replaced *cons* and *nil* in the description of the list by the first two arguments to *reduce*. If you replace *cons* by *cons* and *nil* by *nil*, you get the same list back. Hence, *reduce cons nil* is the *identity* function on lists. The identity function is not a reducer, since a list is returned. The reason is that *cons* constructs a list and therefore balances the reducing effect of *reduce*. You can define other list handling functions, which not are reducers, using *reduce*. Can you define *map*, for instance?? The recursive definition of *map* is

```
 —  fun map f nil  =  nil
     |  map f (x :: xs)  =  cons (f x) (map f xs);
 >  val  map  =  fn  :  ('a —> 'b) —> 'a list —> 'b list
```

Comparing this definition with that of *append*, you see that you first apply *f* to the elements and then "cons" them.

```
 —  fun map f xs  =  reduce (cons o f) nil xs ;
 >  val  map  =  fn  :  ('a —> 'b) —> 'a list —> 'b list
```

Left-to-right reduction

For non-associative operators, you can use either right-to-left or left-to-right reduction, but not both. For associative operators you have a choice. Often one choice is better than the other from an efficiency point of view. The function *reduce* is often called *foldr* since it uses right-to-left reduction. Symmetrically, left-to-right reduction is called *foldl*.

```
 —  fun foldl f u nil  =  u
     |  foldl f u (x :: xs)  =  foldl f (f u x) xs ;
 >  val  foldl  =  fn  :  ('a —> 'b —> 'a) —> 'a —> 'b list —> 'a
```

It uses the second argument as an accumulator, whose initial value is the "identity element".

$$foldl\ add\ 0\ [7,3,13]\ \longrightarrow$$
$$foldl\ add\ 7\ [3,13]\ \longrightarrow$$
$$foldl\ add\ 10\ [13]\ \longrightarrow$$
$$foldl\ add\ 23\ []\ \longrightarrow$$
$$23$$

This reduction should be contrasted to the one using *foldr*.

$$foldr\ add\ 0\ [7,3,13]\ \longrightarrow$$
$$add\ 7\ (foldr\ add\ 0\ [3,13])\ \longrightarrow$$
$$add\ 7\ (add\ 3\ (foldr\ add\ 0\ [13]))\ \longrightarrow$$
$$add\ 7\ (add\ 3\ (add\ 13\ (foldr\ add\ 0\ [])))\ \longrightarrow$$
$$add\ 7\ (add\ 3\ (add\ 13\ 0))\ \longrightarrow$$
$$add\ 7\ (add\ 3\ 13)\ \longrightarrow$$
$$add\ 7\ 16\ \longrightarrow$$
$$23$$

In the second reduction, the size of the expression first grows and then shrinks. The larger the expression you reduce, the larger is the biggest intermediate expression. Using *foldl*, the expression has the same size, regardless the size of the argument list. In an ML system, a stack is needed for *foldr*, but *foldl* can be implemented in a constant amount of space. The details are explained in the next chapter.

Defining functions having no identity elements

The function *maxl* selects the greatest number in a list. It cannot be directly defined using *foldr*, since there is no obvious number to return for the empty list. One may use the smallest representable number, but in systems with "bigints" that may be difficult. A better solution is to raise an error if *maxl* is applied to *nil*. By defining a variant of *foldr*, you can define *maxl*. It raises an error on the empty list and uses the last element of the list as start value.

```
      exception foldr1 ;

   −  fun  foldr1 f nil  =  raise foldr1
       |  foldr1 f (x :: nil)  =  x
       |  foldr1 f (x :: xs)  =  f x (foldr1 f xs);
   >  val  foldr1  =  fn  : ('a −> 'a −> 'a) −> 'a list −> 'a

   −  val  maxl  =  foldr1 max ;
   >  val  maxl  =  fn  : int list −> int
```

The name *foldr1* is intended to hint at the fact that at least one element is needed in the argument list.

General list reducers

Although *reduce* is powerful, there are some list handling functions that cannot be defined by a direct use of *reduce*. Suppose you want a function *duplicates* that checks if there are duplicates in a list. This can be done by checking if any element is a member of the list appearing after itself. The reason that *reduce* cannot be used directly is that the reduction function (the first argument to *reduce*) is provided only with the head of the list but not its tail. If you provide also the tail you get a general list reducer, which by definition captures what is meant by *primitive recursion over lists*. The function *listrec* is mostly of theoretical interest; the use of *reduce* or explicit recursion is most often to be preferred.

>   −   **fun** *listrec f u nil = u*
> | *listrec f u (x :: xs) = f x xs (listrec f u xs)*;
>   >   **val** *listrec* = **fn** :
>   *('a −> 'a list −> 'b −> 'b) −> 'b −> 'a list −> 'b*

Using *listrec*, we can define a function *inrest* that for each element checks if this element occurs once more in the list.

>   −   **local fun** *mem' x xs = mem xs x*
>   **in fun** *inrest xs = listrec (cons oo mem') nil xs*
>   **end**;
>   >   **val** *inrest* = **fn** : *"a list −> bool list*

For instance, *inrest* [1, 2, 3, 3, 2, 5] ⟶ [*false, true, true, false, false, false*]. A list contains duplicates if some element in the list returned by *inrest* is true.

>   −   **val** *duplicates = disjl o inrest*;
>   >   **val** *duplicates* = **fn** : *"a list −> bool*

Exercises

17.11. Define the functions *conjl* (sometimes called *all*) and *disjl* (sometimes called *some*) for the conjunction and disjunction of the elements of a list using *reduce*, *conj*, and *disj*. What can be said about their efficiency?

17.12. Define *forall* (*exists*) that checks if all (some) elements in a list satisfy a given predicate. Define one version using *conjl*, one version using *reduce*, and one version using explicit recursion. Make use of the compose operator. Compare their time complexities.

17.13. Define *len* and *rev* using *reduce* (and perhaps *K* and *postfix*).

17.14. Define *flat* using *foldl*. Compare efficiency with the version using *foldr*.

17.5 Equations, Algebra, and Efficiency

Equations are fundamental to functional programming. In fact, a functional program is essentially a set of equations. When you evaluate an expression, the equations are used as rewrite rules; you replace the left-hand side of an equation by the right-hand side. Also when you specify functions, you use equations. For instance, *sqrt* can be specified by *sqrt x * sqrt x = x*; you specify a property you want *sqrt* to have. Similarly, you use equations to state algebraic properties of functions, for instance, commutativity, associativity, and distributivity. Such properties are important when you want to reason about programs and convince yourself that they work properly. By deriving useful facts about a function you define and also its relation to other functions, you learn about how to use it in the best way. You may sometimes find that a slight change in the definition yields a function with more pleasant properties.

Efficiency

Some equations can be used to transform programs into logically equivalent, but more efficient, programs. The first equation below, for instance, lets you reduce two traversals of a list into only one.

$$(map\ f)\ o\ (map\ g)\ =\ map\ (f\ o\ g)$$
$$flat\ o\ map\ (map\ f)\ =\ map\ f\ o\ flat$$
$$filter\ p\ o\ flat\ =\ flat\ o\ map\ (filter\ p)$$
$$filter\ p\ o\ map\ f\ =\ filter\ (p\ o\ f)$$

The functions *foldr* and *foldl* give the same result when applied to an associative operator and its identity element. Their time or space requirements can vary much, however. Also for non-associative operators, both reducers can be used after some rewriting. Consider the following definitions of *rev*.

$$prefix\ xs\ x\ =\ x :: xs \qquad postfix\ x\ xs\ =\ xs\ @\ [x]$$
$$rev\ =\ foldl\ prefix\ nil \qquad rev\ =\ foldr\ postfix\ nil$$

The version using *foldl* has linear time dependence, whereas the other has a quadratic dependence; you have to traverse the whole list to postfix an element. For other functions it may turn out that *foldr* is better. There is a nice symmetry between the two definitions. If *f* and *g* satisfy

$$f\ x\ (g\ y\ z)\ =\ g\ (f\ x\ y)\ z \qquad \text{and} \qquad f\ x\ u\ =\ g\ u\ x$$

for all *x*, *y*, and *z*, then

$$foldr\ f\ u\ =\ foldl\ g\ u$$

The equations express in a condensed form the conditions that must hold when you shift between uses of *foldr* and *foldl*.

Exercises

17.15. Prove that *prefix*, *postfix*, and *nil* satisfy the conditions above.

17.16. Define *append* using *foldl* and compare the efficiency with the version using *foldr*.

17.6   The Use of Explicit Recursion

Sometimes, it is better to use explicit recursion than trying to bend the definition of some function to fit a certain computation pattern. In addition, when you try to solve some harder programming problem, the formulation of the recursion assumption can help you. Let us define *perms* that generates all permutations of a list; a permutation is a reordering of its elements. For instance, *perms* $[1, 2] =$ $[[1, 2], [2, 1]]$. Can you see how the recursion assumption can help you to find a solution??

If you want all permutations of $x :: xs$, you are allowed to assume that *perm xs* yields all permutations of *xs*. If you, for each list in this list of lists, insert the object x at all places, you get all possible permutations. Working top-down, we assume that *interleave* inserts x at all places in one list. Using *map*, we can insert x into all lists in *perm xs*. The result is a list of list of lists, since *interleave* yields a list of lists. Using *flat*, we get the required list of permutations.

In this exceptional example, the base case requires some thought. We want all permutations of the empty list. It is tempting to believe that there are no such permutations, but since the empty list is a permutation of itself, the result must be $[nil]$, and not *nil*. There is good mathematical evidence of this fact: the number of permutations of n objects equals the factorial of n, and since 0! is 1, the empty list should have one permutation.

```
—  fun  perms nil  =  [nil]
       |  perms (x :: xs)  =  flat (map (interleave x) (perms xs));
   >  val  perms  =  fn  :  'a list −> 'a list list
```

Suppose you want to *interleave* the number 1 into $[2, 3, 4]$. The recursion assumption gives *interleave* $1 [3, 4] = [[1, 3, 4], [3, 1, 4], [3, 4, 1]]$. We now have to put back the number 2 in the front of all these lists, which can be done by *map* (*cons* 2). The result is $[[2, 1, 3, 4], [2, 3, 1, 4], [2, 3, 4, 1]]$. Still missing is the list starting with 1, which must be added to the other lists.

```
—  fun  interleave a nil  =  [[a]]
       |  interleave a (xxs as x :: xs)  =
              (a :: xxs) :: map (cons x) (interleave a xs);
   >  val  interleave  =  fn  :  'a −> 'a list −> 'a list list
```

    — $perms$ $[1, 2, 3]$;
      $[[1, 2, 3], [2, 1, 3], [2, 3, 1], [1, 3, 2], [3, 1, 2], [3, 2, 1]]$: $int\ list\ list$

For both these functions, the recursion assumptions lead us towards the goal, and this is the case for many problems requiring recursion.

Using recursion to achieve efficiency

With a lazy evaluation strategy, you evaluate only those subexpressions that have to be evaluated. In ML, the disjunction using **orelse** is evaluated lazily. If you define a function $disj$ corresponding to **orelse**, however, both arguments will be evaluated.

    — **fun** $disj$ x y = x **orelse** y;
    > **val** $disj$ = **fn** : $bool$ $->$ $bool$ $->$ $bool$

    — $disj$ $true$ $(hd\ nil = 3)$;
    Failure : hd

    — $true$ **orelse** $(hd\ nil = 3)$;
      $true$: $bool$

The function $disjl$ computes the disjunction of a list of truth values.

    — **fun** $disjl$ bs = $reduce$ $disj$ $false$ bs;
    > **val** $disjl$ = **fn** : $bool\ list$ $->$ $bool$

The whole list will be scanned even if a true element is found. Using recursion, you can define an efficient version.

    — **fun** $disjl$ nil = $false$
      | $disjl$ $(b :: bs)$ = b **orelse** $disjl$ bs;
    > **val** $disjl$ = **fn** : $bool\ list$ $->$ $bool$

Exercises

17.17. Define $sort$ by selecting a sorted permutation out of all permutations of the list to be sorted. Use the predicate $sorted$ from Exercise 17.5. What is the time complexity of $sort$?

17.18. Define $allwords$ that computes all strings you get by picking letters out of a string in any order. For instance, $allwords$ "ab" = ["ab", "ba", "a", "b", ""]. No duplicates are allowed.

17.7   Some Data Structures

When modelling the real world, you need a variety of data structures. ML provides you with tuples, lists, and functions, but using them you can represent structures like sets, tables, matrices, and files. The way you look at lists, for instance, crucially depends on which operations you use. By providing new operations, you can look at lists through other glasses and make them look like something else. By forgetting about the old operations, you introduce an *abstraction barrier*: you hide the representation of the structure.

The properties of the structure you represent are usually not the same as those of the representation. For instance, some real objects may be represented by *several* data objects, and some possible data objects of the representation type may not represent any real object at all. In Chapter 21, these issues are considered in more detail.

17.7.1   Sets

Two sets are considered equal if they have the same members. When listing the members of a set, the order and the number of times they occur are irrelevant in contrast to what is the case for lists. We will represent a set by a list without duplicates. Several lists can now represent the same set, since the elements can occur in any order. The main way of analysing a set is to test if an element is a member of the set or not. You can use the function *mem* for this purpose. The union of two sets is the set whose elements are members of at least one of the sets. You cannot just append the two lists representing the sets, since that can yield a list with duplicates.

> ```
> -  fun union s1 s2 = s1 @ filter (not o mem s1) s2 ;
> >  val union = fn : ''a list -> ''a list -> ''a list
> ```

A property like the non-duplicate property is often called an **invariant**. For each new operation, you have to check that it preserves the invariant.

Exercises

17.19. Define the function *intersection* that computes the set whose elements are members of two other sets. Then prove the relation *intersection* (*union x y*) *z* = *union* (*intersection x z*) (*intersection y z*).

17.20. Define the function *difference* that computes the set of all members of a set that are not members of another set. Can you relate *difference* to the other set operations?

17.7.2   Tables

A table is a set of entries, each with a key and some information. The telephone book is one example. You can represent a table by a list of pairs, where the first component is the key and the second component the information. The most important operations on tables are *insert*, *delete*, and *lookup*.

> **exception** *lookup*;

> $-$ **fun** *lookup key nil* $=$ **raise** *lookup*
> | *lookup key* ((*key'*, *info*) :: *ps*) $=$
>   **if** *key* = *key'* **then** *info* **else** *lookup key ps*;
> $>$ **val** *lookup* $=$ **fn** : *''a* $->$ (*''a* $*$ *'b*) *list* $->$ *'b*

Exercises

17.21. Define *insert* and *delete*. Make sure no entries have the same key.

17.22. Each member in an association has a member number between 1 and 999. The address file is a table mapping member numbers to addresses. Can you find a way of improving the efficiency of *lookup* by storing the table in a better way than a list of pairs? Estimate the efficiency.

17.7.3   Vectors and matrices

A vector is a fixed-length sequence of objects. The important operation is indexing by which you select an element at a given position. A vector can be represented by a list. The scalar product of two vectors is the sum of the pairwise products of their elements.

> $-$ **fun** *scalprod v1 v2* $=$ *sum* (*map* **op** $*$ (*combine*(*v1*, *v2*)));
> $>$ **val** *scalprod* $=$ **fn** : *int list* $->$ *int list* $->$ *int*

A matrix can be described as a vector of vectors, all of the same length, where each vector is a row in the matrix. A matrix can be represented by a list of lists. However, only lists whose sublists are non-empty and of equal length represent matrices. Let us define *addmatrices* for element-wise addition of matrices. Like for many other functions on lists of lists, we use *map* twice.

> $-$ **fun** *addmatrices m1 m2* : *int list list* $=$
>   *map* (*map* **op** $+$ *o combine*) (*combine*(*m1*, *m2*));
> $>$ **val** *addmatrices* $=$ **fn** :
>   *int list list* $->$ *int list list* $->$ *int list list*

Other functions on matrices use *map* once and then recursion. The function *diagonal* extracts the diagonal out of a square matrix.

- **fun** *diagonal nil* = *nil*
  | *diagonal* ((x :: _) :: *xss*) = *x* :: *diagonal* (*map tl xss*);
  > **val** *diagonal* = **fn** : *'a list list* −> *'a list*

Exercises

17.23. Define *indexm* that selects an element at a given row and column in a matrix.

17.24. Define *transpose* that converts all rows of a matrix into columns.

17.7.4   Files

When you store data in a computer for some time, you usually use its file system. A file and a list are both sequences of data objects, but their operations differ slightly. When you manipulate a file, you can view it as a list[3] and use all list handling functions.

Assume a company has a file describing employees by their name, salary per hour, and number of hours worked during the week.

- **val** *example_file* =
  [("Adams", 3.50, 36.0), ("Johnson", 3.20, 40.0), ("Jones", 3.90, 39.0),
  ("Nilson", 3.10, 35.0), ("Smith", 3.45, 42.0), ("White", 3.90, 39.0)];
  > **val** *example_file* = ⋯ : (*string* * *real* * *real*) *list*

Now suppose you want to raise the salary of all employees by 10 %. Since you want to do the same thing to all triples, *map* is the natural candidate.

- **fun** *up perc* =
  map (**fn** (*name*, *sal*, *hrs*) => (*name*, *sal* * (1.0 + *perc*/100.0), *hrs*));
  > **val** *up* = **fn** : *real* −> (*'a* * *real* * *'b*) *list* −> (*'a* * *real* * *'b*) *list*

To compute the total amount to be paid in salary to all employees for one week, we sum the total amount per week for each employee.

- **val** *total* = *sum'r* o *map* (**fn** (_ , *sal*, *hrs*) => *sal* * *hrs*);
  > **val** *total* = **fn** : (*'a* * *real* * *real*) *list* −> *real*

We can now, for instance, compute the total amount after a potential raise.

---

[3]In ML, there are special input/output commands to transfer data from/to the file system.

— *total*(*up* 10.0 *example_file*);
  892.76 : *real*

The average salary per week is the total amount divided by the number of employees.

— *total example_file/real*(*len example_file*);
  135.266666667 : *real*

Next, suppose you want to find out how many low-salary employees there are, if a salary under 3.50 per hour is considered as low. You then have to filter out the low-salary employees and count them.

— *len*(*filter* (**fn** (_, *sal*, _) => *sal* < 3.50) *example_file*);
  3 : *int*

As a final example, let us pick out the record describing the employee Smith using *find*. We use a tuple selector to select the name component of a tuple.

— *find* (*eq* "Smith" *o* #1) *example_file*;
  ("Smith", 3.45, 42.0) : *string* * *real* * *real*

The examples show that the list handling functions take care of many common computation patterns occurring in administrative programs.

Updating a file

A common file operation is to update a file. Suppose you want to change the salaries for some persons or add some persons to a personnel file. Usually, you have an update file containing records of the same kind as the main file. For each update record, you replace the corresponding record in the main file with the update record. If such a record does not exist, you add the update record to the resulting file. To make updating simple, you sort both files according to some key, like name or identification number, before you update. The idea behind the update algorithm is to scan the two files in parallel and consume records from the file having the lowest key. If the keys are the same, the main record is replaced by the update record. Since there may be several update records with the same identification, the update record that replaces the main record is not consumed, but used for comparison with the next update record.

To make the function suitable for updating in general, we pass a selector function *key*, which picks out the key of a record and a comparison function, which tests if one key is less than another key. We use the symbolic identifier < as the name of the comparison function. Since it is normally used as an infix symbol, we have to precede it by **op**.

```
— fun update key (op <) mainfile nil  =  mainfile
    | update key (op <) nil updatefile  =  updatefile
    | update key (op <) (mrf as mr :: mf) (urf as ur :: uf)  =
        if key mr < key ur
        then mr :: update key (op <) mf urf
        else  if key mr = key ur
              then update key (op <) (ur :: mf) uf
              else ur :: update key (op <) mrf uf;
> val update = fn  :
  ('a -> "b) -> ("b * "b -> bool) -> 'a list -> 'a list -> 'a list
```

Exercises

17.25. What is the time complexity of *update* if the lists are of length n and m. What would be the case if the lists were not sorted.

Summary

List handling functions can be divided into *generators, transformers, reducers,* and *search* operations. They capture most of the common list manipulations. Sometimes, you still use explicit recursion because it is simpler or more efficient. Using *equations*, you can capture many properties of list functions as well as useful relations between them. They can be used to derive new functions, to reason about them, and to transform them into more efficient versions.

Lists can be used to represent many other structures. By forgetting about the ordinary operations on lists and defining new ones, you can view lists as, for instance, sets and matrices; you perform a em data abstraction and forget about the particular representation of the structure.

Exercises

17.26. One way to generate primes is to use the sieve of Eratosthenes. Starting with a list of all numbers from 2 to n, you select the first number, which will always be a prime. Next, you remove all numbers from the rest of the list which has this prime number as a factor. The procedure is repeated on the result of the previous step until the list is exhausted. Define the function *primes*.

17.27. Two numbers are prime twins if they are prime and their difference is 2. Compute the number of prime twins of numbers less than 2000.

17.28. A perfect number is a number such that the sum of its factors is equal to the number. The number 1 is considered as a factor, but not the number itself.

For instance, 6 is a perfect number since $1+2+3 = 6$. Define a predicate *isperfect*. Use it to compute a list of all perfect numbers less than 1000.

17.29. Every prime except 2 and 3 can be written on the form $\sqrt{1 + 24 * i}$, where i is some integer. Use this knowledge to generate a list of possible primes for i values up to some number k, and then select the real primes out of this list.

17.30. Define *perm* that given a list of objects returns a random permutation of the list.

17.31. Define *matmul* for multiplying two matrices. The element in row i and column j is the scalar product of the ith row of the first matrix and the jth column of the second matrix. The number of columns in the first matrix must equal the number of rows in the second matrix.

17.32. The list recursion function *reduce'* is specified by the recursive equations *reduce' u f g nil* $= u$ and *reduce' u f g* $(x :: xs) = f (g x) (reduce'\ u\ f\ g\ xs)$. Investigate its properties and use it to define *map, len, sum, prod, append, flat*, and *rev*. You may find use of I and K. Also, relate it to *reduce*.

17.33. In Exercise 17.2, a function generating a random walk was defined. Define a function that checks if a walk contains a return to zero. Then, define a function that performs a number of experiments with a given number of steps and compute for how many percent of the experiments that zero was reached again.

17.34. Consider a circle and a square that circumscribes the circle. You can compute an approximation to π by generating points evenly within the square and investigating how many points also fall within the circle. Investigate how the accuracy depends on the number of points. Redo the computation with points generated randomly.

17.35. In a magic square, the sums of all rows, columns, and the two diagonals are equal. Generate one (all) magic squares with side n for $n = 1, 2, \ldots, 10$ such that it contains the numbers 1 through n^2.

17.36. Write a program that decides how many magic squares nine given numbers can form.

17.37. In a diagonal Latin square of order n, each row, column, and diagonal contain the numbers 1 through n. Generate all Latin squares of order 1 through 10.

Chapter 18

Classes of Recursive Functions

Recursive functions can be classified according to their termination properties as well as their efficiency properties. Let us look at some important classes.

18.1 Primitive Recursive Functions

You have seen templates for defining recursive functions over lists and natural numbers. A function definition on that form is said to be on primitive recursive form. By definition, a function is primitive recursive if it *can* be defined on primitive recursive form. We are interested in primitive recursive functions because they have nice properties. They always terminate, since the argument in the recursive application either is the tail of a list or the predecessor of a number and, finally, it must reach *nil* or 0. Further, we have a good grasp of how many reduction steps are needed to evaluate an application, since the argument steadily approaches the base case.

Sometimes, it is uncomfortable to define a primitive recursive function on primitive recursive form. Luckily, we can use more general forms and, once and for all, prove that they are transformable to primitive recursive form. To reason about such functions, we have to use more general induction principles.

18.1.1 Course-of-values recursion

With course-of-values recursion, all smaller arguments, and not only the immediate predecessor, can be used. The semifactorial of an integer n is $1 * 3 * 5 \cdots * n$ if n is odd, and $2 * 4 * 6 \cdots * n$ if n is even. The domain of the function is the non-negative integers. From the specification we get $semifac(n) = n * semifac(n - 2)$ for $n > 2$. The recursive application here goes two steps back, but is otherwise similar to ordinary recursion. The main difference emerges in the base case—you have to give start values for both 0 and 1.

```
 —  fun semifac 0  =  1
      | semifac 1  =  1
      | semifac n  =  n * semifac (n − 2);
 >  val semifac  =  fn  : int −> int

 —  semifac 7;
    105 : int
```

This type of recursion is called course-of-values recursion or **history** recursion, since the function can be used recursively for all smaller arguments.

For *semifac*, it is clear that all even numbers are reached by starting from zero and then repeatedly adding 2. In the same way all odd numbers are reached by starting from one. The general induction principle for course-of-values recursion says that if you can prove $P(n)$ under the assumption that $P(k)$ is true for all $k < n$, then $P(n)$ is true for all n. The base case or base cases are now subsumed in the induction step. For instance, you have to prove $P(0)$ under the assumption that $P(k)$ is true for all $k < 0$, but there are no natural numbers less than zero, so you have to prove $P(0)$ unconditionally. The proof you give in the induction step must be valid for all n; in particular, you must give enough base cases. Several examples are given below.

Exercises

18.1. Define *semifac* without explicit recursion using *genlist*.

18.2. Define a function *powerset* that gives the set of all subsets of a set. Represent sets by lists. For instance, *powerset* $[1, 2] = [[1, 2], [1], [2], []]$. Also derive how many subsets there are of a set with n elements.

18.3. Define a function *cutvector* that splits a vector into vectors of equal length n and puts them into a list. The length of the last vector may be shorter than the others. Use it to define a function generating an identity matrix with n rows and columns. Its diagonal elements are 1 and the other elements are 0.

18.1.2   Multiple recursion

Suppose you represent the denominations of coins in some currency as a list of integers in decreasing order and want a function *change* that given an amount finds the smallest number of coins that adds to that amount. We assume that all but the smallest coin can be exchanged by smaller coins. For instance, you cannot have only coins 2 and 5, since 5 is not divisible by 2. Can you define the function??

Now, the formulation of the recursion assumption is not straightforward any longer. A good way to solve a problem is to try some example by hand. Obviously, you first select the biggest possible coin. Next, you have to repeat the procedure with the amount decreased by the value of the selected coin. The recursion is a multiple recursion over a natural number and a list. If the amount reaches zero, the task is done. If the list of coins reaches *nil* before the amount reaches zero, the amount cannot be changed with the given kinds of coins.

exception *change*;

– **fun** *change* 0 *cs* = *nil*
  | *change m nil* = **raise** *change*
  | *change m* (*ccs* **as** *c* :: *cs*) = **if** $m \mathrel{>=} c$
                                             then *c* :: *change* $(m - c)$ *ccs*
                                             else *change m cs* ;
> **val** *change* = **fn**   : *int* $->$ *int list* $->$ *int list*

– *change* 1280 [500, 100, 50, 10];
  [500, 500, 100, 100, 50, 10, 10, 10] : *int list*

Note that the argument $m - c$ can never become negative thanks to the condition $m \mathrel{>=} c$. The recursion is a combination of multiple recursion and course-of-values recursion in which the sequence of successive arguments strongly depends on the original arguments. Since either the amount is decreased or the list is shortened on each call, the recursion must reach one of the base cases eventually.

Termination of recursive functions

When defining a recursive function, you have to convince yourself that

1. any recursive use of the function has arguments that in some sense are smaller than the arguments to the function and

2. for any allowed argument, the recursion finally reaches some base case.

A good technique for proving termination is to map the arguments onto the natural numbers in some way and prove that that number always decreases when the function is used recursively. For the coin example, we can use the sum of the amount and the length of the list, since at least one of them always decreases. Since they both also remain non-negative, the sum must reach zero unless the recursion stops before. Hence, the function is defined for all arguments.

Exercises

18.4. A partition of a natural number is a list of positive numbers whose sum equals the given number. For instance, *partitions* 3 = [[1, 1, 1], [1, 2], [3]]. Define *partitions*.

18.1.3 Mutual recursion

Any non-trivial ML program contains many function declarations. Nothing prevents you from defining functions that use each other in a mutual fashion.

```
- fun  even 0  =  true
   |   even n  =  odd(n − 1)
  and  odd 0  =  false
   |   odd n  =  even(n − 1);
> fun even  :  int −> bool
> and odd  :  int −> bool
```

An application now results in an alternating sequence of applications.

$$even\ 4\ \longrightarrow\ odd\ 3\ \longrightarrow\ even\ 2\ \longrightarrow\ odd\ 1\ \longrightarrow\ even\ 0\ \longrightarrow\ true$$

The use of a multiple definition (using **and**) is necessary when defining mutually recursive functions. Whichever function you define first, the name of the other one must be known, and that is not possible if you use separate function declarations. The functions *even* and *odd* are defined for all natural numbers, since any positive argument is decreased by one on each call and, in the end, must reach zero.

Exercises

18.5. Redefine *even* and *odd* using conjunction and disjunction expressions.

18.1.4 Branching recursion

All recursion so far has been *linear*: each recursive application gives rise to at most one new application. You can also define functions in which one application can give rise to two new applications, which we call *double* recursion.

The Fibonacci numbers appears every now and then both in mathematics and computer science. They are a sequence of natural numbers starting with zero and one. You get a new number by adding the two previous ones. Let us define *fib* for computing the nth Fibonacci number (starting to count from 0).

```
- fun fib 0  =  0
   |  fib 1  =  1
   |  fib n  =  fib (n − 1) + fib (n − 2);
> val fib  =  fn  :  int −> int

- map fib (0 −− 10);
  [0, 1, 1, 2, 3, 5, 8, 13, 21, 34, 55] : int list
```

The recursion is a form of course-of-values recursion, since the argument $n-2$ is used. This double recursion can be described as *tree recursion* or branching recursion. To illustrate this fact we reduce *fib* 6 in a special order.

$$
\begin{array}{ll}
\textit{fib } 6 & \longrightarrow \\
\textit{fib } 5 + \textit{fib } 4 & \longrightarrow \\
\textit{fib } 4 + \textit{fib } 3 \quad + \quad \textit{fib } 3 + \textit{fib } 2 & \longrightarrow \\
\textit{fib } 3 + \textit{fib } 2 \; + \; \textit{fib } 2 + \textit{fib } 1 \; + \; \textit{fib } 2 + \textit{fib } 1 \; + \; \textit{fib } 1 + \textit{fib } 0 & \longrightarrow \\
\cdots \longrightarrow 13 &
\end{array}
$$

Each application branches into two new applications.

Divide and conquer

To look for a name in the telephone book by starting from the beginning is extremely slow. Instead, you split the book into two parts, select the appropriate part, and then repeat the procedure: you use a divide-and-conquer strategy. If there are 60 000 entries in the catalogue, the average search time in the first case is 30 000 and in the second case around 16 (the base-2 logarithm of 60 000).

Example: Quicksort

You can use a divide-and-conquer strategy also to sort a list of numbers. To divide the task, the numbers are split into two groups containing "small" and "big" numbers. To make the splitting, the first element of the list is used as comparator. These sublists can now be sorted separately and the final result is obtained by putting the results together. To sort the sublists, the function is used recursively. Each sublist is split into two new lists, and the recursion stops when the length of a list is less than or equal to 1. There are some traps you can fall in when you define this function. Below three algorithms are presented. Which one is correct and what are the errors in the others??

```
fun quicksort nil : int list = nil
  | quicksort [x] = [x]
  | quicksort xs = let val small = filter (fn y => y < hd xs) xs
                       and large = filter (fn y => y >= hd xs) xs
                   in quicksort small @ quicksort large
                   end;

fun quicksort nil : int list = nil
  | quicksort (x :: xs) = let val small = filter (fn y => y < x) xs
                              and large = filter (fn y => y > x) xs
                          in quicksort small @ [x] @ quicksort large
                          end;
```

```
fun quicksort nil : int list = nil
  | quicksort (x :: xs) = let val small = filter (fn y => y < x) xs
                              and large = filter (fn y => y >= x) xs
                          in quicksort small @ [x] @ quicksort large
                          end
```

The first algorithm does not always terminate. If the smallest element occurs first in the list, all elements will be classified as big and no progress will be made. The second algorithm works correctly for lists with unique numbers, but it removes all duplicates. The third algorithm is correct. Here you pick out one element and split the remaining elements into two lists, which will always be shorter than the argument list, since the first element is excluded. The recursion is a form of course-of-values recursion: you assume you can sort all lists whose length is shorter than the original list. The recursion always stops, since the lists become shorter at each call.

Is this sorting method really quicker than, for instance, insertion sort? Suppose the list has length n. In insertion sort, you search a list whose length is $n/4$ on average for each element; when you start insertion, the list has length zero and when you stop it has length n, and you search half the list on average for each insertion. Since there are n elements, the overall time is of order n^2.

Quicksort works best if all lists are always split into two equal halves. This does not, of course, happen very often, but let us derive the behaviour if it does. For each recursive application, you go through all elements of all current sublists when you compare them against the comparator, an operation of order n. Since you split the lists into equal halves on each call, you obtain empty lists after $log_2 n$ splittings. Hence, the overall time is of order $n * log_2 n$, which is very much better than n^2. Somewhat surprisingly, the *average* behaviour of *quicksort* is the same as the *best* behaviour. In the *worst* case, however, *quicksort* uses a time proportional to n^2; if the list you start with is already sorted, you will always get one empty sublist, so the size of the argument list decreases linearly only.

Example: The towers of Hanoi

This old problem amounts to moving a set of disks with holes from one peg to another peg using a third, auxiliary peg. All disks are of different sizes and at the start they are on the first peg on top of each other in decreasing size. Only one disk at a time may be moved from a peg to another, and a larger disk is never allowed to be on top of a smaller disk. The solution should work for any number of disks. Try to define a function solving this problem before you continue!!

To represent the problem in ML, we name the pegs 1, 2, and 3 with 1 as start peg and 2 as goal peg. A move is a pair of integers (*from*, *to*) and the solution a list of such pairs. There is no need to name the individual disks, since you always have to move the top disk—the origin and destination pegs are therefore sufficient. The number of disks at the start must be given as an argument, however.

The recursion assumption allows us to assume that a tower with $n-1$ disks can be moved from one peg to another peg. With this knowledge the solution is not far away. To move a tower with n disks from peg 1 to peg 2, all disks but the bottom one are moved to peg 3 (using the recursion assumption), then the bottom disk is moved from peg 1 to peg 2, and, finally, using recursion, the tower now on peg 3 is moved over to peg 2.

As disks have to be moved between various pegs, *towers* must take the pegs as arguments in addition to the number of disks n. The problem with five disks, for instance, is computed by $towers(5, 1, 2, 3)$.

$$- \quad \textbf{fun } towers\ (0,\ \_,\ \_,\ \_) \ = \ nil$$
$$\mid \ towers\ (n, from, to, help) \ = \ towers(n-1, from, help, to)\ @$$
$$[(from, to)]\ @$$
$$towers(n-1, help, to, from)\,;$$
$$> \quad \textbf{val } towers \ = \ \textbf{fn} \ : \ int * {'a} * {'a} * {'a} \ -> \ ({'a} * {'a})\ list$$

$$- \quad towers(3, 1, 2, 3)\,;$$
$$[(1,2),(1,3),(2,3),(1,2),(3,1),(3,2),(1,2)] \ : \ (int * int)\ list$$

Exercises

18.6. Use a divide-and-conquer technique to compute $i ** j$, where i and j are natural numbers.

18.7. Define a function that counts the number of ways you can exchange a given amount with some denominations of coins.

18.8. Redefine *quicksort* so that the list is scanned only once when it is split.

18.9. Define *select* that selects the ith smallest element out of a list. Use a technique similar to the one in quicksort to locate the element. Then, use *select* to define *median* that selects the "middle" element.

18.10. How does the time requirement for *towers* vary with the number of disks? Use induction to prove the derived formula.

18.2   General Recursion

Let us now look at functions that are not primitive recursive and therefore never can be given a definition on primitive recursive form.

18.2.1   The Ackermann function

Many interesting results in recursion theory were, in fact, produced during the 1930s before the advent of modern computers. For instance, it was proved that most interesting functions are primitive recursive. However, the logician Ackermann invented a function that is not primitive recursive. It grows exceedingly fast, and you cannot in any simple way give an upper bound for the number of reductions needed when applying it to an argument. Arguments around 6 are usually the largest you can use on a normal computer. The function uses double recursion with one recursive application *nested* within the other. Here is a simple version of it.

```
- fun ackermann 0 m  =  m + 1
    | ackermann n 0  =  ackermann (n − 1) 1
    | ackermann n m  =
              ackermann (n − 1) (ackermann n (m − 1));
> val ackermann  =  fn  : int −> int −> int

- ackermann 3 6;
  509 : int
```

To prove that *ackermann* terminates, you can no longer map the arguments onto the natural numbers. Instead, you can consider the lexicographic ordering on pairs of numbers mentioned in Section 7.3. For all n, m, and k we have that $(n, m − 1) < (n, m)$ and that $(n − 1, k) < (n, m)$, however large k is. Using these two inequalities, you can see that both recursive applications in the third alternative use arguments that are smaller than (n, m) according to this ordering. The recursion must stop, since there are no infinite chains of pairs that all the time become smaller. The tricky part is that when the first argument is decreased in the third alternative, the second argument makes a big, but finite, jump up. Since the first argument is finite, there will be only a finite amount of such jumps. Fortunately, the Ackermann function was constructed to show that there are non-primitive recursive, total functions. In practice, you very rarely meet such functions.

Exercises

18.11. Trace the recursive calls of *ackermann* by printing each pair of arguments.

18.2.2   Partial recursive functions

Normally, you want a function to terminate for all arguments. A recursive function is really a solution to a recursive equation. Some recursive equations have no solutions, however.

```
 -   fun circle x  =  circle x ;
 >   val circle  =  fn  :  'a -> 'b
```

This function does not terminate for any argument; you say it is *undefined* for all arguments.

The domain of a function is the set of values of the argument type for which it is defined. For a partial function, the domain is only a subset of the argument type. Good examples are *hd* and *div* that are not defined for *nil* and 0, respectively. A computation with an undefined result can show up in several disguises. An exception can be raised, as for *hd*. If the patterns for a function definition are not exhaustive, the function is not defined for some arguments; the system will tell you this when you enter the definition, however. A third possibility is a non-terminating computation, as for *circle*. Finally, a non-terminating computation may lead to memory exhaustion. Note that you cannot tell if a computation running out of memory is really non-terminating or if it only requires more resources than those available.

For some functions, it can be difficult to tell if they are defined for all arguments or not, that is, you do not know if they are total or partial.

```
 -   fun oscillate 1  =  1
   |  oscillate n  =  if odd n
                       then oscillate(3 * n + 1)
                       else oscillate(n div 2) ;
 >   val oscillate  =  fn  :  int -> int
```

In fact, no one has found an argument for which *oscillate* does not terminate, but, on the other hand, no proof has been given that it terminates for all natural numbers.

It is quite possible to write a program that proves general mathematical theorems. You give the program a theorem as argument, and if the theorem is true it will give a proof of it. If the theorem is false, however, the theorem prover may be able to tell you so, but it may also loop forever. By the very nature of theorem-proving, any general theorem-prover must behave in this way. In this case, there is nothing to do about the partiality, but in most cases you can, and should, define only total functions or functions that generate exceptions for undefined arguments. It may be best to add that, even though theorem-proving programs seem attractive, the problem is that even simple theorems lead to very long computations. In fact, very few theorems of interest have been proved mechanically.

Example: Euclid's algorithm

When defining a primitive recursive function, it is sometimes easier to use a more general form for the definition. Euclid discovered an algorithm for computing the greatest common divisor of two natural numbers.

```
—   fun gcd n m  :  int = if n = m then n
                          else if n < m then gcd n (m − n)
                          else gcd (n − m) m ;
>   val gcd = fn  :  int −> int −> int

—   gcd 126 70 ;
    14 : int
```

In this definition, there is no definite base case. Instead, the recursion stops if the
two arguments become equal. We trust old Euclid that the algorithm computes the
greatest common divisor, but let us show that it terminates for all positive integers.
For each recursive application one of the arguments decreases: the numbers are not
equal and we subtract the smaller from the bigger. They cannot decrease below
1, however, since the differences are always positive. If the two arguments do not
become equal before reaching 1, they must do so when they become 1, and they
must become 1, because they cannot be decreased indefinitely without reaching 1.
Thus, the algorithm terminates for positive integers.

   As you see, there are two quite different things to prove for a function using
some general recursion scheme. You have to prove that it terminates for all arguments you want it to terminate for, and you have to prove that it in these cases
gives the right result. If you do not prove termination, but only that the function
gives the right result should it terminate, you have given a proof of **partial correctness**. Hence, a program that never terminates is partially correct for every
specification. If you prove also termination for the whole domain, you have given
a proof of **total correctness**.

Example: The queens problem

A queen in chess can walk along rows, columns, and diagonals. Can you place 8
queens on a chess board so they do not threaten each other??

   A computer cannot do problem solving in an intelligent way, but using its speed
you can test a large amount of cases in a short time. One way to proceed is to
try all ways of putting 8 queens on the board, but that is an extremely inefficient
method. You can immediately see that there can be only one queen on each row.
You can now let the program place one queen after the other on each row. It is
no use to place a new queen if the existing ones can hit it. If they do, you have to
go back and try another alternative.

   Let us work in a top-down fashion. Suppose that *board* is the representation
of the board and the positions of the queens placed so far. Further suppose that
ok is a predicate for deciding if the queens on a given board are threatened, that
complete checks if all queens are placed on the board, that *addqueen* is a function
that places a queen in the first column on the next free row, and, finally, that

new is a function that moves the last queen, if it can be moved, and, otherwise, removes it and tries to move the previous queens. This can happen only if you have just placed a new queen on the board and you then have to move it until it is not threatened.

$$\textbf{fun } queens \; board \; = \; \textbf{if } ok \; board$$
$$\textbf{then } \; \textbf{if } complete \; board$$
$$\textbf{then } board$$
$$\textbf{else } queens(addqueen \; board)$$
$$\textbf{else } queens(new \; board)$$

Since there will be one queen on each row, you can represent the board by a list of numbers telling the columns of the queens. The length of the list tells how many queens have been placed so far. We can now define the auxiliary functions.

```
−   fun complete board  =  len board = 8;
>   val complete  =  fn  :  int list −> bool
```

```
−   fun addqueen board  =  1 :: board;
>   val addqueen  =  fn  :  int list −> int list
```

Next, let us elaborate *ok*. A queen can hit along rows, columns, and diagonals. We also know that it is only the last placed queen that possibly can hit any other one, since we do not place new queens if the existing ones can hit. To investigate if the new queen can hit along a column it is enough to see if there is a queen in the same column. To investigate if it can hit along a diagonal you can simulate that it moves along the two diagonals and look for hits.

```
−   fun ok nil  =  true
  |   ok (q :: qs)  =  not(mem qs q) andalso
                       not(hit (q − 1) (q + 1) qs);
>   val ok  =  fn  :  int list −> bool
```

The function *hit* takes three arguments. The first two are the fictive queens that move along the diagonals, and the third is the board with the remaining queens. For each recursive call, the queens are moved along the diagonals.

```
−   fun hit ql qr nil  =  false
  |   hit ql qr (q :: qs)  =  ql = q orelse qr = q orelse
                              hit (ql − 1) (qr + 1) qs;
>   val hit  =  fn  :  int −> int −> int list −> bool
```

Finally, we must refine *new* which generates new positions. If the last queen is not in column 8, you move it to the next column. If it already is in column 8, you have to remove it and recursively generate a new position for the remaining queens. This procedure might lead to the removal of several queens.

```
—  fun new nil  =  [1]
     | new (x :: xs)  =  if x < 8 then x + 1 :: xs else new xs;
>  val new  =  fn :  int list −> int list
```

This completes our program and we can now find out whether there is a solution to the problem or not. We start with an empty board.

```
—  queens [];
   [4, 2, 7, 3, 6, 8, 5, 1] : int list
```

If no solution had existed, the program would have looped forever. To remove this deficiency, you can stop the search when the program comes to a stage in which the first queen is removed.

Exercises

18.12. Consider the definition $f\ x\ =\ \textbf{if}\ x\ =\ 0.0\ \textbf{then}\ 1.0\ \textbf{else}\ f(x/2.0)$. For which arguments does f terminate?

18.13. The *gcd* function is better defined using the *mod* operator instead of subtraction. Define it as simply as possible. Also prove that it terminates. Can you say anything about the efficiency of the two versions?

18.3 Iteration and Tail Recursion

To iterate means to repeat. You start with some start state or start material, and then you repeat the same manipulation either a given number of times, called *number controlled* iteration, or until some condition becomes true, called *condition controlled* iteration, The manipulation can be described by a function with the same argument and result type. If *start* is the start state and *next* is the manipulation, the result of the iteration is $next(next(next \cdots next(start)))$. Using condition controlled iteration, you can define partial functions, but every number controlled iteration always terminates.

18.3.1 Number controlled iteration

In imperative languages, number controlled iteration is performed with a special **for** construct. The corresponding function is seldom needed in functional programs; you use the *fromto* function to generate a list of indices, and then you manipulate them directly. Often, you do not need the counter itself; you only want to transform an initial state a fixed numer of times.

```
-   fun iter 0 next s  =  s
      | iter n next s  =  iter (n − 1) next (next s);
>   val iter  =  fn :  int −> ('a −> 'a) −> 'a −> 'a
```

Example: An efficient version of Fibonacci

The *fib* function (Section 18.1.4) is extremely inefficient, since you compute most Fibonacci numbers several times. When you compute the numbers by hand, you start with the smallest ones and work upwards having no problems at all. Try to define *fib* using iteration!!

To compute one Fibonacci number, you need the two previous ones. The state must therefore contain two successive numbers, and the state transforming function must compute the next pair. The pair $(0,1)$ is the obvious start state. The function *snd* selects the second component of the resulting pair.

```
-   local fun next(i, j)  =  (j, i + j)
    in fun  fib 0  =  0
          | fib n  =  snd (iter (n − 1) next (0, 1))
    end;
>   val fib  =  fn :  int −> int
```

Let us reduce *fib* 5.

$$fib\ 5 \longrightarrow$$
$$snd\,(iter\ 4\ next\ (0, 1)) \longrightarrow$$
$$snd\,(iter\ 3\ next\ (1, 1)) \longrightarrow$$
$$snd\,(iter\ 2\ next\ (1, 2)) \longrightarrow$$
$$snd\,(iter\ 1\ next\ (2, 3)) \longrightarrow$$
$$snd\,(iter\ 0\ next\ (3, 5)) \longrightarrow$$
$$snd\,(3, 5) \longrightarrow 5$$

No duplicate computations are now performed. Compare this reduction with the one using the previous definition of *fib* (page 235).

Exercises

18.14. Define *for* that performs an iteration with an index running between two limits. The state transforming function now takes the counter as first argument and the state as second argument. For instance, *sum1to* $n = for\ 1\ n\ add\ 0$. Use *for* to define *fac*.

18.15. Use *for* to define *expn* (Exercise 15.15). Let the state be a pair of the last term and the accumulated sum. Compare the efficiency of the two versions.

18.3.2 Tail recursion

The functions *iter* and *for* have a very special form: the result of the function is either computed without a recursive call or *is* the immediate result of a recursive call. Such a function is said to be tail recursive. Let us compare with a definition of *fac*.

$$\textbf{fun } fac\ 0 = 1$$
$$|\quad fac\ n = n * fac(n-1)$$

Here, $fac\ n \longrightarrow n*fac(n-1)$, that is, the result is a product of two expressions and not only the result of a recursive call. A good system can compute tail recursive functions in an efficient way: no stack is needed. Some systems may even be able to transform some non-tail recursive definitions into tail recursive form, but usually you have to do it by hand.

For a tail recursive function, the result is *accumulated* in one of the arguments. Sometimes, you have to introduce an extra argument to transform a function into tail recursive form. Let us define *fac* using an auxiliary function *fac'* with an extra accumulating argument.

```
—   local fun fac' 0 acc  =  acc
              |  fac' n acc  =  fac' (n − 1) (n * acc)
    in fun fac n  =  fac' n 1
    end;
>   val fac  =  fn : int −> int
```

Now, the result of *fac'* for $n > 0$ is the direct result of a recursive call. Another example of a tail recursive function is *foldl*, which accumulates the result in the argument containing the identity element at the start.

When you call a recursive function with a big argument, you may get a stack overflow. If your system takes care of tail recursive functions appropriately, they never lead to overflow, since they are computed in a constant amount of space; the computations of the arguments may lead to overflow, though. A linearly recursive function can always be transformed into tail recursive form. For doubly recursive functions this is, in general, not possible.

Exercises

18.16. Define the *sum* function in tail recursive form.

18.17. The function *rev* is defined by *rev nil* = *nil* and *rev* $(x :: xs)$ = *rev xs* @ $[x]$. Transform it into tail recursive form. Compare the efficiency of the two versions.

18.3.3   Condition controlled iteration

Let us define an iteration function that transforms a state *until* a condition p becomes true.

> —   **fun** *until* p *next* s =   **if** p s
> **then** s
> **else** *until* p *next* $(next\ s)$;
> > **val** *until* = **fn** : $('a -> bool) -> ('a -> 'a) -> 'a -> 'a$

This function is a partial function and will loop forever for some arguments. You must therefore always give a termination proof when you use it. Note that *until* is tail recursive and, therefore, can be computed using a constant amount of space.

Example: The square root of a number

In the subject of numerical analysis, methods for computing mathematical quantities are studied. Many such methods are iterative. To find the root of an equation $f(x) = 0$, you can produce successive approximations using the recurrence relation

$$x_{n+1} = x_n - \frac{f(x_n)}{f'(x_n)}$$

until an acceptable value is obtained. The function f' is the derivative of f. You can define a general function performing this *Newton* iteration (cf. Exercise 18.19), but here we use it to define a function computing the square root of a number x by letting $f(x) = x^2 - a$ and $f'(x) = 2x$. The iteration is stopped when the number x and the square of the computed root differ little. As start value any positive number can be used and we choose 1.

> —   **fun** *sqrt* a = *until* $(\mathbf{fn}\ x => abs(x * x - a) < 1E\tilde{}14)$
> $(\mathbf{fn}\ x => 0.5 * (x + a/x))$
> 1.0;
> > **val** *sqrt* = **fn** : $real -> real$

> —   *sqrt* 2.0;
> 1.414213562373095 : *real*

It has been proved that this method converges, that is, really computes better and better approximations to the square root of a number. There can still be problems using it on a computer. For instance, you may get problems if you try to compute as many correct digits as the computer uses internally; small errors may then keep the condition false.

Example: Bubble sort

When you bubble sort a list of integers, you repeatedly sweep through the list and exchange neighbours out of order, until the whole list is sorted. Let us define a function *bubble* sweeping a list once and exchanging neighbours out of order.

```
—  fun bubble nil  =  nil
    |  bubble [x  :  int]  =  [x]
    |  bubble (x :: y :: xs)  =  if x <= y
                                 then x :: bubble(y :: xs)
                                 else y :: bubble(x :: xs);
>  val bubble  =  fn   :  int list −> int list
```

Using the predicate *sorted* (Exercise 17.5), we can now define another sorting algorithm in an elegant way.

```
—  val sort  =  until sorted bubble;
>  val sort  =  fn  :  int list −> int list
```

Does this function always terminate?? The functions *sorted* and *bubble* always do, since they both use primitive recursion over lists. If the list is not sorted, *bubble* will exchange at least two neighbours. Any two values can be exchanged at most once, since both of them cannot be less than the other. The process must therefore terminate.

Exercises

18.18. Define *while* that transforms a state as long as a given condition is true.

18.19. Differentiation is in mathematics defined by $\frac{d[f(x)]}{dx} = \lim_{\epsilon \to 0} \frac{f(x+\epsilon)-f(x)}{\epsilon}$. Define a higher order function *derivative* that gives the derivative of f at x using $\epsilon = 1E\tilde{}12$. Then, define a general version of Newton iteration taking only a function and a start value as arguments. Can you find arguments for which it does not terminate?

Summary

We have described three classes of recursive functions: *primitive recursive*, *recursive*, and *partial recursive*. The partial recursive functions include the other two classes, and the recursive functions include the primitive recursive ones. A partial function may not terminate for some arguments. The Ackermann function is an example of a total, non-primitive recursive function. You cannot give any simple bound on its time complexity. The simplest form of recursion is primitive recursion over a natural number, a list, or a tree (*branching recursion*). Often, you use derived forms like *course-of-values* recursion, *multiple recursion*, and *mutual recursion* and must then prove that the function *terminates* for all arguments in the domain. In an iteration, you transform a state either a fixed number of times or until some condition becomes true. For a *tail recursive* function, the result of the function either is computed without a recursive call or it is the immediate result of a recursive call. A tail recursive function can be evaluated in constant space.

Exercises

18.20. Define a function *to_bin* that given a positive integer yields a string which is the binary representation of the integer. For instance, *to_bin* $12 = $ "1100".

18.21. One method for sorting is called *merge sort*. The list to be sorted is split into two lists of lengths as equal as possible. These lists are sorted using the same method. After sorting, the lists are merged together. Define *mergesort*.

18.22. What is the value, if any, of the infinite sum $\sum_{i=1}^{\infty} \frac{1}{i}$?

18.23. The real Ackermann function is defined by the equations

$ackermann\,(0,0,k) = k$
$ackermann\,(0,j+1,k) = ackermann\,(0,j,k) + 1$
$ackermann\,(1,0,k) = 0$
$ackermann\,(i+2,0,k) = 1$
$ackermann\,(i+1,j+1,k) = ackermann\,(i, ackermann\,(i+1,j,k),k)$

Prove that $ackermann\,(0,j,k) = k + j$, that $ackermann\,(1,j,k) = k * j$, and that $ackermann\,(2,j,k) = k ** j$. What function is $ackermann\,(3,j,k)$?

18.24.* Reading a palindrome forwards and backwards, you get the same thing. For instance, 373 and 12321 are palindrome numerals. Define a function that given any positive integer, finds the numeral with the digits reversed and adds the corresponding number to the given number. This procedure is repeated until the result is a palindrome numeral. Does the function always terminate? Also investigate how many additions you need for all arguments less than 200.

18.25.* Define a function for computing the following difference: given a numeral, say 537, reorder the digits to get the smallest and the largest corresponding number, here 357 and 753, and subtract the smaller from the bigger. Now repeat the procedure with the numeral you obtain, until you get the numeral from the previous step back. If you get 87 as difference, for instance, you use the numeral 087. Show that the procedure terminates for all three-digit numerals. Which numerals do you end up with? What is the case for numerals with two digits, four digits, and five digits?

18.26.* Simulate how many times you have to throw a dice on average to obtain all possible results at least once. Try dice of different sizes.

18.27. Simulate how many times you have to throw a dice on average to get the number six. What is the mean value and the standard deviation of 100 experiments?

18.28. Write a program to generate a line on a pools coupon with 13 games. As input you provide the probabilities for 1, x, and 2, respectively. Next, extend the program to generate several lines in such a way that all pairs of lines differ in at least a given number of positions.

18.29. Write a program for generating a knight's tour, that is, a walk by a knight on a chess board in such a way that each square is visited exactly once. Try boards of various sizes.

18.30. In how many ways can you place 8 knights on a 4x4 board so that they do not threaten each other?

18.31. How many knights are needed to dominate all squares on a 8x8 board? How many queens are needed for the same task?

18.32. Consider the definition

$$\textbf{fun } f91 \; n \; = \; \textbf{if } n > 100 \textbf{ then } n - 10 \textbf{ else } f91(f91(n+11))$$

Try to show that *f91* terminates for all natural numbers or find an argument for which it does not terminate.

18.33. To find the root of a polynomial, an interval splitting method can be used. Define a function *root* that takes three arguments a, b, and f and locates the root of f in the interval $[a, b]$ by splitting the interval into two equal halves, choosing the interval in which the function changes sign, and repeating this until the interval is shorter than 10^{-9}.

18.34. Define a function that evaluates simple arithmetic expressions. An expression is represented by a string. It can contain one-digit numbers and the four common operators. The operators have their normal priorities. Then extend the evaluator to handle parentheses expressions and numbers with many digits.

Chapter 19

Concrete Data Types

Each data object in ML is assigned a type and the system checks the consistency of the types of subexpressions in an expression. A language with this property is called a *typed language*. In most typed languages, you have to give the types explicitly; in ML, the system derives the types of all expressions for you. If you make some programming error it may well lead to a type error, and the system can detect it at an early stage of the program development. Since the cost of correcting an error increases drastically the longer it takes to detect it, the type system in ML saves a lot of effort.

Modelling the real world

You use a computer to get new information about the real world. First, you describe your application with data objects—you build a model of the real world. Next, you write a program that describes how you compute new data objects from the constructed objects—the program is a model describing how real objects are related. Finally, you can run the program on some input data and interpret the computed data to get new information.

Much of the usefulness of a programming language is coupled to the ease by which you can model the real world. In ML, there are powerful modelling means that can help you to produce programs that are easy to read and modify.

Describing the problem

Top-down design really involves two different activities: to find a way of representing the objects of interest and to find a suitable algorithm. A danger in all design is to make decisions about details too early; first you have to understand the problem well, then you can solve it.

One way to start solving a problem is to draw a diagram describing it. The diagram describes the problem in general terms. Suppose a company wants to register what it has in store and then regularly compute what to order.

$$STORE \quad\xrightarrow{\quad create\_order \quad}\quad ORDER$$

The input and output are described in very general terms with no reference to possible representations in ML; they describe real-life *concepts*. When you refine the function *create_order*, you have to refine the data types as well and choose suitable representations. Until now we have almost exclusively used the standard types of ML. A store may, of course, be represented by a list of tuples, where each tuple describes items of some kind. In this chapter, we will look at how you can introduce new types and new data objects that describe the real world more closely. You have, in fact, already seen the enumeration types, which we used to introduce concepts like colours, suits, and directions into ML. Remember that a data type describes some concept and that the data objects of this type are examples of this concept. For instance, red and blue are colours, and *Red* and *Blue* are data objects of the data type *COLOUR*.

Construction and analysis of data objects

A data type consists of a set of data objects and operations for manipulating the objects. Normally, we use the word *type* to denote the set of data objects by themselves and the word *data type* to denote the type together with the operations.

For any data type, there are *constructors* used to construct the data objects of the type. For instance, *true* and *false* are the constructors of truth values and *nil* and :: the constructors of lists. When you define a new type you have to define all its constructors. Note that the constructors in general decide only the type, not the data type.

The general tool for *analysing* data objects in ML is pattern matching. For each way of constructing a new data object, there is a corresponding way of analysing the object through pattern matching. An exception is functions, which can be analysed only by applying them to arguments. Using pattern matching, you can define *selectors* and *predicates* for the type as well as other operations. For most types of data objects, the ML system in addition automatically provides the operators = and <>.

The properties of a data type are given by its operations. Different sets of operations working on the same type give you different data types. The *regular* view of a type is the data type you get by using pattern matching and the equality operations defined by the system. Such a data type will be called a **regular data type** and is what you get by a **datatype** definition. If you are not satisfied by the regular view, you can put on other "glasses" by defining a new set of operations.

Usually, you also want to forget about your old view of the objects: you want to perform a *data abstraction* and introduce an *abstraction barrier*. The new data type is usually called an *abstract* data type (described in Chapter 21) in contrast to the *concrete* data type you start with.

Example: Three-valued logic

There are only two truth values, *true* and *false*. In some applications you cannot always tell whether a condition is true or false, and you would like a data type containing a third alternative "don't know".

```
-  datatype LOGIC3 = True  |  False  |  Undef;
>  datatype LOGIC3 = True  |  False  |  Undef
```

There are three constructors for the type *LOGIC3* and, in the general case, you therefore need three alternative patterns to analyse these objects.

```
-  fun not3 True  = False
   | not3 False = True
   | not3 Undef = Undef;
>  val not3 = fn  : LOGIC3 -> LOGIC3
```

When defining the function *and3* taking two arguments, there are nine combinations, but you can reduce the number of alternatives using wild-cards.

```
-  fun and3 (True, True) = True
   | and3 (False, _) = False
   | and3 ( _ , False) = False
   | and3 ( _ , _ ) = Undef;
>  val and3 = fn : LOGIC3 * LOGIC3 -> LOGIC3

-  infix and3 ;

-  True and3 Undef;
   Undef : LOGIC3
```

Note how pattern matching allows you to make a complete analysis of the arguments. If you fail to make it complete, or if you use redundant patterns, the system will complain.

Exercises

19.1. Define the operator *or3* for disjunction in three-valued logic. Also define *disjl3* for disjunction of a list of *LOGIC3* values.

19.1 Types with Structured Objects

In ML, you can construct compound data objects like tuples and lists. In the same way, you can define new types whose objects have an internal structure. Constructors like *true* or *nil* construct atomic data objects; they are *constructor constants*. The constructors in an enumeration type are all constructor constants, for instance. The :: constructor for lists, on the other hand, is a *constructor function*: it takes an element and a list as arguments and constructs a compound object.

Example: Coordinates of points in the plane

A point in the plane can be described in several ways. You can give its x and y coordinates, its *rectangular coordinates*, or the distance r from origin and the angle v between the x axis and the vector from origin to the point, its *polar coordinates*. A pair like (2.3, 7.04) can be interpreted both as rectangular and polar coordinates. By introducing separate types *RECT* and *POLAR* you can differentiate between them. We use the constructors *Rect* and *Polar* to construct coordinates from pairs of real numbers.

$\quad$ — **datatype** $RECT = Rect$ **of** $real * real$;
$\quad$ > **datatype** $RECT = Rect$ **of** $real * real$
$\qquad$ **con** $Rect = $ **fn** $: real * real -> RECT$

$\quad$ — **datatype** $POLAR = Polar$ **of** $real * real$;
$\quad$ > **datatype** $POLAR = Polar$ **of** $real * real$
$\qquad$ **con** $Polar = $ **fn** $: real * real -> POLAR$

$\quad$ — $Rect(2.3, 7.04)$;
$\qquad$ $Rect(2.3, 7.04) : RECT$

$\quad$ — $Polar(2.3, 7.04)$;
$\qquad$ $Polar(2.3, 7.04) : POLAR$

The word **of** indicates that a constructor function is introduced and the word **con** that a constructor has been defined. Note that a constructor function is not a function in the ordinary sense. When an ordinary function is applied to an argument a computation is performed, and the result is the value of the application. When a constructor function is "applied" to its argument, a new data object is created; no computation other than the evaluation of the operand is performed. The created data object is denoted by the name of the constructor followed by the argument. Hence, $Polar(2.3, 7.04)$ is a new data object, which can be used in the program.

Pattern matching against constructor functions

For any way of constructing a data object there is a corresponding form of pattern matching. Let us define a function that transforms rectangular coordinates to polar coordinates. (If you are not familiar with this transformation you can skip the details.) We assume for simplicity that x and y are positive.

```
-  fun to_polar (Rect(x, y)) = Polar(sqrt(x * x + y * y), arctan(y/x));
>  val to_polar = fn : RECT -> POLAR
```

```
-  to_polar(Rect(2.3, 7.04));
   Polar(7.406186603104191, 1.255023497951054) : POLAR
```

Note how the constructor function is used in the pattern. In fact, the same mechanism is used for the :: operator in list patterns, but it is placed in infix position.

```
fun  hd nil = raise hd
   |  hd (x :: xs) = x
```

Example: A file of person records

The advantage with user-defined data types is increased readability and modifiability. The price you pay is that you have to write a little more, but that is a low price. Suppose you want to describe a set of persons, where each person is described by name, sex, age, and weight. We introduce a type for each of these quantities. To represent a set of persons we use a list.

```
datatype NAME     = Name of string;
datatype SEX      = Male | Female;
datatype AGE      = Age of int;
datatype WEIGHT   = Weight of int;
datatype PERSON   = Person of NAME * SEX * AGE * WEIGHT;
datatype PERSONS = Persons of PERSON list;
val john  = Person(Name "John", Male, Age 27, Weight 73);
val mary  = Person(Name "Mary", Female, Age 23, Weight 58);
```

```
-  val persons = Persons[john, mary];
>  val persons = Persons[
      Person(Name "John", Male, Age 27, Weight 73),
      Person(Name "Mary", Female, Age 23, Weight 58)]  : PERSONS
```

Each data object is now self-explanatory. Let us next define a function for finding all females under 18 in a set of persons.

> - **local fun** *isgirl*(*Person*(_ , *Female*, *Age age*, _)) = *age* < 18
> | *isgirl* _ = *false*
>   **in fun** *girls*(*Persons ps*) = *Persons*(*filter isgirl ps*)
>   **end** ;
> > **val** *girls* = **fn** : *PERSONS* −> *PERSONS*

Note that you have to use pattern matching to get access to the list of persons, since the constructor function *Persons* constructs an object which is not a list. After filtering, you have to convert the resulting list to an object of type *PERSONS* using the constructor *Persons*.

Exercises

19.2. Define *to_rect* that transforms polar to rectangular coordinates. The x and y coordinates are given by $r * cos \ v$ and $r * sin \ v$.

19.3. Define a function for computing the average weight of a *PERSONS* object.

19.2 Union Types

In an enumeration type no data objects have internal structure. A constructor function, on the other hand, constructs objects with internal structure. In a *union type*, you have several constructors, some of which may construct composite objects. Thus, an enumeration type is really a special case of a union type. Each constructor in a union type constructs a set of "structurally equal" data objects; the union type is the *union* of all these sets.

Let us define data objects describing vehicles, where a vehicle can be a car, a truck, or a bike. A car is described by its kind, its registration number, and its weight (defined as above). A truck is described by its registration number, its weight, and its maximum weight with load. A bike has no attributes.

datatype *REGNUM* = *Regnum* **of** *int* ;
datatype *KIND* = *Kind* **of** *string* ;

> - **datatype** *VEHICLE* = *Car* **of** *KIND* * *REGNUM* * *WEIGHT*
> | *Truck* **of** *REGNUM* * *WEIGHT* * *WEIGHT*
> | *Bike* ;
> > **datatype** *VEHICLE* = *Car* **of** *KIND* * *REGNUM* * *WEIGHT*
> > | *Truck* **of** *REGNUM* * *WEIGHT* * *WEIGHT*
> > | *Bike*
> **con** *Car* = **fn** : *KIND* * *REGNUM* * *WEIGHT* −> *VEHICLE*
> **con** *Truck* = **fn** : *REGNUM* * *WEIGHT* * *WEIGHT* −> *VEHICLE*
> **con** *Bike* = *Bike* : *VEHICLE*

Note that in the system response, the constructor functions are described as functions and the constructor constant as an object having itself as value.

Suppose a ferry company wants a function that computes the *total weight* of all vehicles in a list of vehicles. First, we define a function that selects the weight of vehicles, assuming that the weight of a bike is 15 kg.

> — **local fun** *weight(Car(_, _, Weight w)) = w*
> | *weight(Truck(_, _, Weight w)) = w*
> | *weight Bike = 15*
>   **in fun** *totalweight vehicles = sum (map weight vehicles)*
>   **end**;
> > **val** *totalweight = **fn** : VEHICLE list −> int*

Note that the patterns in *weight* correspond directly to the alternatives in the type definition.

Keeping track of units

The union types can be used to differentiate between units. Let us define a type *LENGTH*, whose objects are lengths measured in meters or millimeters.

> **datatype** *LENGTH =| Meter* **of** *int | Mm* **of** *int*

Let us now define a function that computes the volume of a sphere given the radius.

> **datatype** *VOL = Liter* **of** *real*;
>
> — **fun** *sphere (Meter r) = Liter(real(4 * (r ** 3) * 1000) * pi/3.0)*
> | *sphere (Mm r) = Liter(real(4 * (r ** 3)) * pi/3.0/1000000.0)*;
> > **val** *sphere = **fn** : LENGTH −> VOL*
>
> — *sphere(Meter 1)*;
>   *Liter 4188.7902047864 : VOL*

When giving the length, you give its unit in the form of a constructor. A constructor also tells us about the unit of the result.

Exercises

19.4. Define a selector *regnum* for vehicles.

19.5. Define the function *totalweight* so that only one traversal of the list is needed. Use the *reduce* function. Can you generalize the optimization and express it in the form of an equation?

19.6. A vehicle register can be represented by a list of pairs describing owners and their vehicles. Define suitable types. Then define a function that selects all truck-owners out of a register.

19.7. Define a function *add_lengths* that, given two lengths in meters or millimeters, yields the result in meters unless both arguments are in millimeters.

19.3   Named Types

A datatype definition introduces a completely new data type into a program. There is also a possibility of giving a name to some type in a **type declaration** in the same way as you name a data object in a value declaration.

```
—   type PERSON =  string * int ;
>   type PERSON =  string * int
```

The name you introduce can be used as a substitute for the type *string * int*, but the system does not use the name itself.

```
—   ("garfield", 9) ;
    ("garfield", 9) : string * int
```

Let us give another name to the same type.

```
—   type CAR =  string * int ;
>   type CAR =  string * int

—   val car1  :  CAR  =  ("ford", 12345) ;
>   val car1  =  ("ford", 12345)  :  CAR
```

Unfortunately, you cannot make the system differentiate between named types.

```
—   fun age (p  :  PERSON )  =  snd p ;
>   val  age  =  fn  :  PERSON  ->  int

—   age car1 ;
    12345 : int
```

Although we prescribed that the function *age* takes a *PERSON* as argument, the system lets it accept a *CAR*. Named types are therefore of limited value, but they are useful when you want to give short names to types. They also help you to produce more readable type definitions.

19.4 Records

The main use of tuples is to collect pieces of data that are related to each other in some way and then treat the collection as a unit. Tuples do not always contribute to the goal of creating readable programs, though. A tuple like $(2341, 14.25, 200)$ can be interpreted in many ways, and you cannot tell its intended meaning only by looking at it. Using labelled tuples, you can name each component in a tuple and make the program more comprehensible. Pattern matching is sometimes also simpler using labelled tuples.

Records

Labelled tuples are usually called records. An example of a record describing an item is $\{id\_nr = 2341, price = 14.25, amount = 200\}$. In a record, a name is associated with each component, and if the name is well-chosen, the intended use of the record can be read directly from the record.

A real object is usually described by various *attributes* like form, weight, size, and price. The records give you the possibility of describing the object by giving both its characteristic attributes and the values of the attributes.

$$- \quad \{name = "Anderson", weight = 67\};$$
$$\{name = "Anderson", weight = 67\} \; : \; \{name : string, weight : int\}$$

The type of a record contains the names of the attributes and not only the types of the components.

Sets of attributes

In contrast to tuples, the order of components in records is unimportant. The records $\{x = 3, y = true\}$ and $\{y = true, x = 3\}$ are therefore equal and so are their types; a record is considered as a *set* of components, not as an ordered sequence. When the system is to print the attributes of a record, there is a choice of order. We will use alphabetical order, but no such requirement is enforced by the system. On the contrary, one of the advantages of records is that the order is inessential.

$$- \quad \{x = 3, \; y = true\} = \{y = true, \; x = 3\};$$
$$true \; : \; bool$$

A requirement on a record is that all its names are *unique*.

$$- \quad \{x = 3, \; x = true\};$$
Parse error:
      Labels not all distinct
In: ... $\{ \; x \; = \; 3 \; , \; x \; = \; true \; \}$

Any number of attributes are allowed in records. Unlike tuples they can have only one component.

  $-$ $\{x = 3\}$;
       $\{x = 3\}$: $\{x : int\}$

  $-$ $\{\}$;
       $\{\}$: $\{\}$

The empty record and its type have the same name: $\{\}$. In fact, this type is the type we earlier have called the *unit* type. In ML, it is defined by

  type *unit* $=$ $\{\}$;

The hermit $\{\}$ can also be written (), which is a derived form of $\{\}$.

Record pattern matching

To select attribute values out of a record you use pattern matching. Suppose you want to work with records describing persons.

  $-$ **type** *PERSON* $=$ $\{name : string, \ height : int, \ weight : int\}$;
  $>$ **type** *PERSON* $=$ $\{height : int, \ name : string, \ weight : int\}$

A possible pattern for this type is $\{name = n, \ height = h, \ weight = w\}$, where n, h, and w are names that will become bound to the attribute values when the pattern is used. Normally, you use a derived form of pattern matching, in which the attribute names themselves are used as pattern names. Suppose you want a function *over_weighted* that tests if the *weight* of a person (in kg) increased by 100 exceeds the *height* of the person (in cm).

  $-$ **fun** *over_weighted* $\{name, height, weight\}$ $=$ $weight + 100 > height$;
  $>$ **val** *over_weighted* $=$ **fn** :
                $\{height : int, \ name : \ 'a, \ weight : int\}$ $->$ *bool*

  $-$ *over_weighted*$\{name =$ "john", $height = 186, weight = 86\}$;
       false : *bool*

The pattern $\{name, \ height, \ weight\}$ is only a shorthand for the full form of pattern $\{name = name, \ height = height, \ weight = weight\}$. In the function definition, the attribute *name* is not used, and the system cannot derive its type. You can omit such attributes if you use the **record wild card** consisting of three dots.

    – **fun** *over_weighted* ({*height, weight, ...*} : *PERSON*) =
              weight + 100 > *height*;
    > **val** *over_weighted* = **fn** :
              {*height* : *int, name* : *string, weight* : *int*} −> *bool*

Note that you now need a type constraint to inform the system about the intended type of the record.

Next, suppose you want a function *taller* that tests if one person is taller than another. Now a problem arises. You cannot write

    fun *taller*({*height*}, {*height*}) = ···

because the system cannot differentiate between the two heights. In such a case you have to use the full form of pattern matching.

    – **fun** *taller* ({*height* = *h1*, ...} : *PERSON*,
                      {*height* = *h2*, ...} : *PERSON*) = *h1* > *h2*;
    > **val** *taller* = **fn** : *PERSON* ∗ *PERSON* −> *bool*

Record selectors

As for tuples, the system automatically provides selector functions for all components of a record. If the name of a label is *label*, the selector function is named #*label*. Let us rewrite *over_weighted* and *taller* using selector functions.

    – **fun** *over_weighted* (*p* : *PERSON*) =
                  #*weight* *p* + 100 > #*height* *p*;
    > **val** *over_weighted* = **fn** : *PERSON* −> *bool*

    – **fun** *taller* (*p1* : *PERSON, p2* : *PERSON*) =
                  #*height* *p1* > #*height* *p2* ;
    > **val** *taller* = **fn** : *PERSON* ∗ *PERSON* −> *bool*

19.5   Selectors and Predicates

Pattern matching is the basic way of analysing data objects in ML. There is one disadvantage, though: extensive use of pattern matching may make changes more difficult. On page 254, the type *PERSON* was defined. Suppose you define a multitude of functions taking *PERSON* arguments like the function *isgirl* on page 255. If you now decide to add an attribute *Length* to the *PERSON* type, you have to change each function definition, since each pattern has to be changed. By defining a suitable set of operations you can hide the actual type. To replace

pattern matching, you have to define a sufficient set of selectors and predicates—
the constructors are defined in the type declaration. The selectors let you select all
components out of the composite data objects, and the predicates let you decide by
which constructor a data object has been constructed. If there are n constructors,
you need $n - 1$ predicates. For lists, for instance, you can use the selectors hd
and tl and the predicate $null$ instead of pattern matching. For the vehicles defined
above, you can define the selectors $kind$, $regnum$, $weight$, and $maxweight$, and the
predicates $iscar$ and $istruck$. Most often, it is good practice to define predicates
for all constructors and therefore define also $isbike$.

> **exception** $vehicle$;

> — **fun** $regnum\ (Car(\ \_,r,\ \_)) = r$
> | $regnum\ (Truck(r,\ \_,\ \_)) = r$
> | $regnum\ Bike = $ **raise** $vehicle$;
> \> **val** $regnum = $ **fn** $: VEHICLE \rightarrow REGNUM$

> — **fun** $iscar\ (Car\ \_) = true$
> | $iscar\ \_ = false$;
> \> **val** $iscar = $ **fn** $: VEHICLE \rightarrow bool$

Next, suppose you define a function $car\_regnums$ that gives a list of the registration
numbers of all cars in a vehicle file.

> — **fun** $car\_regnums\ vf = map\ regnum\ (filter\ iscar\ vf)$;
> \> **val** $car_regnums = $ **fn** $: VEHICLE\ list \rightarrow REGNUM\ list$

If you now add new attributes or new alternatives to the $VEHICLE$ type, only the
selectors and predicates have to be changed; functions like $car\_regnums$ can be left
unchanged.

When you introduce selectors and predicates instead of pattern matching, you
perform a data abstraction: you no longer have to know all the details about the
data objects and how they are represented. Even if you have introduced selectors
and predicates, nothing prevents you from using pattern matching. Through the
use of abstract data types described in Chapter 21, the system can help you to
hide the representation completely.

If the objects you work with can be constructed in only one way, you can use
records and the record wild card to avoid the described problem.

19.6 Non-regular Types

Sometimes, you want to model real objects or phenomena that do not match the
regular view of any concrete type. In such a case, you are forced to introduce

an abstraction by defining new operations and view the concrete data type in a
new way. Often, the selectors you want are not the inverses of the constructors.
Sometimes, you also want new constructors. What you need to redefine depends
on the objects you want to model. There are really three different levels involved
when you perform such an abstraction: the type of real objects you want to
model, the abstract data type, which is the new *view* of the concrete type, and
the concrete data itself, which is the type you define in ML. By introducing an
abstraction barrier, you can hide the bottom level.

Example: Queues

The idea of a queue is familiar to everyone. Queues are frequently used in the
operating system of a computer; for instance, they are used to line up users waiting
for resources like line printers, processing power, etc. A queue is a sequence of
objects with the rules that you enter the queue at the end and leave it at the
front, that is, it obeys the FIFO (First-In-First-Out) principle. The two main
operations are to enter and to leave a queue. You also need an operation that
creates an empty queue and an operation that tests if a queue is empty. Note that
a queue as well as a list is a *sequence* of objects. The regular view of a sequence
is what we call a list; a queue is an example of a non-regular view of a sequence.

Let us define a data type for representing queues. For simplicity we assume
that the elements of the queue are integers; we will relieve this restriction later.
Since a queue is a sequence of objects, a natural choice of representation is a list.
A list is not a queue, however, so we introduce a constructor *Queue* that constructs
a queue given a list.

```
-  datatype QUEUE  =  Queue of int list;
>  datatype QUEUE  =  Queue of int list
   con Queue  =  fn  :  int list  ->  QUEUE
```

Our task is now to define suitable operations on queues. There are three types
of operations: *constructors*, *selectors*, and *predicates*. As a rule, you start with
the constructors. The constructor *Empty* constructs an empty queue and *Enter*
inserts an element at the end of the queue. We choose here to put that element
last also in the list representing the queue, but that is not necessary.

```
-  val Empty  =  Queue nil;
>  val Empty  =  Queue []  :  QUEUE

-  fun Enter e (Queue es)  =  Queue(es @ [e]);
>  val Enter  =  fn  :  int  ->  QUEUE  ->  QUEUE
```

We use pattern matching to get access to the list representing the queue. Let us
now construct a queue with the number 7 first and 11 second.

> — *Enter* 11 (*Enter* 7 *Empty*);
> *Queue* [7, 11] : *QUEUE*

To handle lists, two selectors *hd* and *tl* are needed. In the same way we need one selector that removes an element from a queue and one selector that yields the rest of the queue, when an element is removed.

> **exception** *remove* **and** *rest*;

> — **fun** *remove* (*Queue nil*) = **raise** *remove*
> | *remove* (*Queue* (*e* :: _)) = *e*;
> > **val** *remove* = **fn** : *QUEUE* –> *int*

> — **fun** *rest* (*Queue nil*) = **raise** *rest*
> | *rest* (*Queue* (_ :: *es*)) = *Queue es*;
> > **val** *rest* = **fn** : *QUEUE* –> *QUEUE*

Note that *remove* yields an element, but *rest* yields a queue as result. The constructors *Empty* and *Enter* starts with capital letters according to our convention, but for selectors we use small letters.

For all data types with more than one constructor, you need a predicate to find out in which way an object of the type has been constructed.

> — **fun** *isempty* (*Queue es*) = *null es*;
> > **val** *isempty* = **fn** : *QUEUE* –> *bool*

These five operations are sufficient to handle queues.

Exercises

19.8. Redefine queues and their operations so that elements are inserted at the front of the list and removed from the end.

19.9. Whether you insert elements first or last, either *Insert* or the selectors have to scan the whole list, which is inefficient. Represent a queue by a pair of lists *entry* and *exit*. Insert elements into *entry* and remove them from *exit*. When *exit* is exhausted, reverse *entry* and make it into the *exit* list. Define all operations using this representation. Compare the efficiency with the list representation.

19.7 Type Functions

Exactly as you have both constructor constants and constructor functions for constructing data objects, you have *type constructor constants* and *type constructor functions* for constructing data types. They are often called type constants and

type functions only. In ML, the standard type constants are *int, real, bool, unit,*
and *string.* The standard type functions are the tuple constructor $(\ldots * \ldots * \ldots)$,
the list constructor *(list),* and the function constructor (−>). A type function
takes other types as argument. For instance, the type *int list* is constructed by
applying the type function *list* to the type *int.* Contrary to normal functions, type
functions are placed in *postfix* position, that is, after their operand.

In ML, you can define your own type functions. The concept of a queue is
really independent of the particular type of element in the queue—you want to
define queues of any type. In a data type definition, you can introduce a type
parameter, which precedes the name of the type function. The parameter must
be a type variable and start with a prime.

> - **datatype** *'a QUEUE = Queue* **of** *'a list* ;
> > **datatype** *'a QUEUE = Queue* **of** *'a list*
> > **con** *Queue =* **fn** : *'a list* −> *'a QUEUE*

The operations on queues are now polymorphic functions.

> - **val** *Empty = (Queue nil)* ;
> > **val** *Empty = Queue* [] : *'a QUEUE*

> - **fun** *Enter e (Queue es) = Queue(es* @ *[e])* ;
> > **val** *Enter =* **fn** : *'a* −> *'a QUEUE* −> *'a QUEUE*

> - *Enter* 11 *(Enter* 7 *Empty)* ;
>   *Queue* [7, 11] : *int QUEUE*

Compare these types with those in the previous section!!

Exercises

19.10. Define a type function *TABLE* for tables with keys and information of the
same, but arbitrary, type. Define the operations *Insert* and *lookup.*

19.8   General Properties of Types

Types play an important role in ML. The possibility of polymorphic types lets you
define very general functions, and the automatic type derivation catches errors
for you, even though you do not specify the types. The possibility of defining
new types lets you model the real world in quite a faithful way. To describe
the properties of types in general, you have to give their syntax, semantics, and
pragmatics.

19.8.1   Syntax: Type expressions

A type expression is a description of a type or polytype. Type expressions occur in three different contexts in ML: in type constraints, in type declarations, and in system responses. A type expression and an ordinary expression can therefore never occur in the same context. They are constructed in much the same way, though. Ordinary expressions are built from variables, constants, functions, operators, and parentheses, and so are type expressions. A difference is that type functions are placed after their operand. The syntax of type expressions is described on page 410 in Appendix B. By convention, the constructions high up in the syntax description have higher precedence than those further down. Thus, type functions (e.g. *list*) have higher precedence than tuple types, which, in turn, have higher precedence than function types ($->$). Hence, $'a * 'a$ *list* $-> 'b * 'c$ is read as $('a * ('a$ *list*$)) -> ('b * 'c)$.

A type expression with a type variable denotes a *polytype*, that is, a whole set of types. Such a type expression is comparable to an expression, whose value depends on the values of its variables. Polytypes are used mainly to describe the possible types of a polymorphic function and as parameters to type functions.

You can take the analogy between expressions and type expressions even further. In the same manner as an ordinary expression has some type, a type expression has a "type", namely the "type" of types. The objects in this "type" are the possible types in ML. The type of types is one level up in a hierarchy of types. An ordinary type is a set of objects; therefore, the type of types must be a set of sets of objects. Constructors for this "type" are type constants like *int* and type functions like *list*. In this "type", all expressions are canonical, since there are no means for analysing a type and taking it into parts; you cannot do computations with types. Such computations are possible in principle, but are not available in ML.

19.8.2   Semantics: The meaning of a type

When you define a new data type, you introduce a set of new data objects. A constructor constant introduces a single data object, and a constructor function introduces as many data objects as the number of possible arguments. The set of objects is also given a name, the name of the type. If you define a type function, you define a whole set of new types.

The constructors of a type decide the symbols used as data objects. The operations you define give these objects their characteristic properties. The system automatically defines equality operators, provided the constituents of the composite objects allow tests for equality. Two queues of integers can be compared for equality, but not two queues of functions, for example. Pattern matching allows a full decomposition of all composite objects and also allows you to find out how an object has been constructed. For regular data types pattern matching suffices, and you need no extra selectors or predicates. For objects with non-regular properties you have to introduce new constructors, selectors, and predicates and forget the underlying representation.

The system treats constructor constants like *true* and *Spades* as new symbols that cannot be further reduced. Thus, a constant on evaluation yields itself as value. When a constructor function, *con*, is applied to an operand, the value of the operand is first computed. If the value is *v*, the result of the "application" is *con v*; no function body is evaluated.

19.8.3 Pragmatics: The use of types

A good program should be easy to read and it should describe the application in a faithful fashion. Types play an important role here. You can always do completely without user-defined data types, but then you may be forced to use codings that make the program less readable and less modifiable.

In the first chapter, it was claimed that a type and a concept are similar. A new type introduces a new concept into your program, and the data objects are symbols describing the objects captured by the concept. As a rule, these objects have some property in common.

Specification and types

A specification of a function usually has the following form: "Find a function f that, given an argument x of type T, computes a result y of type T' in such a way that some desired relation holds between x and y". For instance, a specification of the square root function says that given a non-negative real number x you want a real number y such that $y * y = x$. In this case, the types of the argument and the result coincide with a standard type in ML, but suppose you want a program that, given a description of the current weather, computes a weather forecast for the next day.

$$\overline{\quad\quad WEATHER \quad\quad} \rangle\!\!\!\overline{forecast}\!\!\!\langle \overline{\quad\quad FORECAST \quad\quad} \rightarrow$$

An equivalent way of expressing the problem is to say that you want a function *forecast* of type *WEATHER* $->$ *FORECAST*. A type consequently plays the role of a *partial specification* of a problem. There are more powerful type systems that allow you to use types as full specifications of problems, but then it is not possible to let the system derive the types automatically.

To solve the problem with the weather forecast, three things have to be done. You have to choose a suitable representation of the current weather and of a forecast, and you have to define the function *forecast*. All three steps can be performed in a top-down fashion, sometimes described as a *step-wise refinement*. However, step-wise refinement is sometimes also used to mean that you start to produce a simple implementation of a given specification and, then, produce better implementations in subsequent steps.

Top-down design of data types

When you define a type for some real objects, the first question to answer is if there are one or several classes of objects. When defining vehicles, for instance, we had three classes: cars, trucks, and bikes. For each such class, you have to introduce a constructor.

The next question is if the objects in a class are compound or not. If they are, you have to decide which are their appropriate attributes. For a car, for instance, we chose registration number, kind, and weight.

When you define the attributes, you are by no means forced to used the standard types of ML. Instead, you can choose a suitable name for a new type. The next step in the top-down design is to define this type in the same manner as the main type. This process continues until all types are defined in terms of the predefined types. The process is consequently similar to top-down design of functions, but deals with types.

In the next chapter, recursive data types will be described. They give you yet another possibility in this design process; you can define new types with, conceptually, an infinite number of data objects.

Models are simplifications

The very idea of a model is that you capture those properties of the application that are important for the problem. For a complicated problem, you usually have to make simplifying assumptions. As a consequence, the result you get is not a true picture of reality. This fact is important to remember when using a computer. There can be aspects of reality you avoid paying attention to just because you have problems finding a model that captures them.

Summary

See the description of the syntax, semantics, and pragmatics of types above.

Exercises

19.11. Define suitable types for describing an organization, if an organization is described by its name, its leader, and its sections. A section can either be a team or a group. A team is described by its name and its members. A group is described by its name, its leader, and its members. All persons are described by their name and their salary. Define a function *map_organization* that applies a given function to all persons in an organization. Then, use it to define a function that raises the salary of all employees by a given percentage. Try to use type definitions, datatype definitions, and labelled records, even if you could do with only some of them.

19.12. Most books have a logical structure. A book can contain chapters, sections, paragraphs, preface, and index, for instance. Define data types reflecting this structure.

19.13. A complex number can be represented by rectangular or polar coordinates. Define a suitable union type *COMPLEX*. Then, define operators for the four common arithmetic operations. If the arguments to an operation have the same representation, the result shall also have this representation. Otherwise, either representation can be used for the result. Finally, define a function giving the two roots of a second degree equation, which can be complex numbers.

Chapter 20

Recursive Data Types

Recursive functions are defined in terms of themselves. They give you the power of defining arbitrarily large computations in a finite way. Similarly, recursive data types give you the power of defining types with an unbounded number of data objects like lists and trees.

20.1 Linearly Recursive Data Types

You can classify recursive data types according to the type of recursion used. Examples of data types using linear recursion are lists and natural numbers. To define tree structures you need double recursion or even more complicated schemes.

20.1.1 Lists

Lists are constructed with the two constructors *cons* and *nil*. The empty list has no components, and a list constructed with *cons* is a pair consisting of an element and another list. This verbal definition is recursive, and so is the type definition of the list type function.

$$
\begin{aligned}
&- \quad \textbf{datatype } 'a \; list \; = \; nil \; \mid \; \textbf{cons of } 'a * 'a \; list; \\
&> \quad \textbf{datatype } 'a \; list \; = \; nil \; \mid \; \textbf{cons of } 'a * 'a \; list \\
&\quad\;\; \textbf{con } nil \; = \; nil \; : \; 'a \; list \\
&\quad\;\; \textbf{con } cons \; = \; \textbf{fn} \; : \; 'a * 'a \; list \; -> \; 'a \; list
\end{aligned}
$$

Obviously, there is an infinite number of lists. Using *nil* you can construct one list, and using *cons* you can construct new lists by inserting elements into already constructed lists indefinitely.

In ML, you use :: instead of *cons*. To place it in infix position, you use the **infix** directive, which can be used both for constructor functions and ordinary functions.

269

infix 5 :: ;
datatype $'a$ $list$ = nil | **op** :: **of** $'a * 'a$ $list$

Note the use of **op**. The bracket notation for lists is introduced into ML as a syntactic convenience; you cannot perform similar extensions yourself.

An important observation is that the template we use for defining recursive functions over lists corresponds directly to the type definition of lists.

fun f nil = ?
 | f $(x :: xs)$ = ??

There are two constructors and therefore two alternative patterns. The constructor :: constructs a composite object, and the pattern is therefore non-atomic. The type definition is recursive, and the pattern for a list therefore contains a subpattern which matches a sublist. Often, a function taking an argument defined by a recursive type is itself recursive. If the type definition is linearly recursive, so often is the function. Since pattern matching is sufficient for a full analysis of a list, the list data type is a regular data type.

Exercises

20.1. Define a type function $QUEUE$ without using lists and with constructors $Empty$ and $Insertq$. Define suitable selectors and predicates. What is the difference between such a queue and a list?

20.1.2   Natural numbers

A natural number is either zero or the successor of some other natural number. If we use $Zero$ and $Succ$ as constructors, the natural numbers are represented by $Zero$, $Succ$ $Zero$, $Succ(Succ$ $Zero)$, etc. This definition corresponds to a unary number system. The type definition of natural numbers is similar to that of lists.

     — **datatype** NAT = $Zero$ | $Succ$ **of** NAT;
     > **datatype** NAT = $Zero$ | $Succ$ **of** NAT
        con $Zero$ = $Zero$: NAT
        con $Succ$ = **fn** : $NAT -> NAT$

Let us now define the factorial function. Its domain is the natural numbers, but in ML you normally use int as argument type. As a consequence, you have to raise an exception for negative arguments. The type NAT has nothing to do with the type int. To type in and print natural numbers in a unary representation is not practical, however, so we need translation functions.

```
—   fun to_int Zero  =  0
      |  to_int (Succ n)  =    1 + to_int n ;
>   val to_int  =  fn  :  NAT −> int

—   to_int(Succ(Succ(Succ Zero)));
      3 : int
```

Note the similarity between the patterns and the type definition. To define the factorial function you have to multiply natural numbers and to multiply them, you have to add them.

```
—   infix 6  +'  ;
—   infix 7  *'  ;

—   fun  Zero +' m  =  m
      |  (Succ n) +' m  = Succ(n +' m);
>   val  +'  =  fn  :  NAT * NAT −> NAT

—   to_int(Succ Zero +' Succ(Succ Zero));
      3 : int

—   fun  Zero *' m  =  Zero
      |  (Succ n) *' m  = m +' n *' m;
>   val  *'  =  fn  :  NAT * NAT −> NAT

—   fun fac Zero  =  Succ Zero
      |  fac (Succ n)  =  Succ n *' fac n;
>   val  fac  =  fn  :  NAT −> NAT
```

The use of *NAT* instead of *int* gives less efficient computations, since integer arithmetic is supported by special machine instructions on all computers.

Circular types

When you define a recursive type, there must be some way to stop the recursion. Suppose you remove the *Zero* alternative in the definition of natural numbers.

```
—   datatype WHAT  =  What of WHAT;
>   datatype WHAT  =  What of WHAT
      con What  =  fn  :  WHAT −> WHAT
```

Which data objects belong to this type?? Since there is no object to start with, you cannot construct any object of the type. Still, you can define a function yielding a *WHAT* as result.

```
  —  fun  f  x  =  What(f  x);
  >  val  f  =  fn  :  'a  ->  WHAT
```

If you apply *f* to any object, the result is a non-terminating computation. This is no surprise, since circular definitions never lead to any goal. In a lazy functional language, this kind of definition is meaningful, though.

Exercises

20.2. Define the function *to_nat* and operators for exponentiation, subtraction, and division. Let the result of subtracting a number from a smaller number be zero.

20.3. What is the type, if any, of the function *f* defined by $f(What\ x) = 1 + f\ x$? What can you use it for?

20.1.3   Stacks

A stack is a common structure in computer science. It is a sequence of objects, in which you are allowed to insert and remove objects only at one end. There are two constructors of stacks: the *Empty* stack constructor and the *Push* constructor pushing one element onto the top of the stack.

$$\textbf{datatype } 'a\ STACK\ =\ Empty\ \ |\ \ Push\ \textbf{of}\ 'a * 'a\ STACK;$$

You do not really need any selectors and predicates for stacks—pattern matching suffices. If you still want these operations you need the *top* operation to get the top element, the *pop* operation to get the stack that remains when you remove the top element, and the predicate *isempty* testing if a stack is empty. Before proceeding, you are urged to ask yourself if you have seen this structure or data type before. Does any other type have similar properties and operations??

The properties of a stack are exactly those of a list. The operations *Empty*, *Push*, *top*, *pop*, and *isempty* do the same thing as *nil*, *cons*, *hd*, *tl*, and *null*, respectively. Usually, you think of a stack as something vertical and a list as something horizontal. Mathematically, they are *isomorphic* structures, that is, they have identical structure. Similar facts can sometimes be revealed by studying other type definitions.

20.1.4   Free and non-free types

In ML, the integers are predefined. Let us still try to define them as a concrete data type. It seems reasonable to start with the natural numbers and add an extra constructor *Pred*, which gives the predecessor of a number. Starting with *Zero*, you can now construct the negative numbers.

datatype *INT* = *Zero* | *Succ* **of** *INT* | *Pred* **of** *INT*

You can continue to define addition and multiplication in a similar way as for natural numbers. There is a problem with this definition, however. The equality operator is automatically defined for all concrete data types.

— *Pred*(*Succ Zero*) = *Zero*;
false : *bool*

You want the predecessor of the successor of zero to be zero. To the system, however, each constructor constructs a unique object, and this object can never be equal to an object created in another way. Thus, the regular view of the type *INT* does not coincide with the properties we want integers to have.

When one of the abstract objects is represented by several data objects, you say that the chosen *representation* is not *free*. If you want to use a non-free representation, you have to forget the regular view of the representation and introduce new operations: you introduce an abstraction barrier. In particular, you have to define a new equality operation that considers all data objects representing the same real object as equal. You say that such an equality relation *partitions* the type into a **quotient** type, since it *divides* the set of all data objects in the type into subsets of objects that you consider equal. If you want to use a non-free representation, you should hide it in an abstract data type (described in Chapter 21).

Another representation of an integer is a pair of a sign and a natural number.

datatype *SIGN* = *Plus* | *Minus*
and *INT* = *Int* **of** *SIGN* * *NAT*

Unfortunately, this representation is not free either, since *Int*(*Plus*, *Zero*) and *Int*(*Minus*, *Zero*) both denote zero.

One way to construct a free representation of the integers is to start with positive integers.

datatype *POSINT* = *One* | *Succ* **of** *POSINT*
and *INT* = *Zero* | *Plus* **of** *POSINT* | *Minus* **of** *POSINT*

This representation is free. We say that a set of abstract objects like the integers is a *free type*, if there exists a free representation of it. Note the distinction between a free type, which is a set of abstract objects to be modelled and a free representation, which is a data type. We will later consider types for which there is no free representation.

In ML, the integers are in effect considered as an enumeration type with the numerals as constructors. This is possible since you never write down the type definition explicitly, but build it into the system from the beginning and consider it as part of the standard environment. Similarly, there are several standard operations on integers.

Structural induction

When you define a recursive function, you use an inductive reasoning. The induction principle you use depends on the type of data objects you do the recursion over. You can, in fact, derive the induction principle directly from the type definition. To prove a property P for all natural numbers, you have to prove $P(0)$ and, under the assumption that $P(k)$ is true for some integer k, prove $P(k+1)$. Since zero and the successor function are all the constructors of natural numbers, you can conclude that P holds for all natural numbers.

To prove a property P for all lists, you have to prove $P(nil)$ and, under the assumption that $P(xs)$ is true for some list xs, you have to prove $P(x :: xs)$ for all x of the right type. Since nil and $::$ are the only constructors of lists, you can conclude that P is true for all lists. This induction principle is often called *structural induction over lists*.

Consider the functions rev and rev' for reversing lists.

> **fun** $rev\ nil\ =\ nil$
> $\ |\quad rev\,(x :: xs)\ =\ rev\ xs\ @\ [x]$

> **fun** $rev'\ nil\ ys\ =\ ys$
> $\ |\quad rev'\,(x :: xs)\ ys\ =\ rev'\ xs\ (x :: ys)$

Let us prove that $rev\ xs = rev'\ xs\ nil$ for all lists xs, that is, we want to prove that the two different ways of reversing lists are equivalent. We start with a lemma.

Lemma: For all xs and ys, $rev'\ xs\ ys = rev\ xs\ @\ ys$.

Proof: We do the proof by induction over xs.

Base case: For $xs = nil$ we have $rev'\ nil\ ys = ys$ and $rev\ nil\ @\ ys = nil\ @\ ys = ys$, which proves the base case.

Inductive step: Assume that $rev'\ xs\ ys = rev\ xs\ @\ ys$. We now must prove that $rev'\,(x :: xs)\ ys = rev\,(x :: xs)\ @\ ys$. Rewriting the left-hand side we get

> $rev'\,(x :: xs)\ ys\ =$
> $rev'\ xs\ (x :: ys)\ =$ by the definition of rev'
> $rev\ xs\ @\,(x :: ys)\ =$ by the inductive assumption

Using the definition of rev and associativity of $@$ we get for the right-hand side $rev\,(x :: xs)\ @\ ys\ =\ rev\ xs\ @\ [x]\ @\ ys\ =\ rev\ xs\ @\,(x :: ys)$, which proves the inductive step. The lemma now follows from the principle of structural induction over lists.   ∎

Theorem: For all xs, $rev\ xs = rev'\ xs\ nil$.

Proof: The lemma gives that $rev'\ xs\ nil = rev\ xs\ @\ nil = rev\ xs$.   ∎

The important lesson of the proof of the lemma is that the type of argument you use to prove properties of lists is similar to the argument you use to convince yourself that a recursive function definition is correct. Furthermore, the argument is an inductive argument, whose form is derivable from the type definition of lists. Below, we will use similar techniques for binary trees.

Exercises

20.4. Three possible representation of integers are suggested above. Define the operations *equal* and *add* for all of them.

20.5. Formulate the induction principle for integers by starting with the last definition of integers above.

20.2 Binary Trees

Natural numbers and lists have a linearly recursive structure. Many objects you want to describe have a doubly recursive structure. An arithmetic expression is one example, since both operands to an operator are subexpressions of the expression. You say they have a tree structure or branching structure. Linearly recursive functions are suitable for linear structures, and you can expect that doubly recursive functions are well suited for work with tree structures.

The simplest form of tree structure is a binary tree. Each time you split a branch of the tree, you split it into two new branches. There are five classes of binary tree, each of them constructed by one type function. For reasons to become clear later, we call these five type functions *BT0* through *BT3*, and *BT*.

20.2.1 Binary branching structures

Every recursive data type must have at least one non-recursive constructor. For natural numbers it is *Zero* and for lists it is *nil*. For a binary branching structure we call this constructor *Tip*. The other constructor called *Node* constructs a branching structure given two other branching structures.

$$
\begin{array}{ll}
- & \textbf{datatype } BT0 \ = \ Tip \ \mid \ Node \textbf{ of } BT0 * BT0; \\
> & \textbf{datatype } BT0 \ = \ Tip \ \mid \ Node \textbf{ of } BT0 * BT0 \\
& \textbf{con } Tip \ = \ Tip \ : BT0 \\
& \textbf{con } Node \ = \ \textbf{fn} \ : \ BT0 * BT0 \ -> \ BT0
\end{array}
$$

The objects are called binary branching structures, because they repeatedly split into two branches until a *Tip* is reached; the objects have a tree structure as shown in the figure.

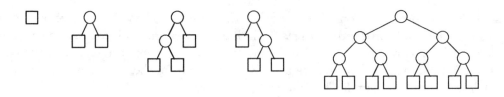

In computer science, it is common practice to draw trees upside down. In this, the simplest type of binary tree, there is no information in the tree but the branching structure itself. This is also evident from the type, which does not depend on any other type. The fourth tree in the picture is constructed by

> — *Node*(*Tip, Node*(*Tip, Tip*));
>   *Node*(*Tip, Node*(*Tip, Tip*)) : *BT0*

Let us for future use define a curried version of the *Node* constructor.

> — **val** *Node'* = *curry Node* ;
> > **val** *Node'* = **fn** : *BT0 −> BT0 −> BT0*

> — *Node' Tip* (*Node' Tip Tip*);
>   *Node*(*Tip, Node*(*Tip, Tip*)) : *BT0*

Some terminology

Often, you say that a tip is a form of node. Sometimes you talk about external nodes (tips) and internal nodes. The topmost node of a tree is called the **root** of the tree. To relate nodes of a tree, family relations are often used. You talk about the parent of a node, the sister (or brother), the children, the siblings, the ancestors, and so on. The root is the ancestor of every other node and the only node without a parent. A **path** is a sequence of nodes from the root to some tip such that each node is a child of the preceding node. The **height** of a tree is the length of its longest path.

In a binary tree you differentiate between the left and the right subtree. If the order of the subtrees in a tree is essential, the tree is said to be **ordered**. The third and fourth tree in the picture above are therefore different. If you consider the subtrees as unordered, however, they are equal. We will consider only ordered trees.

In a list, the essential constructor is the *cons* constructor; *nil* does not give any information, since all lists contain an empty sublist. The essential structure of a branching structure is given by its nodes; the tips give no extra information. In the figure below, we redraw the binary trees above without the tips.

The skeleton of the tree completely decides its tips, so you can leave them out. You can convince yourself of this by filling in the tips of the trees. The leftmost tree does not contain any node and is therefore "invisible".

Some of the trees above have the property that each (internal) node has either none or two subnodes. Such trees are called a **full** trees. We do not count a tip as a full tree, since it contains no nodes at all.

Structural induction over branching structures

The definition of a concrete type suggests in a direct way the structure of definitions of functions over the type. For binary trees there are two constructors, so you need two alternatives. The recursion assumption allows you to assume that you can use the function recursively for the two subtrees. Let us define a function that counts the number of tips in a branching structure.

```
-   fun nroftips Tip = 1
      | nroftips (Node(left, right)) = nroftips left + nroftips right;
>   val nroftips = fn : BT0 -> int
```

Note the use of double recursion in this function. There are two recursive applications, one for the left and one for the right subtree. Thus, the recursion corresponds to how a binary tree is constructed. This type of recursion is therefore called *primitive recursion* over a binary tree. The recursion must always terminate since you always use the function on immediate subtrees; finally, you must reach the tips.

As for lists, the underlying principle is a form of structural induction. To prove a property P for all binary trees, you first have to prove that $P(Tip)$ is true, and, under the assumption that $P(l)$ and $P(r)$ are true for some trees l and r, you have to prove $P(Node(l, r))$.

Let us prove that the number of tips in a binary tree is one more than the number of (internal) nodes. It is certainly true for a *Tip*. Assume that there are j nodes and $j + 1$ tips in l, and k nodes and $k + 1$ tips in r. The number of nodes in $Node(l, r)$ is now $j + k + 1$ and the number of tips $j + 1 + k + 1$. Hence, there is one more tip than there are nodes in $Node(l, r)$.

A reducer for binary branching structures

Using *reduce*, you can define almost any function on lists without explicit recursion (Section 17.4). You can define a similar function *redbt0* for binary branching structures. For a tree created by the constructors *Tip* and *Node'* (the curried version of *Node*), the effect of applying the function *redbt0 f u* to that tree is to replace *Tip* by *u* and *Node′* by *f*. As for *reduce*, the definition of *redbt0* follows directly from the definition of the data type and the structural induction principle.

```
-  fun redbt0 f u Tip  =  u
     | redbt0 f u (Node(l, r))  =  f (redbt0 f u l) (redbt0 f u r);
>  val redbt0  =  fn :  ('a -> 'a -> 'a) -> 'a -> BT0 -> 'a
```

Compare the definitions of *reduce* and *redbt0* with their corresponding types, and make sure you understand the idea of defining reducing functions!! We can now redefine *nroftips*.

```
-  fun nroftips bt  =  redbt0 add 1 bt;
>  val nroftips  =  fn :  BT0 -> int
```

To illustrate the effect of *redbt0*, you can replace the constructors of a tree by the arguments to *redbt0*. The number of tips in the tree

$$Node' \ (Node' \ (Node' \ Tip \ Tip) \ Tip) \ (Node' \ Tip \ Tip)$$

is given by *add*(*add*(*add* 1 1) 1) (*add* 1 1), which reduces to 5.

Exercises

20.6. Define a data type for ternary branching structures.

20.7. Define a predicate *full* that tests if a binary tree is full or not.

20.8. Prove by structural induction that a full binary tree always has an odd number of nodes.

20.9. Define *nrofnodes* both without and with the use of *redbt0*.

20.10. Define a function *maxheight* on branching structures using *redbt0*.

20.11. Define a predicate *balanced* that tests if all tips in a tree occur at the same depth.

20.2.2 Labelled binary trees

Branching structures capture the idea of a binary tree, but are too simple to be of real use. You want to associate data objects with nodes, tips, or both. In a labelled binary tree, each node contains a data object, but the tips are atomic. The type of the data objects is not essential to the idea of a binary tree, so we define a type function.

datatype *'a BT1 = Tip | Node of 'a * 'a BT1 * 'a BT1*

As for branching structures, the tips do not give any information, so the labelled trees can be drawn without their tips.

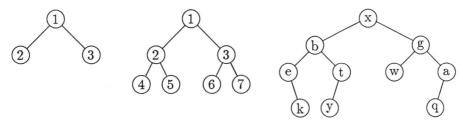

A common kind of labelled tree is an ancestor tree, which shows the parents and ancestors of a person. The labels are then persons.

Labelled tree handling functions

A reducer for labelled binary trees is similar to that for branching structures, but the function argument now takes one extra argument, which is a label.

```
 — fun redbt1 f u Tip = u
  | redbt1 f u (Node(a,l,r)) = f a (redbt1 f u l) (redbt1 f u r);
 > val redbt1 = fn :
   ('a –> 'b –> 'b –> 'b) –> 'b –> 'a BT1 –> 'b
```

The *sum* function on lists can be defined using *reduce*, and in the same way you can use *redbt1* to sum all numbers in the nodes of a labelled binary tree. You need a function adding three numbers: the number in a node and the sum of all nodes in the two subtrees, which are computed by recursive applications. Composing *add* with itself you get a function adding three numbers.

```
 — fun sumbt1 lbt = redbt1 (add oo add) 0 lbt;
 > val sumbt1 = fn : int BT1 –> int
```

You can also define a function *mapbt1* that maps a function to all labels in a labelled binary tree. If *Node'* is the curried version of the *Node* constructor, *mapbt1* can be defined using *redbt1* (cf. page 220).

```
 — fun mapbt1 f lbt = redbt1 (Node' o f) Tip lbt;
 > val mapbt1 = fn : ('a –> 'b) –> 'a BT1 –> 'b BT1
```

Let us look at how the tree *Node'* 1 (*Node'* 2 *Tip Tip*) *Tip* is transformed by *mapbt1 f*. All occurrences of *Node'* are replaced by *Node' o f*.

$$(Node' \ o \ f) \ 1 \ ((Node' \ o \ f) \ 2 \ Tip \ Tip) \ Tip \longrightarrow$$
$$Node' \ (f \ 1) \ (Node' \ (f \ 2) \ Tip \ Tip) \ Tip$$

Tree traversal

When you describe a tree, you draw a graph with nodes and arcs. In this way, you show the hierarchical structure of the tree. Sometimes, you want to list only the labels of the nodes in some order. There are three natural ways to list the labels. Due to the recursive nature of a tree, you want to list the subtrees in the same order as the whole tree. It remains only to decide if the root shall be listed before, in between, or after the subtrees, which always are listed from left to right. The three ways are called **preorder**, **inorder**, and **postorder** traversal of trees. Let us define *preorder* and apply it to the second of the labelled trees above. We assume a description of it is bound to *tree2*.

- **fun** *preorder Tip* = *nil*
  | *preorder* (*Node*(*a, l, r*)) = [*a*] @ *preorder l* @ *preorder r* ;
> **val** *preorder* = **fn** : *'a BT1* −> *'a list*

- *preorder tree2* ;
  [1, 2, 4, 5, 3, 6, 7] : *int list*

The definition of *preorder* shows clearly in which order the nodes are listed. The same is true of *inorder* and *postorder*.

- **fun** *inorder Tip* = *nil*
  | *inorder* (*Node*(*a, l, r*)) = *inorder l* @ [*a*] @ *inorder r* ;
> **val** *inorder* = **fn** : *'a BT1* −> *'a list*

- *inorder tree2* ;
  [4, 2, 5, 1, 6, 3, 7] : *int list*

- **fun** *postorder Tip* = *nil*
  | *postorder* (*Node*(*a, l, r*)) = *postorder l* @ *postorder r* @ [*a*] ;
> **val** *postorder* = **fn** : *'a BT1* −> *'a list*

- *postorder tree2* ;
  [4, 5, 2, 6, 7, 3, 1] : *int list*

All three traversal functions can be defined using *redbt1*, but only the one for preorder is simple.

- **val** *preorder* = *redbt1* (*append oo cons*) *nil* ;
> **val** *preorder* = **fn** : *'a BT1* −> *'a list*

One-dimensional representations of trees

By flattening a tree using one of the three orders, you loose information about the structure of the tree. You cannot reconstruct a tree from only one listing of any order. This is easily seen by observing that several trees can have the same listing. The preorder listings of the trees in the figure below are all $[1, 2, 4, 6, 7, 5, 3]$. Given the inorder listing and one other listing you can reconstruct the tree, however.

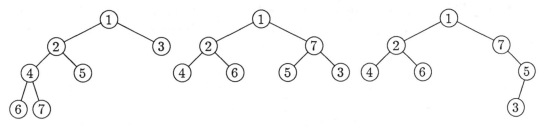

A tree has a hierarchical structure. A common way to show such a structure in one dimension is to use parentheses. Let us give the traversals of the rightmost tree in the figure. The tree is not a full tree, so we use dots to indicate that one but not both subtrees are tips.

Preorder:	(1 (2 4 6) (7 . (5 3 .)))
Inorder:	((4 2 6) 1 (. 7 (3 5 .)))
Postorder:	((4 6 2) (. (3 . 5) 7) 1)

For full trees, the dots are not needed.

Exercises

20.12. Define a function *membt1* that checks if a given label occurs in a tree.

20.13. Define a function *eqstruct* that decides if two labelled binary trees have the same structure. The labels may differ.

20.14. Which tree has the preorder listing 1 3 4 5 7 6 2 8 and the inorder listing 4 3 7 5 6 1 2 8?

20.15. Give two different trees whose preorder listings are the same and whose postorder listings are the same, too.

20.16. Define a function *printtree* that generates the parentheses form of preorder of a labelled binary tree in the form of a string.

20.2.3   Binary leaf trees

In a labelled tree, each node contains a label of some kind. In a leaf tree only the tips, which we now call leaves, contain labels.

datatype $'a\ BT2\ =\ \ Leaf$ **of** $'a\ \ |\ \ Node$ **of** $'a\ BT2 * 'a\ BT2$

One application of leaf trees is to use them as binary decoding trees. A binary code is a set of sequences of zeros and ones. To each sequence, called a *code word*, some information is associated. The *code words* need not be of the same length. A code word can be represented by a path through a leaf tree, where a zero means "go left" and a one means "go right". The associated information is contained in the leaf you reach when following the path. Let us define a function which, when given a list of zeros and ones, gives the associated information from a decoding tree.

exception *decode*;

```
—    fun  decode nil (Leaf info)  = info
     |  decode (0 :: t) (Node(l, r))  =  decode t l
     |  decode (1 :: t) (Node(l, r))  =  decode t r
     |  decode _ _  =  raise decode;
>    val  decode : int list −> 'a BT2 −> 'a
```

In a *prefix* code, no code word is an initial sequence of another code word. For instance, both 01 and 011 cannot be code words. For a prefix code, you can uniquely decode all code words. Telephone numbers, area codes included, form a prefix code. The Morse alphabet, on the other hand, is a non-prefix code. You can still use it because it has a third letter, the pause.

LISP lists

The language LISP was designed around 1960 and is a LISt Processing language. By definition, a LISP list is either an atom or a sequence of LISP lists surrounded by parentheses. An atom is either a number or an identifier. In LISP, not only data, but also programs are represented by LISP lists. The expression $2 + f(g(x, y), z+1)$, for instance, is given by $(add\ 2\ (f\ (g\ x\ y)\ (add\ z\ 1)))$. A function application is always denoted by a list, and you do not use infix operators[1]. You cannot use ML lists to represent LISP lists, because all elements of an ML list must be of the same type. In fact, a LISP list is not a list at all, but a binary tree structure, where the left subtree corresponds to the head of the list and the right subtree to its tail. Hence, the appropriate view of a LISP list is a binary tree, which you can represent in one dimension as a parentheses expression in the way described. In a LISP list, some elements can be atoms, some lists. An atom in a LISP list is represented by a leaf occurring as the left subtree of a node. To mark the end of a list, you introduce the atom *Nil*, often written (), which is the

---

[1]Modern dialects of LISP have many extensions to this simple view.

only atom that can occur as the right subtree of a node in our simple view of LISP lists. For instance, the list $(f\ (g\ x))$ is given by the tree in the figure.

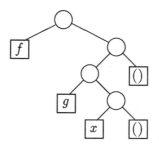

Let us first define the type of atoms and a function for printing atoms.

datatype *ATOM* $=$ *Nil* $\mid$ **Num of** *int* $\mid$ **Id of** *string*;

```
— fun printatom Nil = ")("
     | printatom (Num n) = makestring n
     | printatom (Id id) = id;
>   val printatom = fn : ATOM −> string
```

A LISP list is represented by a tree of type *ATOM BT2*. The leaves can be printed by *printatom*. To print a node, you scan along the right subtree until a *Nil* list is encountered and print each sublist recursively. We use the auxiliary function *printlist* to do the scanning; *print* only surrounds the list by parentheses. They have to be mutually recursive, since a list can contain sublists.

exception *print*;

```
— fun printlist (Leaf Nil) = ""
     | printlist (Leaf _) = raise print
     | printlist (Node(l, Leaf Nil)) = print l
     | printlist (Node(l, r)) = print l ^ " " ^ printlist r
  and print (Leaf a) = printatom a
     | print tree = "(" ^ printlist tree ^ ")";
>   val printlist = fn : ATOM BT2 −> string
>   and print = fn : ATOM BT2 −> string
```

Note that *Nil* atoms are printed by *printatom* and not by *printlist*. The list $(()())$, for instance, is a list of two *Nil* lists. In the corresponding tree there are three *Nil* atoms, but the third one is the empty list and is never printed.

Exercises

20.17. Are there decoding trees that represent non-prefix codes?

20.18. Define a function that lists the labels of a leaf tree from left to right.

20.19. Define *redbt2* and *mapbt2* for leaf trees.

20.20. Define *car* and *cdr* that take the head and tail of a LISP list and also *cons*, *null*, and *isatom*. LISP lists are represented by trees.

20.2.4   Full binary trees

A full binary tree is a labelled tree, in which every node has either zero or two immediate subnodes, but never one tip and one node. You can use labelled trees to represent them, but then some labelled trees do not represent full trees. Instead, you can label both nodes and tips. The leaves then play the role of nodes with zero subnodes.

$$\textbf{datatype } \textit{'a BT3} \;=\; \textit{Leaf } \textbf{of } \textit{'a} \;\mid\; \textit{Node } \textbf{of } \textit{'a} * \textit{'a BT3} * \textit{'a BT3}$$

We have now defined four kinds of binary tree. You can interpret the number suffix as a binary number with two bits, the first one associated with the leaves and the other one with the nodes. A zero denotes that no information is associated with the leave or node, and a one denotes that it is.

Huffman codes

One use of full binary trees is in the design of optimal binary codes. Given the relative frequences of some messages, you want to construct a code of minimum cost. Frequent messages should be given short code words and infrequent ones long code words. The cost is the weighted sum of the lengths of the code words, where the weight is the relative frequency of the code word. Let us draw one optimal and one non-optimal tree for the weights 2, 2, 4, and 8. In the nodes we put the sum of all leaf descendents of that node.

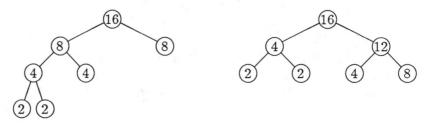

Cost: $2 * 3 + 2 * 3 + 4 * 2 + 8 * 1 = 28$ $2 * 2 + 2 * 2 + 4 * 2 + 8 * 2 = 32$

The cost of the left tree is smallest since the most frequent message has the shortest code word (1), and the two most infrequent ones have the longest code words (000 and 001).

The question now arises how you find an optimal code given a set of weights in the general case. This problem was solved by D. A. Huffman with a nice algorithm. First note that the numbers in the nodes give the total frequency for that subtree. Huffman observed that if sister nodes have as equal frequency as possible, then the code is optimal. To achieve this, you first sort the weights. Then, you transform the list of weights into a list of leaves (really trees) containing the weights. Now, you take the first two leaves (the smallest ones) and combine them into a tree by creating a node. The weight of the node is the sum of the leaves. The leaves are removed from the list of trees, and the new node (tree) is inserted at the right place according to its weight. You continue to combine the two first trees of the list until all nodes (or leaves) have been combined. The resulting tree is then optimal.

To construct an optimal tree for the weights [2, 2, 4, 8] you first combine the two smallest weights to give a tree with inorder (2 4 2). You now have the list [(2 4 2), 4, 8]. Next, you combine the two 4 weights to give [((2 4 2) 8 4), 8]. Combining these two trees now yields the left tree above.

Let us define a function *huffman* that constructs an optimal tree. We first have to create a list of leaves from the weights. Then, the *huff* function combines the trees with smallest weights and inserts the result into the list of subtrees. The function *insert* performs the inserting and *weight* selects the weight from the root of a tree.

```
-  local  exception huffman
          fun  huff (t :: nil)  =  t
            |  huff (t1 :: t2 :: ts)  =
                    huff(insert(Node(weight t1 + weight t2, t1, t2)) ts)
          and  weight (Leaf w)  =  w
            |  weight (Node(w, _, _))  =  w
          and  insert (t : int BT3) nil  =  [t]
            |  insert s (t :: ts)  =  if weight s <= weight t
                                      then s :: t :: ts
                                      else t :: insert s ts
       in fun huffman nil  =  raise huffman
            |  huffman xs  =  huff(map Leaf (sort xs))
       end ;
>  val huffman  =  fn   : int list -> int BT3

-  huffman [2, 2, 4, 8];
   Node(16, Node(8, Node(4, Leaf 2, Leaf 2), Leaf 4), Leaf 8) : int BT3
```

The left tree on page 284 is, indeed, optimal. Nothing else is really to be expected, since all sister nodes have exactly the same weights.

Exercises

20.21. Define the three traversal functions for full binary trees.

20.22. Construct by hand an optimal Huffman tree for the weights 1, 1, 3, 4, 4, 6, and 9.

20.23. Define a function *cost* that gives the cost of a Huffman tree. You can do it either with explicit recursion or with *redbt3*.

20.2.5   General binary trees

You have seen four kinds of binary trees, but a further possibility is to have trees with different types of data objects in nodes and leaves.

> **datatype** $('a, 'b)$ BT $=$ $Leaf$ **of** $'a$ $\mid$
> $\qquad\qquad\qquad\qquad Node$ **of** $'b * ('a, 'b)$ $BT * ('a, 'b)$ BT

Note that if a type function has two parameters, they must be enclosed within parentheses. Let us define a reducer for this most general type of binary tree.

```
 -  fun  redbt f g (Leaf x)  =  g x
      |  redbt f g (Node(x, l, r))  =  f x (redbt f g l) (redbt f g r);
 >  val  redbt  =  fn  :  ('a -> 'b -> 'b -> 'b) ->
                         ('c -> 'b) -> ('c, 'a)BT -> 'b
```

This reducer must be given two functions as arguments, since both nodes and leaves contain data objects.

Arithmetic expressions

General binary trees are suitable for representing arithmetic expressions with binary operators. The nodes contain the operators and the leaves the constants.

Let us define an enumeration type for operators.

> **datatype** OPS $=$ $Plus$ $\mid$ $Minus$ $\mid$ $Times$ $\mid$ $Divide$

Now, *Node(Times, Node(Plus, Leaf 2, Leaf 3), Node(Divide, Leaf 9, Leaf 3))* constructs the right tree above. Note the similarity to the prefix form of this expression, which is *times(plus(2, 3), divide(9, 3))*.

Let us now define a function *eval* that gives the value of a tree representing an arithmetic expression. For each operator of type *OPS*, we then need the corresponding function in ML, so we first define a translation function.

```
—  fun getop Plus   = curry (op +)
   |  getop Minus  = curry (op −)
   |  getop Times  = curry (op *)
   |  getop Divide = curry (op div);
>  val getop : OPS −> int −> int −> int
```

```
—  fun eval (Leaf c) = c
   |  eval (Node(oper, l, r)) = getop oper (eval l) (eval r);
>  val eval = fn : (int, OPS) BT −> int
```

To evaluate an expression, you traverse the tree from left to right. You may therefore suspect that *eval* can be defined in a simple way using *redbt*.

```
—  val eval = redbt getop I;
>  val eval = fn : (int, OPS) BT −> int
```

The second argument to *redbt* is the identity function, since the leaves contain constants that have themselves as values.

redbt getop I (Node(Plus, Leaf 2, Leaf 3)) ⟶
getop Plus (redbt getop I (Leaf 2))(redbt getop I (Leaf 3)) ⟶
(curry (op +)) (I 2) (I 3) ⟶ *(curry (op +)) 2 3* ⟶ 5

Traversal of arithmetic expression trees

We have given the labels of a tree in three different orders. All these orders have illustrative readings for expression trees.

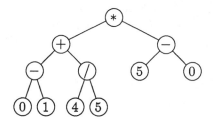

Expression:	$((0-1)+(4/5))*(5-0)$
Preorder:	$*+-0\ 1/4\ 5-5\ 0$
Inorder:	$0-1+4/5*5-0$
Postorder:	$0\ 1-4\ 5/+5\ 0-*$

The preorder listing is similar to the ordinary functional notation. If you insert commas and parentheses at appropriate places in the listing, you get the expression $*(+(-(0,1),/(4,5)),-(5,0))$. Interestingly enough, you can reconstruct the tree given the preorder of the tree only. This contradicts what we have earlier observed. The reason is that you now can tell operators from constants, and operators occur only in nodes and constants only in leaves.

The inorder listing is the original expression with parentheses removed. Since parentheses are significant in an expression, you cannot reconstruct the tree from the inorder listing; in fact, many trees have the same listing.

The postorder listing has properties analogous to the preorder one, and the tree can be reconstructed from it, too. The postorder listing is sometimes used to simplify the evaluation of an expression. By using a stack for storage of intermediate values, the postorder (postfix form) can be read left to right. Operands are pushed onto the stack, and operators are applied to the two top values on the stack. The result is pushed onto the stack. At completion, the single value on the stack is the value of the expression. By the use of recursion, you avoid this explicit manipulation of a stack; the system uses one, though.

Exercises

20.24. Define a function *printexpr* that transforms a tree representing an arithmetic expression into a string. Do not consider precedences. Instead, surround all subexpressions by parentheses.

20.25. How many trees representing arithmetic expressions have the inorder listing $1+4*5-0$?

20.26. A boolean expression can contain the operators *and*, *or*, and *not*, together with *true* and *false*. Define a suitable tree representation of such expressions and define an evaluation function. You need a new type of node having only one subtree.

20.27. Define a function that constructs a tree from a string with an arithmetic expression in preorder. Assume all numbers contain only one digit. Hint: Let the function that builds a tree return a pair consisting of the tree built and the string that has not yet been examined.

20.28. Define a tail recursive function that evaluates an arithmetic expression represented by a string with a postorder listing of the expression. Assume all numbers contain only one digit.

20.3 Trees and Forests

A node in a binary tree has at most two subtrees. In a general tree, a node can have any number of subtrees. A tree can be said to be a label and a list of subtrees.

> **datatype** $'a$ $TREE$ $=$ $Node$ **of** $'a * ('a\ TREE)\ list$

In this definition, there is only one alternative and the definition may seem circular, since there is no base case. However, the empty list provides such a base case. For each new recursive type you define, you should state the corresponding induction principle. Assume you want to prove that a property P holds for all trees. As base case you have to prove that P is true for a node with no subtrees. The inductive step amounts to assuming that P holds *for all* lists ts of subtrees and proving that P then also holds for all trees $Node(x, ts)$, where x is an element of the right type.

Let us use this induction principle to define a function $maxdepth$ over trees. The maximum depth of a node without subtrees is zero. We now assume that we can compute the maximum depth of all subtrees. To get these depths we map $maxdepth$ to the list of trees.

```
−   fun maxdepth (Node(x, nil))   =   0
      |  maxdepth (Node(x, trees))  =  1 + maxl(map maxdepth trees);
 >  val maxdepth  =  fn  :  'a TREE −> int
```

The use of map comes naturally. We have a list of trees, and we want to do something to all trees.

Another way of viewing a tree is to say that a tree is a label and a *forest*, and a forest is a list of trees. Trees and forests are now defined in terms of each other: they are *mutually recursive*. Let us define the list of trees with two constructors *Empty* and *Addtree*, which correspond to *nil* and *cons*.

> **datatype** $'a$ $TREE$ $=$ $Node$ **of** $'a * 'a\ FOREST$
> **and** $'a$ $FOREST$ $=$ $Empty$ $|$ $Addtree$ **of** $'a\ TREE * 'a\ FOREST$

Now substituting the first definition into the second you get

> **datatype** $'a$ $FOREST$ $=$ $Empty$ $|$
> $\qquad\qquad\qquad\qquad Addtree$ **of** $'a * 'a\ FOREST * 'a\ FOREST$

Do you recognize this structure??

The given type definition is isomorphic to labelled binary trees. This may seem surprising, but can be easily explained. Suppose we consider the list of subtrees of a tree as a list of sisters of increasing age. The left subtree of a node in the binary tree is then the youngest daughter, and the right subtree is the next older sister of that node. This correspondence is often called the *natural correspondence* between trees and binary trees.

Exercises

20.29. Define a function for deciding if two trees have the same structure.

20.30. Suppose the nodes in a tree contain strings. Define a function *print* that generates a string with the tree listed in preorder and with parentheses to show its structure.

20.31. Draw a forest of three trees where the trees have 2, 1, and 3 subtrees. Then draw the corresponding binary tree. What can you say about a binary tree corresponding to a forest containing one tree only?

20.4 Abstract Syntax Trees

A type definition defines a set of data objects, and a grammar defines a set of sentences. Hence, they both define sets of objects, and a closer examination reveals that type definitions and grammars have much in common. A grammar describes the **concrete syntax** of a language, that is, a set of strings, whereas a type definition describes the **abstract syntax** of a language, that is, the structural properties of the sentences disregarding unimportant details of how they are written. If the objects have a doubly recursive nature, the corresponding data objects will have a tree structure. Such trees are often called abstract syntax trees. We can make the following list of correspondences between grammars and type definitions.

BNF grammar	*Type definition*
non-terminal symbol	type
terminal symbol	constructor
concatenation	tuple
alternative	union
iteration	list
recursion	recursive data types
mutual recursion	mutually recursive types

Abstract syntax trees for expressions

Let us define a data type for arithmetic expressions extended with conditional expressions, whose concrete syntax is chosen to make programs simple (they are written with "?" and "!"). We start with the BNF grammar for the expressions (| denotes alternative and {...} zero or more repetitions).

```
EXPR    ::=  TERM {ADDOP   TERM }
TERM    ::=  FACTOR {MULOP   FACTOR }
FACTOR  ::=  CONST  |  VAR  |  ( EXPR )  |  ( EXPR ? EXPR ! EXPR )
CONST   ::=  DIGIT { DIGIT }
```

$$\begin{array}{lll}
\text{VAR} & ::= & \text{LETTER} \; \{ \; \text{LETTER} \; \} \\
\text{ADDOP} & ::= & + \; | \; - \\
\text{MULOP} & ::= & * \; | \; /
\end{array}$$

Multiplication operators have higher precedence than addition operators. The intended meaning of the condition in the conditional expression is that it is true if it is greater than zero. This is nothing that the grammar tells you, however.

To evaluate an expression with variables, you have to know their values. We therefore introduce environments, which contain bindings of variables, and represent them by lists of pairs of identifiers and their values. Such lists are nothing but tables, and we can use the *lookup* function to find the value of an identifier.

To work with expressions, you have to define a suitable data type for them. The grammar above describes the concrete syntax of expressions. In that grammar, precedences are described by the use of three syntactic categories: factors, terms, and expressions. In a tree, however, precedences are not needed; they are useful only for telling in which way to build a tree from an expression represented by a string. We therefore define a simpler grammar, which reflects only the structure of the trees we will use.

$$\begin{array}{lll}
\text{EXPR} & ::= & \text{CONST} \; | \; \text{VAR} \; | \; \text{EXPR OP EXPR} \; | \\
& & (\; \text{EXPR} \; ? \; \text{EXPR} \; ! \; \text{EXPR} \;) \\
\text{OP} & ::= & + \; | \; - \; | \; * \; | \; /
\end{array}$$

This grammar contains concrete details like the use of "?" and "!". We now abstract from such details and define a data type *EXPR* reflecting the grammar.

$$- \quad \textbf{datatype } EXPR = Const \textbf{ of } int \; | \; Var \textbf{ of } string \; | \\
Op \textbf{ of } string * EXPR * EXPR \; | \; If \textbf{ of } EXPR * EXPR * EXPR$$

The abstract syntax reflects the structure of the expressions very closely: a conditional expression contains three subexpressions, and therefore the constructor *If* takes three expressions as arguments.

Parsing expressions

To make a program modifiable, the dependence on the concrete syntax should be restricted. We therefore need functions for building trees from strings representing expressions. The syntax of the strings is given by the first BNF grammar above. To analyse a string and check that it agrees with a given grammar is called *parsing* of the string. When defining parsing functions, you can start by looking at the grammar, since parsing functions to a large extent can be derived from the grammar.

Strings are difficult to work with, so we explode them into a lists of characters before parsing them. In the course of building the tree, the parsed part of the expression is represented by a tree and the remaining part by the list of the characters not yet parsed. Hence, during parsing an expression will be represented by a *pair* of a tree and a string. Most parsing functions will yield such pairs as result. First, we define two functions parsing constants and variables. The first argument is an accumulator. We assume the existence of predicates to check if a character is a letter, a digit, an addition operator, or a multiplication operator.

```
-  fun bldconst (acc, nil)  =  (Const acc, nil)
   |  bldconst (acc, c :: cs)  =
          if digit c
          then bldconst(10 ∗ acc + digitval  c, cs)
          else (Const acc, c :: cs);
>  val bldconst  =  fn  :  int ∗ string list −> EXPR ∗ string list

-  fun bldvar (id, nil)  =  (Var id, nil)
   |  bldvar (id, c :: cs)  =
              if letter  c orelse digit c
              then bldvar(id ˆ c, cs)
              else (Var id, c :: cs);
>  val bldvar  =  fn  :  string ∗ string list −> EXPR ∗ string list
```

The definitions of expressions, terms, and factors are mutually recursive. In such cases, it is most often best to define also the parsing functions as mutually recursive. To parse an expression, you first parse a term and, then, iteratively look for additional operators and terms. Therefore, you need an auxiliary function performing this iteration. Its argument is the tree built so far and the remaining characters, that is, the same type of pair as the results of the parsing functions. We also define a function *rem* that removes the head of a list of characters if it satisfies a given predicate and raises an exception otherwise.

```
   exception syntaxerror;

-  fun rem p (x :: xs) = if p x then xs else raise syntaxerror;
>  val rem  =  fn  :  ('a −> bool) −> 'a list −> 'a list

-  fun bldexp  cs  =  bldexp'(bldterm cs)  (∗ TERM { ADDOP TERM } ∗)
   and bldexp' (l, nil)  =  (l, nil)        (∗ { ADDOP TERM } ∗)
    |  bldexp' (l, c :: cs)  =
              if addop c
              then let val (r, cs)  =  bldterm cs
                      in bldexp' (Op(c, l, r), cs) end
              else (l, c :: cs)
```

```
and  bldterm cs  =  bldterm'(bldfact cs) (* FACTOR { MULOP FACTOR } *)
and  bldterm' (l, nil)  =  (l, nil)         (* { MULOP FACTOR } *)
  |  bldterm' (l, c :: cs)  =
          if mulop c
          then let val (r, cs)  =  bldfact cs
                  in bldterm' (Op(c, l, r), cs) end
          else (l, c :: cs)

and  bldfact nil  =  raise syntaxerror
  |  bldfact (c :: cs)  =
        if c = ")("
        then let val (t1, cs)  =  bldexp cs
                in  if hd cs = ")"
                    then (t1, rem (eq ")") cs)
                    else  let val (t2, cs)  =  bldexp (rem (eq "?") cs)
                            in  let val (t3, cs)  =  bldexp (rem (eq "!") cs)
                                  in (If(t1, t2, t3), rem (eq ")") cs) end
                          end
                end
        else  if digit c
              then bldconst(0, c :: cs)
              else bldvar(c, cs);
```

```
>  val bldexp    =  fn :  string list -> EXPR * string list
   val bldexp'   =  fn :  EXPR * string list -> EXPR * string list
   val bldterm   =  fn :  string list -> EXPR * string list
   val bldterm'  =  fn :  EXPR * string list -> EXPR * string list
   val bldfact   =  fn :  string list -> EXPR * string list
```

Finally, we define a function that given a string gives the corresponding tree.

```
-  fun build s  =  fst(bldexp(explode s));
>  val build = fn :  string -> EXPR
```

Our next task is define a print function, which converts a tree into a string. We now have to insert some parentheses. To simplify, we surround all subexpressions by parentheses, many of which are really unnecessary.

```
-  fun print (Const i)  =  makestring i
  |  print (Var id)  =  id
  |  print (Op(oper, l, r))  =  "(" ^ print l ^ oper ^ print r ^ ")"
  |  print (If(cond, thn, els))  =
          "(" ^ print cond ^ "?" ^ print thn ^ "!" ^ print els ^ ")";
>  val  print  =  fn :  EXPR -> string
```

The function *print* is the inverse of *build*, except for unnecessary parentheses and syntax errors.

$$- \quad print(build \text{ "(x-y?x!y)"});$$
$$\text{"((x-y)?x!y)"} : string$$

We always have that *build o print* = *I*, though. Once you can construct trees from strings, you can do all work with expressions as trees. By the use of special *parser generators*, you can use a program to generate a parser for you. Such a parser generator is a tool that should accompany an ML system for production use.

Evaluation of expressions

An expression with variables must always be evaluated in an environment, so an environment must be given to the *eval* function. To find the value of a variable, we use the table operation *lookup*. The *eval* function is a simple case analysis of the different forms of tree.

exception *eval*;

```
—  fun  eval env (Const i)        =  i
     |  eval env (Var id)          =  lookup id env
     |  eval env (Op (" + ", l, r)) =  eval env l + eval env r
     |  eval env (Op (" − ", l, r)) =  eval env l − eval env r
     |  eval env (Op (" * ", l, r)) =  eval env l * eval env r
     |  eval env (Op ("/", l, r))   =  eval env l div eval env r
     |  eval env (Op ( _, _, _))    =  raise eval
     |  eval env (If(be, thn, els)) =  if eval env be > 0
                                       then eval env thn
                                       else eval env els;
>  val  eval  =  fn  :  (string * int) list −> EXPR −> int
```

$$- \quad eval \text{ [("x", 3), ("y", 5)]} (build \text{ "(x-y?x!y)"});$$
$$5 : int$$

The *eval* function is really an interpreter for expressions. By extending the expressions with functions, you get an interpreter for a small functional language.

Formal differentiation

The great advantage of constructing abstract syntax trees is that it simplifies whatever you want to do with expressions. Suppose you want to find the derivative of an expression with respect to some variable. The first argument to *diff* is the differentiation variable. Conditional expressions cannot be differentiated and, for simplicity, we omit also division.

$$
\begin{aligned}
- \quad \textbf{fun} \;\; &diff \;\; v \;\; (Const \; i) \qquad\qquad = \; Const \; 0 \\
| \;\; &diff \; (Var \; id) \; (Var \; id') \;\; = \; \textbf{if} \; id = id' \; \textbf{then} \; Const \; 1 \\
& \qquad\qquad\qquad\qquad\qquad\qquad\quad \textbf{else} \; Const \; 0 \\
| \;\; &diff \; v \; (Op \, (" + ", \; l, \; r)) \;\; = \; Op \, (" + ", \; diff \; v \; l, \; diff \; v \; r) \\
| \;\; &diff \; v \; (Op \, (" - ", \; l, \; r)) \;\; = \; Op \, (" - ", \; diff \; v \; l, \; diff \; v \; r) \\
| \;\; &diff \; v \; (Op \, (" * ", \; l, \; r)) \;\; = \\
& \qquad Op \, (" + ", \; Op \, (" * ", \; diff \; v \; l, \; r), \; Op \, (" * ", \; l, \; diff \; v \; r)); \\
> \quad \textbf{val} \;\; &diff \; = \; \textbf{fn} \; : \; EXPR \; -> \; EXPR \; -> \; EXPR
\end{aligned}
$$

Let us differentiate $x * x * 2 + x * y$ with respect to x.

$$
\begin{aligned}
- \quad &print \; (diff \; (Var \; "x") \; (build \; "x*x*2+x*y")); \\
&"(((((1*x)+(x*1))*2)+((x*x)*0))+((1*y)+(x*0)))" \; : \; string
\end{aligned}
$$

Exercises

20.32. Formulate the induction principle for the type *EXPR*. Then, define a function *nr_of_constants* that counts the number of constants in an expression.

20.33. Define a *print* function that prints only those parentheses that are really needed in an expression. Do not consider conditional expressions.

20.34. Extend *diff* to handle division.

20.35. After differentiation, an expression is usually more complicated than necessary. Define *simplify* that simplifies an expression according to the following rules.

$$
\begin{array}{llll}
0 + e = e & e + 0 = e & 0 * e = 0 & e * 0 = 0 \\
1 * e = e & e * 1 = e & e - 0 = e & e/1 = e
\end{array}
$$

You may also add the rule $e - e = 0$, but it is a bit more difficult.

Summary

Using recursive data types, you can define types with an infinite number of data objects. A type definition gives useful information about the type: what patterns look like, the *structural induction principle* to use, and the definition of a *reducer*. The most important *regular linear types* are natural numbers and lists. A *binary tree* is a doubly recursive structure. There are five regular types of binary trees. A BNF grammar gives the *concrete syntax* of a language. The objects defined by a grammar are strings. The corresponding data type defines the *abstract syntax* of the language. Its objects are *abstract syntax trees*. In a *free representation* of some abstract objects, there is a unique data object representing each abstract object. A data type is *free*, if there exists a free representation for it. A non-free representation of a type is called a *quotient type*, since the data objects are divided into classes of equal data objects, called *equivalence classes*.

Exercises

20.36. Label a balanced tree by the numbers $1, 2, \ldots$ starting with the root and traversing the nodes "row-wise". What is the relation between the number in a node and its two children?

20.37. Define a function that given two lists of the labels of a labelled binary tree in preorder and inorder constructs the tree. Assume all labels are unique.

20.38. Define a function *encode* that given some information yields the associated code out of a decoding tree, which is a leaf tree.

20.39. In Section 20.2.5, the function *eval* is defined. In the nodes, objects of type *OPS* are stored. Redefine *eval* supposing that the curried functions themselves are stored in the nodes. Is this a good representation of arithmetic expressions?

20.40. Define a predicate *leftskew* that checks that, for all nodes, the maximal depth of its left subtree is at least as big as that of its right subtree.

20.41. Define a function that builds a decoding tree given a sorted list of pairs of code words and associated data. A code word is a list of zeros and ones, and the sorting order is the corresponding numerical order.

20.42. Define a function *alltrees* that constructs a list of all binary branching structures with a given number of nodes. Then compute how many trees there are with n nodes for $n = 1, 2, \ldots, 10$. Check that the number agees with the formula $\frac{bin(2*n,n)}{n+1}$, where *bin* is the function computing the binomial coefficients.

20.43. Extend expressions with functions taking one argument. Their syntax is given by FACTOR ::= ID(EXPR). Change *build*, *eval*, *print*, *diff*, and *simplify* accordingly. In *eval* you can, for instance, introduce *sin* and *sqrt*.

20.44. Extend expressions with function constants and function applications.

$$\text{FACTOR} \quad ::= \quad \% \text{ VAR . EXPR}$$
$$\text{EXPR} \quad ::= \quad \text{EXPR (EXPR)}$$

Extend *build*, *eval*, and *print* accordingly. You now, in fact, have an interpreter for a functional language, which you can expand to handle other expressions and operators. You may also try to define one strict and one lazy version. The formal semantics of ML can be of help.

20.45. Define a lexical scanner, that is, a parsing function handling tokens like numbers, identifiers, delimiters, and reserved words. Its argument is the string to be parsed and its result a list of tokens represented in a suitable way.

20.46. Find a book on LISP and define an interpreter for a small subset of LISP. You may also select some other programming language.

20.47. A small imperative language has the following grammar.

```
PROGRAM    ::= { STATEMENT ; }
STATEMENT ::= VAR = EXPR                              (* Assignment *)
           |  ( EXPR ? STATEMENT ! STATEMENT )        (* Conditional *)
           |  "{" EXPR ! STATEMENT "}"                (* While *)
           |  > VAR                                    (* Input *)
           |  < EXPR                                   (* Output *)
```

The expressions are as given in the text. A positive expression is considered as true in the conditional and while statement. Define functions which build abstract syntax trees and print them in the form of strings. Define a function *run* which takes a list of numbers and a program tree and runs the program with the number list as input. Each time an input statement is executed a new number is taken from the list. The output is the list of numbers which has been produced by the output statements. Try the functions on some sample programs.

20.48. Adapt the Huffman algorithm to construct codes allowing only code words of even length. Use quaternary trees, in which each node has four subnodes and find out how to interpret them in an appropriate manner.

20.49. The functions *diff* and *simplify* constitute an embryo of a formula manipulation system. Extend it with, for instance, more predefined functions, possibilities for integration, or the like.

20.50. Define a data type that represents the type definitions used in ML. Make ·simplifying assumptions if you want. Define a function that, given a type definition, produces a definition of the reducer for this type definition. To represent the result, you need a data type representing function definitions in ML.

20.51. Define a function that prints the nodes and leaves of a general binary tree as they appear in the graphical representation of the tree, so that you later can fill in the arcs, boxes, and circles by hand. The result can be a list of strings, where each string is a line.

20.52. Consult the paper Turner 79 about combinators. Define an interpreter for a small functional language using the ideas described in the paper.

Chapter 21

Abstract Data Types

For any programming problem, you have to decide how to represent the information about the application in your program. A desired goal is that the inherent structure of the real concepts is well reflected in the data objects you use. Concrete data types work fine until you encounter real objects with properties that cannot be described using only concrete types and pattern matching. You solve this problem by defining a concrete type to be used as a representation and by introducing new operations with the right properties working on this representation. Using abstract data type definitions, you can hide the properties of the representation and export a view of them that suits your application. In this chapter we will look at, for instance, queues, files, sets, relations, tables, and graphs. They are all candidates for the inclusion in an ML system as predefined data types.

21.1 Data Abstraction

If you can limit the dependence of some particular representation, your program is easier to change, for instance, if you want a more efficient implementation of an operation. To hide the details of a representation and make visible only the important properties is to make an abstraction. Such an abstraction is called a *data abstraction*. There are two independent reasons for performing data abstraction: the need to limit the dependence of a particular representation and the need to model real concepts with non-regular properties.

Example: Queues

A concrete type definition introduces new constructors used to construct objects of the type. The regular view of these objects is what you get through pattern matching. We have looked at queues in Section 19.6. The constructors of queues are *Empty* and *Enter*, the selectors are *remove* and *rest*, and the predicate is *isempty*. We can represent queues by lists. To define an abstract data type we need a concrete data type as representation, for which we use the constructor *Queue*. Since queues can contain elements of any type, we define an abstract type function.

      exception *remove* **and** *rest*;

      abstype $'a$ *QUEUE* $=$ *Queue* **of** $'a$ *list*
      with **val** *Empty* $=$ *Queue nil*
            fun *Enter e (Queue es)* $=$ *Queue* $(e :: es)$
            fun *remove (Queue nil)* $=$ **raise** *remove*
              | *remove (Queue* $[e]$*)* $=$ e
              | *remove (Queue* $(e :: es)$*)* $=$ *remove (Queue es)*
            fun *rest (Queue nil)* $=$ **raise** *rest*
              | *rest (Queue* $[e]$*)* $=$ *Queue nil*
              | *rest (Queue* $(e :: es)$*)* $=$ *Enter e (rest (Queue es))*
            fun *isempty (Queue nil)* $=$ *true*
              | *isempty (Queue* $\_$*)* $=$ *false*
    end

This definition introduces the new **abstract** data type function *QUEUE* with the five operations *Empty, Enter, remove, rest,* and *isempty*. The objects of type *QUEUE* are represented by another type, the **representation** type, which is the concrete type after the equal sign.

The representation of the objects is hidden in the sense that a program containing this definition can manipulate the objects only by the use of the five exported operations. The constructor of the representation type, sometimes called a **concrete constructor**, is not visible outside the definition.

    $-$ *Queue* $[1, 2, 3]$;
    Unbound identifier : *Queue*

There are no special selectors or predicates for the representation type; pattern matching is used instead, as you see in the definition.

Pictorially, you can imagine that the (abstract) constructors *Empty* and *Enter* construct a representation of an object, and then put it into a black box. You are allowed to pass the black box around in your program, but you cannot look inside it. If you try to evaluate an expression whose type is an abstract type, the system prints only a hyphen.

    $-$ *Enter 7 Empty*;
    $-$: *int QUEUE*

When you apply one of the selectors to the "black box", however, the representation is taken out of the box and matched against the pattern.

> — *remove it*;
> 7 : *int*

Hence, you can only see the properties of an abstract data object through the use of the abstract operations, that is, the operations exported from the abstract type definition.

The given implementation of queues is not very efficient. In Exercise 19.9, a better implementation is suggested. It uses two lists to represent a queue.

> **abstype** $'a\ QUEUE\ =\ Queue\ \textbf{of}\ 'a\ list * 'a\ list$
> **with val** $Empty\ =\ Queue\ (nil, nil)$
>   **fun** $Enter\ e\ (Queue\ (es, fs))\ =\ Queue\ (e :: es, fs)$
>   **exception** *remove* **and** *rest*
>   **fun** $remove\ (Queue\ (nil, nil))\ =\ \textbf{raise}\ remove$
> | $remove\ (Queue\ (es, nil))\ =\ remove\ (Queue\ (nil,\ rev\ es))$
> | $remove\ (Queue\ (\ \_, f :: \_))\ =\ f$
>   **fun** $rest\ (Queue\ (nil, nil))\ =\ \textbf{raise}\ rest$
> | $rest\ (Queue\ (es, nil))\ =\ rest\ (Queue\ (nil,\ rev\ es))$
> | $rest\ (Queue\ (es, f :: fs))\ =\ Queue\ (es, fs)$
>   **fun** $isempty\ (Queue\ (nil, nil))\ =\ true$
> | $isempty\ (Queue\ (\ \_,\ \_))\ =\ false$
> **end**

The types of the operations are the same as in the previous definition, and however much you compare the two implementations of queues, the operations will yield the same results for all arguments; the representation is not visible outside the definition. You say that the implementations have the same behaviour or that they are *observationally equivalent*.

Implementation descriptors

There are two types involved in an abstract data type definition: the abstract type and the concrete (representation) type. In order to understand better the relation between these types, you can define (on paper) the two implementation descriptors *abstr* and *valid* of type $REPTYPE\ ->\ ABSTYPE$ and $REPTYPE\ ->\ bool$, respectively. The function *valid* tells whether a data object in the representation type represents an abstract object or not, and *abstr* gives the abstract object represented by some valid representation. For the first definition of queues we get

> $abstr(Queue\ nil)\ =\ Empty$
> $abstr(Queue\ (e :: es))\ =\ Enter\ e\ (abstr(Queue\ es))$
> $valid(\ \_) = true$

and for the second definition we get

$$
\begin{aligned}
abstr(Queue\ (nil, nil)) &= Empty \\
abstr(Queue\ (e :: es, fs)) &= Enter\ e\ (abstr(Queue\ (es, fs))) \\
abstr(Queue\ (nil, fs)) &= abstr(Queue\ (rev\ fs, nil)) \\
valid(\_) &= true
\end{aligned}
$$

It is good practice to specify the implementation descriptors for all abstract data types, since they clarify the actual representation and its relation to the abstract objects.

Quotient types

For a concrete type, equality operators are defined automatically, but that equality is not always the one you want. Suppose you represent sets of integers by lists of integers without duplicates.

> **datatype** SET = Set **of** $int\ list$;

> — $Set\ [1, 2] = Set\ [2, 1]$;
> $false : bool$

The equality operator tests if the two concrete objects have been constructed in the same way, not if they represent the same set, which is what we really want. The problem is that the chosen representation is not free; many objects represent the same real object. To solve this problem, we define an abstract data type. As constructors for sets we use $Empty$ and $Insert$.

> **abstype** SET = Set **of** $int\ list$
> **with** **val** $Empty$ = $Set\ nil$
>   **fun** $Insert\ e\ (Set\ es)$ =
>   **if** $mem\ es\ e$ **then** $Set\ es$ **else** $Set\ (e :: es)$
>   **fun** $member\ (Set\ es)\ e$ = $mem\ es\ e$
>   **fun** $eqset\ (Set\ es)\ (Set\ fs)$ = $sort\ es = sort\ fs$
>   **end**

Using $eqset$ to test if sets are equal, you will find that $[1, 2]$ and $[2, 1]$ represent the same set; you cannot differentiate them within their black boxes with the operations provided. The equality operation $eqset$ partitions the concrete data objects constructed by $Empty$ and $Insert$ into equivalence classes, in which all objects represent the same set. We can appoint one of these objects as a representative for each such equivalence class. For instance, we can use $Set(sort\ es)$ as a representative for $Set\ es$; you say it is a **canonical** element of the class. To define the implementation descriptor $abstr$, we need such canonical elements. To describe sets, we use the conventional notation with curly brackets.

$$abstr(Set\ es)\ =\ \{x_1, x_2, \ldots, x_n\} \qquad where\ [x_1, x_2, \ldots, x_n] = sort\ es$$
$$valid(Set\ es)\ =\ not(duplicates\ es)$$

The predicate *duplicates* tests if a list contains duplicates (Section 17.4). Note, that for this type there are invalid concrete objects; they represent no sets at all. On the other hand, you can never construct lists with duplicates using only the exported constructors.

Specification and implementation

For any specification of a data type, there are many possible *implementations*. If no operations are left undefined for some arguments in the specification, all (correct) implementations will behave logically in the same way. The time and memory space needed to perform an operation in different implementations may very well vary, though; they can still satisfy the same specification. If your specification also contains *performance requirements*, only some of the logically equivalent implementations satisfy the specification; some have operations using too much time or too much space.

Unfortunately, you can seldom find an implementation for which all operations are both fast *and* use little space. Instead, you have to favour some operations at the expense of others. Ideally, you want the implementation that favours the operations used most frequently. Often, your programming work is easier if you choose simplicity before efficiency in your first implementation, unless you get efficiency almost for free. Once your program is working, you can make it more efficient by changing the implementation, if you find your first choice unacceptable.

Exercises

21.1. Implement sets without using lists.

21.2   Linear Structures

A data type consists of a set of objects (the type) and a set of operations. Different data types can be based on the same type. For instance, many data types like lists, stacks, queues, strings, and files are all sequences of objects; the operations differentiate them. A sequence is constructed by starting with an empty sequence and then inserting elements into it. The regular view of such structures is lists, which are often used to implement various linear structures. By using the concrete constructors *Empty* and *Insert* instead of lists, you just simulate lists.

21.2.1   Ordered sequences

When you select the first element out of an ordered sequence, you always get the smallest element according to some given order relation. Simple examples of order relations are $<$ and $\leq$. Some order relations are only *partial* and do not give any particular order between some pairs of objects; the objects are uncomparable. The subset relation on sets, for instance, partially orders the set of all subsets of some given set. Let us here work only with *total* or *linear* order relations, for which all objects are comparable. We give the order relation as an argument to the operations.

> **abstype** $'a\ ORDSEQ\ =\ Empty'\ \mid\ Insert'$ **of** $'a * 'a\ ORDSEQ$
> **with** **val** $Empty\ =\ Empty'$
>   **fun** $Insert\ order\ a\ seq\ =\ Insert'(a, seq)$
>   **exception** $smallest$ **and** $rest$
>   **fun** $smallest\ order\ Empty'\ =\ $**raise** $smallest$
> $\mid\ smallest\ order\ (Insert'(a,\ Empty'))\ =\ a$
> $\mid\ smallest\ order\ (Insert'(a,\ Insert'(b,\ seq)))\ =$
>   **if** $order\ a\ b$
>   **then** $smallest\ order\ (Insert'(a,\ seq))$
>   **else** $smallest\ order\ (Insert'(b,\ seq))$
>   **fun** $rest\ order\ Empty'\ =\ $**raise** $rest$
> $\mid\ rest\ order\ (Insert'(a,\ Empty'))\ =\ Empty'$
> $\mid\ rest\ order\ (Insert'(a,\ Insert'(b,\ seq)))\ =$
>   **if** $order\ a\ b$
>   **then** $Insert'(b,\ rest\ order\ (Insert'(a,\ seq)))$
>   **else** $Insert'(a,\ rest\ order\ (Insert'(b,\ seq)))$
>   **fun** $isempty\ seq\ =\ seq = Empty'$
> **end**

This type is not free, since an ordered sequence can be constructed in several ways. For instance, $Insert\ (curry$ **op** $<)\ 3\ (Insert\ (curry$ **op** $<)\ 7\ Empty)$ and $Insert\ (curry$ **op** $<)\ 7\ (Insert\ (curry$ **op** $<)\ 3\ Empty)$ denote the same ordered sequence. In the implementation, all representations are valid. As canonical elements, you can use the data objects you get when you insert the elements in decreasing order according to the order relation.

Simplification at construction or selection

The given definition is one implementation of ordered sequences, a quite straightforward one. Let us now investigate its properties. Insertion is done in constant time, but selection uses linear time. Sorting at construction and not at selection reverses the situation.

abstype $'a\ ORDSEQ\ =\ Empty'\ \mid\ Insert'$ **of** $'a * 'a\ ORDSEQ$
with val $Empty\ =\ Empty'$
    fun $Insert\ order\ a\ Empty'\ =\ Insert'(a, Empty')$
      $\mid\ Insert\ order\ a\ (Insert'(b, seq))\ =$
          if $order\ a\ b$ **then** $Insert'(a, Insert'(b, seq))$
          else $Insert'(b, Insert\ order\ a\ seq)$
    exception $smallest$ **and** $rest$
    fun $smallest\ order\ Empty'\ =$ **raise** $smallest$
      $\mid\ smallest\ order\ (Insert'(a, \_))\ =\ a$
    fun $rest\ order\ Empty'\ =$ **raise** $rest$
      $\mid\ rest\ order\ (Insert'(\_, seq))\ =\ seq$
    fun $isempty\ seq\ =\ seq = Empty'$
end

Here, the order relation is used at construction and not at selection. We now face the important question whether the two implementations logically behave in the same way in all situations. Let us just give a very informal argument. In the first implementation you sort at selection and in the second implementation you sort at insertion. Since you use the same order relation, the two data types are the same; to be sure, however, you have to check many more details and look at different classes of order relations.

Since you order the objects at insertion in the last implementation, each abstract object has a unique representation. On the other hand, many concrete objects do not represent any abstract objects, that is, they are non-valid.

Exercises

21.2. Define a function $sort$ using ordered sequences. Some relations are of type "precedes", others of type "precedes or equals". Does it make any difference which you use when you sort?

21.3. Investigate the properties of sorting numbers with an order relation $shorter$, which is the relation $\leq$ on the number of digits in the numbers.

21.2.2 Sequential files

Files are used in most operating systems and are also available in many programming languages. A file is similar to a queue, since you insert elements at the end of the file. When you read a file, you scan the elements in order and keep track of the current position. Again, we will use $Empty$ and $Insert$ as concrete constructors. For keeping track of the current position when reading a file, we introduce a third constructor $Cursor$. A file containing the numbers 3, 7, and 9,

and with current position in front of the second element, will be represented by
$Insert(9, Cursor(Insert(7, Insert(3, Empty))))$.

The abstract operation *Rewrite* constructs an empty file, *Reset* sets the cursor
before the first element, *Put* appends an element at the end of the file provided
the cursor is at the end of the file, *get* retrieves the current element, *Advance* steps
the cursor to the next element, and *eof* tests if the cursor is at the end of the file.
Note that we consider *Reset* and *Advance* as constructors, since we have to use
them to get files where the cursor is not at the end of the file.

Hidden functions

When you try to implement this structure, you encounter a problem. You need
an auxiliary function to remove the cursor from a file when you reset it to the first
element, but this function shall not be seen outside the definition. Such a function
is called a *hidden* function and can be defined in a local declaration. It is a good
exercise to define this structure!!

```
abstype 'a FILE  =  Empty  |  Insert of 'a * 'a FILE  |
                    Cursor of 'a FILE
with  exception Put and Advance and get and Reset
      val  Rewrite  =  Cursor Empty
      fun  Put x (Cursor Empty)  =  Insert(x, Cursor Empty)
        |  Put x (Insert(y, f))  =  Insert(y, Put x f)
        |  Put _ _  =  raise Put
      fun  Advance (Cursor (Insert(x, f)))  =  Insert(x, Cursor f)
        |  Advance (Insert(x, f))  =  Insert(x, Advance f)
        |  Advance _  =  raise Advance
      local fun remove (Cursor f)  =  f
             |  remove (Insert(x, f))  =  Insert(x, remove f)
             |  remove _  =  raise Reset
      in fun Reset (Cursor f)  =  Cursor f
          |  Reset (Insert(x, f))  =  Cursor(Insert(x, remove f))
          |  Reset _  =  raise Reset
      end
      fun  get (Cursor (Insert(x, _)))  =  x
        |  get (Insert( _, f))  =  get f
        |  get _  =  raise get
      fun  eof (Cursor Empty)  =  true
        |  eof (Cursor _)  =  false
        |  eof (Insert( _, f))  =  eof f
end
```

Let us now verbally describe the implementation descriptors. In a *valid* representation, there must be exactly one *Cursor*. The *abstr* function is more complicated. The type is not free, since you can reset and advance the cursor in different ways and still get the same file. We can easily select canonical elements, though. If the cursor is at the end of the file, you can construct the file using only *Rewrite* and *Put*. Otherwise, you can first insert all elements using *Put*, then *Reset* the file, and, finally, *Advance* the cursor the right amount of steps.

The given implementation is inefficient, so let us define a better one. We can represent a file by two lists in such a way that the first list contains the scanned elements and the second list the elements to be scanned. When you advance the cursor, you move the first element of the second list to the front of the first list. Try to define this data type before you proceed!!

```
abstype 'a FILE  =  File of 'a list * 'a list
with  exception Put and Advance and get
      val   Rewrite  =  File(nil, nil)
      fun   Put x (File(xs, nil))  =  File(x :: xs, nil)
       |    Put x _  =  raise Put
      fun   Advance (File( _, nil))  =  raise Advance
       |    Advance (File(xs, y :: ys))  =  File(y :: xs, ys)
      fun   Reset (File(xs, ys))  =  File(nil, rev xs @ ys)
      fun   get (File( _, nil))  =  raise get
       |    get (File( _, y :: ys))  =  y
      fun   eof(File( _, ys)) = null ys
end
```

Convince yourself that this data type implements the same data type as the previous implementation!!

Exercises

21.4. The operation *back* moves the cursor one step backwards. Introduce it into the two implementations of files above.

21.5. In a *direct-access* file, you can read and write elements at any position in the file. You can also move the cursor to an arbitrary position in the file by giving the order number of the element you want to move to. To write at the end of the file, you first move the cursor to the position immediately after the file. As for ordinary files, a *Put* causes the cursor to move one step forwards. Implement such files.

21.3 Sets

For a sequence, you can talk about the first, the last, the second element, and so forth. Sometimes you want to consider collections of elements without the need to have them in sequence. A *set* is a collection of objects in which the number of occurrences of an object is insignificant. In a **bag**, on the other hand, the number of occurrences of an object is significant. The central operation on a set is to test whether an object is an element of the set or not. Other common operations are to form the *union* and *intersection* of sets.

We will first define a data type for sets with only the most essential operations and then extend this definition with other operations. We represent sets by lists without duplicates.

```
abstype 'a SET  =  Set of 'a list
with  val  Empty  =  Set nil
      fun  Insert e (Set es)  =
               if mem es e then Set es else Set (e :: es)
      fun  member (Set es) e  =  mem es e
      fun  union (Set es) (Set fs)  =
               Set(es @ filter(not o mem es) fs)
      fun  intersect (Set es) (Set fs)  =
               Set(filter(mem fs) es)
end
```

The definitions of set operations below are given as if they were defined within this type definition. Some of them can also be defined outside it, but not all of them.

Let us define a function *mkset* that creates a set of all elements in a list. (Remember that *reduce cons nil* is the identity function.)

```
−   fun mkset es  =  reduce Insert Empty es ;
>   val mkset  =  fn  :  'a list −> 'a SET
```

Note that duplicates will be removed by *Insert*.

Exercises

21.6. Add the operation *difference* to the implementation of sets above.

21.7. Implement sets using ordered lists. Some operations must now be given an order relation. Compare the time complexity of the operations with the previous version.

21.3.1   Set abstraction

In mathematics, sets are often formed by the use of set abstraction. In its simplest form, it defines a set by selecting all elements satisfying a given condition.

$$\{ x \mid P(x) \}$$

The expression is read: "The set of all elements x such that $P(x)$ is true". This definition leads to problems, however, since too little is said about from which set you can select elements. By telling which **universe** you work with, this problem is avoided. (The symbol $\wedge$ means conjunction.)

$$\{ x \mid x \in S \wedge P(x) \}$$

Let us define a corresponding operation which selects those elements of a set that satisfy a given condition. It is essentially the *filter* operation on lists.

```
   -  fun setfilter p (Set es) = Set(filter p es);
   >  val setfilter = fn : ('a -> bool) -> 'a SET -> 'a SET
```

The condition p can, of course, be any boolean expression containing both conjunctions and disjunctions. Another form of set abstraction uses a function for forming the set elements.

$$\{ f(x) \mid x \in S \}$$

The idea behind this expression is the same as that of *map* on lists.

```
   -  fun setmap f (Set es) = mkset(map f es);
   >  val setmap = fn : ('a -> 'b) -> 'a SET -> 'b SET
```

Yet another form of set abstraction forms those pairs of objects that satisfy a given condition. The elements of the pairs are taken from two sets.

$$\{ (x, y) \mid x \in S1 \wedge y \in S2 \wedge P(x, y) \}$$

One way to implement this form of set abstraction is to form all possible pairs and then filter out those satisfying the condition. If there are many elements in *S1* and *S2*, but few elements in the resulting set, much space is needed to form the list of all pairs. Therefore, we build the result list directly. We assume that the condition is given as a partially applicable function.

```
   -  fun pairabstr p (Set nil) _   =  Set nil
      |  pairabstr p (Set(x :: xs)) (Set ys) =
             let val Set xys  =  pairabstr p (Set xs) (Set ys)
             in Set(map (pair x) (filter (p x) ys) @ xys)
             end ;
   >  val pairabstr = fn : ('a -> 'b -> bool) ->
                           'a SET -> 'b SET -> ('a * 'b) SET
```

Exercises

21.8. Define an operation for triple abstraction.

21.3.2   Operations on finite sets

The implementation given above uses lists and thus implements finite sets only. All operations, however, can be used also for implementations of infinite sets, as will be described below. Let us now look at some useful operations that can be implemented only for finite sets, since they require that all elements in the set are inspected. The **cardinality** of a set is the number of elements in the set.

```
-  fun cardinality (Set es) =  len es;
>  val cardinality = fn : 'a SET -> int
```

Finite sets can also be compared for equality, if their elements can.

```
-  fun eqset (Set es) (Set fs) =  len es = len fs andalso
                                       conjl(map (mem fs) es);
>  val eqset = fn : 'a SET -> 'a SET -> bool
```

Quantifiers

Given a set and a condition, you sometimes pose the question whether all elements of the set satisfy the condition or whether there exists an element in the set that satisfies the condition. The symbols normally used are an upside down A (from *All*) and a reversed E (from *Exist*).

$$(\forall x \in S) \ P(x) \qquad\qquad (\exists x \in S) \ P(x)$$

The functions *forall* and *exists* can now be defined by mapping the condition on the elements in the set.

```
-  fun forall p (Set es) =  conjl(map p es);
>  val forall = fn : ('a -> bool) -> 'a SET -> bool
```

```
-  fun exists p (Set es) =  disjl(map p es);
>  val exists = fn : ('a -> bool) -> 'a SET -> bool
```

A problematic operation

Sometimes, you want an operation that gives you all elements of a set. A simple way of achieving this is to provide an operation *members* that yields a list of all elements of a given set. This operation, however, spoils the essential idea behind a set, namely that the order you insert the elements is immaterial. The *members* operation must list the elements of the set in some order, and this order may depend on how the set was constructed. Thus, two equal sets can give different lists of members. By using the implementation of sets with ordered sequences (Exercise 21.7), this problem is avoided. To pass an order relation to all operations complicates the code, and since we only use *members* to inspect sets at the end of a computation, we use an unsafe version.

> ```
> -   fun members (Set es) = es;
> >   val members = fn : 'a SET -> 'a list
> ```

Example: Egyptian triangles

Many problems can be specified using the different forms of set abstraction and quantification. By providing the *members* operation, you can print sets formed by *setmap*, *setfilter*, *pairabstr*, and other set operations. An Egyptian triangle is a right-angled triangle with integer sides. Let us specify the set of all Egyptian triangles with sides less than 10.

$$\{ (x, y, z) \mid x \in [1 \ldots 10] \land y \in [1 \ldots 10] \land x^2 + y^2 = z^2 \land z \in NAT \}$$

We compute only the smaller sides of the triangles, since the hypotenuses are derivable from them. We first define a predicate for the condition of being an Egyptian triangle.

> ```
> -   fun egypt x y = let val z = sqrt(real(x * x + y * y))
>                     in z == real(round z)
>                     end;
> >   val egypt = fn : int -> int -> bool
> ```

Using pair abstraction, we can now find all Egyptian triangles with sides less than 10.

> ```
> -   members(pairabstr egypt (mkset(1 -- 10)) (mkset(1 -- 10)));
>     [(3,4),(4,3),(6,8),(8,6)] : (int * int) list
> ```

This example shows a technique that can be used for many problems: specify a problem using set abstraction and then implement it with the set operations.

Exercises

21.9. Define *subset* that decides if one set is a subset of another set. A set is considered a subset of itself.

21.10. Define efficient versions of *forall* and *exists*. Are these versions in all respects equivalent to the implementations above?

21.11. Find all pairs of two-digit numerals such that the product of their corresponding numbers equals their product when you have reversed the digits of the numerals. For instance, $12 * 42 = 21 * 24$. Use the techniques described above.

21.12. Are there any numbers less than 1000 that are both prime numbers and perfect numbers (cf. Exercise 17.28)?

21.3.3   Sets as binary search trees

Using binary trees, the membership operation for sets can be performed in logarithmic time, which is considerably better than the linear time required for the list implementation. A requirement is that you can totally order the elements of the set. We use labelled binary trees and store the elements of the set in the nodes of the tree in such a way that the inorder listing of the elements is sorted.

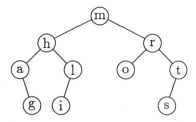

If you, for instance, want to test if "o" is a member of the set represented by the tree above, you start comparing it with the root element. Since "o" is greater than "m" (in alphabetical order), you go to the right and compare "o" with "r". Now you have to go left and, since you now find a node with the element "o", "o" belongs to the set. If you come to a tip, the element does not belong to the set.

The insertion order is essential. When you insert, you do the same search as when you look up, and when you come to a tip, you replace it by a node with the element to be inserted. If the element already occurs in the tree, you do nothing. In the tree in the figure, "m" was inserted first. A possible insertion sequence for the tree is "mhaglirots", but other sequences lead to the same tree.

Let us implement sets as binary search trees. To simplify, we assume that the elements are integers. In the general case, you have to give a comparison function as argument as was done for ordered sequences.

```
abstype SET = Set of int BT1
with  val  Empty  =  Set Tip
      local fun insert' i Tip  =  Node(i, Tip, Tip)
            | insert' i (t as Node(i', l, r))  =
                  if i = i' then t
                  else if i < i' then Node(i', insert' i l, r)
                  else Node(i', l, insert' i r)
```

in fun *Insert i (Set t)* =   *Set(insert' i t)*
end
fun *member (Set Tip) i* =   *false*
    | *member (Set(Node(i', l, r))) i* =
         if $i = i'$ **then** *true*
         else if $i < i'$ **then** *member (Set l) i*
         else *member (Set r) i*
end

The average search time depends strongly on the shape of the tree. If the tree is balanced, the time for both insertion and lookup is logarithmic. If you insert the elements in sorted order, however, the resulting tree degenerates to a "list", and the search time is linear instead. To avoid unbalanced trees, you can reorder the tree at insertion so that it remains balanced.

Exercises

21.13. What changes are needed to the definition of sets with binary search trees to handle objects of arbitrary type? Define the *union* operation for this definition. You are allowed to use the *members* operation.

21.14. Assume the sets represented as binary search trees can contain elements of arbitrary type. Define a function *sort* by defining a *members* operation. Compare with Exercise 21.2. What is the time complexity?

21.3.4   Infinite sets

In some applications, you want to work with infinite sets. At first, it may seem impossible to represent infinite sets. Remember, however, that a definition of a function with an infinite domain is a finite description of an infinite set of computations. The idea behind the representation of infinite sets is to use a boolean function to represent the set of all elements for which the function yields *true* as result. For instance, the predicate *even* can be used as a representation of the set of even numbers and *prime* of the set of prime numbers. In set theory, you call such a function the **characteristic** function of the set.

The definition of the operations on sets using functions turns out to be astonishingly simple. An empty set is represented by a function that always gives the value *false*. To check if an element belongs to a set, you simply apply the representation function to that element. The union operation is implemented using conjunction and the intersection using disjunction. The *set_of* operation makes it possible to start with an infinite set like the prime numbers and then continue to manipulate it with the other operations. The complement of a set is the set of elements not belonging to the type.

```
abstype 'a SET  =  Set of 'a ->  bool
with  val  Empty  =  Set(fn e =>  false)
      fun  Insert e (Set f)  =  Set(fn x =>  e = x orelse f x)
      fun  member (Set f) e  =  f e
      fun  union (Set f) (Set g)  =  Set(fn x =>  f x orelse g x)
      fun  intersect (Set f) (Set g)  =  Set(fn x =>  f x andalso g x)
      fun  set_of p  =  Set p
      fun  complement (Set f)  =  Set(not o f)
end
```

The reason for the extreme simplicity is, of course, the close correspondence between a set and its characteristic function. With this representation of sets, operations like *eqset*, *cardinality*, and *members* cannot be defined, though.

The use of functions for the representation of infinite data objects is a further indication of the power of functions. As has been said before, functions can be used to represent all other types of data objects.

Exercises

21.15. Define the operations *difference* and *setfilter* for infinite sets. What can be said about the time complexity of these and the other operations?

21.3.5   Relations

There are several standard relations in ML like $<$ and $=$. Associated with such relations are boolean functions taking pairs as arguments.

```
-  (op <) (7, 3);
   false : bool
```

Since any boolean function can be regarded as a characteristic function, there must exist some set corresponding to the function. As the function takes pairs as arguments, the set is a set of pairs. This is to be expected, since a binary *relation* by definition is a set of pairs. The *less than* relation, for instance, is the infinite set of pairs

$$\{(0,1), (0,2), (1,2), (0,3), (1,3), (2,3), (0,4), \ldots\}$$

Infinite relations can be represented by functions in the same way as infinite sets. In fact, we can use infinite sets to implement relations.

```
-  val lt = set_of (op < : int * int -> bool);
>  val lt = - : (int * int) SET
```

```
-   member lt (2,3);
    true : bool
```

Since the complement operation is defined on sets represented by functions, we can now define the *greater than or equal* relation.

```
-   val gte = complement lt;
>   val gte = - : (int * int) SET
```

Also the union and intersection of relations are meaningful.

```
-   val universal = union lt gte;
>   val universal = - : (int * int) SET

-   val eq = intersect (set_of (op <=)) gte;
>   val eq = - : (int * int) SET
```

The **universal** relation holds for all pairs, that is, it corresponds to the everywhere true function.

Finite relations

The use of functions is required when representing infinite sets or relations, but in many applications you want operations that can be defined only for finite sets. Let us therefore define finite binary relations represented by lists of pairs.

```
abstype ('a,'b) REL = Rel of ('a * 'b) list
with   val Empty = Rel nil
       fun Insert p (Rel ps) =
               Rel(if mem ps p then ps else p :: ps)
       fun related (Rel ps) x y = mem ps (x, y)
       fun relset (Rel ps) = mkset ps
       fun domain (Rel ps) = mkset(map fst ps)
       fun range (Rel ps) = mkset(map snd ps)
       fun inverse (Rel ps) = Rel(map swap ps)
end
```

For relations, the membership operation is called *related*, since it tests if two objects are related under the given relation. Many operations like *union, intersection, forall,* and *exists* can be defined in the same way as for sets. In fact, it is fully possible to use sets to implement relations, as a relation is a set.

The *domain* of a binary relation is the set of all first components of the pairs of the relation, and the *range* is the set of all the second components. The *inverse* of a binary relation is the set of all pairs, in which the first and second components have been exchanged. For example, the *less than* relation is the inverse of the *greater than* relation, but the *less than or equal* relation is its complement.

Equivalence relations

Let us now consider binary relations whose first and second components have the same type. We define the **base set** of such a relation to be the union of its domain and the range. A relation is said to be **reflexive**, if all elements in the base set are related to themselves. A relation is said to be **symmetric**, if for all x and y that are related, y and x are also related. A relation is said to be **transitive**, if for all x, y, and z such that x is related to y, and y is related to z, x is also related to z. You can define three predicates that test if a finite relation is reflexive, symmetric, and transitive, respectively. A relation that satisfies all these three properties is said to be an **equivalence** relation. Such a relation always partitions a set into equivalence classes, that is, subsets in which all elements are equivalent under the relation. The classes are *disjoint*, that is, they have no elements in common. Note the similarity to quotient types: a type is a set, and it is partitioned by any equivalence relation into a quotient type. Let us define an operation that partitions a finite set (represented as a list without duplicates) into equivalence classes given an equivalence relation. The result is a list of lists.

```
fun refl r    =  forall (fn x => related r x x)
                      (union (domain r) (range r)) ;
fun symm r =  forall (fn (x, y) => related r y x) (relset r);
fun trans r =  forall (fn (x, y) => forall (fn (z, w) =>
                  y <> z orelse related r x w) (relset r)) (relset r);
exception partition;
local fun  part eq nil = nil
      |  part eq (x :: xs) =
          (x :: (filter (eq x) xs)) :: part eq (filter (not o eq x) xs)
in fun partition eq s  =
              if not(refl eq andalso symm eq andalso trans eq)
              then raise partition
              else part (related eq) s
end
```

```
—  partition (reduce Insert Empty [(1, 1), (2, 2), (3, 3), (4, 4), (1, 2), (2, 1)])
              (0 −− 4);
  [[1, 2], [3], [4]] : int list list
```

The elements 1 and 2 are equivalent under this relation, since both (1,2) and (2,1) belongs to the relation.

Exercises

21.16. Relations can be composed in a similar way as functions. Define an operation *compose* for finite relations.

21.17. An order relation must be transitive. You get the *transitive closure* of a relation *r* by repeatedly adding all pairs (x, z) such that *related r x y* and *related r y z* for some *y*, until no more pairs can be added. For instance, to a relation with pairs $[(1,2),(2,3),(3,4)]$ you add $(1,3)$ and $(2,4)$ in the first iteration and $(1,4)$ in the second; no more iterations are then needed. Define a function for computing the transitive closure of a relation.

21.18. What changes are needed to the definition above to handle *n*-ary relations for any *n*. Can you give an example of a ternary relation?

21.3.6   Tables and finite mappings

In set theory, a function is defined as a special kind of relation, in which no two pairs have the same first component. This restriction is needed in order to guarantee the uniqueness of a function for a given argument. Functions with finite domains can be represented in other ways than by function expressions. A *table* is a finite mapping from some type of key to some data associated with the key. When you view a table as a function, the key is the argument to the function and the associated data its result. The operation of looking up in a table is the same as applying a function to an argument.

It is illustrative to compare different implementations of tables with respect to the efficiency of the operations. In an implementation with lists of pairs, table lookup has linear time complexity, which is bad for large tables. It does not help much to sort the entries. Another implementation is to define tables with functions from keys to the information in the table.

```
abstype ('a, 'b) TABLE  =  Table of 'a -> 'b
with   val Empty  =  Table(fn x => raise lookup)
       fun Insert key info (Table f) =
             Table(fn x => if x = key then info else f x)
       fun delete key (Table f) =
             Table(fn x => if x = key then raise lookup else f x)
       fun lookup key (Table f)  =  f key
       fun mktab f  =  Table f
end
```

We have here added a function *mktab* that constructs a table given any function. This makes it possible to start with an infinite table. The *Insert* operation constructs a new function object for each insertion. A sequence of insertions therefore leads to a sequence of function objects, which is similar to a list. Table lookup will therefore have linear time complexity, unless you use *mktab*, in which case it may be considerably faster; no search is then needed.

Using binary search trees, you can implement tables so that both insertion and lookup use only logarithmic time. The implementation is essentially the same as the one for sets using binary search trees (page 311).

Exercises

21.19. Describe how binary search trees can be used to implement tables.

21.3.7   Graphs

A graph is really a pictorial representation of a relation. Hence, a *graph* can be defined as a base set and a relation over that set. To each element in the base set, there is a node in the graph. In a *directed graph*, there is an **arc** from node *a* to node *b* if and only if *a* is related to *b*. Pictorially, you draw an arc as an arrow between the two nodes. A binary tree is an example of a directed graph. An *undirected graph* corresponds to a symmetric relation, where you replace two inverse arcs between two nodes by one undirected **edge**. The directed graphs are most common in computer science, however.

There are several ways of representing graphs. The obvious one is to use one of the implementations of relations above. However, many operations on graphs then become extremely inefficient. The best implementations of graphs use so called *arrays*, but they are not a part of ML[1]. As a substitute, you can use tables implemented with balanced binary search trees.

A node *a* is *adjacent* to *b* if there is an arc (edge) from *a* to *b*. An *adjacency list* is a list of all nodes adjacent to a given node. A graph can also be represented by a table with node names as keys and adjacency lists as associated data. Usually, you represent nodes by small positive integers.

Summary

Abstract data types are used both to hide representations and to define non-regular data types. Here is a procedure for defining them in a program.

Abstraction. Investigate your application and try to find its inherent properties. Abstract from details and identify useful data types. This phase is the most important in a programming project and can be very time-consuming. Never stop until the abstractions and types really suit the application.

Specification. Specify your data types in detail. You may use equations to specify the operations. Convince yourself that the specification describes what you want, that is, *validate* it.

---

[1]Work is going on to include them as an extension, though.

Properties. Investigate the logical properties of each type. Is it regular? If not, is it free or non-free? Does it have nice algebraic properties? If not, can you redefine it in a better way?

Implementation. Define abstract data types in ML.

Implementation descriptors. Define or describe the implementation descriptors *valid* and *abstr*.

Correctness. Prove or convince yourself that the implementation satisfies the specification, that is, *verify* it.

Efficiency. Is the implementation efficient enough? What is the time and space complexity of the operations? If efficiency is critical, try to find a more efficient implementation and repeat the last three steps above.

Exercises

21.20. Big integers can be implemented by lists of digits. Define an abstract data type for big integers providing the ordinary arithmetic operations. This implementation is not efficient. Can you make it more efficient?

21.21. Implement lists using functions. The representation is a pair of an integer and a function. The integer is the number of elements in the list, and the function yields the *i*th element when applied to *i*. Implement the five ordinary operations and the *len* and *append* functions. Also define an operation which allows you to give a number and a function and get a list in this representation.

21.22. Specify bags and then implement them using functions. Replace the membership function for sets by a function giving the number of times an element occurs. What is the reasonable interpretation of *union* and *intersection* for bags?

21.23.* Define an abstract data type for rational numbers with operations for creating rational numbers and for doing arithmetic and comparisons. A straightforward implementation is to use pairs of integers. A better representation, however, is to use a canonical form of rational numbers, where the numbers in the pairs never have common factors and where the first, but never the second, component can be negative. What are the advantages with this representation?

21.24.* In interval arithmetic, the arithmetic operations are defined on intervals of the real number axis. If you perform an operation on two intervals, the resulting interval is the one containing all numbers you can get as result by using any pair of numbers in the argument intervals. Define a data type for interval arithmetic.

21.25.* In the last section of Chapter 20, a data type *EXPR* is defined. In Exercise 20.35, a function *simplify* was defined. An alternative way of performing simplification of expressions is to introduce new constructors, which perform the simplifications directly when an expression is constructed. Define these operations and use them for defining the function *diff*.

21.26. Redefine the *Insert* function for sets represented as binary search trees so that the trees are kept balanced after an insertion. This usually requires a reorganization of the tree. The height of subtrees may differ by one at most.

21.27. Define an abstract data type for representing polynomials and then define operations for adding and multiplying them.

21.28. Define an abstract data type for handling BNF grammars. You need functions for building and printing them. Can you define a function that generates the corresponding data type definition in ML (the abstract syntax) in the form of a string? Can you even derive the definition of appropriate print functions?

21.29. For this exercise, you may want to consult some book describing graphs in more detail. Implement graphs as lists of pairs (relations) or as tables with nodes as keys and adjacency lists as associated data. Define a suitable set of basic operations. Then, define functions corresponding to the following concepts. A graph contains a *cycle* if there is a path from a node back to itself. A graph is *connected* if you can go from any node in the graph to any other node by following arcs (edges). A *Hamiltonian circuit* is a cycle which visits each node exactly once. An *Eulerian circuit* is a cycle that uses each arc (edge) exactly once. The *shortest path length* between two given nodes is the length of the shortest of all paths between the two nodes.

Chapter 22

Input and Output

In an imperative language, input and output commands are a necessity. They allow you to input data from and output data to files and terminals. In an interactive environment, as provided by an ML system, you can often do without them. There are occasions, however, when a more traditional mode of working is to be preferred. When you work with large data sets, you want to store data in and retrieve data from the file system of your computer. When you want an interactive program, you need a program that communicates with the terminal during the execution. Examples are game playing programs, editors, command interpreters, and monitors of various kinds.

The I/O (Input/Output) commands in ML are not functional. When you use them, you loose the important property of *referential transparency*, which guarantees that an expression has the same value wherever it occurs within a fixed context in a program. If a language is referentially transparent, an expression like $f(1) = f(1)$ always has the value *true*, provided the computation terminates. In most languages, ML included, this is not certain. For instance, the ML expression $input(std\_in, 1) = input(std\_in, 1)$ is true if you input two equal characters, otherwise it is false. An input command has a *side-effect*: it changes something in the environment, and when you perform the same command again, it may well give another result. Since it is more difficult to reason about programs without the referential transparency property, you should try to isolate the non-functional parts as much as possible. Functions which have or can give rise to side-effects will be called *commands* below, since they are not functions in the mathematical sense.

Streams

The word "stream" usually denotes a continuous flow of objects like a water stream or a stream of words. A stream is potentially infinite, in contrast to a sequence or list that is finite. In ML, you use streams of characters for input and output.

320

You can think of them as lists of characters that potentially can be infinitely long. There are two types of streams: input streams and output streams. If you want a program that inputs data from the outside world, you need a *producer* of data from which you can consume them. The producer can be an existing file in the file system, another program, a data communication link, or the like. If you give the name of some producer to the *open_in* command, you get an input stream from which you can input characters. Thus, a stream in ML is an abstract concept that captures the essential properties of a producer.

In the same way you can connect an ML program to a *consumer* that consumes the data you output. Like the producer, the consumer can be a file, a program, etc. To connect a program to a consumer you use the *open_out* command.

When you start running an ML program, it is connected to your keyboard through the standard input stream *std_in* and to your screen through the standard output stream *std_out*; the keyboard is the standard producer and the screen the standard consumer. Consequently, you can communicate with the terminal without opening any streams.

22.1 Standard Input and Output Commands

If you want to input n characters from an input stream s, you use the command $input(s, n)$. The result is a string, normally of size n. If there are less than n characters left in the input stream, you get those that are left[1]. To check if you have reached the end of a stream, you can use the *end_of_stream* operation, which yields *true* only if you have consumed the whole stream. Sometimes, you want to look at the first character of a stream without consuming it. The *lookahead* operation yields the next character of a stream, but leaves the stream unchanged. If you have reached the end of the stream, the *null* string is returned. To output a string x on a stream s, you perform the command $output(s, n)$.

Any time you perform an I/O command that is not valid, the exception *io_failure* will be raised. The type of this exception is not *unit* as our previous exceptions, but *string*. The string associated with the exception tells you about the error. If you, for instance, try to open a file *myfile* which does not exist, the string "Cannot open myfile" will be associated with the exception.

Example: An echo command

Let us write a program that echoes every character it consumes. The echoing shall stop when a period is encountered. The program is best written as a recursive

---

[1] If your program is connected to a producer, which may produce data at a later point, your program will be put to wait until n characters are available.

function, which on each recursive application echoes one character. It cannot work completely as an ordinary recursive function, however.

In the *echo* program, you first want to output a character and then continue echoing. You can then use a *sequence* expression, which is a sequence of expressions separated by semicolon and surrounded by parentheses. Its value is the value of its last expression. The preceding expressions are evaluated because they have side-effects; otherwise, it would be pointless to evaluate them.

The *echo* command is performed solely for the I/O commands it performs, but since a function must have some argument and yield some result, we use the hermit {} or () of type *unit* for both purposes.

> $-$ **fun** *echo* () $=$ **if** *lookahead std_in* $=$ ".".
>   **then** ()
>   **else** (*output*(*std_out*, *input*(*std_in*, 1));
>   *echo*()) ;
> $>$ **val** *echo* $=$ **fn** : *unit* $->$ *unit*

This function is programmed in a non-functional style. The reason is that the I/O commands are non-functional.

Opening and closing streams

The standard I/O streams can be used without opening them; they are opened by the system. If you want to connect your program to any other file in the file system, you have to open it before you can use it. The result of opening a file is a stream.

> $-$ **val** *infile1* $=$ *open_in* "salaries" ;
> $>$ **val** *infile1* $=$ $-$: *instream*

> $-$ **val** *outfile1* $=$ *open_out* "newsalaries" ;
> $>$ **val** *outfile1* $=$ $-$: *outstream*

A value of type *stream* is printed as a hyphen, exactly as abstract values are. Note that "salaries" is the name of a real, physical file, but *infile1* is the name you use when you want to refer to that file. Such a logical file name can be bound to different physical files at different executions of a program or even at different points in a program.

Let us define a command for copying a file to another file and then use it to copy "salaries" to "newsalaries". Copying is similar to echoing, but the input stream is consumed until the end of the stream is reached.

— **fun** *copy infile outfile* = **if** *end_of_stream infile*
                                    then ()
                                    else (*output*(*outfile, input*(*infile,* 1)));
                                          copy infile outfile);
> **val** *copy* = **fn** : *instream* −> *outstream* −> *unit*

— *copy infile1 outfile1* ;
    () : *unit*

Streams can also be closed, but normally closing is performed automatically by the ML system. If you want to reuse a file for a different purpose in a program, you can close it and then open it again. For instance, you may produce a temporary file in the first part of a program and then consume in the last part.

— *close_out outfile1* ;
    () : *unit*

— **val** *infile2* = *open_in* "newsalaries" ;
> **val** *infile2* = − : *instream*

The commands described above are those that every ML system should provide as a standard. Most systems will provide more commands. They are not part of the kernel of ML, but of your particular implementation of ML. You have to consult your local manual to find out which they are.

Exercises

22.1. Change *copy* so that 80 characters are input and output each time.

22.2   Input and Output of Data Objects

All I/O commands process strings. When you work interactively in the normal way, you can input and output objects of almost any type. Let us therefore define a set of commands which provides more flexible I/O than the standard ones, which only allow I/O of strings. When you extend a language with a set of operations for some application, you should select them to obtain both generality and ease of use. In ML, most data objects are written in the same way in a program and on your screen when they are input or output. One alternative is to use the same format also when you communicate over streams. Then, there is only one format to learn, and you can use the different I/O commands interchangeably. Another desired property is that input and output commands should be symmetrical; they should be the inverses of each other.

A critical choice when defining an input command is how far you shall read before stopping. Using the *lookahead* command, you can look at the next character without consuming it. We therefore introduce the convention that the input commands consume as few characters as possible. To be able to use an arbitrary stream in a command, the stream is passed as argument.

In an ML program, you can put space, tabulation, and new-line characters between data objects and delimiters. Since this opportunity provides a simplification for the user, we define a command that consumes the longest sequence of any of these characters.

```
-  fun skip s = if lookahead s  =  " "  orelse
                   lookahead s  =  "\t"  orelse
                   lookahead s  =  "\n"
               then (input(s, 1);
                       skip s)
               else ();
>  val skip = fn : instream -> unit
```

Let us next define I/O commands for some data types. To input a number, we first have to check if the number to be input is negative. Then we consume characters as long as they are digits.

```
exception getint;
-  local fun getint' s n =
              if digit(lookahead s)
              then getint' s (10 * n + digitval(input(s, 1)))
              else n
          fun getposint s  =  if digit(lookahead s) then getint' s 0
                              else raise getint
    in fun getint s  =  (skip s;
                         if lookahead s  =  " ~ "
                         then (input(s, 1);
                               ~(getposint s))
                         else getposint s)
    end;
>  val getint  =  fn : instream -> int
```

Note that an exception is raised if there are no digits or a single ˜. To output an integer, you can use the *makestring* function.

```
-  fun putint s (n : int) = output(s, makestring n);
>  val putint = fn : outstream -> int -> unit
```

Let us now turn to compound data objects. The problem with these is that the components can be of any type. The solution is to pass suitable I/O commands as arguments. To input a pair, two input commands are needed. When inputting a pair, it must be checked that it contains parentheses and a comma at the right place. For this purpose, we define a command *have* that consumes the next character if it is equal to its argument and raises an exception otherwise.

```
      exception have;
   —  fun have s c  =  if c = lookahead s then input(s, 1)
                        else  (output(std_out,"Did not get " ^ c);
                              raise have);
   >  val have  =  fn : instream —> string —> string

   —  fun getpair get1 get2 s  =  (skip s;
                                   have s "(";
                                   let val e1  =  get1 s
                                   in skip s;
                                      have s ",";
                                      let val e2  =  get2 s
                                      in skip s;
                                         have s ")";
                                         (e1, e2)
                                      end
                                   end);
   >  val getpair = fn :
      (instream —> 'a) —> (instream —> 'b) —> instream —> 'a * 'b
```

Note that parentheses can be omitted around sequence expressions in local declarations.

Let us finally define a command for outputting a list. It takes a command for outputting the individual elements as argument.

```
   —  local fun  putlist' put s nil          = ()
                | putlist' put s (x :: nil)  =  put s x
                | putlist' put s (x :: xs)   =  ( put s x;
                                                 output(s,",");
                                                 putlist' put s xs)
      in fun putlist put s xs  =  ( output(s,"[");
                                    putlist' put s xs;
                                    output(s,"]"))
      end;
   >  val putlist = fn :
      (outstream —> 'a —> unit) —> outstream —> 'a list —> unit
```

Exercises

22.2. Define *putint* without using *makestring*. Next, define *putpair*.

22.3. Define the command *getstring* for reading a string within quotes and the command *getlist* for reading lists on square bracket form. Assume that strings do not contain escape sequences.

22.4. Define *putmatrix* that prints matrices represented by lists of lists.

22.3   Example: A Vocabulary Examiner

Let us now put to use many of the described techniques and construct a program that can examine a person's knowledge of words in a foreign language. The program keeps a lexicon and picks words at random out of it. The program will contain a command interpreter which accepts the following commands:

- *Add*: After this command the program reads two words and adds them to the lexicon. The first word is the word to be questioned, and the second word is the correct translation.

- *Remove*: The program reads one word. The corresponding pair is removed from the lexicon.

- *Ask*: The program prints a word at random, inputs your answer, and tells you if your translation was right.

- *Statistics*: The program prints the number of right answers and the total number of words examined.

- *Restart*: The program starts counting from zero again.

- *Store*: The program reads a file name and stores the lexicon in that file.

- *Load*: The program reads a file name and replaces the current lexicon with the contents of the named file.

- *Help*: The program prints helpful information about how to use it.

- *Stop*: The program stops.

The specification describes a simple examination program. You can surely think of other features you would like, for instance, examination in both directions, repetition of words not correctly translated, etc. In general, it is better to start with a simple version of a program and get it working; then, you can add more advanced features.

A command interpreter

When you are posed with a big problem, you should try to examine it and find parts which can be handled separately—you should try to decompose the problem. The present problem consists really of three parts: the interpretation of commands, the examination of words, and the communication with the terminal and the file system.

Almost all interactive programs contain one part for handling commands. Therefore, we first try to *abstract* from individual interactive programs and define a command interpreter for general use. Such an interpreter can be included in a library and used in many different applications.

First, we have to find the essential parts of a command interpreter. For each command, you manipulate some state and get a new state, which is manipulated by the next command. A command interpreter is therefore iterative in nature. It takes a start *state*, which is manipulated by different commands until a stop command is encountered. We assume that the manipulation of a state is performed by a function called *do_cmd*. This function must also compute the result to be printed after the command is performed, so the result of *do_cmd* must be a pair. We further assume that the function *nextcmd* consumes the next command from the standard input, that *printreply* prints the obtained result, and that *prompt* is the symbol to be printed when the system is ready to accept a command. The structure of the command interpreter is quite similar to that of the *echo* program.

```
—   fun cmdint isstop do_cmd state nextcmd printreply prompt =
        (output(std_out, "\n" ^ prompt);
       let val cmd = nextcmd()
       in  if isstop cmd then ()
            else let  val (result, newstate) = do_cmd cmd state
                 in  (printreply result;
                          cmdint isstop do_cmd newstate nextcmd
                               printreply prompt)
                 end
       end);
>  val cmdint = fn : ('a -> bool) -> ('a -> 'b -> 'c * 'b) ->
        'b -> (unit -> 'a) -> ('c -> 'd) -> string -> unit
```

The function *cmdint* captures what is common to command interpreters. By applying it to suitable arguments, you specialize it to a particular application.

The structure of the vocabulary examiner

In addition to the command interpreter, the main modules in the program are an abstract data type *LEXICON* handling the lexicon, an abstract data type *REPLY* for printing the system replies to commands, and an abstract data type *COMMAND* for reading and interpreting commands. One part of the *COMMAND* type is an abstract data type *STATE* with the function *do_cmd* for the execution of commands.

fun *cmdint isstop do_cmd state nextcmd printreply prompt* = ...
local abstype *LEXICON* = ...
    with fun *getlexicon file* = ...
        fun *putlexicon file lex* = ...
        ...
    end
    abstype *REPLY* = ...
    with fun *printreply reply* = ...
        ...
    end
    abstype *COMMAND* = ...
    with abstype *STATE* = ...
        with fun *do_cmd cmd state* = ...
        ...
        end
        fun *isstop* = ...
        fun *nextcmd* () = ...
        ...
    end
in fun *startexam seed* = *cmdint isstop do_cmd (Initstate seed)*
                       nextcmd printreply "− > "
end

The whole program is shown on page 330 and in it you will find the details of what is described below. It is given in the way it is typed on a terminal.

The lexicon

The lexicon is nothing but a table with some added operations. Constructors are *Emptylex* and *Insertlex*. Selectors are *deletelex* and *ask*, which selects an entry at random using a random number generator and then questions a word. Its result is a truth value telling if the answer was correct or not. The additional operations are *getlexicon*, which reads a lexicon from a file and *putlexicon*, which writes a lexicon to a file. Outside the *LEXICON* module, you see neither how lexicons are represented internally nor on files. Hence, you can easily change these representations at a later stage.

The type of commands and replies

Commands were described informally in the specification of the problem. We now have to decide both how you type commands on your keyboard and how you represent them in ML. For the latter, we use a union type with one constructor for each command. Those commands that take extra arguments will be represented by compound objects. A problem arises with the ask command, since you do not give your answer until the system has questioned you a word. Consequently, the answer cannot be given as argument to the *Ask* constructor. Instead, you have to treat it separately.

$$
\begin{aligned}
\textbf{abstype } COMMAND \;=\; & Add \textbf{ of } string * string \;\mid\; Remove \textbf{ of } string \\
\mid\; & Ask \;\mid\; Statistics \;\mid\; Restart \\
\mid\; & Store \textbf{ of } string \;\mid\; Load \textbf{ of } string \\
\mid\; & Help \;\mid\; Stop
\end{aligned}
$$

with ...

Next, we have to define the type of the replies. To most commands, the system remains silent, which we represent by the constructor *Empty*. After *Ask*, however, you are told if your *Answer* was correct or wrong, and after *Statistics* you are told your achievements.

$$
\begin{aligned}
\textbf{abstype } REPLY \;=\; & Empty \;\mid\; Answer \textbf{ of } bool \\
\mid\; & Stat \textbf{ of } int * int \;\mid\; Inform
\end{aligned}
$$

with ...

The *Inform* reply is used when the user wants help.

Concrete and abstract syntax

We have now defined suitable types for handling commands and replies. These data objects capture the essential properties of what you type in and what you see on the screen, but we have to decide what you really type and see. You want a command to be short to save time when you use the program. You also want it to be self-explanatory and easy to remember, which may require it to be a bit longer. Between these conflicting requirements we choose here single character commands for simplicity.

+	Store	−	Remove
?	Ask	!	Statistics
<	Load	>	Save
0	Restart	.	Stop

To simplify further, we require that all strings are given within string quotes. The described syntax is one of many possible choices of a *concrete syntax* of commands. The type definition of commands given above is a description of their *abstract syntax* (cf. Section 20.4). Whatever concrete syntax you choose, you can use the same type definition.

If you make your program largely independent of the concrete syntax, it is easy to change it by changing only a small part of the program. In the program, the only functions that are concerned with communication with the terminal and the file system are *nextcmd* for reading commands, *printreply* for printing replies, *ask* for asking for an answer to a question, *getlexicon*, and *putlexicon*. All other functions are independent of the concrete syntax.

Transforming the current state

The command interpreter is an iterative command, which means that it successively transforms some state. There are two main components of the state in the vocabulary examiner: the current lexicon and the statistics counters. The operation *ask* in the type *LEXICON* needs a seed for the random number generator, so we also include a seed in the state.

The function *do_cmd* takes a *COMMAND* and a *STATE* as argument and yields a *REPLY* and the new *STATE* as result, that is, it yields a pair. It can receive any command but a stop command, which is taken care of by the command interpreter.

To use the program, we use the function *startexam*, which is the only function exported from the local declaration in the program. To be able to make the examiner behave differently at different executions, an initial seed is given to *startexam* as argument.

The whole program

```
fun cmdint isstop do_cmd state nextcmd printreply prompt =
  (output(std_out, "\n" ^ prompt);
   let val cmd = nextcmd ()
   in if isstop cmd then ()
      else let val (result, newstate) = do_cmd cmd state
           in (printreply result;
                 cmdint isstop do_cmd newstate nextcmd printreply prompt)
           end
   end);
(* This vocabulary examiner is based on four abstract data types:    *)
(* LEXICON, REPLY, STATE, and COMMAND. STATE is local to COMMAND     *)
(* in order to allow pattern matching in the function do_cmd         *)
(* against the constructors of the COMMAND type.                     *)
(* The exported function startexam lets you use the examiner.        *)
```

```
local

  abstype LEXICON = Lexicon of (string * string) list
  with fun getlexicon file = Lexicon(getlist(getpair getstring getstring)
                                             (open_in file))
       fun putlexicon file (Lexicon ps) =
               putlist (putpair putstring putstring) (open_out file) ps
       val Emptylex = Lexicon nil
       fun Insertlex (w, w') lex = let val (Lexicon ps) = deletelex w lex
                                   in Lexicon((w, w')::ps)
                                   end
       and deletelex w (Lexicon nil) = Lexicon nil
         | deletelex w (Lexicon ((w', w'')::ps)) =
               if w=w' then Lexicon ps
               else Insertlex (w', w'') (deletelex w (Lexicon ps))
       fun ask seed (Lexicon ps) =
               let val (w1,w2) = index (randint 1 (len ps) seed) ps
               in (output(std_out, w1 ^ "==>");
                   getstring std_in = w2)
               end
  end  (* LEXICON *)




  abstype REPLY = Empty' | Answer' of bool | Stat' of int * int | Inform'
  with val Empty  = Empty'
       val Answer = Answer'
       val Stat   = Stat'
       val Inform = Inform'

       fun printreply Empty' = ()
         | printreply (Answer' correct) =
               output (std_out, if correct then "correct" else "wrong")
         | printreply (Stat'(total, correct)) = output(std_out,
               makestring correct ^ " out of " ^ makestring total)
         | printreply Inform' = output(std_out,
               "+ Add\n"        ^ "- Remove\n" ^ "? Ask\n"   ^
               "! Statistics\n" ^ "0 Restart\n" ^ "> Store\n" ^
               "< Load\n"       ^ ". Stop\n"    ^ "* Help"    )
  end  (* REPLY *)
```

```
abstype COMMAND = Add of string * string | Remove of string
                | Ask                     | Statistics
                | Restart                 | Store of string
                | Load of string          | Help
                | Stop
with
    abstype STATE = State of (int * int) * real * LEXICON
    with
        fun Initstate seed = State((0, 0), seed, Emptylex)
        fun do_cmd cmd (state as State(stat, seed, lex)) =
            case cmd of
                Add(w1,w2) => (Empty, State(stat,seed,Insertlex (w1,w2) lex))
              | Remove w   => (Empty, State(stat,seed,deletelex w lex))
              | Ask        => let val correct = ask seed lex
                                in (Answer correct,State((fst stat+1, snd stat+
                                    if correct then 1 else 0), random seed,lex))
                                end
              | Statistics => (Stat stat, state)
              | Restart    => (Empty, State((0, 0), seed, lex))
              | Store file => (putlexicon file lex;
                                 (Empty, state))
              | Load file  => (Empty, State(stat, seed, getlexicon file))
              | Help       => (Inform, state)
    end   (* STATE *)

    fun isstop Stop = true
      | isstop _    = false
    fun nextcmd () =
        (skip std_in;
            case input(std_in, 1) of
                "+" => Add(getstring std_in, getstring std_in)
              | "-" => Remove(getstring std_in)
              | "?" => Ask
              | "!" => Statistics
              | "0" => Restart
              | ">" => Store(getstring std_in)
              | "<" => Load(getstring std_in)
              | "." => Stop
              | _   => Help)
end   (* COMMAND *)
in
    fun startexam seed =
            cmdint isstop do_cmd (Initstate seed) nextcmd printreply "->"
end;
```

What is a good program?

We have now completed a non-trivial program. There are many steps to go through when you design such a program. Almost always, you try many different ideas before you arrive at a program you are satisfied with. Which criteria can be used to decide whether a program is good or not? The essential property is that the structure of the program corresponds well to the inherent properties of the problem. Furthermore, different aspects of the problem should be as isolated from each other as possible. In the examine program, communication with the environment, the command interpreter, and the command evaluation are separated. Moreover, the main program is isolated from the concrete syntax of commands through a small set of operations. One remaining disturbing property is that the *ask* command has to be treated in a special way; further improvements may resolve this problem.

When you start looking at a problem, you cannot see all of its properties and inherent structure. The more you work with it, the more you discover. At some point, you hopefully feel that you understand all aspects of the problem and that your program reflects in a nice way the properties of the problem. Ideally, you should not stop until you feel proud of what you have produced and can explain to someone else why the choices you have made are the right ones. Programming is a difficult activity, and without care you cannot produce good programs.

Summary

Input and *output commands* in ML have side-effects and are therefore not functional. They should be isolated from the remaining parts of a program as much as possible. With open commands, a program can be connected to physical files and other programs.

Exercises

22.5.* Type in all definitions of the examine program and try it. Extend the program with a command for printing the current lexicon. Also change the *ask* function so that it tries three times before it gives up.

22.6.* Design a program that helps schoolchildren to practice arithmetic. You tell the program which of the four operators to practice and how big are the numbers you want. The program shall count how many correct answers have been given.

22.7.* Select a small part of the commands of some text editor and write a program implementing such a text editor.

22.8.* Design a program that can play tic-tac-toe, master mind, four in a row, or any other of your favourite games. If you are working in a group, you can even play your programs against each other.

22.9.* Design a graphics package suitable either for ordinary graphics or turtle graphics.

22.10.* Use the package in the previous exercise to draw, for instance, Hilbert or Sierpinski curves (see page 141 in Wirth 86). The paper "Functional Geometry" (Henderson 82) also describes what you can do with graphics and functional programming.

22.11.* A screen of a simple terminal can be represented by a list of list of characters, each sublist representing a line. Define suitable operations for building and printing screens. For example, you may want operations to centre and to left and right justify a string on a line. You may also want operations for creating and combining square subpictures. Try to select a small, but useful and easy-to-use, set of operations.

22.12.* In Exercise 20.44, a small interpreter for a functional language is described. Define an abstract data type for such expressions containing a current position, that is, a cursor. Define operations for moving the cursor, for adding and deleting subexpressions at the cursor position, and other operations you want in an interactive system. Then add a command interpreter for the system.

Chapter 23

Programming Methodology

The development of a program is a demanding activity. Without a good methodology it is difficult to achieve a good result. The area of programming methodology or *software engineering* is large, and here we will only scratch its surface. In particular, we will look at how a very high-level language like ML can support the development of good programs at a lower cost.

Programming is sometimes considered as an art and the programmer as an artist. There will always be difficult problems and there will always be good programmers, so part of the programming activity will surely remain an art. However, due to the increasing role of programs in society, it is a necessity to make programming into an engineering discipline. In traditional engineering disciplines like house and bridge building, many development phases precede the construction itself: architecture, model construction , material selection, calculation of strength of materials, etc. When a bridge has been built, cars loaded with sand are sometimes driven out on the bridge to test it before it is used—nobody expects it to fall down, though. In many programming projects, little time is spent on the phases that precede the construction of the program. In consequence no programmers, except for the real optimists, believe that their program will stand its testing. In contrast to the bridge building enterprise, much time is spent on the phases after construction, that is, debugging, testing, and changing. There are many steps involved in the whole *life-cycle* of a large program. Let us look at some of the phases in the program development process.

23.1 Specification

The most important step towards a programming discipline is the separation of the specification and programming activities: you have to know *what* to do before you do it. In many projects, finding out what you want is the difficult part and can require the involvement of many categories of persons and take long time. In the end of such a process, a specification of the intended system must be produced. A specification is a precise description of requirements on the intended system. It can also serve as a documentation of the program you want. Furthermore, it can act as a *contract* between the people wanting the system and those who are going to realize it. Those who order a system want a specification that is easy to read, and the implementors want a specification that is a good start for the program development. Both parties want it to be clear and precise. Today, natural language is often used, but efforts are made to design more precise specification languages. Often, mathematical or logical languages like *predicate logic* are used.

23.1.1 Validation

However precise a specification is, it is of no use if it does not express what you want. Therefore, you have to validate the specification and convince yourself that it expresses your intentions. By necessity, validation is an informal activity; you compare the specification against ideas in your head. By the use of a good specification language, it is easier to see that all cases are taken care of and that no parts contradict each other.

By spending much time on specification and validation, you decrease the time needed for program development. An error detected in this phase is simple to remove; to remove an error in a system that is already in use can be very expensive.

23.1.2 Rapid prototyping

Sometimes, it is difficult to decide what kind of system you want, if you are not allowed to try alternatives. But that means that you have to implement the system *before* you have a specification. However, if you could very simply produce a system that gives you a feel for a real system, the idea would be fruitful. The following facts support the idea. Using a very high-level language like ML, a program can be developed in a shorter time than with a traditional language. Furthermore, some 90 % of the main functions in a system are often taken care of by 10 % of the code. By implementing only the main functions, you can get a working system much faster. By choosing the simplest implementation possible in each situation, the resulting system may be inefficient, but still allow small-scale experiments. If you, in addition, have access to good libraries of functions and data types suited to the application, the work may be speeded up further. This working method is often called rapid prototyping, *experimental system development*, or *explorative programming*.

Once you have experimented with the prototype, you can throw it away: a technique sometimes called *iterative design* or *throw-away programming*. However, you can also continue and develop the prototype itself into a production system.

Often you have to replace some modules by more efficient ones and add new modules that were not present in the prototype. Developing a system in this way, there is a risk that you construct a program without a real specification, which is in conflict with our earlier statement that the specification should be developed before the program is designed. This can be avoided in the following way. First, you specify what you intend to implement first. When you are ready, you can experiment with that program and, from the experience you gain, develop a new specification, which you realize in a second phase. You continue this process of switching between specification and implementation until you are content with the result. It is tempting to skip the specification phase and perhaps also the the effort of convincing yourself that the the additions really do what you want. Resist such temptations, since the end result is usually bad.

Executable specifications

A desirable goal is to have a language that is both a good specification language and a good programming language. It is unlikely that such a language can be found. In a specification, you want to state exactly what you require of a program, but nothing more, since that would limit the freedom of the implementor of the specification. In a program, you make very specific choices, often to get a time and space efficient program. Furthermore, the details of a program make it less useful as a specification. On the other hand, the executability of a program is a great advantage. Therefore, the use of high-level languages as specification languages is sometimes advocated. In some applications this may be a good compromise, but, in general, special specification languages allow better specifications.

23.1.3 Automatic programming

A very attractive solution would be to give a specification to the computer and let it derive the program for you, that is, let the computer program itself. To achieve this goal, you need a general problem solving program that can find a satisfactory program for any specification. It is theoretically possible to write such programs, but the time it takes to find the solution is usually enormous for all but trivial problems. If you limit the range of problems to be handled, if you limit the power of your specification language, and if you guide the program in its search for a solution, you can decrease the time considerably. However, these activities are really a form of programming, since you guide the computer in its work. One example of this character is a kind of programming called *logic programming*, in which you write "programs" in a subset of predicate logic and then guide the search for a solution to the specified problem. For some problems, this is a powerful technique; for others, functional programming is more straightforward.

23.2   Programming

Once you have a specification, you have to implement it, that is, write a program that satisfies the specification. Let us look at some of the problems encountered and some of the techniques used to meet them.

23.2.1   Programming in the large

We have mainly looked at techniques for *programming in the small*. For *programming in the large*, you need techniques for mastering the complexity of large problems and large programs. A large project may involve tens or hundreds of programmers. The resulting program may be several ten thousands or even hundred thousands lines of code, and it may be in use for many years. The problem to be solved may be difficult to grasp and involve many details. To carry through such a project, the problem must be broken down into well-defined parts, which can be handled by small programmer groups. In the end, the resulting program pieces, often called *modules*, must be integrated into one large program. A central problem is to define the interfaces between the modules in such a clear way that all programmers understand them in the same way and make the same assumptions about them. To get as small interfaces as possible, it is important to make the modularization in such a way that the module structure matches the inherent structure of the problem. It is no exaggeration to say that by a good analysis and modularization, the cost of a whole project can decrease by several orders of magnitude. Therefore, do not start coding until you have fully understood the problem and the modularization is complete.

Program maintenance

A problem of great proportions is the maintenance of old programs. They are often ill-structured and when changing one small part, large parts of the program have to be changed, too. The reason is that there are few abstraction barriers isolating different parts of the program from each other. Through the use of abstract data types, you can hide details and make each module largely self-contained. Many changes will then influence only small parts of the program, and the resulting program will have its nice properties preserved. Today, some programs have to be thrown away because nobody can understand them any longer.

Reusable programs

Many times, programmers invent the wheel again and again. They write programs that are but slight variations of other programs. Through the use of higher order functions, polymorphism, and good abstraction mechanisms, you can define modules that are general enough to be used in a large variety of contexts. The use of libraries of predefined modules and functions, possibly adapted to a particular application, promises program development with much less effort. The main tool in ML to achieve this goal is the **modules**. They are not described in this book, though. Many times you can instead use abstract data types, which give many of the advantages that modules give.

23.2.2   Top-down design

The main problem solving technique in programming is to decompose a problem into subproblems. There are three ways of doing it: sequential decomposition, decomposition into cases, and recursive decomposition. When you work top-down, you assume that you already have solutions to the subproblems and then put together a solution to the whole problem under this assumption. In the resulting program, the three decomposition methods correspond respectively to function composition, conditional or case expressions, and recursive function definitions.

When you work top-down, the only assumptions you make about the solutions to the subproblems are those stated in their specifications; if you use properties of a particular solution, you break the rules of the game. Working according to this *principle of least commitment*, you obtain modifiability, since any solution satisfying the specification can be replaced by any other correct solution.

As described in Chapter 19, data types can also be designed in a top-down fashion. Here, too, three methods of composition are used. A structured data object is a sequence of other data objects. A union type is the union of a set of other types, and a recursive type is defined inductively. As mentioned, the analysis of data objects is the inverse process of their construction. The analysis of data objects of union types is performed by case analysis and of objects of recursive types by recursive functions. The analysis of tuples has nothing to do with function composition, however; rather, it corresponds to matching against a structured pattern.

23.2.3   Bottom-up design

ML consists of a kernel extended with some standard types and functions. Most ML systems also contain a set of other useful predefined functions. A language really defines an abstract machine. The ML system, for instance, can be viewed as an ML machine. When you predefine functions and types, you extend it and provide the user with a more powerful machine. Such extensions are often performed in a bottom-up fashion, and you do not always have a particular application in mind.

23.2.4   Structured growth

Even if your intention is to produce an advanced program, there is a point in starting with a simple version. If you select the most important parts of the task and implement them first, you can get a working program at an early stage. Now you can add new features one after the other. Since you understand the other parts better, it is easier to make the additions and be convinced they are correct. Should you still find bugs, they are most probably in the added parts. This technique is sometimes called *structured growth*. Very often, your program contains a case analysis, and you add new cases according to your needs.

23.2.5   Program derivation

An attractive way of developing a program is to start with a precise specification and gradually derive the program from the specification. In essence, that is what you do at present, but you do it informally and usually not in a systematic fashion. There exist program derivation systems, however, in which you write your specification in a formal language and, then, interactively derive a program from the specification. In this way, you can only derive programs that satisfy the specification; the system does not allow anything else. In fact, in some systems, the specification has the form of a mathematical theorem, and by giving a proof of that theorem, the system can automatically derive a program. This close correspondence between programming and mathematical theorem proving is yet another indication that a good mathematical maturity is useful for a programmer. Since most decisions you make when constructing a program are routine decisions, there is hope that large parts of programs can be derived automatically. Some parts, however, require ingenuity, and there is little evidence that all programming can be done automatically.

23.3   Verification

Most production programs contain errors. Some errors cause considerable problems, for instance, when a space rocket is lost due to errors in a program. The earlier during the program development an error is detected, the lower is the cost of removing it. For each phase like specification, programming, testing, and production use that is reached before detection, the cost of removing the error increases by about an order of magnitude. It is therefore cost effective to spend much time on finding errors at an early stage. Even if you have formally proved that your program is correct, it is important to test it, since you can never validate your specification 100 %. By combining a careful examination of a program with systematic testing, you can produce good programs.

There are many methods for verifying the correctness of a program ranging from rigorous mathematical proofs to ad hoc testing. Formal proofs are often both difficult and time-consuming, but informal proofs of the crucial parts of a program are often well worth the effort. Just to read through your program and try to convince yourself of its correctness is often a good help. In many companies, a technique called *code reading* is used: some other programmer reads the program and tries to find errors before it is put to testing. In addition, this is of great psychological value, because you know that someone else will be suffering if you are careless when writing your program.

23.3.1 Bottom-up testing

When you have scrutinized your program in all ways, you start testing it. If the program is not very small, it should be tested one piece at a time. If you test the whole program at once and something does not work correctly, you have few clues to where to look for the error. When you designed your program, you worked top-down. Now you reverse the order and start with those functions that do not depend on any other functions than the predefined ones—you work *bottom-up*. This works particularly well with an interactive system, since you can test each function without writing extra code.

Choosing test examples

For testing to be effective, the test examples must be chosen so that all parts of the program are tested and all main combinations of input data examined. If the input is a number, you must test, for instance, positive and negative numbers, zero, even and odd numbers, very small and very large numbers, and all other numbers that may cause trouble.

A problem that appears when choosing test examples is that you are familiar with the problem. Therefore, you tend to select those test values you consider typical, and omit values you do not think will appear. Experience shows that much more can appear than you think. Similar to the technique of code-reading, programmers can construct test examples for each other in order to avoid this problem.

Many programs that are used for some time are changed. A good idea is to save the test examples you have chosen. It saves you a lot of work the next time you test your program, and you can accumulate good test examples.

23.3.2 Debugging

Working with a large program, debugging can be time consuming; some bugs may take days to find. Bottom-up testing is one technique that makes it easier to find bugs—you limit yourself to small parts of the program at a time. Some errors, however, may result from unfortunate combinations of several program parts and may require considerable effort to find. If you are careful in the early phases of the development, you make the time for removing all bugs short: your program has a better structure, and there are fewer bugs to look for.

23.3.3   Efficiency and optimization

A specification of a program often consists of one functional part and one part describing requirements on time and space efficiency. A program that does not meet the performance requirements can be said to contain an "efficiency bug".

Very often, the simplest program for a problem is inefficient. There are still reasons for starting with a simple solution. First, it is difficult to tell in advance which parts of a program will make the program inefficient. If you try to make it very efficient in the first place, you may very well waste time on program parts that are not crucial. Second, by trying to produce an efficient version directly, it may be difficult to get a program of good quality; you have to think of several things at the same time.

One way to handle the efficiency problem is to start to write a simple program without considering efficiency. In this way you will, in a shorter time, get a program that works. If you find your program unacceptably slow, you can now try to find those parts that make it slow. Usually, there are tools with which you can measure in which parts most execution time is spent. Now, you can put your efforts into replacing the inefficient algorithms by more efficient ones. In this way you know your work will be worth the effort and, if you now introduce new errors, they are easier to find, since you have changed only a very small part of the program. In addition, experience shows that you often accept a program that works, even if it is less efficient than you first intended. As a rule, programs take longer to produce than you estimate, and the choice might very well be between an inefficient, but working, program and no program at all. A prerequisite for working in this way, however, is that your programs are well-modularized and, as a consequence, modifiable.

23.4   What is a Good Program?

To become a really good programmer is like becoming a good piano player or a good craftsman. You need both talent and a lot of practice, and there is really no short cut to that goal. The reason is that programming is a form of problem solving, which is a difficult task. There are some rules of thumb, however, that at least to some extent can improve your programming capability. Let us state some of these rules and also some of the properties that characterize nice programs.

Readability and clarity

Most programs of value are read and perhaps also changed by many persons. Clarity and readability are therefore two important properties of a good program. Many programmers have had the experience that, if they do not keep these goals in mind, they cannot even read their own programs after a couple of weeks.

Program layout

In an ML program, you can insert space, tabulation, and new line characters between entities like identifiers, numerals, and special symbols. This freedom can be used to make programs easier to read. Primarily, this is achieved by *indentation* (page 72), whereby the layout of the program is made to correspond to the structure of the program. There are several, in essence, equally good conventions for indentation. Most important is that you stick to one set of conventions all the time and, if you are working together with other programmers, to the same conventions as they use.

Comments

A comment is any sequence of characters surrounded by (* and *). It can be inserted at any place where a space can be inserted. The ML system treats a comment as if it were a space.

When you write a program you should always try to make the program itself as readable as possible. Sometimes, however, you can increase the readability of it by inserting comments at suitable places. Comments can improve the readability considerably, but their overuse can have the opposite effect: commenting something that equally well can be understood directly from the program is an annoying habit.

A good use of comments is to make short descriptions of function and type definitions. The names of the functions and types should say as much as possible, but in comments you can give *complete specifications* of them. The rule is that the comment should say only what they do, not how they do it. If some algorithm is complicated, however, a description of it might be useful, too.

A problem with comments is that they duplicate the code. You express the same thing in other words. When you later change the program, you have to change the comments accordingly; otherwise, the comments may lead to problems. Thus, again, make the code readable in the first place, then use comments.

Chosing names

Certainly, the choice of names is important for program readability. This subject has been treated in Chapter 3, so we here just repeat that expressive, excessively long, names should be used, unless the name is used very locally, for instance, as parameter in a function. In such a case, a shorter name might be as good.

Naming constants

An extremely good, but still easy way, of making a program both readable and modifiable is to name constants. A numeral like 1000 or a pair like $(true, "0037")$ does not give much information to the reader. By naming them in value declarations, more information can be conveyed. An important consequence is that, if you now want to change the constant 1000 to 10000, you have to change only the declaration and not every occurrence of the constant 1000 concerned.

Information hiding

In a large program, many names are used. Usually, many programmers are involved in its production. To avoid name clashes and misconceptions about the use of names, names should be known only in small parts of the program, if possible. In this way, programs are easier to change, since different parts do not depend on each other more than necessary. This programming technique is one aspect of what is called *information hiding*.

Well-structured programs

The rules given above are easy to learn and can be used as rules of thumb. The difficult part of the programming task is, as mentioned, to find a good solution to the given problem and then produce a program that in a nice way reflects the properties of this good solution. Such a program can be said to be *well-structured* which is something more than just being structured—the fact that a program is split into small parts is a necessary, but not a sufficient, condition for being a good program. The production of a good program is a demanding task, but it is also a rewarding one. It is my hope that you will find functional programming as stimulating as I find it and give you as many pleasures.

References

Abelson, H. and Sussman, G.J. with Sussman, J., *Structure and Interpretation of Computer Programs*, The MIT Press, 1985.

Augustsson, L., "SMALL, A small interactive functional system", Programming Methodology Group, Report 28, Göteborg, 1986.

Backus, J. "Can Programming Be Liberated from the von Neumann Style? A Functional Style and Its Algebra of Programs", *CACM*, Vol 21, pp. 613-641, Aug. 1978.

Burge, W.H., *Recursive Programming Techniques*, Addison-Wesley, 1975.

Burstall, R., MacQueen, D., and Sanella, D., "HOPE: An Experimental Applicative Language", Edinburgh University Internal Report CSR-62-80, 1980.

Cardelli, L. and Wegner, P., "On Understanding Types, Data Abstraction, and Polymorphism", *Computing Surveys*, Vol 14, pp. 471-522, Dec. 1985.

Church, A., *The Calculi of Lambda-Conversion*, Princeton University Press, 1941.

Glaser, H., Hankin, C., and Till, D., *Principles of Functional Programming*, Prentice-Hall, 1984.

Gordon, M.J., Milner, R., and Wadsworth, C., *Edinburgh LCF: A Mechanised Logic of Computation*, LNCS 78, Springer-Verlag, 1979.

Harper, R., MacQueen, D., and Milner, R. , *Standard ML*, Edinburgh University Internal Report ECS-LFCS-86-2, 1986.

Harper, R. and Mitchell, K., *Introduction to Standard ML*, Laboratory for Foundations of Computer Science, Edinburgh, 1986.

Henderson, P., *Functional Programming: Application and Implementation*, Prentice-Hall, 1980.

Henderson, P., "Functional Geometry", Proceedings of the 1982 ACM Conference on LISP and Functional Programming, Pittsburgh.

Hofstadter, D.R., *GÖDEL, ESCHER, BACH: an Eternal Golden Braid*, Basic Books, New York, 1979.

Knuth, D.E., *The Art of Computer Programming*, Vol 1: *Fundamental Algorithms*, Addison-Wesley, 1969.

Landin, P., "The Mechanical Evaluation of Expressions", *Computer Journal*, Jan. 1964.

Landin, P., "The Next 700 Programming Languages", *CACM*, Vol 9, pp. 157-164, March 1966.

McCarthy, J., "Recursive Functions of Symbolic Expressions and Their Computation by Machine", *CACM*, pp. 184-195, April 1960.

McCarthy, J., "A Basis for a Mathematical Theory of Computation", in *Computer Programming and Formal Systems*, eds P. Brafford and D. Hirshberg, North Holland, 1963.

McCarthy, J., "Towards a Mathematical Science of Computation", in *Information Processing*, Proceedings IFIP Congress 1962, pp. 21-28, North Holland, 1963.

Milner, R., "A Theory of Type Polymorphism in Programming", *Journal of Computer System Science*, Vol 17, pp. 348-375, 1978.

Milner, R., "The Standard ML Core Language", Edinburgh University Internal Report CSR-168-84, 1984.

MacQueen, D., "Modules for Standard ML", AT&T Bell Laboratories, May 1985.

Polya, G., *How to Solve It*, Princeton University Press, 1971.

Polymorphism, The ML/LCF/Hope Newsletter, ed D. MacQueen, AT&T Bell Laboratories, Murray Hill, NJ 07974, USA.

Turner, D., "A New Implementation Technique for Applicative Languages", *Software—Practice and Experience*, Vol 9, pp. 31-49, 1979.

Turner, D., "Recursion Equations as a Programming Language", *Functional Programming and its Applications*, eds. J. Darlington, P. Henderson, and D. Turner, Cambridge University Press, 1981.

Wirth, N., *Algorithms and Data Structures*, Prentice-Hall, 1986.

Glossary

In this glossary, important concepts as well as pairs of concepts are explained. Some of the concepts have no absolute meaning and other authors may well define them differently. The words are divided into groups under a few main headings. Further, related concepts occur near each other. Some entries contain words in bold, which are important concepts without separate entries. All entries are referred to from the index.

General Concepts

Information—Data. A **datum** (plur. data) is any physical phenomenon or object that carries information. The information is obtained by interpreting the datum. In contrast to data, information is something abstract.

Algorithm—Program. An algorithm is a method for computing a desired result from some input data in a finite number of steps. A program is a *description* of an algorithm.

Abstraction—Concept—Type. Abstraction is the process of paying special attention to the similarities of the objects in a set of objects. The idea captured by the abstraction process is called a concept or a type.

Language. A language is a set of sentences (programs) that can be described by strings of characters. A full description of a language consists of a description of its **syntax**, **semantics**, and **pragmatics**, that is, its form, meaning, and usage, respectively.

Programming Languages

Compiler—Interpreter—Computer. A compiler is a translator from one programming language to another, often to machine code. An interpreter is a program (or machine) that executes programs in some programming language. A computer is an "interpreter" realized by electronic circuits that interprets programs in machine code.

Language level. Programming languages are often described on a scale where a low-level language is near the machine code of a computer and a high-level language near the way humans express algorithms.

Referential transparency. A notation is referentially transparent, if the only thing that matters about an expression is its value. Within a part of a program with a fixed set of bindings, the value of a subexpression is the same wherever it occurs, and the subexpression can be replaced by its value without changing the value of the whole expression.

Side effect. Many languages have notations that resemble expressions syntactically but, in addition to yielding values, the evaluation of the expressions have side effects such as performing I/O operations or storing new values in memory cells. Such languages are not referentially transparent.

Imperative language. A program in an imperative language is a sequence of **commands** that expresses how an initial **state** is to be transformed into a final state. State changes are either changes of the contents of memory cells or the result of I/O operations. Execution of commands gives rise to side effects; hence, imperative languages are not referentially transparent.

Functional language. A functional or **applicative** language is a very high-level, referentially transparent, language. A functional program is normally a sequence of declarations and expressions. The values of the expressions are computed when the program is executed. Functions are first class objects in a functional language and can be used in similar ways as other data objects.

Programs

Expressions

Expression. An expression is a sequence of symbols describing a computation. The most important kinds of symbols are constants, variables, operators, and parentheses.

Canonical expression—Value. A canonical expression is an expression that cannot be further reduced. Any expression (like 3+5) describing a terminating computation denotes a value. A canonical expression (like the numeral 8) is a canonical description of a value (like the number 8).

Declarations

Identifier. An identifier is a special kind of symbol used to denote an object like a function or a type.

Declaration. With a declaration, a name is bound to an object. A pair of a name and an object is called a **binding**. An **environment** is a set of bindings. The **scope** of a name is the part of a program in which the binding introduced in a declaration is valid.

Constant—Variable. A constant is a special kind of symbol denoting a value. Its meaning is fixed and cannot be changed with a declaration. A variable is a symbol (identifier) denoting a value. The value of a variable is obtained from a binding in the current environment (if it is bound).

Functions

Function—Relation. A relation is a set of pairs of values. A function is a relation in which no pairs have the same first components. For a function, the first component in a pair is called the **argument** and the second component the **result**.

Domain—Range. The set of arguments for which a function is defined is called the domain of the function and the set of possible results its range. The type of the elements in the domain is called the **argument type**, and the type of the elements in the range is called the **result type**. The domain and range can be proper subsets of the argument and result types.

Function—Procedure. A function is characterized by the relation between its arguments and results. Nothing has to be said about how to compute the results. A procedure is a method for computing the result of a function for a given argument. Different procedures can compute the same function. (In many imperative languages, the words function and procedure are defined in a different way.)

Functional abstraction—Procedural abstraction. Functional abstraction is to abstract away from the particular procedure used to evaluate function applications. Procedural abstraction is to abstract away from the the use of different arguments and consider only the computation pattern (method) used.

Partial function—Total function. A function is defined for an argument if the function has a result for that argument. A total function is defined for all arguments of the argument type, that is, the domain is equal to the argument type. A partial function is undefined for some arguments of the argument type.

Pattern matching. A pattern is used to analyse the structure of a data object. If the pattern contains variables, the variables become bound to parts of the data object when matched. A **match** is a sequence of rules, where a **rule** is a pair of a pattern and an expression. When applying a match to an argument, the first rule whose pattern matches the argument is used. The result is the value of the corresponding expression, which can contain variables that have been bound to values during the last pattern matching.

Function expression.   A (canonical) function expression is an expression describing a function. It consists of a match that is matched against the argument, when the function is applied to an argument.

Bound variable—Free variable.   In a rule of a match, the bound variables are those that occur in the pattern of the rule; the other variables are said to be free. An **open** expression is an expression containing free variables. By associating an environment containing bindings of all free variables to the expression, the expression is closed and a **closure** is formed.

Argument—Parameter.   The variables occurring in the patterns of the match in a function expression are called parameters. They are matched against, and bound to, an argument (or part of it), when the function is applied to the argument.

Operator—Operand.   An **application** is an expression consisting of an **operator** and one or two operands. The value of the operator must be a function. The value of an operand is called an argument to the function. In a **prefix** application, the only operand follows the operator. In an **infix** application, the two operands surround the operator. The word operator is also used for symbols like + and *.

Polymorphic function.   A **type expression** is an expression that denotes a type. A type expression containing **type variables** denotes all types that are obtained when a type is substituted for each type variable. Such a type is called a **polytype**. A polymorphic function is a function with a polytype; it can be applied to arguments of all types of the polytype. A polymorphic function is always defined with one single definition.

Overloaded function.   An overloaded function symbol is a symbol that denotes several different functions. The function that is to be used in a function application is decided from the type of the argument(s). The term "overloaded function" is really improper since it is the function symbol that is overloaded, not the function itself.

Higher order function.   A higher order function is a function taking a function as argument or yielding a function as result. A function yielding a function as result is also called a **partially applicable** function or a **curried** function.

Combinator.   The term combinator is normally used to denote a function that is useful when defining other functions. Formally, it is a function expression without free variables. Usually, a combinator is polymorphic and often also higher order.

Primitive recursion. A function is primitive recursive if it can be defined in **primitive recursive form**. A function is defined in primitive recursive form if the patterns used in the function definition directly correspond to the constructors of the argument type and if all recursive uses of the function have an argument that is an immediate "predecessor" of the argument to the function. In addition, all auxiliary functions used in the definition must be primitive recursive. A primitive recursive function is always total. **Course-of-values** recursion is a more general form of primitive recursion in which all "predecessors" of the function argument can be used in the recursive calls.

General recursion. There are no restrictions on the form of the definition of a general recursive function. Almost all interesting recursive functions that are total are also primitive recursive. A **partial recursive** function is a general recursive function that may not terminate for all arguments of the argument type.

Linear recursion. For a linearly recursive or **iterative** function, each call can generate at most one new call of the function. Iteration can be described as the transformation of a state either a fixed number of times, called **number controlled** iteration, or until a given condition becomes true, called **condition controlled** iteration. A **tail recursive** function is an iterative function, for which the result of the function either is computed without a recursive call or is the immediate result of a recursive call.

Types

Type— Data type. A type is a set of data objects of similar kind. A data type is a type together with operations for working with the data objects of the type. The operations are often split into three classes: **constructors**, which are used to construct all objects of the type; **selectors**, which are used to select parts of the data objects; and **predicates**, which are used to decide which constructor was used to construct a data object. The selectors and predicates are sometimes called **analysers**.

Constructor—Type constructor. A constructor (like *nil* and *cons*) constructs a data object, whereas a type constructor (like *bool* and *list*) constructs a type. A **constructor constant** constructs an **atomic** data object and a **constructor function** constructs a **compound** data object. A **type constant** (like *bool*) constructs one single type, whereas a **type function** (like *list*) yields a type when applied to some other type.

Regular data type.   A regular data type is a data type for which the selectors and predicates are the converses of the constructors. For a regular data type, no selectors and predicates have to be defined, since pattern matching achieves the same purpose.

Free type—Quotient type.   A free type is a type for which there exists a free representation of the real objects. In a **free representation** of a type, there is only one data object for each real object to be modelled. For a non-free type, you cannot use the equality provided by the system, since different data objects are considered as different by this equality, even though they may represent the same real object. A non-free type is also called a quotient type, since the data objects can be divided into **equivalence classes** containing objects to be considered equal in the sense that they represent the same real object.

Abstract data type—Concrete data type.   In a concrete data type, the real objects are modelled by one particular representation, which is visible to the user of the data type. In an abstract data type, the representation is hidden and can therefore be replaced by another representation without changing the external behaviour of the operations. In an abstract data type, an abstraction away from particular representations is performed.

Syntax

Grammar.   A grammar is a device describing the syntactic part of a language, which is a set of sentences (programs). A **syntax chart** is a graphical representation of a grammar. The grammatical structure of a language is often split into the **lexical structure**, which is concerned with the individual symbols, and the general structure of the sentences.

Parsing.   To parse a sentence is to recognize its structure. The analysis of the lexical structure is called **lexical analysis** and the analysis of the general structure is called **syntax analysis**.

Abstract syntax—Concrete syntax.   A grammar is a description of all syntactic details of all sentences of a language; it describes the concrete syntax. The result of abstracting away from the particular symbols used to make the structure of a sentence visible is the structure itself. Such a structure can be represented by an **abstract syntax tree**. The abstract syntax of a language can be described by a type definition in ML, if the particular choice of constructor names is disregarded.

Semantics

Operational semantics—Abstract machine. The meaning of a programming language can be given by describing how programs are evaluated. Such a semantics is called an operational semantics. Essentially, it is a description of how an abstract machine for executing the programs works. One choice of abstract machine for a functional langauge is a **reduction machine** consisting of a program store, an environment store, and a control. The operational semantics is then given by **axioms** and **derivation rules** that describe how the control is to guide the reduction of an expression.

Computation. A computation in a reduction machine is the process of reducing a program to a canonical expression representing a value. The computation may not terminate for some programs.

Strict evaluation—Lazy evaluation. The reduction of a function application can be performed in two ways: with strict (**applicative**) evaluation order, the value of an operand is computed before the body of the function is evaluated, whereas with lazy (**normal**) evaluation order, the value of an operand is computed when it is needed during the evaluation of the function body. Often, a distinction is made between normal and lazy evaluation order: lazy evaluation is a normal evaluation order in which each operand is evaluated at most once.

The Program Development Process

Specification. A specification of a programming problem is a description of the task that a program satisfying the specification is expected to perform. A specification must tell only *what* a program shall do, not *how* it is to perform the task. A specification may also contain **performance requirements** that set limits to the time and space that a program is allowed to use.

Validation. To validate a specification is to check that it really expresses what you want it to express, that is, that it describes the problem correctly. Validation is, by necessity, an informal activity.

Programming. Programming is the activity of finding a method (an algorithm) for solving a programming problem as well as finding suitable representations of the available and desired information. Programming can be described as a form of problem solving. **Coding** is the activity of describing a solution to a programming problem in a particular programming language.

Problem decomposition. Most problem solving is performed by decomposing a problem into subproblems, solving the subproblems, and then putting the solutions together. Each solution to a subproblem describes a computation. There are three ways of decomposing a problem, each of which corresponds to a different way of putting computations together. Using **sequential decomposition**, you split a problem into subproblems, whose solutions are composed sequentially. Using **decomposition into cases**, you split a problem into subproblems, whose solutions are branches in a **case analysis**. Using **recursive decomposition** you decompose a problem into a number of **base cases** and **inductive** or **recursive cases**. In the solution to the recursive cases, you are allowed to assume that the solution works for arguments that in some sense are smaller than the original argument. The correctness of this way of reasoning is based on the principle of **mathematical induction**, which usually is performed over natural numbers. A similar argument for objects like lists and trees is called **structural induction**.

Abstraction.   Abstraction is the main vehicle for dealing with large programming problems and for obtaining modular and easy-to-change programs. Through **functional abstraction** you abstract away from the particular procedure used to compute a function, and through **data abstraction** you abstract away from the actual representation of some type of real objects.

Program derivation.   Program derivation is the process of a systematic derivation of a program from a formal specification in such a way that the correctness of the derived program is guaranteed.

Top-down design—Bottom-up design.   When deriving a program in a top-down fashion, you solve a problem under the assumption that the subproblems are already solved. Then, subproblems are repeatedly tackled until problems with known solutions are reached. In the same manner, suitable data types needed in the program are derived. When deriving a program in a bottom-up fashion, the primitives in the language are used to define new functions and data types, normally for use in a variety of applications. The term **step-wise refinement** is sometimes used synonymously with top-down design, but is sometimes also used to denote the process of successive replacement of definitions of functions and data types by more efficient versions.

Structured growth—Iterative design.   When you develop a program with structured growth, you start implementing a small, but essential, part of the problem. Then, new cases are added successively until the whole problem is solved. Iterative design means that you first implement a problem or part of it and, then, when you have gained experience from this implementation, start all over again with a new implementation.

Rapid prototyping.   Rapid prototyping is the idea of developing a test implementation of a system to gain experience of a potential system before the final specification is produced. To minimize the work, a very high-level language is used and only the most important parts of the potential system are implemented. This way of working is also called **explorative programming** or **experimental system development**.

Verification. Verification is the process of convincing oneself that a program satisfies its specification. Examples of verification methods are **program proving** and **testing**. A property of testing is that it can show the presence of errors but never their absence. An **implementation** of a specification is a program or data type satisfying the specification. To show **partial correctness** of a program, one has to show that the program gives the right result if it terminates. To show **total correctness**, you have to show partial correctness *and* that the program terminates for all arguments in the domain.

Implementation descriptor. The implementation of an abstract data type can be described by two implementation descriptors. The descriptor *valid* tells which representation objects really represent abstract objects and *abstr* maps a representation object to the corresponding abstract object.

Well-structured program. A well-structured program is a program whose structure is a good reflection of the inherent structure of the problem.

Time complexity—Space complexity. The complexity of a program is measured by how fast the time or space requirements increase when the "size" of input data is increased. The **order** concept is used to tell the overall speed of this increase; for instance, it can grow logarithmicly, linearly, quadraticly, or exponentially.

Optimization. If a program does not meet the performance requirements in the specification, it has to be optimized by finding an implementation that uses less time or space.

Divide and conquer. In an algorithm using the divide and conquer technique, the problem is split into two or more subproblems of comparable size, which are solved using the same method. This technique often reduces a linear complexity into a logarithmic complexity.

Answers to Exercises

To some exercises, only part of the answer or some hint is given. Often, a function is described by a set of equations, instead of a full definition, but it should be easy to transform the equations into an ML definition. For some equations, the order of the equations is important, since the equations contain overlapping patterns. Furthermore, the names of exceptions are not declared before they are used.

Chapter 1.

1.1. 1) No, only if you know how to interpret it. 2) Not really, only data can be on a paper; these data can give you information, though. 3) Usually, you want the objects to have at least some property in common. 4) No, they are not comparable. 5) No, it is an instance of the concept *red*, which is an instance of the concept *colour*. 6) Yes.

1.2. 1) No, a computer is a data processing machine, but sometimes you say it processes information. 2) Usually, you consider a program as a description of an algorithm, but sometimes the words denote the same thing. 3) Yes. 4) Yes. 5) No, the value of a numeral is a number, not an expression. For instance, the value of the numeral 3 is the number 3.

1.3. 1, 11, 111, ..., 1111111111 and 0, 1, 2, 10, 11, 12, 20, 21, 22, 100.

1.4. 1001, 100000, 1100100 and 15, 42, 512.

Chapter 2.

2.1. Since $41451 \bmod 123 \longrightarrow 0$, the number 123 divides 41451.

2.2. $(3 ** 4) ** 4 \longrightarrow 43046721$.

2.3. 256, 65 536, and 4 294 967 296.

2.4. $8 ** 3 \longrightarrow 512$. (Really $1 * 8 ** 3 + 0 * 8 ** 2 + 0 * 8 ** 1 + 0 * 8 ** 0$.)

2.5. $1000.0 * 1.07 * 1.07 * 1.07 \longrightarrow 1225.043$.

2.6. 6.0.

2.7. In one system, $sin(3.1415927/2.0) \longrightarrow 0.9999999999999998$, but $sin(3.14159265/2.0) \longrightarrow 1.0$ and $sin(3.14159265/2.0) - 1.0 \longrightarrow 8.326672684688674E\tilde{}17$.

2.8. $1000 * (1000 + 1) \ div \ 2 \longrightarrow 500500$.

2.9. 9 223 372 036 854 775 808.

2.10. Use $floor(2.6 * real \ m - 0.2) + d + y + y \ div \ 4 + c \ div \ 4 - 2 * c$ to compute A. Take the result modulo 7 using the *mod* operator. Note that A can be negative, but a correct implementation of the *mod* operator yields the right result.

Chapter 3.

3.1. 1) Yes. 2) No. Consider the declaration sequence **val** $x = 3$; **val** $y = x * 2$; **val** $x = 4$. Now $y \longrightarrow 6$, but $x * 2 \longrightarrow 8$. 3) No, the system does not "interpret" identifiers in any way.

3.2. **val** $e = exp\, 1.0$. $exp\, 1.0 \longrightarrow 2.718281828459045$.

Chapter 4.

4.1. 1) Yes. 2) Yes. 3) Normally, but in some countries you can have several wives.

4.2. $real \rightarrow real$ and $int \rightarrow real$.

4.3. $f(f\, 345) \longrightarrow f((\textbf{fn}\ x\ =>\ x\ div\ 10)\, 345) \longrightarrow f(345\ div\ 10) \longrightarrow$
    $f(34) \longrightarrow \ldots \longrightarrow 34\ div\ 10 \longrightarrow 3$.

4.4. $double\ interest = ln\, 2.0/ln(1.0 + interest/100.0)$. (As remarked above, function definitions are given as equations. In ML, you write: **fun** $double\ interest = ln\, 2.0/ln(1.0 + interest/100.0)$).

Chapter 5.

5.1. 1) Yes, if the number of values of the argument type is finite. 2) No, not with our definition of correct; we only know that the program meets its specification, but the specification can be wrong. 3) See previous answer.

Chapter 6.

6.1. $odd\ n\ =\ n\ mod\ 2 <> 0$ or $odd\ n = not(even\ n)$, where not is explained in Section 6.2.

6.2. $invert\ x\ =\ $ **if** $x = 0.0$ **then** $maxreal$ **else** $1.0/x$.

6.3. $anniversary\ age\ =\ age\ mod\ 10 = 0$.

6.4. $issquare\ i\ =\ sq(round(sqrt(real\ i))) = i$, where $sq\ x\ :\ int\ =\ x * x$.

6.5. $anniversary\ age\ =\ $ **if** $age\ mod\ 10 = 0$ **then** $true$ **else** $age\ mod\ 25 = 0$.

6.6. You have to test all cases. The first test is
$false = false$ and $false = not(not\ false\ or\ not\ false) = not(true\ or\ true) = not\ true = false$.
All the other cases are similar.

6.7. The same as $anniversary$, that is, 0 is an anniversary, too.

6.8. $is\_leapyear\ y\ =\ y\ mod\ 4 = 0$ **andalso** $(y\ mod\ 100 <> 0$ **orelse** $y\ mod\ 400 = 0)$.

6.9. We define one version for $n < 100$ and one for $n < 1000$.
    $peep99\ n\ =\ n\ mod\ 7 = 0$ **orelse** $n\ mod\ 10 = 7$ **orelse** $n\ div\ 10 = 7$.
    $peep999\ n\ =\ n\ mod\ 7 = 0$ **orelse** $n\ mod\ 10 = 7$
                orelse $n\ div\ 10\ mod\ 10 = 7$ **orelse** $n\ div\ 100 = 7$.

6.10. Since $sqr(n + 1) = n * (n + 2) + 1$ we get $semisum\ n\ =\ (n * (n + 2) + n\ mod\ 2)\ div\ 4$. I prefer the first solution, since the case analysis is visible there.

6.11. $ceiling\ x = $ **if** $x - real(floor\ x) = 0.0$ **then** $floor\ x$ **else** $floor\ x + 1$.

Chapter 7.

7.1. $digitval\ d\ =\ ord\ d - ord\ "0"$. Note that this solution works for any code having the digits occurring consequtively.

7.2. $to\_capital\ c\ =\ chr(ord\ c + ord\ "A" - ord\ "a")$.

7.3. $digit\ c\ =\ c >= "0"$ **andalso** $c <= "9"$,
$lower\_case\ c\ =\ c >= "a"$ **andalso** $c <= "z"$,
$upper\_case\ c\ =\ c >= "A"$ **andalso** $c <= "Z"$, and
$letter\ c\ =\ lower\_case\ c$ **orelse** $upper\_case\ c$.

Chapter 8.

8.1. $(real\ ->\ real) * (int * bool)$.

8.2. $'a\ ->\ 'a$, $'a * ('b * 'c)\ ->\ 'b$, and $'a * 'b\ ->\ 'b * 'a$.
Some instantiations are $int\ ->\ int$, $int * (real * bool)\ ->\ real$, and $int * real\ ->\ real * int$.

8.3. $power(a, b)\ =\$ **if** $a = 0.0$ **then** 0.0 **else** $exp(b * ln(a))$, since $ln(0.0)$ is undefined.

8.4. $max3(x, y, z)\ =\ max(x, max(y, z))$.

8.5. $real * real\ ->\ real$, $bool * 'a * 'a\ ->\ 'a$, and $'a * ('b * 'c)\ ->\ ('a * 'b) * 'c$. A type
constraint must be added to the last definition. It will yield a type error, if you type it in as it is.

8.6. $compladd((x1 : int, y1 : int), (x2,\ y2))\ =\ (x1 + x2,\ y1 + y2)$ and
$complmul((x1 : int,\ y1), (x2,\ y2))\ =\ (x1 * x2 - y1 * y2,\ x1 * y2 + x2 * y1)$.
$complroots(a, b, c)\ =\$ **if** $b * b - 4.0 * a * c < 0.0$
                    then $((\tilde{}b/(2.0 * a),\ sqrt(4.0 * a * c - b * b)/(2.0 * a)),$
                          $(\tilde{}b/(2.0 * a),\ \tilde{}(sqrt(4.0 * a * c - b * b))/(2.0 * a)))$
                    else $(((\tilde{}b + sqrt(b * b - 4.0 * a * c))/(2.0 * a),\ 0.0),$
                          $((\tilde{}b - sqrt(b * b - 4.0 * a * c))/(2.0 * a),\ 0.0))$.

8.7. $fak\ n\ =\ round(sqrt(2.0 * pi) * power(real\ n,\ real\ n + 0.5) * exp(\tilde{}(real\ n)))$.
It differs from fac for $n = 5$ and upwards.

Chapter 9.

9.1. 1) True. 2) False. Some forms of recursion cannot be described by iteration. 3) False. There
are more powerful forms of grammars that can describe context dependencies. 4) True.

9.2.

GRAMMAR	::=	{ PRODUCTION }
PRODUCTION	::=	SYNTAXCATEGORY "::=" { ALTERNATIVE "newline" }
ALTERNATIVE	::=	{ ITEM }
ITEM	::=	TERMINALSYMBOL
		SYNTAXCATEGORY

Chapter 10.

No exercises.

Chapter 11.

11.1. **fun** $tanh\ x\ =\$ **let val** $e1 = exp\ x$; **val** $e2 = exp(\tilde{}x)$ **in** $(e1 - e2)/(e1 + e2)$ **end**.

11.2. **datatype** $CARMAKE\ =\ Ford\ |\ Jaguar\ |\ Volvo$
        datatype $SHAPE\ =\ Round\ |\ Square\ |\ Oval$
        datatype $SEX\ =\ Female\ |\ Male$

11.3. $complroots(a, b, c)\ =\$ **let val** $x = \tilde{}b/(2.0 * a)$ **and** $d = b * b - 4.0 * a * c$ **in**
        if $d < 0.0$ **then let val** $y = sqrt(\tilde{}d)/(2.0 * a)$ **in** $((x, y), (x, \tilde{}y))$ **end**
        else let val $y = sqrt\ d/(2.0 * a)$ **in** $((x + y, 0.0), (x - y, 0.0))$ **end end**

Chapter 12.

12.1.

```
–  fun  f (0.0, 0.0)  =  2.0
      |  f (0.0, _)  =  1E30
      |  f ( _, 0.0)  =  1E30
      |  f (x, y)  =  x/y + y/x ;
>  val  f  =  fn  :  real ∗ real –> real
```

```
val f  =  fn (0.0, 0.0)  =>  2.0
         |  (0.0, _)  =>  1E30
         |  ( _, 0.0)  =>  1E30
         |  (x, y)    =>  x/y + y/x
```

```
fun f (x, y)  =  case (x, y) of  (0.0, 0.0)  =>  2.0
                  |  (0.0, _)  =>  1E30
                  |  ( _, 0.0)  =>  1E30
                  |  (x, y)    =>  x/y + y/x
```

Chapter 13.

13.1. *bool list list*, *'a list list*, and *int list*. The last expression does not have any type, since $tl[3, []]$ is not a type correct expression.

13.2. *second (_ :: x :: xs)* = *x* and *second _* = **raise** *second*.

13.3. *remlast nil* = **raise** *remlast* and *remlast xs* = *rev(tl(rev xs))*.

13.4. *palindrome xs* = *xs = rev xs*.

13.5. 1) Yes, but all real computers have limitations. 2) No. It is total, since it can handle all lists. 3) No. It can only handle integer lists. 4) No, :: takes an element and a list as arguments. 5) No. The elements of the sublists must have the same type, too.

13.6. $bin(n, m)$ = $fac\ n\ div\ (fac(n - m) * fac\ m)$. Note that the binomial coefficients are always integers. A better solution is: $bin(n, m)$ = $prod(n - m + 1 -- n)\ div\ fac\ m$. An even better solution is: $bin(n, m)$ = $prod(max(n - m, m) + 1 -- n)\ div\ fac(min(n - m, m))$.

Chapter 14.

14.1. *sum nil* = 0 and *sum (x :: xs)* = *x + sum xs*.
prod nil = 1 and *prod (x :: xs)* = *x ∗ prod xs*.

14.2. $sum[1, 2, 3] \longrightarrow 1 + sum[2, 3] \longrightarrow 1 + 2 + sum[3] \longrightarrow 1 + 2 + 3 + sum[] \longrightarrow 1 + 2 + 3 + 0 \longrightarrow 6$.

14.3. We do the induction over n.
Base case: Since $x^0 = 1$ we get $x^m * x^0 = x^m$ and also $x^{m+0} = x^m$, which proves the base case. Inductive step: Assume that for $k > 0$ we have $x^m * x^k = x^{m+k}$ for all m. Now, $x^m * x^{k+1} = x^m * x^k * x = x^{m+k} * x = x^{m+k+1}$, which proves the inductive step.

14.4. We do the induction over n. For $n = 0$, both formulas give 1 as result, which proves the base case. Assume that $S_{k-1} = \frac{r^k - 1}{r - 1}$. Now, $S_k = S_{k-1} + r^k = \frac{r^k - 1}{r - 1} + r^k = \frac{r^k - 1 + r^{k+1} - r^k}{r - 1} = \frac{r^{k+1} - 1}{r - 1}$, which proves the inductive step.

14.5. *sql nil* = *nil* and *sql ((x : int) :: xs)* = *x ∗ x :: sql xs*.

14.6. *flat nil* = *nil* and *flat (xs :: xss)* = *xs @ flat xss*. Note that *xss* is used to tell that *flat* takes a list of lists as argument. Its type is *'a list list –> 'a list*.

14.7. $count(nil, a) = 0$ and $count(x :: xs, a) = ($**if** $a = x$ **then** 1 **else** $0) + count(xs, a)$.

14.8. The function $prodlists$ is defined similarly to $addlists$.
$scalprod(xs, ys) = sum(prodlists(xs, ys))$. Its type is $int\ list * int\ list \rightarrow int$.

14.9. $merge(nil, nil) = nil$, $merge(nil, ys) = ys$, $merge(xs, nil) = xs$, and
$merge(xxs$ **as** $x :: xs, yys$ **as** $y :: ys) =$ **if** $x <= y$ **then** $x :: merge(xs, yys)$
$\qquad\qquad\qquad\qquad\qquad\qquad\qquad$ **else** $y :: merge(xxs, ys)$.
Note that we use xxs to name the list $x :: xs$.

14.10. $initsegment(nil, nil) = true$,
$initsegment(nil, ys) = true$,
$initsegment(xs, nil) = false$, and
$initsegment(x :: xs, y :: ys) = x = y$ **andalso** $initsegment(xs, ys)$.
Its type is $''a\ list * ''a\ list \rightarrow bool$. The elements must allow tests for equality, which is denoted by type variables starting with two primes.

14.11. This function does not have any type.

14.12. $to\_dec\ bin = td(rev(explode\ bin))$, where $td\ nil = 0$, $td("0" :: bs) = 2 * td\ bs$, and
$td("1" :: bs) = 1 + 2 * td\ bs$.

14.13. We use $initsegment$ above. $position(s, t) = pos(explode\ s, explode\ t)$, where
$pos(nil, ys) = 1$, $pos(x :: xs, nil) =$ **raise** pos, and
$pos(xs, yys$ **as** $y :: ys) =$ **if** $initsegment(xs, yys)$ **then** 1 **else** $1 + pos(xs, ys)$.

14.14. $power2\ 0 = 1$ and $power2\ n = 2 * power2(n - 1)$.

14.15. $duplicate(a, 0) = nil$ and $duplicate(a, n) = a :: duplicate(a, n - 1)$. The type is
$'a * int \rightarrow 'a\ list$.

14.16. $take(0, xs) = nil$, $take(n, nil) =$ **raise** $take$, and
$take(n, x :: xs) = x :: take(n - 1, xs)$.
$drop(0, xs) = xs$, $drop(n, nil) =$ **raise** $drop$, and
$drop(n, x :: xs) = drop(n - 1, xs)$.

14.17. $substring(size, pos, s) = implode(ss(size, pos, explode\ s))$, where $ss(0, 1, xs) = nil$,
$ss(size, 1, x :: xs) = x :: ss(size - 1, 1, xs)$,
$ss(size, pos, x :: xs) = ss(size, pos - 1, xs)$, and
$ss(\_, \_, \_) =$ **raise** ss.

14.18. For $n = 0$, the formula yields zero, which proves the base case. Suppose that $S(n) = n * (n + 1) * (2 * n + 1)/6$. We now assume that $S(k)$ gives the right result. Since we, by some manipulation, get $S(k + 1) = S(k) + (k + 1)^2$, the correctness is proved.
$sumsq\ n = n * (n + 1) * (2 * n + 1)/6$ and $sumsq\ n = sum(sql(1 - -n))$.
The first solution uses constant time and space, but the second one uses linear time and space. Hence, the first solution is much better.

14.19. $average'r\ xs = sum'r\ xs/real(len\ xs)$, $sq'r(x : real) = x * x$,
$sql'r\ nil = nil$, $sql'r\ ((x : real) :: xs) = x * x :: sql'r\ xs$, and
$stand\_dev\ xs =$ **let val** $n = real(len\ xs)$
$\qquad\qquad\qquad$ **in** $sqrt((sum'r(sql'r\ xs) - n * sq'r(average'r\ xs))/(n - 1.0))$ **end**.

Chapter 15.

15.1. **fun** $times\ x\ y : int = x * y$, **fun** $times\ x =$ **fn** $y : int \Rightarrow x * y$,
val $times =$ **fn** $x : int \Rightarrow$ **fn** $y \Rightarrow x * y$, **fun** $double\ x = times\ 2\ x$,
val $double =$ **fn** $x \Rightarrow times\ 2\ x$, and **val** $double = times\ 2$.

15.2. $int * int \rightarrow 'a\ list \rightarrow int$, read as $(int * int) \rightarrow (('a\ list) \rightarrow int)$. Given a pair, f returns a function that, given a list, returns an integer.

15.3. $bool \rightarrow 'a \rightarrow 'a \rightarrow 'a$. When you use *what*, all three arguments will be computed. When you evaluate a conditional expression, only two expressions will be evaluated. Therefore, **if** $1 = 0$ **then** 1 *div* 0 **else** $3 \longrightarrow 3$, but *what* $(1 = 0)$ $(1$ *div* $0)$ $3 \longrightarrow$ Failure: *div*.

15.4. *curry3* $f =$ **fn** $x =>$ **fn** $y =>$ **fn** $z => f(x, y, z)$ or *curry3* $f\ x\ y\ z = f(x, y, z)$. Its type is $('a * 'b * 'c \rightarrow 'd) \rightarrow 'a \rightarrow 'b \rightarrow 'c \rightarrow 'd$.
uncurry3 $f(x, y, z) = f\ x\ y\ z$. Its type is $('a \rightarrow 'b \rightarrow 'c \rightarrow 'd) \rightarrow 'a * 'b * 'c \rightarrow 'd$.

15.5. *thrice* $f\ x = f(f(f\ x))$. Its type is $('a \rightarrow 'a) \rightarrow 'a \rightarrow 'a$. *thrice double* $3 \longrightarrow$ $double(double(double\ 3)) \longrightarrow double(double\ 6) \longrightarrow double\ 12 \longrightarrow 24$.

15.6. $f1$: $(int \rightarrow int \rightarrow 'a) \rightarrow 'a$
$f2$: $(string \rightarrow 'a) \rightarrow string \rightarrow string \rightarrow 'a$
$f3$: $('a \rightarrow 'b \rightarrow 'c) \rightarrow 'a \rightarrow 'b \rightarrow 'c$
$f4$: $'a \rightarrow 'a\ list \rightarrow 'b \rightarrow 'a\ list$

15.7. *len xs* $= sum(map\ ($**fn** $x =>\ 1)\ xs)$. Both use linear time, but the last definition makes two traversals of a list and, in addition, creates a list of ones.

15.8. *swapl xs* $= map\ swap\ xs$ or *swapl* $= map\ swap$, where $swap(x, y) = (y, x)$. The type of *swapl* is $('a * 'b)\ list \rightarrow ('b * 'a)\ list$.

15.9. *map2* $f\ xs = map\ (map\ f)\ xs$ or *map2* $f = map\ (map\ f)$. Its type is $('a \rightarrow 'b) \rightarrow 'a\ list\ list \rightarrow 'b\ list\ list$.

15.10. *compose* $f\ g\ x = f(g\ x)$ or *compose* $f\ g = f\ o\ g$ with type $('a \rightarrow 'b) \rightarrow ('c \rightarrow 'a) \rightarrow 'c \rightarrow 'b$.
compose2 $f\ g\ x\ y = f(g\ x\ y)$ or *compose2* $f\ g = f\ oo\ g$ with type $('a \rightarrow 'b) \rightarrow ('c \rightarrow 'd \rightarrow 'a) \rightarrow 'c \rightarrow 'd \rightarrow 'b$.

15.11. *map2* $= map\ o\ map$.

15.12. *map* $f\ (map\ g\ xs) = map\ (f\ o\ g)\ xs$.

15.13. $(('a * 'b) * 'c \rightarrow 'd) \rightarrow 'a \rightarrow 'b \rightarrow 'c \rightarrow 'd$.

15.14. *invert* : $real \rightarrow real$, $\qquad\qquad$ *pair* : $'a \rightarrow 'b \rightarrow 'a * 'b$,
divides : $int \rightarrow int \rightarrow bool$, $\qquad$ *cons* : $'a \rightarrow 'a\ list \rightarrow 'a\ list$,
hasfactor : $int \rightarrow int \rightarrow bool$, $\qquad$ *append* : $'a\ list \rightarrow 'a\ list \rightarrow 'a\ list$,
conj : $bool \rightarrow bool \rightarrow bool$, $\qquad$ *postfix* : $'a \rightarrow 'a\ list \rightarrow 'a\ list$,
disj : $bool \rightarrow bool \rightarrow bool$, $\qquad$ *eq* : $''a \rightarrow ''a \rightarrow bool$.
fromto : $int \rightarrow int \rightarrow int\ list$, $\qquad$ *neq* : $''a \rightarrow ''a \rightarrow bool$.

15.15. *expn* $x\ n = sigma'r\ ($**fn** $i => power(x, real\ i)/real(fac\ i))\ 0\ n$.
$exp\ 1.0 \longrightarrow 2.718281828459045$, *expn* $1.0\ 4 \longrightarrow 2.70\ldots$,
expn $1.0\ 8 \longrightarrow 2.71827\ldots$, and *expn* $1.0\ 12 \longrightarrow 2.7182818282\ldots$.

15.16. **fun** *simp* $f\ x0\ xn\ n =$ **let val** $h = (xn - x0)/real\ n$
$\qquad\qquad\qquad$ **fun** $f'\ i = ($**if** $odd\ i$ **then** 4.0 **else** $2.0) * f(x0 + real\ i * h)$
$\qquad\qquad$ **in** $h/3.0 * (f\ x0 + sigma'r\ f'\ 1\ (n - 1) + f\ xn)$ **end**.

15.17. For all x, $I\ x = x$ and $S\ K\ K\ x = K\ x\ (K\ x) = x$. Also, for all n, $S(S(K\ add)(K\ 1))\ I\ n = S\ (K\ add)\ (K\ 1)\ n\ (I\ n) = K\ add\ n\ (K\ 1\ n)\ n = add\ 1\ n = succ\ n$.

15.18. *semifac* $n =$ **if** $odd\ n$ **then** $prod(map\ ($**fn** $i => 2 * i + 1)\ (0 -- (n\ div\ 2)))$
else $prod(map\ (times\ 2)\ (1 -- (n\ div\ 2)))$.

15.19.

n	$log_2 n$	n	$n * log_2 n$	n^2	n^3	2^n
1	0	1	0	1	1	2
10	3	10	33	100	1000	1024
100	7	100	664	10000	1000000	10^{30}
1000	10	1000	9966	1000000	10^9	10^{301}
10000	13	10000	132877	10^8	10^{12}	10^{3010}

15.20. *Pascal n* $=$ *map2 bin* (*map* (**fn** i $=>$ *map* (*pair i*) (*fromto* 0 i)) (*fromto* 0 n)).

15.21. *pii n* $=$ (*sqrt o* (*times'r* 6.0) *o sigma'r* (*invert o sq'r o real*) 1) n. You need 145 terms.

15.22. *sine x n* $=$ *sigma'r*
(**fn** i $=>$ **let val** $j = 2 * i + 1$ **in** *real*(($\tilde{}$1) ** i) $*$ *power*(x, *real* j)/*real*(*fac* j) **end**) 0 n.

15.23. (($'a$ $->$ $'b$) *list*) $->$ ($'a$ *list* $->$ $'b$ *list*) *list*

15.24. *stop f i* $=$ **if** $i < 0$ **then raise** *stop* **else** f i
fac n $=$ *stop* (**fn** 0 $=>$ 1 $|$ n $=>$ $n * fac(n-1)$) n.

15.25. The Y-combinator "unfolds" its first argument, that is, replaces the recursive call by the whole definition of the recursive function. Let $H =$ **fn** *len'* $=>$ (**fn** *nil* $=>$ 0 $|$ _ $::$ l $=>$ $1 + len'$ l).

len $[2, 4]$ $\longrightarrow$ Y H $[2, 4]$ $\longrightarrow$ H (Y H) $[2, 4]$ $\longrightarrow$
$1 + (Y$ $H)$ $[4]$ $\longrightarrow$ $1 + (1 + (Y$ $H)$ $nil)$ $\longrightarrow$ $1 + (1 + 0)$ $\longrightarrow$ 2

The unfolding process stops thanks to the second argument; the expression Y H is not reduced until the second argument to Y is supplied. If you remove the parameter x from the definition of Y, an application of Y to an argument leads to a non-terminating computation. If you use a lazy language, the parameter x can be removed. You can then also define so called recursive data structures using Y. You can read more about this combinator in, for instance, Burge 75, but it is really outside the scope of this book.

Chapter 16.

16.1. **infix** 3 o; **fun** (f o g) x $=$ $f(g$ $x)$; **infix** 3 oo; **fun** (f oo g) x y $=$ $f(g$ x $y)$;

16.2. **val** $>|$ $=$ *take*;   **infix** 4 $>|$;   **infix** 4 $|>$;   **val op** $|>$ $=$ *drop*;

Chapter 17.

17.1. We use *duplicates* defined in Section 17.4 that checks if a list contains duplicates.
birthtest n seed $=$ *randintlist* 1 365 n *seed*
proportion size $=$ *count true* (*map duplicates* (*experiments* (*birthtest size*) 100)).
map proportion (20 $--$ 29) $\longrightarrow$ $[47, 49, 53, 57, 59, 61, 67, 70, 71, 73]$.
Hence, this simulation indicates that the proportion is greater than 50 % for group sizes of 22 persons and upwards. You can show theoretically that with a group of 23 persons, the probability exceeds one half.

17.2. To use *genlist*, the state must include both the current position and the current seed. By mapping *fst* to the result, the seeds are eliminated.
fun *next*(*pos*, *seed*) $=$
if *seed* $>=$ 0.5 **then** (*pos* $-$ 1, *random seed*) **else** (*pos* $+$ 1, *random seed*)
fun *rwalk n seed* $=$ *map fst* (*genlist* (0, *seed*) *next n*)
rwalk 20 (*sin* 0.1) $\longrightarrow$ $[0, 1, 0, 1, 2, 3, 2, 1, 0, 1, 2, 1, 0, 1, 2, 3, 4, 5, 6, 7]$.

17.3. *sigma2 term n m k l* $=$ *sum*(*map term* (*allpairs* ($n - -m$) ($k - -l$))).

17.4. $combine(nil, nil) = nil$ and $combine(x :: xs, y :: ys) = (x, y) :: combine(xs, ys)$
$split\ nil = (nil, nil)$
$split\ ((x, y) :: xys) =$ **let val** $(xs, ys) = split\ xys$ **in** $(x :: xs, y :: ys)$ **end**
$split(combine(xs, ys)) = (xs, ys)$ and $combine(split\ xys) = xys$.

17.5. $conjl\ nil = true$ and $conjl\ (t :: ts) = t$ **andalso** $conjl\ ts$.
$sorted\ (xs\ :\ int\ list) = conjl(map\ (\text{op} <=)\ (combine(take\ (len\ xs - 1)\ xs, tl\ xs)))$.

17.6. $pairwise\ f\ nil\ nil = nil$
$pairwise\ f\ (x :: xs)\ (y :: ys) = f\ x\ y :: pairwise\ f\ xs\ ys$.

17.7. $moveupleft(k, l) = (k + 1, l - 1)$
$diagonals\ n = map\ (\textbf{fn}\ i => genlist\ (0, i)\ moveupleft\ (i + 1))\ (0 - -n)$.

17.8. $count\ a\ xs = len(filter\ (eq\ a)\ xs)$. For the recursive version, only one traversal of the list is needed; this version needs two. Both versions have linear time complexity, though.

17.9. $prime\ n = null(findl\ (divides\ n)\ (2 - - round(sqrt\ n)))$, since if there is a factor greater than the square root of the number, there must also be one less than the square root.

17.10. $digits\ 0 = nil$ and $digits\ n = digits(n\ div\ 10)\ @\ [n\ mod\ 10]$.
$sumcube\ n = sum(map\ (\textbf{fn}\ i => i * i * i)\ (digits\ n))$.
$filter\ (\textbf{fn}\ i => i = sumcube\ i)\ (1 - - 1000) \longrightarrow [1, 153, 370, 371, 407]$.

17.11. $conjl\ xs = reduce\ conj\ true\ xs$ and $disjl = reduce\ disj\ false$, where we have used the possibility of omitting the argument xs on both sides in the last equation. Note that $true$ and $false$ are identity elements of $conj$ and $disj$, respectively. In particular, $all\ nil \longrightarrow true$, which may look surprising, but is mathematically well supported.

17.12. We consider only $forall$; $exists$ is similar. Two versions based on reduction are:
$forall\ p\ xs = conjl(map\ p\ xs)$ or $forall\ p = conjl\ o\ map\ p$ and
$forall\ p\ xs = reduce\ (conj\ o\ p)\ true\ xs$.
Explicit recursion using **andalso** is more efficient, since the whole list need not always be traversed.
$forall\ p\ nil = true$ and $forall\ p\ (x :: xs) = p\ x$ **andalso** $forall\ p\ xs$.
The laziness of **andalso** saves unnecessary calls.

17.13. $len = reduce\ (add\ o\ K\ 1)\ 0$ and $rev = reduce\ postfix\ nil$.

17.14. $flat\ xss = foldl\ append\ nil\ xss$. Using $foldl$, you evaluate the expression
$append\ (append\ \ldots(append\ nil\ l_1)\ \ldots l_{n-1})\ l_n$
The last list is never manipulated, the next last broken down and built up once, the next next last twice, and so on. Using $foldr$, each list will be taken into pieces and inserted into the result list exactly once, since you evaluate the expression
$append\ l_1\ (append\ l_2\ \ldots(append\ l_n\ nil))$.
In fact, you need not break down the last list, if the equation $append\ xs\ nil = xs$ is used in the definition of $append$. Hence, the version with $foldr$ is to be preferred.

17.15. $postfix\ x\ (prefix\ y\ z) = (z :: y)\ @\ [x]$ and
$prefix\ (postfix\ x\ y)\ z = z :: (y\ @\ [x]) = (z :: y)\ @\ [x]$. Also,
$postfix\ x\ nil = [x] = prefix\ nil\ x$.

17.16. Let $hangon\ xs\ x = xs\ @\ [x]$. Now, we have $append\ xs\ ys = foldr\ cons\ ys\ xs$ and $append\ xs\ ys = foldl\ hangon\ xs\ ys$. If n and m are the lengths of the lists, the first version is of order n, but the second of order $(n + m/2) * m$. Unless m is very small compared to n, the version with $foldl$ has a quadratic time behaviour. (The combinator C is defined $C\ f\ x\ y = f\ y\ x$. Hence, we can use the expression $C\ postfix$ instead of the function $hangon$.)

17.17. $sort\ xs = find\ sorted\ (perms\ xs)$. There are $n!$ permutations of a list of length n, and since the factorial function grows like n^n (cf. Stirling's formula, Exercise 8.7), this is an extremely inefficient method.

17.18. $remdupl\ nil\ =\ nil$
$remdupl\ (x :: xs)\ =\ \textbf{if}\ mem\ x\ xs\ \textbf{then}\ remdupl\ xs\ \textbf{else}\ x :: remdupl\ xs$
$allw\ nil\ =\ [nil]$
$allw\ (c :: cs)\ =\ \textbf{let\ val}\ acss = allw\ cs\ \textbf{in}\ flat(map\ (interleave\ c)\ acss)\ @\ acss\ \textbf{end}$
$allwords\ s\ =\ map\ implode\ (remdupl(allw(explode\ s))).$

17.19. $intersection\ s1\ s2\ =\ filter\ (mem\ s2)\ s1\,.$
The elements in $intersection\ (union\ x\ y)\ z$ are all elements in z that are also in x or y. The elements in $union\ (intersection\ x\ z)\ (intersection\ y\ z)$ are the elements both in x and z *and* the elements both in y and z, but that is all elements in z that are also in x or y.

17.20. $difference\ s1\ s2\ =\ filter\ (not\ o\ mem\ s2)\ s1\,.$ Two relations are
$union\ (difference\ s1\,s2)\ (intersection\ s1\,s2)\ =\ s1$ and
$intersection\ (difference\ s1\,s2)\ (intersection\ s1\,s2)\ =\ nil.$

17.21. $insert\ key\ info\ table\ =\ (key, info) :: delete\ key\ table$
$delete\ key\ nil\ =\ nil$
$delete\ key\ ((key', info) :: table)\ =$
$\quad\quad \textbf{if}\ key = key'\ \textbf{then}\ table\ \textbf{else}\ (key', info) :: delete\ key\ table.$

17.22. We can store the table as a list of lists of lists, where each list on all levels contains 10 elements. On the bottom level, the elements are the addresses. The function $digits$ is defined in the solution to Exercise 17.10.
$lookup\ key\ tab = \textbf{let\ val}\ [i, j, k]\ =\ digits\ key\ \textbf{in}\ index\ k\ (index\ j\ (index\ i\ tab))\ \textbf{end}.$
On average, you will traverse 15 elements in the lists, and at most 30, compared to 500 and 999 in the ordinary case.

17.23. $indexm\ i\ j\ m\ =\ index\ j\ (index\ i\ m)$

17.24. We select the columns of the matrix and make them into rows.
$transpose\ nil\ =\ nil,\ transpose\ (nil :: \_)\ =\ nil,$ and
$transpose\ xss\ =\ map\ hd\ xss :: transpose(map\ tl\ xss).$
$transpose[[1,2,3],[4,5,6]]\ \longrightarrow\ [1,4] :: transpose(map\ tl[[1,2,3],[4,5,6]])\ \longrightarrow$
$[1,4] :: transpose[[2,3],[5,6]]\ \longrightarrow\ [1,4] :: [2,5] :: [3,6] :: nil\ \longrightarrow\ [[1,4],[2,5],[3,6]].$
The second equation is needed to stop the recursion, but a list of empty lists does not represent a matrix.

17.25. The complexity is of order $n + m$. If they are not sorted, it is of order $n * m$.

17.26. $sieve\ x\ xs\ =\ filter\ (not\ o\ hasfactor\ x)\ xs$
$primes'\ nil\ =\ nil$ and $primes'\ (x :: xs)\ =\ x :: primes'(sieve\ x\ xs)$
$primes\ n\ =\ primes'(2\ \textrm{--}\ n).$

17.27. $len(filter\ (\textbf{fn}\ i\ =>\ prime\ i\ \textbf{andalso}\ prime\ (i+2))\ (2\ \textrm{--}\ 1997))\ \longrightarrow\ 61.$

17.28. $isperfect\ n\ =\ 1 + sum(factors\ n) = n.\quad filter\ isperfect\ (1\ \textrm{--}\ 1000)\ \longrightarrow\ [1, 6, 28, 496].$
Euclid proved that if $2^m - 1$ is a prime, then $2^{m-1}(2^m - 1)$ is a perfect number. This happens for $m = 2, 3, 5, 7, 13, 17, 19, 31, 61, 89, 107,$ and 127 only. One does not know of any other perfect numbers than those constructed in this way.

17.29. $primes\ k = 2 :: 3 :: filter\ prime\ (map\ (\textbf{fn}\ i\ =>\ round(sqrt(real(1 + 24 * i))))\ (1\ \textrm{--}\ k)).$

17.30. We need a function that removes an element at position n in a list.
$remove\ n\ xs\ =\ take\ (n - 1)\ xs\ @\ drop\ n\ xs.$
$perm\ nil\ seed\ =\ nil$
$perm\ xs\ seed\ =\ \textbf{let\ val}\ i = randint\ 1\ (len\ xs)\ seed$
$\quad\quad\quad\quad\quad \textbf{in}\ index\ i\ xs :: perm(remove\ i\ xs)\ (random\ seed)\ \textbf{end}.$

17.31. $matmul\ m1\ m2\ =$

map (**fn** row => map (**fn** col => $scalprod\ row\ col$) ($transpose\ m2$)) $m1$.

17.32. $map = reduce'\ nil\ cons$, $len = reduce'\ 0\ add\ (K\ 1)$, $sum = reduce'\ 0\ add\ I$
$prod = reduce'\ 1\ times\ I$, $append\ xs\ ys = reduce'\ ys\ cons\ I\ xs$
$flat = reduce'\ nil\ append\ I$, and $rev = reduce'\ nil\ postfix\ I$.
$reduce\ f\ u\ xs\ =\ reduce'\ u\ f\ I\ xs$.

Chapter 18.

18.1. $semifac\ n\ =\ prod(genlist\ n\ (subtract\ 2)\ (n\ div\ 2))$.

18.2. $powersets\ nil\ =\ [nil]$
$powersets\ (x :: xs)\ =\ $ **let val** $pxs = powersets\ xs$ **in** $map\ (cons\ x)\ (pxs)\ @\ pxs$ **end**.
We claim there are 2^n subsets of a set with n elements. Base case: $2^0 = 1$, which proves the base case since the empty set is a subset of the empty set. Inductive step: Assume that a set with k elements has 2^k subsets. If you now add one element, all the old subsets are still subsets, but also all sets you get by adding the new element to the old subsets, that is, we get $2^k + 2^k = 2*2^k = 2^{k+1}$ subsets, which proves the inductive step. Note the similarity between the function definition and the proof.

18.3. $cutvector\ n\ xs\ =\ $ **if** $len\ xs <= n$ **then** $[xs]$ **else** $take\ n\ xs :: cutvector\ n\ (drop\ n\ xs)$.
$idmatrix\ n\ =\ cutvector\ n\ (flat(duplicate\ (1 :: (duplicate\ 0\ n))\ (n-1))\ @\ [1])$,
where $duplicate$ duplicates its first argument the number of times given by its second argument.
$idmatrix\ 3\ \longrightarrow\ ...\ \longrightarrow\ cutvector\ 3\ [1,0,0,0,1,0,0,0,1]\ \longrightarrow\ [[1,0,0],[0,1,0],[0,0,1]]$.

18.4. There are several ways to solve this, slightly difficult, problem. We observe that we can group the resulting lists according to their greatest element. Our solution is to generate these groups separately and then put them together. We define a function $parts$ to help us. Its first argument max is the greatest number we are allowed to use. Its second argument is the sum we still have to partition. Its third argument is the list of lists obtained by partitioning the remaining amount $n - sum$. We first generate the list $1 -- min\ max\ sum$, which are all numbers we can use. For each number i in this list, we use the function recursively to generate all solutions to the subproblem with new sum $sum - i$ and i as the new greatest number allowed. The number i is added to all previous sets using $cons$.
$parts\ max\ 0\ xss\ =\ xss$
$parts\ max\ sum\ xss\ =$
$flat(map\ ($**fn** i => $parts\ i\ (sum - i)\ (map\ (cons\ i)\ xss))\ (1 -- min\ max\ sum))$
$partitions\ n\ =\ parts\ n\ n\ [nil]$.

18.5. **fun** $even\ n\ =\ n = 0$ **orelse** $odd(n-1)$ **and** $odd\ n\ =\ n <> 0$ **andalso** $even(n-1)$.

18.6. $i ** 0\ =\ 1$
$i ** j\ =\ $ **let val** $k = i ** (j\ div\ 2)$ **in if** $even\ j$ **then** $k * k$ **else** $i * k * k$ **end**.
Note that this implementation is much better than the one in Chapter 16; this one has logarithmic and the other one linear time behaviour. In fact, it also handles negative js correctly.

18.7. We observe that the number of ways must be the sum of all ways of changing without using the largest coin less than or equal to the amount and the number of ways using that coin.
$nr\_of\_ways\ 0\ coins\ =\ 1$
$nr\_of\_ways\ amount\ nil\ =\ 0$
$nr_of_ways\ amount\ (coins\ $**as**$\ coin :: smallercoins)\ =$
    if $amount < coin$ **then** $nr\_of\_ways\ amount\ smallercoins$
    else $nr\_of\_ways\ (amount - coin)\ coins + nr\_of\_ways\ amount\ smallercoins$.

18.8. Replace the bindings between **let** and **in** by **val** $(small, large)\ =\ split\ (x, xs)$, where

$$split(x \ : \ int, nil) \ = \ (nil, nil)$$
$$split(x, y :: ys) \ = \ \textbf{let val} \ (small, large) = split(x, ys)$$
$$\textbf{in if} \ y < x \ \textbf{then} \ (y :: small, large) \ \textbf{else} \ (small, y :: large) \ \textbf{end}.$$

18.9. We use the function *split* from the previous exercise.

$$select \ i \ nil \ = \ \textbf{raise} \ select$$
$$select \ i \ (x :: xs) \ = \ \textbf{let val} \ (small, large) \ = \ split(x, xs); \ \textbf{val} \ n = len \ small$$
$$\textbf{in if} \ i <= n \ \textbf{then} \ select \ i \ small$$
$$\textbf{else if} \ i = n + 1 \ \textbf{then} \ x \ \textbf{else} \ select \ (i - n - 1) \ large \ \textbf{end}$$
$$median \ xs \ = \ select \ ((len \ xs + 1) \ div \ 2) \ xs.$$

18.10. If n is the number of disks, the number of moves needed is given by the recurrence formula $M_n = 2 * M_{n-1} + 1$, where $M_0 = 1$. The first numbers in this series are 1, 3, 7, 15, 31, 63, 127, etc. That is, $M_n = 2^{n+1} - 1$. Proof: $M_0 = 1 = 2^{0+1} - 1$, and if $M_k = 2^{k+1} - 1$ then $M_k = 2 * (2^{k+1} - 1) + 1 = 2^{k+2} - 2 + 1 = 2^{k+2} - 1$.

18.11. $ackermann \ 0 \ m \ = \ (print \ 0; \ print \ ","; \ print \ m; \ print \ "\backslash n"; \ m + 1)$
$ackermann \ n \ 0 \ = \ (print \ n; \ print \ ","; \ print \ 0; \ print \ "\backslash n"; \ ackermann \ (n-1) \ 1)$
$ackermann \ n \ m \ = \ (print \ n; \ print \ ","; \ print \ m; \ print \ "\backslash n";$
$ackermann \ (n-1) \ (ackermann \ n \ (m-1))).$

18.12. On any normal computer, it will terminate for all arguments, since repeatedly dividing a number by 2 will finally yield 0. In theory, however, the function does not terminate for non-zero arguments, since the divisions by 2 can go on forever.

18.13. $gcd \ n \ m \ = \ \textbf{if} \ m = 0 \ \textbf{then} \ n \ \textbf{else} \ gcd \ m \ (n \ mod \ m)$. If $n < m$, the next recursive call will be $gcd \ m \ n$, that is, the arguments are swapped. Hence we can assume that $n \geq m$. If $n = m$, the next call will be $gcd \ m \ 0$, and the result is, correctly, m. If $n > m > 0$, $n \ mod \ m$ is less than both n and m, but always non-negative, a property of the remainder at division. Hence, both arguments decrease and must either become equal or reach zero after a finite number of calls. In general, the last version is faster, in particular, if the two arguments differ much in magnitude. Consider $gcd \ 100 \ 2 \ \longrightarrow \ gcd \ 98 \ 2 \ \longrightarrow \ gcd \ 96 \ 2 \ \longrightarrow \ \ldots \ \longrightarrow \ gcd \ 2 \ 2 \ \longrightarrow \ 2$ and $gcd \ 100 \ 2 \ \longrightarrow \ gcd \ 2 \ 0 \ \longrightarrow \ 2$.

18.14. $for \ n \ m \ next \ s \ = \ \textbf{if} \ n > m + 1 \ \textbf{then raise} \ for$
$\textbf{else if} \ n = m + 1 \ \textbf{then} \ s \ \textbf{else} \ for \ (n+1) \ m \ next \ (next \ n \ s)$
$fac \ n \ = \ for \ 1 \ n \ times \ 1.$

18.15. $expn \ x \ n \ = \ \textbf{let fun} \ next \ i \ (lastterm, sum) = \textbf{let val} \ newterm = lastterm * x/real \ i$
$\textbf{in} \ (newterm, sum + newterm) \ \textbf{end}$
$\textbf{in} \ snd(for \ 1 \ n \ next \ (1.0, 1.0)) \ \textbf{end}.$
This version is much more efficient, since no products and quotients are computed several times.

18.16. $sum \ xs = sum' \ xs \ 0$, where $sum' \ nil \ acc = acc$ and $sum' \ ((x :: xs) \ acc = sum' \ xs \ (x + acc)$.

18.17. $rev \ xs = rev' \ xs \ nil$, where $rev' \ nil \ ys = ys$ and $rev' \ (x :: xs) \ ys = rev' \ xs \ (x :: ys)$. For the first version, $rev \ [1, 2, 3] \ \longrightarrow \ \ldots \ \longrightarrow \ nil \ @ \ [1] \ @ \ [2] \ @ \ [3]$. Now, after having appended [1] and [2] to give [1, 2], you have to break it down again to append [3]. Hence, the time complexity is quadratic. In the second version you break down the list once and build it up once, that is, you get a linear time complexity.

18.18. $while' \ p \ next \ s \ = \ \textbf{if} \ p \ s \ \textbf{then} \ while' \ p \ next \ (next \ s) \ \textbf{else} \ s.$

18.19. $epsilon \ = \ 1E\tilde{} 12, \quad derivative \ f \ x \ = \ (f(x + epsilon) - f \ x)/epsilon$, and
$newton \ f \ x = until \ (\textbf{fn} \ x \ => \ abs(f \ x) < 1E\tilde{} 14) \ (\textbf{fn} \ x \ => \ x - f \ x/derivative \ f \ x) \ x.$
The function does not terminate if there are no roots. For instance, the evaluation of the expression $newton \ (\textbf{fn} \ x \ => \ x * x + 1.0) \ 1.0$ does not terminate.

18.20. $to\_bin\ 0\ =\ "0"$, $to\_bin\ 1\ =\ "1"$, and
$to_bin\ n\ =\ to_bin(n\ div\ 2) \ \hat{}\ $ **if** $odd\ n$ **then** $"1"$ **else** $"0"$.

18.21. We use the function $merge$ defined in Exercise 14.9.
$mergesort\ nil\ =\ nil$
$mergesort\ [x]\ =\ [x]$
$mergesort\ xs\ =\ $ **let val** $n = len\ xs\ div\ 2$
                in $merge\ (mergesort\ (take\ n\ xs))\ (mergesort\ (drop\ n\ xs))$ **end**.

18.22. The value of the sum is infinite. To test large values, you need a tail recursive function.
$sumn\ 0\ x\ =\ x$ and $sumn\ n\ x\ =\ sumn\ (n-1)\ (x + invert(real\ n))$.
The value of the sum for 1, 10, 100, 1000, 10000, and 100000 is 1.0, 2.9, 5.2, 7.5, 9.8, and 12.1,
respectively. As you see, the difference is constantly 2.3 (except for the first pair), and one can
suspect that the series does not converge. There are mathematical proofs showing this fact.

18.23. We first have to prove that $ackermann(0, j, k) = sum(k, j)$. However, sum can be defined
by $sum(k, 0) = k$ and $sum(k, j+1) = sum(k, j)+1$, which are the same equations as the first two
of $ackermann$ if we ignore the zero argument. If the first argument to $ackermann$ is 1, only the
third and fifth equations apply, and in the fifth, i must equal 0, which yields:
$ackermann(1, 0, k) = 0$ and $ackermann(1, j+1, k) = ackermann(0, ackermann(1, j, k), k)$.
The last equation can be rewritten using sum as
$ackermann(1, j+1, k) = sum(k, ackermann(1, j, k))$,
which essentially is the definition of multiplication. The proof of the exponentiation case is similar.
If the first argument is 3, the result is k raised to k raised to k raised to ... j times. As you see, it
is difficult even to explain how fast $Ackermann$ grows when the first argument is greater than 3.

18.24. Nobody has been able to prove that the procedure always reaches a palindrome numeral
or proved that for some number the procedure will never reach one. Many numbers have been
checked, however. Nobody yet knows if you reach a palindrome numeral for the number 196.

Chapter 19.

19.1. **infix** $or3$; $False\ or3\ False = False$, $True\ or3\ \_ = True$, $\_\ or3\ True = True$, and
$\_\ or3\ \_ = Undef$. $disjl3\ ls\ =\ reduce\ (curry$ **op** $or3)\ False\ ls$.

19.2. $to\_rect(Polar(r, v))\ =\ Rect(r * cos\ v,\ r * sin\ v)$.

19.3. $weight(Person(\ \_,\ \_,\ \_,\ Weight\ w))\ =\ w$
$average_weight(Persons\ nil)\ =\ $ **raise** $average\_weight$
$average\_weight(Persons\ ps)\ =\ real(sum(map\ weight\ ps))/real(len\ ps)$.

19.4. $regnum(Car(\_, r, \_)) = r$, $regnum(Truck(r, \_, \_)) = r$, and $regnum\ Bike = $ **raise** $regnum$.

19.5. $totalweight\ vs = reduce\ (add\ o\ weight)\ 0\ vs$. $sum(map\ f\ xs) = reduce\ (add\ o\ f)\ 0\ xs$,
or, more generally, $reduce\ f\ u\ (map\ g\ xs) = reduce\ (f\ o\ g)\ u\ xs$.

19.6. **datatype** $VEHICLEREG\ =\ Vehiclereg$ **of** $(PERSON * VEHICLE)$ list;
$owner(p, v) = p$, $vehicle(p, v) = v$, $istruck(Truck\ \_) = true$, $istruck\ \_ = false$,
$truckowners(Vehiclereg\ vs)\ =\ map\ owner\ (filter\ (istruck\ o\ vehicle)\ vs)$.

19.7. $add\_lengths(Mm\ l1,\ Mm\ l2)\ =\ Mm(l1 + l2)$
$add\_lengths(Mm\ l1,\ Meter\ l2)\ =\ Meter(l1\ div\ 1000 + l2)$
$add\_lengths(Meter\ l1,\ Mm\ l2)\ =\ Meter(l1 + l2\ div\ 1000)$
$add\_lengths(Meter\ l1,\ Meter\ l2)\ =\ Meter(l1 + l2)$.

19.8. $Enter\ e\ (Queue\ xs) = Queue(e :: xs)$, $remove\ (Queue\ nil) = $ **raise** $remove$,
$remove\ (Queue\ [e]) = e$, $remove\ (Queue\ (e :: es)) = remove\ es$.
$rest\ (Queue\ nil) = $ **raise** $rest$, $rest\ (Queue\ [e]) = Queue\ nil$, and

$rest\ (Queue\ (e :: es)) = Enter\ e\ (rest\ es).$
The other operations are unchanged.

19.9. **datatype** $QUEUE\ =\ Queue$ **of** $int\ list * int\ list;$
$Empty\ =\ Queue(nil, nil),\quad Enter\ e\ (Queue(entry, exit))\ =\ Queue(e :: entry, exit),$
$remove(Queue(nil, nil))\ =\ $ **raise** $remove,\quad remove(Queue(entry, nil))\ =\ last\ entry,$
$remove(Queue(\_, e :: es))\ =\ e,\ rest(Queue(entry, nil))\ =\ Queue(nil, tl(rev\ entry)),$
$rest(Queue(entry, e :: es))\ =\ Queue(entry, es),$
$isempty(Queue(nil, nil))\ =\ true,$ and $isempty(Queue\ \_)\ =\ false.$

The remarkable thing is that, on average, all operations now use only constant time. The reverse operation takes a time proportional to the length of *entry* at that time, but, on the other hand, it is a delayed action of the corresponding number of entries into the queue. Of course, if you remove the same elements many times from the same queue, the *last* operation can consume more than constant time.

19.10. **datatype** $'a\ TABLE\ =\ Table$ **of** $('a * 'a)\ list;$
$Insert\ key\ info\ (Table\ pairs)\ =\ Table\ ((key, info) :: pairs)$
$lookup\ key\ (Table\ nil)\ =\ $ **raise** $lookup$
$lookup\ key\ (Table((key', info) :: pairs))\ =\ $ **if** $key = key'$ **then** $info$
$\qquad\qquad\qquad\qquad\qquad\qquad\qquad\qquad\qquad\qquad$ **else** $lookup\ key\ (Table\ pairs).$

19.11. **type** $PERSON\ =\ \{name = string,\ salary = real\};$
datatype $LEADER = Leader$ **of** $PERSON;$
type $NAME\ =\ \{name = string\};$
datatype $SECTION\ =\ Team$ **of** $NAME * PERSON\ list$
$\qquad\qquad\qquad\qquad\quad |\ \ Group$ **of** $NAME * LEADER * PERSON\ list;$
datatype $ORGANIZATION\ =\ Org$ **of** $NAME * LEADER * SECTION\ list;$
$map\_organization\ f\ (Org(name,\ Leader\ leader,\ sections))\ =$
$\qquad Org(name,\ Leader(f\ leader),\ map\ (map\_section\ f)\ sections)$
$map\_section\ f\ (Team(name,\ members))\ =\ Team(name,\ map\ f\ members)$
$map\_section\ f\ (Group(name,\ Leader\ leader,\ members))\ =$
$\qquad\qquad\qquad Group(name,\ Leader(f\ leader),\ map\ f\ members),$
$up\ percentage\ organization\ =\ map\_organization$
$\qquad ($ **fn** $\{name, salary\}\ =>\ \{name, (1.0 + percentage/100.0) * salary\})\ organization.$
There are many other ways of defining these types.

Chapter 20.

20.1. **datatype** $'a\ QUEUE\ =\ Empty\ \ |\ \ Insert$ **of** $'a * 'a\ QUEUE;$
$remove\ Empty\ =\ $ **raise** $remove,\quad remove\ (Insert(e, Empty))\ =\ e,$
$remove\ (Insert(e, q))\ =\ remove\ q,\quad rest\ Empty\ =\ $ **raise** $rest,$
$rest\ (Insert(e, Empty))\ =\ Empty,\quad rest\ (Insert(e, q))\ =\ Insert(e, rest\ q),$ and
$isempty\ q\ =\ q = Empty.$

There is no real difference between the type of a list and the type of this queue; the names of the constructors are different, but they do the same thing. The data types are quite different, though, since the selectors do different things for lists and for queues.

20.2. $to\_nat\ Zero\ =\ 0,\quad to\_nat(Succ\ n)\ =\ to\_nat\ n + 1,$
infix $6\ -\ ';$ **infix** $7\ /\ ';$ **infixr** $8\ **\ ';$
$n\ **'\ Zero\ =\ Succ\ Zero,\quad n\ **'\ Succ\ m\ =\ n\ *'\ n\ **'\ m,$
$n\ -'\ Zero\ =\ n,\quad Zero\ -'\ m\ =\ Zero,\quad Succ\ n\ -'\ Succ\ m\ =\ n\ -'\ m,$
$n\ /'\ Zero\ =\ $ **raise** $/',\quad Zero\ /'\ m\ =\ Zero,\quad n\ /'\ m\ =\ 1\ +'\ (n\ -'\ m)\ /'\ m.$

20.3. The type is $WHAT \rightarrow int$, but the problem is that you cannot use it in an application, because you cannot write down any object of type $WHAT$.

20.4. For the first version, we first simplify the representation of an integer to a form not containing both *Succ* and *Pred*.

$simplify\ Zero\ =\ Zero$

$simplify(Succ\ n)\ =\ $**let val** $n = simplify\ n$
       in case n **of** $Pred\ m\ =>\ m\ \mid\ \_\ =>\ Succ\ n$ **end**

$simplify(Pred\ n)\ =\ $**let val** $n = simplify\ n$
       in case n **of** $Succ\ m\ =>\ m\ \mid\ \_\ =>\ Pred\ n$ **end**

$equal\ n\ m\ =\ equal'\ (reduce\ n)\ (reduce\ m),$

$equal'\ Zero\ Zero\ =\ true,\quad equal'\ (Succ\ n)\ (Succ\ m)\ =\ equal'\ n\ m,$

$equal'\ (Pred\ n)\ (Pred\ m)\ =\ equal'\ n\ m,\quad equal'\ \_\ \_\ =\ false,$

$add\ n\ m\ =\ add'\ (reduce\ n)\ (reduce\ m),$

$add'\ Zero\ m\ =\ m,\quad add'\ (Succ\ n)\ m\ =\ Succ(add'\ n\ m),$ and

$add'\ (Pred\ n)\ m\ =\ Pred(add'\ n\ m).$

For the second version, we make use of the operations defined for NAT. We also assume that the relational operator $>='$ is defined.

$equal\ (Int(s, Zero))\ (Int(t, Zero))\ =\ true,$

$equal\ (Int(s, i))\ (Int(t, j))\ =\ s = t$ **andalso** $i = j,$

$add\ (Int(Plus, i))\ (Int(Plus, j))\ =\ Int(Plus, i\ +'\ j),$

$add\ (Int(Minus, i))\ (Int(Minus, j))\ =\ Int(Minus, i\ +'\ j),$

$add\ (Int(Minus, i))\ (Int(Plus, j))\ =\ add\ (Int(Plus, j))\ (Int(Minus, i)),$

$add\ (Int(Plus, i))\ (Int(Minus, j))\ =\ $**if** $i\ >='\ j$ **then** $Int(Plus, i\ -'\ j)$
                              else $Int(Minus, j\ -'\ i).$

The third version is free so $equal = eq$. We assume that $>='$ and $possub$ has been defined for $POSINT$.

$posadd\ One\ j\ =\ Succ\ j$ and $posadd\ (Succ\ i)\ j\ =\ Succ(posadd\ i\ j).$

$add\ Zero\ j\ =\ j,\quad add\ i\ Zero\ =\ i,\quad add\ (Plus\ i)\ (Plus\ j)\ =\ Plus(posadd\ i\ j),$

$add\ (Minus\ i)\ (Minus\ j)\ =\ Minus(posadd\ i\ j),$

$add\ (Minus\ i)\ (Plus\ j)\ =\ add\ (Plus\ j)\ (Minus\ i),$

$add\ (Plus\ i)\ (Minus\ j)\ =\ $**if** $i\ >='\ j$ **then** $Plus(possub\ i\ j)$ **else** $Minus(possub\ j\ i).$

20.5. To prove $P(n)$ for all integers n, you first have to prove $P(Zero)$, $P(Plus\ One)$, and $P(Minus\ One)$. Next, under the assumption $P(Plus\ k)$, you have to prove $P(Plus(Succ\ k))$, and, under the assumption $P(Minus\ k)$, you have to prove $P(Minus(Succ\ k))$.

20.6. **datatype** $TT0\ =\ Tip\ \mid\ Node$ **of** $TT0 * TT0 * TT0.$

20.7. $full\ Tip = false,\quad full(Node(Tip, Tip)) = true,\quad full(Node(Tip, Node\ \_)) = false,$

$full(Node(Node\ \_, Tip))\ =\ false,\quad full(Node(l, r))\ =\ full\ l$ **andalso** $full\ r.$

20.8. A tree with a single node is full and has an odd number of nodes. Suppose that l and r are full trees with n and m nodes, where n and m are odd. The tree $Node(l, r)$ then has $n + m + 1$, which is odd. Hence, all full trees have an odd number of nodes.

20.9. $nrofnodes\ Tip\ =\ 0$ and $nrofnodes(Node(l, r))\ =\ nrofnodes\ l + nrofnodes\ r + 1.$

$nrofnodes\ bt\ =\ redbt0\ (succ\ oo\ add)\ 0\ bt.$

20.10. $maxheight\ bt\ =\ redbt0\ (succ\ oo\ max)\ 0\ bt.$

20.11. We use a trick and represent unbalanced trees by ~1:

$balanced\ bt\ =\ baldepth\ bt >= 0,$ where $baldepth\ Tip\ =\ 0$ and

$baldepth(Node(l, r))\ =\ $**let val** $b = baldepth\ l$

in if $b = baldepth\ r$ **andalso** $b >= 0$ **then** $b + 1$ **else** $\tilde{}1$ **end**.
It is questionable whether the use of a trick like this one is good programming practice. Can you define *balanced* without using a trick?

20.12. $membt1\ Tip\ x\ =\ false$
$membt1\ (Node(a,l,r))\ x\ =\ x = a$ **orelse** $membt1\ l\ x$ **orelse** $membt1\ r\ x$.

20.13. $eqstruct\ Tip\ Tip = true,\quad eqstruct\ Tip\ \_ = false,\quad eqstruct\ \_\ Tip = false,$
$eqstruct\ (Node(\ \_\ , l1, r1))\ (Node(\ \_\ , l2, r2)) = eqstruct\ l1\ l2$ **andalso** $eqstruct\ r1\ r2$.

20.14. We give the preorder and mark a missing node by a dot: $(1\ (3\ 4\ (5\ 7\ 6))\ (2\ .\ 8))$.

20.15. The trees with dot preorder $(1\ 2\ .)$ and $(1\ .\ 2)$ have preorder $1\ 2$ and postorder $2\ 1$.

20.16. $printtree\ Tip\ =\ ".",\quad printtree(Node(a, Tip, Tip))\ =\ makestring\ a$, and
$printtree(Node(a, l, r)) = "("\ \hat{}\ makestring\ a\ \hat{}\ "\ "\ \hat{}\ printtree\ l\ \hat{}\ "\ "\ \hat{}\ printtree\ r\ \hat{}\ ")"$.

20.17. No, since information is associated only with the leaves, this is not possible. If you associate information also with internal nodes, the path to an internal node is a prefix of the path to some tips. Then, you are not using leaf trees, however.

20.18. $labels(Leaf\ a)\ =\ makestring\ a$ and $labels(Node(l, r))\ =\ labels\ l\ \hat{}\ "\ "\ \hat{}\ labels\ r$.

20.19. $redbt2\ f\ g\ (Leaf\ a) = g\ a$ and $redbt2\ f\ g\ (Node(l, r)) = f\ (redbt2\ f\ g\ l)\ (redbt2\ f\ g\ r)$.
$mapbt2\ f\ bt\ =\ redbt2\ Node'\ f\ bt$, where $Node'\ =\ curry\ Node$.

20.20. $car(Leaf\ \_\ )\ =$ **raise** car and $car(Node(l, r))\ =\ l$.
$cdr(Leaf\ \_\ )\ =$ **raise** cdr and $cdr(Node(l, r))\ =\ r$.
$cons\ l1\ l2\ =\ Node(l1, l2),\quad null\ (Leaf\ Nil)\ =\ true,\quad null\ \_\ =\ false,$
$isatom(Leaf\ \_\ )\ =\ true$, and $isatom\ \_\ =\ false$.

20.21. $preorder(Leaf\ a) = [a],\quad preorder(Node(a, l, r)) = [a]\ @\ preorder\ l\ @\ preorder\ r$.
$inorder(Leaf\ a) = [a],\quad inorder(Node(a, l, r)) = inorder\ l\ @\ [a]\ @\ inorder\ r$.
$postorder(Leaf\ a) = [a],\quad postorder(Node(a, l, r)) = postorder\ l\ @\ postorder\ r\ @\ [a]$.

20.22. $[1, 1, 3, 4, 4, 6, 9],\quad [(1\ 2\ 1), 3, 4, 4, 6, 9],\quad [4, 4, ((1\ 2\ 1)\ 5\ 3), 6, 9],\quad [((1\ 2\ 1)\ 5\ 3), 6, (4\ 8\ 4), 9],$
$[(4\ 8\ 4), 9, (((1\ 2\ 1)\ 5\ 3)\ 11\ 6)],\quad [(((1\ 2\ 1)\ 5\ 3)\ 11\ 6), ((4\ 8\ 4)\ 17\ 9)],$
$[((((1\ 2\ 1)\ 5\ 3)\ 11\ 6)\ 28\ ((4\ 8\ 4)\ 17\ 9))]$.

20.23. $cost(Leaf\ i)\ =\ 0$ and $cost(Node(i, l, r))\ =\ i + cost\ l + cost\ r$.
$cost\ bt\ =\ redbt3\ (add\ oo\ add)\ (K\ 0)\ bt$.

20.24. $printoper\ Plus\ =\ "+",\quad printoper\ Minus\ =\ "-",$
$printoper\ Times\ =\ "*",\quad printoper\ Divide\ =\ "/"$.
$printexpr(Leaf\ i)\ =\ makestring\ i$ and
$printexpr(Node(oper, l, r))\ =\ "("\ \hat{}\ printexpr\ l\ \hat{}\ printoper\ oper\ \hat{}\ printexpr\ r\ \hat{}\ ")"$.

20.25. Five trees. Note that, in an inorder listing, no parentheses are present to denote precedences, so even the tree corresponding to the expression $(1 + 4) * (5 - 0)$ has the given inorder listing.

20.26. We define a type *EXPR* that can be used for many types of expressions.
datatype $BINOP\ =\ And\ |\ Or;$ **datatype** $UNOP\ =\ Not;$
datatype $('a, 'b, 'c)\ EXPR\ =\ Leaf\ \textbf{of}\ 'a\ |\ Node1\ \textbf{of}\ 'b * ('a, 'b, 'c)\ EXPR$
$|\ Node2\ \textbf{of}\ 'c * ('a, 'b, 'c)\ EXPR * ('a, 'b, 'c)\ EXPR;$
$eval(Leaf\ b)\ =\ b,\quad eval(Node1(Not, tree))\ =\ not(eval\ tree),$
$eval(Node2(And, l, r))\ =\ eval\ l$ **andalso** $eval\ r$, and
$eval(Node2(Or, l, r))\ =\ eval\ l$ **orelse** $eval\ r$.

20.27. $build\ s\ =' $ **let val** $(expr, rest) = bld(explode\ s)$
in if $rest = nil$ **then** $expr$ **else raise** $build$ **end**,
$bldop\ "+"\ =\ Plus,\quad bldop\ "-"\ =\ Minus,$
$bldop\ "*"\ =\ Times,\quad bldop\ "/"\ =\ Divide,\quad bldop\ \_\ =$ **raise** $build$,
$bld\ ""\ =$ **raise** $build$ and

$bld\ (c :: cs)\ =\ \mathbf{if}\ digit\ c\ \mathbf{then}\ (digitval\ c,\ cs)$

$\qquad\qquad\qquad \mathbf{else\ let\ val}\ (left, ds) = bld\ cs;\ \mathbf{val}\ (right, es) = bld\ ds$

$\qquad\qquad\qquad\qquad \mathbf{in}\ (Node(bldop\ c,\ left,\ right),\ es)\ \mathbf{end}.$

20.28. $eval\ s = ev\ nil\ (explode\ s)$, where

$\qquad ev\ [result]\ nil\ =\ result,\quad ev\ \_\ nil\ =\ \mathbf{raise}\ eval,$

$\qquad ev\ (x :: y :: es)\ ("+" :: cs)\ =\ ev\ (x + y :: es)\ cs$

$\qquad ev\ (x :: y :: es)\ ("*" :: cs)\ =\ ev\ (x * y :: es)\ cs$

$\qquad ev\ stack\ (c :: cs)\ =\ \mathbf{if}\ digit\ c\ \mathbf{then}\ ev\ (digitval\ c :: stack)\ cs\ \mathbf{else\ raise}\ eval.$

20.29. $eqstruct\ (Node(\ \_, trees), Node(\ \_, trees'))\ =$

$\qquad len\ trees = len\ trees'\ \mathbf{andalso}\ conjl(map\ eqstruct\ (combine(trees, trees'))).$

20.30. $insertblanks\ nil = nil,\quad insertblanks\ [s] = [s]$, and

$insertblanks\ (s :: ss) = s ::\ "\ " :: insertblanks\ ss.$

$print(Node(x, nil)) = x$ and

$print(Node(x, ts)) = "("\ \hat{}\ x\ \hat{}\ "\ "\ \hat{}\ implode(insertblanks(map\ print\ ts))\ \hat{}\ ")".$

Note the similarity to LISP lists and the function *printlist* on page 283.

20.31. We show such a forest and the corresponding binary tree using preorder:

$\qquad [(+ [5\ 7])\ (- [5])\ (if\ [(> [2\ 3])\ 4\ 6])]$ and $(+ (5\ .\ 7)\ (- 5\ (if\ (> (2\ .\ 3))\ (4\ .\ 6))\ .))).$

A forest with only one tree corresponds to a binary tree whose root has no right subtree.

20.32. To prove $P(e)$ for all expressions e, you have to prove: 1) $P(Const\ i)$ for all integers i, 2) $P(Var\ id)$ for every id, 3) $P(Op(oper, l, r))$ under the assumptions $P(l)$ and $P(r)$ for every $oper$, and 4) $P(If(be, thn, els))$ under the assumptions $P(be)$, $P(thn)$, and $P(els)$.

$\qquad nr\_of\_constants(Const\ \_) = 1,\quad nr\_of\_constants(Var\ \_) = 0,$

$\qquad nr\_of\_constants(Op(\ \_, l, r)) = nr\_of\_constants\ l + nr\_of\_constants\ r$, and

$\qquad nr\_of\_constants(If(be, thn, els)) =$

$\qquad\qquad nr\_of\_constants\ be + nr\_of\_constants\ thn + nr\_of\_constants\ els.$

20.33. We have to take precedences into consideration and we therefore introduce an extra argument telling the precedence of the parent of an expression.

$\qquad print\ expr\ =\ prt\ 0\ expr,\ prec\ "+"\ =\ 6,\quad prec\ "*"\ =\ 7$, etc. and

$\qquad prt\ \_\ (Const\ i)\ =\ makestring\ i,\quad prt\ \_\ (Var\ id)\ =\ id$, and

$\qquad prt\ parentprec\ (Op(oper, l, r))\ =\ (\mathbf{if}\ parentprec > prec\ oper\ \mathbf{then}\ "("\ \mathbf{else}\ "")\ \hat{}$

$\qquad\qquad\qquad\qquad\qquad\qquad prt\ (prec\ oper)\ l\ \hat{}\ oper\ \hat{}\ prt\ (prec\ oper)\ r\ \hat{}$

$\qquad\qquad\qquad\qquad\qquad\qquad (\mathbf{if}\ parentprec > prec\ oper\ \mathbf{then}\ ")"\ \mathbf{else}\ "").$

20.34. $diff\ v\ (Op("/", l, r))\ =\ Op("/", Op("-", Op("*", diff\ v\ l, r), Op("*", l, diff\ v\ r)),$

$\qquad\qquad\qquad\qquad\qquad\qquad\qquad Op("*", r, r)).$

20.35. $simplify(Const\ i)\ =\ Const\ i,\quad simplify(Var\ id)\ =\ Var\ id,$

$simplify(Op(oper, l, r)) = \mathbf{let\ val}\ (ll, rr) = (simplify\ l,\ simplify\ r)\mathbf{in}$

$\qquad\qquad\qquad \mathbf{case}\ (oper, ll, rr)\ \mathbf{of}$

$\qquad\qquad\qquad\qquad ("+",\ Const\ 0,\ e)\ =>\ e\ \mid\ ("+",\ e,\ Const\ 0)\ =>\ e\ \mid$

$\qquad\qquad\qquad\qquad ("*",\ Const\ 0,\ e)\ =>\ 0\ \mid\ ("*",\ e,\ Const\ 0)\ =>\ 0\ \mid$

$\qquad\qquad\qquad\qquad ("*",\ Const\ 1,\ e)\ =>\ e\ \mid\ ("*",\ e,\ Const\ 1)\ =>\ e\ \mid$

$\qquad\qquad\qquad\qquad ("-",\ e,\ Const\ 0)\ =>\ e\ \mid\ ("/",\ e,\ Const\ 1)\ =>\ e\ \mid$

$\qquad\qquad\qquad\qquad ("-",\ e,\ f)\ =>\ \mathbf{if}\ e = f\ \mathbf{then}\ Const\ 0\ \mathbf{else}\ Op("-", e, f)\ \mid$

$\qquad\qquad\qquad\qquad triple\ =>\ Op\ triple\ \mathbf{end}.$

20.36. If the number of a node is n, its children have numbers $2 * n$ and $2 * n + 1$.

20.37. We first define *split* that gives the list to the left and to the right of a symbol in a list.

$\qquad split\ s\ xs\ =\ \mathbf{let\ val}\ pos = position\ s\ xs\ \mathbf{in}\ (take\ (pos - 1)\ xs,\ drop\ pos\ xs)\ \mathbf{end}.$

$\qquad bld\ nil\ nil\ =\ Tip$

$bld\ (s :: pre)\ inn\ =\ $**let val** $(left, right) = split\ s\ inn\ $**in**
$\qquad Node(s,\ bld\ (take\ (len\ left)\ pre)\ left,\ bld\ (drop\ (len\ left)\ pre)\ right)\ $**end.**

20.38. We first have to go down in the tree to find the appropriate leaf and then return the path expressed in zeros and ones as result. We use a small trick and return a string with the path if we succeed and an empty string if we fail. At each stage, we can now concatenate the results, and only the correct path will contribute to the result string.

$encode\ info\ tree\ =\ enc\ ""\ info\ tree,$ where
$enc\ path\ info\ (Leaf\ info')\ =\ $**if** $info = info'\ $**then** $path\ $**else** $""$
$enc\ path\ info\ (Node(l,r))\ =\ enc\ (path\ \hat{\ }\ "0")\ info\ l\ \hat{\ }\ enc\ (path\ \hat{\ }\ "1")\ info\ r.$

20.39. Surprisingly, $eval$ now is extremely simple to define: $eval\ =\ redbt\ I\ I.$
$\qquad redbt\ I\ I\ (Node(add,\ Leaf\ 2,\ Leaf\ 3))\ \longrightarrow\ I\ add\ (I\ 2)\ (I\ 3)\ \longrightarrow\ add\ 2\ 3\ \longrightarrow\ 5.$
The serious drawback of this representation is that you cannot find out which operator a node contains, since you cannot compare functions for equality. Hence, you cannot define functions like $print$ and $diff$.

Chapter 21.

21.1.   **abstype** $SET\ =\ Empty'\ |\ Insert'\ $**of** $int * SET$
$\qquad$**with val** $Empty = Empty'$
$\qquad\qquad$**fun** $Insert\ e\ s\ =\ $**if** $member\ s\ e\ $**then** $s\ $**else** $Insert'(e, s)$
$\qquad\qquad$**and** $member\ Empty'\ e\ =\ false$
$\qquad\qquad\quad|\ member\ (Insert'(x, s))\ e\ =\ e = x\ $**orelse** $member\ s\ e$
$\qquad$**end**

21.2. $gen_until\ p\ next\ s\ =\ $**if** $p\ s\ $**then** $nil\ $**else** $s :: gen\_until\ p\ next\ (next\ s)$
$\qquad sort\ order\ xs\ =\ $**let val** $sortseq = reduce\ (Insert\ order)\ Empty\ xs$
$\qquad\qquad\qquad\qquad\quad$**in** $map\ smallest\ (gen_until\ isempty\ rest\ sortseq)\ $**end.**
Some order relations can consider different objects as equal; the objects form equivalence classes. If you use a "precedes" relation, equivalent, but not equal, objects will shift place; you say that the sorting method is not stable.

21.3.   Numbers with few digits always occur before numbers with many digits. Numbers with an equal number of digits will occur in the same order as in the argument list.

21.4. $back(Cursor\ _)\ =\ $**raise** $back,\ back(Insert(x,\ Cursor\ f))\ =\ Cursor(Insert(x,\ f)),$
$\qquad back(Insert(x,\ f))\ =\ Insert(x,\ back\ f),$ and, for the second implementation,
$\qquad back'(File(nil, _))\ =\ $**raise** $back',\quad back'(File(x :: xs, ys))\ =\ File(xs, x :: ys).$

21.5.   The current position is always at the head of the second list. The extra counter tells which position number that element has.

$\qquad$**abstype** $'a\ FILE\ =\ File\ $**of** $int * 'a\ list * 'a\ list$
$\qquad$**with val** $Rewrite\ =\ File(1, nil, nil)$
$\qquad\qquad$**fun** $Put\ x\ (File(pos, xs, nil))\ =\ File(pos + 1, x :: xs, nil)$
$\qquad\qquad\quad|\ Put\ x\ (File(pos, xs, y :: ys))\ =\ File(pos + 1, x :: xs, ys)$
$\qquad\qquad$**fun** $Advance\ (File(_, _, nil))\ =\ $**raise** $Advance$
$\qquad\qquad\quad|\ Advance\ (File(pos, xs, y :: ys))\ =\ File(pos + 1, y :: xs, ys)$
$\qquad\qquad$**fun** $Reset\ (File(\_, xs, ys))\ =\ File(1, nil, rev\ xs\ @\ ys)$
$\qquad\qquad$**fun** $get\ (File(pos, xs, nil))\ =\ $**raise** get
$\qquad\qquad\quad|\ get\ (File(pos, xs, y :: ys))\ =\ y$
$\qquad\qquad$**fun** $move\ newpos\ (File(1, nil, nil))\ =\ $**if** $newpos = 1\ $**then** $File(1, nil, nil)$
$\qquad\qquad\qquad\qquad\qquad\qquad\qquad\qquad\qquad\qquad$**else raise** $move$
$\qquad\qquad\quad|\ move\ newpos\ (File(pos, x :: xs, nil))\ =\ $**if** $newpos > pos\ $**then raise** $move$

$$\textbf{else if } newpos = pos \textbf{ then } File(pos, x :: xs, nil)$$
$$\textbf{else } move\ newpos\ (File(pos - 1, xs, [x]))$$
$$\mid\ move\ newpos\ (File(1, nil, y :: ys)) = \textbf{if } newpos < 1 \textbf{ then raise } move$$
$$\textbf{else if } newpos = 1 \textbf{ then } File(1, nil, y :: ys)$$
$$\textbf{else } move\ newpos\ (File(2, [y], ys))$$
$$\mid\ move\ newpos\ (File(pos, x :: xs, y :: ys)) =$$
$$\textbf{if } newpos < pos \textbf{ then } move\ newpos\ (File(pos - 1, xs, x :: y :: ys))$$
$$\textbf{else if } newpos = pos \textbf{ then } File(pos, x :: xs, y :: ys)$$
$$\textbf{else } move\ newpos\ (File(pos + 1, y :: x :: xs, ys))$$
$$\textbf{fun } eof\ (File(\ \_,\ \_, ys)) = null\ ys$$
$$\textbf{fun } length(File(xs, ys)) = len\ xs + len\ ys$$
$$\textbf{end.}$$

21.6. $difference\ (Set\ es)\ (Set\ fs) = Set(filter\ (not\ o\ mem\ fs)\ es)$

21.7. Only some operations have to be changed.
$Insert\ (\textbf{op} <)\ e\ (Set\ nil) = Set\ [e]$
$Insert\ (\textbf{op} <)\ e\ (Set\ (x :: xs)) = \textbf{if } e < x \textbf{ then } Set(e :: x :: xs)$
  $\textbf{else if } e = x \textbf{ then } Set(x :: xs) \textbf{ else } Insert\ (\textbf{op} <)\ x(Insert\ (\textbf{op} <)\ e\ (Set\ xs))$
$member\ (\textbf{op} <)\ (Set\ nil)\ e = false$
$member\ (\textbf{op} <)\ (Set\ (x :: xs))\ e = \textbf{if } e < x \textbf{ then } false$
  $\textbf{else if } e = x \textbf{ then } true \textbf{ else } member\ (\textbf{op} <)\ (Set\ xs)\ e$
$union\ (\textbf{op} <)\ (Set\ es)\ (Set\ fs) = Set(merge\ (\textbf{op} <)\ es\ fs), \text{where}$
$merge\ (\textbf{op} <)\ nil\ ys = ys, merge\ (\textbf{op} <)\ xs\ nil = xs, \text{and}$
$merge\ (\textbf{op} <)\ (x :: xs)\ (y :: ys) = \textbf{if } x < y \textbf{ then } x :: merge\ (\textbf{op} <)\ xs\ (y :: ys)$
  $\textbf{else if } x = y \textbf{ then } x :: merge\ (\textbf{op} <)\ xs\ ys \textbf{ else } y :: merge\ (\textbf{op} <)\ (x :: xs)\ ys.$
Since you now have to search only up to an element larger than the one you look for, searching is faster, but still linear. The union operation was formerly quadratic, but is now linear.

21.8. $triple\ x\ (y, z) = (x, y, z),\quad tripleabstr\ p\ (Set\ nil)\ \_\ \_ = Set\ nil$
$tripleabstr\ p\ (Set\ (x :: xs))\ s\ t =$
  $\textbf{let val } Set\ yzs = pairabstr\ (p\ x)\ s\ t;\ \textbf{val } Set\ xyzs = tripleabstr\ p\ (Set\ xs)\ s\ t$
  $\textbf{in } Set(map\ (triple\ x)\ (filter\ (\textbf{fn}\ (y, z)\ =>\ p\ x\ y\ z)\ yzs)\ @\ xyzs)\ \textbf{end.}$

21.9. $subset\ (Set\ nil)\ \_ = true \text{ and}$
$subset\ (Set\ (e :: es))\ s = member\ s\ e \textbf{ andalso } subset\ (Set\ es)\ s.$

21.10. $forall\ p\ (Set\ nil) = true \text{ and}$
$forall\ p\ (Set\ (e :: es)) = p\ e \textbf{ andalso } forall\ p\ (Set\ es).$
The expression $forall\ even\ [2, 3, 1\ div\ 0]$ will give the result $false$ with the implementation here, but will raise an exception with the implementation in the text. The predicate $exists$ is defined similarly and has similar properties.

21.11. $switch\ i = 10 * i\ mod\ 10 + i\ div\ 10\quad (*\ 0 \leq i \leq 99\ *)$
$check\ i\ j = i * j = switch\ i * switch\ j$
$members(pairabstr\ check\ (mkset(0 - -99))\ (mkset(0 - -99))).$

21.12. $members(setfilter\ (\textbf{fn}\ x\ =>\ prime\ x \textbf{ andalso } perfect\ x)\ (mkset(1\ --\ 999))).$

21.13. You have to pass an order relation to operations like $Insert$ and $member$.
$union\ (\textbf{op} <=)\ s\ t = reduce\ (Insert\ (\textbf{op} <=))\ t\ (members\ s).$

21.14. You can sort by inserting all elements into a set and then let the $members$ operation list the elements in the search tree in inorder.
$members(Set\ Tip) = nil,\ members(Set(Node(e, l, r))) = members\ l\ @\ [e]\ @\ members\ r.$
If the tree is balanced, sorting will have time complexity $n * log(n)$ instead of n^2 for insertion sort.

21.15. *difference* (*Set f*) (*Set g*) = *Set*(**fn** *x* => *f x* **andalso** *not*(*g x*))
$\qquad$ *setfilter p* (*Set f*) = *Set*(**fn** *x* => *f x* **andalso** *p x*).

If you insert the elements one after the other, the time complexity of *member* will be linear. If you, however, form a set by successive unions of equally big sets the time complexity for *member* will be logarithmic. If you form a set with the *set_of* operation, *member* will only take the time it takes to apply the argument function to *set_of* to an argument.

21.16. *compose* (*Rel ps*) (*Rel qs*) = *Rel*(*flat*(*map* (**fn** (*x, y*) => *map* (*pair x o snd*)
$\qquad\qquad\qquad\qquad\qquad\qquad\qquad$ (*filter* (**fn** (*y′, z*) => *y* = *y′*) *qs*)) *ps*)).

21.17. Suppose that *relunion* computes the union of two relations, that *releq* decides if two relations are equal, and that *compose* is the function defined in the previous exercise.

$\qquad$ *transitive_closure s* = **let val** *t* = *relunion s* (*compose s s*)
$\qquad\qquad\qquad\qquad\qquad\qquad$ **in if** *releq s t* **then** *s*
$\qquad\qquad\qquad\qquad\qquad\qquad\qquad\quad$ **else** *transitive_closure t* **end**

A more efficient, but also more complicated solution is

$\qquad$ *transitive_closure* (*Rel nil*) = *Rel nil* **and**
$\qquad$ *transitive_closure* (*Rel*((*x, y*) :: *ps*)) =
$\qquad\qquad$ **let val** *Rel qs* = *transitive_closure* (*Rel ps*)
$\qquad\qquad\qquad$ **val** *newps* = *filter* (**fn** (*z, w*) => *y* = *z* **andalso** *not*(*related* (*Rel qs*) *x w*)) *qs*
$\qquad\qquad$ **in if** *null newps* **then** *Rel*((*x, y*) :: *qs*)
$\qquad\qquad\qquad$ **else** *transitive_closure*(*Rel*(*map* (*pair x o snd*) *newps* @ ((*x, y*) :: *qs*))) **end**.

21.18. This is possible only if all arguments to the relation have the same type. One solution then is to change the representation of a relation from a list of pairs to a list of lists. You have to store also the "arity" of the relation, since you cannot decide it for an empty relation. The operations *domain*, *range*, and *inverse* have no immediate interpretations now. An example of a ternary relation is the relation *add* with triples (*x, y, z*) such that $x + y = z$. This relation is infinite, though.

21.19. When you implement sets with binary search trees you store only the elements. To implement tables you store both keys and associated data, but you compare only the keys. The *lookup* operation now corresponds to the *member* operation.

21.20. We use lists of digits (numbers between 0 and 9) with the least significant digits first, since that simplifies the definitions.

$\qquad$ **abstype** *BIGINT* = *Int* **of** *int list*
$\qquad$ **with local fun** *add* 0 *nil ys* = *ys*
$\qquad\qquad\qquad\qquad$ | *add* 0 *xs nil* = *xs*
$\qquad\qquad\qquad\qquad$ | *add* 1 *xs nil* = *add* 0 *xs* [1]
$\qquad\qquad\qquad\qquad$ | *add* 1 *nil ys* = *add* 0 [1] *ys*
$\qquad\qquad\qquad\qquad$ | *add carry* (*x* :: *xs*) (*y* :: *ys*) = **let val** *sum* = *x* + *y* + *carry*
$\qquad\qquad\qquad\qquad\qquad\qquad$ **in** *sum mod* 10 :: *add* (*sum div* 10) *xs ys* **end**
$\qquad\qquad$ **in fun** *bigadd xs ys* = *Int*(*add* 0 *xs ys*)
$\qquad\qquad\qquad$ **end**
$\qquad$ **end**.

The other operations are left to the reader. To gain efficiency, you can store larger numbers as elements of the list and use the property that arithmetic is very fast on computers.

21.21. The representation type is defined by *'a LIST* = *List* **of** *int* ∗ (*int* −> *'a*). The operations are defined by

$\qquad$ *Nil* = *List*(0, **fn** *x* => **raise** *error*),
$\qquad$ *Cons x* (*List*(*n, f*)) = *List*(*n* + 1, **fn** 1 => *x* | *i* => *f*(*i* − 1)),
$\qquad$ *hd* (*List*(*n, f*)) = **if** *n* < 1 **then raise** *hd* **else** *f* 1,

$tl\ (List(n, f))\ =\ $ **if** $n < 1$ **then raise** tl **else** $List(n - 1,$ **fn** $i\ =>\ f(i + 1))$,
$null\ (List(n, f))\ =\ n = 0,\quad len\ (List(n, f))\ =\ n,\quad Mklist\ n\ f\ =\ List(n, f)$
$append\ (List(n, f))\ (List(m, g))\ =$
$\qquad List(n + m,$ **fn** $i\ =>\$ **if** $i <= n$ **then** $f\ i$ **else** $g(i - n))$

Note that you with this representation can represent lists in which some elements are undefined (leading to non-terminating computations); as long as you do not try to compute those elements by applying the function to their indices, nothing happens.

21.22. The representation type is defined by $'a\ BAG\ =\ Bag\ $ **of** $'a\ ->\ int$. Its operations are defined by

$Empty\ =\ Bag($ **fn** $x\ =>\ 0)$
$Insert\ x\ (Bag\ f)\ =\ Bag($ **fn** $y\ =>\$ **if** $y = x$ **then** $f\ y + 1$ **else** $f\ y)$
$number\_of\ x\ (Bag\ f)\ =\ f\ x$
$union\ (Bag\ f)\ (Bag\ g)\ =\ Bag($ **fn** $x\ =>\ f\ x + g\ x)$
$intersection\ (Bag\ f)\ (Bag\ g)\ =\ Bag($ **fn** $x\ =>\ min\ (f\ x)\ (g\ x))$

Chapter 22.

22.1. Change the constant 1 to 80. During the last input, as many characters as are left are input.

22.2. $convert\ 0\ =\ ""$ and $convert\ n\ =\ convert(n\ div\ 10)\ \widehat{}\ chr(ord\ "0" + n\ mod\ 10)$.
$\ \ . putint\ s\ 0\ =\ output(s, "0")$ and
$putint\ s\ n\ =\ $ **if** $n < 0$ **then** $(output(s, "\widetilde{}\ "); putint\ s\ (\widetilde{}\ n))$ **else** $output(s,\ convert\ n)$.
$putpair\ put1\ put2\ s\ (x, y)\ =\ (output(s, "("); put1\ s\ x; output(s, ",");$
$\qquad\qquad\qquad\qquad\qquad\qquad\qquad\qquad put2\ s\ y; output(s, ")"))$.

22.3. $getchars\ s = $ **if** $lookahead\ s = "\backslash""$ **then** $""$ **else** $input(s, 1)\ \widehat{}\ getchars\ s$
$getstring\ s = (skip\ s;\ have\ s\ "\backslash"";\ $ **let val** $str = getchars\ s\ $ **in** $(have\ s\ "\backslash"";\ str)\ $ **end**$)$
$getelements\ get\ s\ =\ (skip\ s;\ $ **if** $lookahead\ s = "]"$ **then** $nil\ $ **else**
$\qquad $ **if** $lookahead\ s = ","$ **then** $(input(s, 1);\ get\ s :: getelements\ get\ s)$
$\qquad $ **else raise** $getlist)$
$getlist\ get\ s = (skip\ s;\ have\ s\ "[";\ skip\ s;\ $ **if** $lookahead\ s = "]"$ **then** $(have\ s\ "]";\ nil)$
$\qquad $ **else let val** $xs = get\ s :: getelements\ get\ s\ $ **in** $(have\ s\ "]";\ xs)\ $ **end**$)$.

22.4. $putvector\ put\ s\ nil\ =\ output(s, "\backslash n")$
$putvector\ put\ s\ (x :: xs)\ =\ (put\ s\ x;\ output(s, "\ ");\ putvector\ put\ xs)$
$putmatrix\ put\ x\ m\ =\ map\ (putvector\ put\ s)\ m$

Appendix A

The ASCII character set

The table on the next page enumerates the code words and the corresponding characters in the ASCII code. In ML, you can transform code words to characters using the *chr* function and characters to code words using the *ord* function.

0	NUL	32	SP	64	@	96	'
1	SOH	33	!	65	A	97	a
2	STX	34	"	66	B	98	b
3	ETX	35	#	67	C	99	c
4	EOT	36	$	68	D	100	d
5	ENQ	37	%	69	E	101	e
6	ACK	38	&	70	F	102	f
7	BEL	39	'	71	G	103	g
8	BS	40	(	72	H	104	h
9	HT	41	)	73	I	105	i
10	LF	42	*	74	J	106	j
11	VT	43	+	75	K	107	k
12	FF	44	,	76	L	108	l
13	CR	45	−	77	M	109	m
14	SO	46	.	78	N	110	n
15	SI	47	/	79	O	111	o
16	DLE	48	0	80	P	112	p
17	DC1	49	1	81	Q	113	q
18	DC2	50	2	82	R	114	r
19	DC3	51	3	83	S	115	s
20	DC4	52	4	84	T	116	t
21	NAK	53	5	85	U	117	u
22	SYN	54	6	86	V	118	v
23	ETB	55	7	87	W	119	w
24	CAN	56	8	88	X	120	x
25	EM	57	9	89	Y	121	y
26	SUB	58	:	90	Z	122	z
27	ESC	59	;	91	[	123	{
28	FS	60	<	92	\	124	|
29	GS	61	=	93	]	125	}
30	RS	62	>	94	^	126	~
31	US	63	?	95	_	127	DEL

Appendix B
The Standard ML Core Language (Revised)

Robin Milner [*]
University of Edinburgh

Contents

1 Introduction   **380**
  1.1 How this proposal evolved 380
  1.2 Design principles 381
  1.3 An example 382

2 The bare language   **384**
  2.1 Discussion 384
  2.2 Reserved words 384
  2.3 Special constants 385
  2.4 Identifiers 385
  2.5 Comments 387
  2.6 Lexical analysis 387
  2.7 Delimiters 387
  2.8 The bare syntax 387

3 Evaluation   **388**
  3.1 Environments and values 388
  3.2 Environment manipulation 390
  3.3 Matching patterns 390
  3.4 Applying a match 391
  3.5 Evaluation of expressions 391
  3.6 Evaluation of value bindings 392
  3.7 Evaluation of type and datatype bindings 393
  3.8 Evaluation of exception bindings 393
  3.9 Evaluation of declarations 393
  3.10 Evaluation of programs 394

---

[*]Reprinted by permission from Robin Milner.

4 Directives   **394**

5 Standard bindings   **395**
  5.1 Standard type constructors   395
  5.2 Standard functions and constants   396
  5.3 Standard exceptions   397

6 Standard derived forms   **397**
  6.1 Expressions and patterns   397
  6.2 Bindings and declarations   399

7 References and equality   **399**
  7.1 References and assignment   399
  7.2 Equality   399

8 Exceptions   **401**
  8.1 Discussion   401
  8.2 Derived forms   402
  8.3 An example   402
  8.4 Some pathological examples   403

9 Type-checking   **404**

10 Syntactic restrictions   **405**

11 Relation between the Core Language and Modules   **407**

12 Conclusion   **407**

References   **408**

13 Changes to the ML Core Language   **412**
  13.1 Numeric record labels   412
  13.2 Selector functions   412
  13.3 Abbreviations in datatype bindings   412
  13.4 Polymorphic equality   413
  13.5 Polymorphic assignment   414
  13.6 Polymorphic exceptions   414

Standard ML Input/Output   **415**
  1 Introduction   415
  2 Basic I/O Primitives   416
  3 Extended I/O Primitives   418

1   Introduction[1]

1.1   How this proposal evolved

ML is a strongly typed functional programming language, which has been
used by a number of people for serious work during the last few years [1].
At the same time HOPE, designed by Rod Burstall and his group, has
been similarly used [2]. The original DEC-10 ML was incomplete in some
ways, redundant in others. Some of these inadequacies were remedied by
Cardelli in his VAX version; others could be put right by importing ideas
from HOPE.

In April 1983, prompted by Bernard Sufrin, I wrote a tentative proposal
to consolidate ML, and while doing so became convinced that this consoli-
dation was possible while still keeping its character. The main strengthen-
ing came from generalising the "varstructs" of ML - the patterns of formal
parameters - to the patterns of HOPE, which are extendible by the declaration of new data types. Many people immediately discussed the initial
proposal. It was extremely lucky that we managed to have several separate
discussions, in large and small groups, in the few succeeding months; we
could not have chosen a better time to do the job. Also, Luca Cardelli
very generously offered to freeze his detailed draft ML manual [3] until this
proposal was worked out.

The proposal went through a second draft, on which there were further
discussions. The results of these discussions were of two kinds. First, it became clear that two areas were still unsettled: Input/Output, and Modules
for separate compilation. Second, many points were brought up about the
remaining core of the language, and these were almost all questions of fine
detail. The conclusion was rather clear; it was obviously better to present
at first a definition of a *Core* language without the two unsettled areas.
This course was further justified by the fact that the Core Language appeared to be almost completely unaffected by the choice of Input/Output
primitives and of separate compilation constructs. Also, there were already
strong proposals, from Cardelli and MacQueen respectively, for these two
vital facilities.

A third draft [4] of the Core Language was discussed in detail in a design
meeting at Edinburgh in June 1984, attended by nine of the people mentioned below; several points were ironed out, and the outcome was reported
in [5]. The meeting also looked in detail at the MacQueen Modules proposal
and the Cardelli Input/Output proposal, and agreed on their essentials.

During the ensuing year, having an increasingly firm design of Mac-
Queen's Modules, we were able to assess the language as a whole. The
Modules proposal, which is the most adventurous part of the language,

---

[1]In April 1987, a few changes were made to the Core Language. They are described on
page 412. The description that follows describes the language *before* these changes.

reached a state of precise definition. At a final design meeting, which was held in Edinburgh in May 1985 and attended by fifteen people (including twelve named below), the Modules design was discussed and warmly accepted. We also took advantage of the meeting to tidy up the Core Language, and to settle finally the primitives for Input/Output. The final versions of these proposals are presented in [6].

The main contributors to Standard ML, through their work on ML and on HOPE, are:

> Rod Burstall, Luca Cardelli, Michael Gordon, David MacQueen, Robin Milner, Lockwood Morris, Malcolm Newey, Christopher Wadsworth.

The language also owes much to criticisms and suggestions from many other people: Guy Cousineau, Bob Harper, Jim Hook, Gerard Huet, Dave Matthews, Robert Milne, Kevin Mitchell, Brian Monahan, Peter Mosses, Alan Mycroft, Larry Paulson, David Park, David Rydeheard, Don Sannella, David Schmidt, John Scott, Stefan Sokolowski, Bernard Sufrin, Philip Wadler. Most of them have expressed strong support for the design; any inadequacies which remain in the Core Language are my fault, but I have tried to represent the consensus.

1.2   Design principles

The proposed ML is not intended to be *the* functional language. There are too many degrees of freedom for such a thing to exist: lazy or eager evaluation, presence or absence of references and assignment, whether and how to handle exceptions, types-as-parameters or polymorphic type-checking, and so on. Nor is the language or its implementation meant to be a commercial product. It aims to be a means for propagating the craft of functional programming and a vehicle for further research into the design of functional languages.

The over-riding design principle is to restrict the Core Language to ideas which are simple and well-understood, and also well-tried — either in previous versions of ML or in other functional languages (the main other source being HOPE, mainly for its argument-matching constructs). One effect of this principle has been the omission of polymorphic references and assignment. There is indeed an elegant and sound scheme for polymorphic assignment worked out by Luis Damas, and described in his Edinburgh PhD thesis; however, it may be susceptible to improvement with further study. Meanwhile there is the advantage of simplicity in keeping to the well-understood polymorphic type-checking discipline which derives from Curry's Combinatory Logic via Hindley.

A second design principle is to generalise well-tried ideas where the generalisation is apparently natural. This has been applied in generalising ML "varstructs" to HOPE patterns, in broadening the structure of declarations (following Cardelli's declaration connectives which go back to Robert Milne's PhD thesis) and in allowing exceptions which carry values of arbitrary polymorphic type. It should be pointed out here that a difficult decision had to be made concerning HOPE's treatment of data types - present only in embryonic form in the original ML - and the labelled records and variants which Cardelli introduced in his VAX version. Each treatment has advantages which the other lacks; each is well-rounded in its own terms. Though a combination of these features was seen to be possible, it seemed at first (to me, but some disagreed!) to entail too rich a language. Thus the HOPE treatment alone was adopted in [5]. However, at the design meeting of June 1984 it was agreed to experiment with at least two different ways of adding labelled records to the Core as a smooth extension. The outcome – decided at the May 1985 meeting – is the inclusion of a form of labelled records (but not variants) nearly identical to Cardelli's, and its marriage with the HOPE constructions now appears harmonious.

A third principle is to specify the language completely, so that programs will port between correct implementations with minimum fuss. This entails, first, precise concrete syntax (abstract syntax is in some senses more important — but we do not all have structure editors yet, and humans still communicate among themselves in concrete syntax!); second, it entails exact evaluation rules (e.g. we must specify the order of evaluation of two expressions, one applied to the other, because of side-effects and the exception mechanism). At a level which is not fully formal, this document and its sister reports on Modules and on Input/Output constitute a complete description; however, we intend to augment them both with a formal definition and with tutorial material.

1.3   An example

The following declaration illustrates some constructs of the Core Language. A longer expository paper should contain many more examples; here, we hope only to draw attention to some of the less familiar ideas.

The example sets up the abstract type 'a dictionary , in which each entry associates an item (of arbitrary type 'a) with a key (an integer). Besides the null dictionary, the operations provided are for looking up a key, and for adding a new entry which overrides any old entry with the same key. A natural representation is by a list of key-item pairs, ordered by key.

```
abstype 'a dictionary =
    dict of (int * 'a)list                (* dict is the datatype      *)
                                          (* constructor, available    *)
with                                      (* only in the with part.    *)
    val nulldict = dict nil
                                          (* The function lookup may   *)
    exception lookup : unit               (*    raise an exception.    *)

    fun lookup (key:int)                  (* 'a is the result type.    *)
            (dict entrylist :'a dictionary) :'a =
        let fun search nil = raise lookup |  (* An auxiliary clausal   *)
                search ((k,item)::entries) = (*  function declaration.  *)
                    if key=k then item
                    else if key<k then raise lookup
                    else search entries
        in search entrylist
        end

    fun enter (newentry as (key, item:'a))  (* A layered pattern.      *)
            (dict entrylist) :'a dictionary =
        let fun update nil = [ newentry ] |  (* A singleton list.      *)
                update ((entry as (k,_))::entries) =
                    if key=k then newentry::entries
                    else if key<k then newentry::entry::entries
                    else entry::update entries
        in dict(update entrylist)
        end
end                                       (* end of dictionary         *)
```

After the declaration is evaluated, five identifier bindings are reported,
and recorded in the top-level environment. They are the **type** binding
of dictionary, the **exception** binding of lookup, and three typed **value**
bindings:

```
nulldict : 'a dictionary
lookup   : int -> 'a dictionary -> 'a
enter    : int * 'a -> 'a dictionary -> 'a dictionary
```

The layered pattern construct "**as**" was first introduced in HOPE, and
yields both brevity and efficiency. The discerning reader may be able to
find one further use for it in the declaration.

2   The bare language

2.1   Discussion

It is convenient to present the language first in a bare form, containing
enough on which to base the semantic description given in Section 3. Things
omitted from the bare language description are:

1. Derived syntactic forms, whose meaning derives from their equivalent
   forms in the bare language (Section 6);

2. Directives for introducing infix identifier status (Section 4);

3. Standard bindings (Section 5);

4. References and equality (Section 7);

5. Type-checking (Section 9).

The principal syntactic objects are expressions and declarations. The
composite expression forms are application, record formation, raising and
handling exceptions, local declaration (using **let**) and function abstraction.

Another important syntactic class is the class of patterns; these are essentially expressions containing only variables and value constructors, and
are used to create value bindings. Declarations may declare value variables
(using value bindings), types with associated constructors or operations
(using type and datatype bindings), and exceptions (using exception bindings). Apart from this, one declaration may be local to another (using
local), and a sequence of declarations is allowed as a single declaration.

An ML program is a series of declarations, called *top-level* declarations,

$$dec_1 \; ; \; \_ \; dec_n \; ;$$

each terminated by a semicolon (where each dec_i is not itself of the form
$dec \; ; \; dec'$). In evaluating a program, the bindings created by dec_1 are
reported before dec_2 is evaluated, and so on. In the complete language,
an expression occurring in place of any dec_i is an abbreviated form (see
Section 6.2) for a declaration binding the expression value to the variable
"it"; such expressions are called *top-level* expressions.

The bare syntax is in Section 2.8 below; first we consider lexical matters.

2.2   Reserved words

The following are the reserved words used in the Core Language. They
may not (except =) be used as identifiers. In this document the alphabetic
reserved words are always shown in boldface.

```
abstype   and   andalso   as   case   do   datatype
else   end   exception   fn   fun   handle   if   in
infix   infixr   let   local   nonfix   of   op   open
orelse   raise   rec   then   type   val   with   while
(  )   [  ]   {  }   ,   :   ;   ...   |   ||   =   =>   _   ?
```

2.3   Special constants

An integer constant is any non-empty sequence of digits, possibly preceded by a negation symbol ($\tilde{\ }$).

A real constant is an integer constant, possibly followed by a point (.) and one or more digits, possibly followed by an exponent symbol (E) and an integer constant; at least one of the optional parts must occur, hence no integer constant is a real constant. Examples: 0.7 , $\tilde{\ }$3.32E5 , 3E$\tilde{\ }$7 . Non-examples: 23 , .3 , 4.E5 , 1E2.0 .

A string constant is a sequence, between quotes ("), of zero or more printable characters, spaces or escape sequences. Each escape sequence is introduced by the escape character \, and stands for a character sequence. The allowed escape sequences are as follows (all other uses of \ being incorrect):

\n	A single character interpreted by the system as end-of-line.
\t	Tab.
\^c	The control character c, for any appropriate c.
\ddd	The single character with ASCII code ddd (3 decimal digits).
\"	"
\\	\
\f_f\	This sequence is ignored, where f_f stands for a sequence of one or more formatting characters (a subset of the non-printable characters including at least space, tab, newline, formfeed). This allows one to write long strings on more than one line, by writing \ at the end of one line and at the start of the next.

2.4   Identifiers

Identifiers are used to stand for six different syntax classes which, if we had a large enough character set, would be disjoint:

value variables	(*var*)	type variables	(*tyvar*)
value constructors	(*con*)	type constructors	(*tycon*)
exception names	(*exn*)	record labels	(*lab*)

An identifier is either *alphanumeric*: any sequence of letters, digits, primes (') and underbars (_) starting with a letter or prime, or *symbolic*: any sequence of the following *symbols*

$$! \quad \% \quad \& \quad \$ \quad + \quad - \quad / \quad : \quad < \quad = \quad > \quad ? \quad @ \quad \backslash \quad \sim \quad ` \quad \hat{} \quad | \quad *$$

In either case, however, reserved words are excluded. This means that for example ? and | are not identifiers, but ?? and |=| are identifiers. The only exception to this rule is that the symbol =, which is a reserved word, is also allowed as an identifier to stand for the equality predicate (see Section 7.2). The identifier = may not be rebound; this precludes any syntactic ambiguity.

A type variable (*tyvar*) may be any alphanumeric identifier starting with a prime. The other five classes (*var, con, exn, tycon, lab*) are represented by identifiers not starting with a prime; the class *lab* is also extended to include the *numeric* labels #1, #2, #3, ...

Type variables are therefore disjoint from the other five classes. Otherwise, the syntax class of an occurrence of identifier id is determined thus:

1. At the start of a component in a record type, record pattern or record expression, id is a record label.

2. Elsewhere in types id is a type constructor, and must be within the scope of the type binding or datatype binding which introduced it.

3. Following **exception, raise** or **handle**, or in the context "**exception** *exn* = id", id is an exception name.

4. Elsewhere, id is a value constructor if it occurs in the scope of a datatype binding which introduced it as such, otherwise it is a value variable.

It follows from (4) that no declaration must make a hole in the scope of a value constructor by introducing the same identifier as a variable; this is because, in the scope of the declaration which introduces id as a value constructor, any occurrence of id in a pattern is interpreted as the constructor and not as the binding occurrence of a new variable.

The syntax-classes *var, con, tycon* and *exn* all depend on which bindings are in force, but only the classes *var* and *con* are necessarily disjoint. The context determines (as described above) to which class each identifier occurrence belongs.

In the Core Language, an identifier may be given infix status by the **infix** or **infixr** directive; this status only pertains to its use as a *var* or a *con*. If id has infix status, then "exp_1 id exp_2" (resp. "pat_1 id pat_2") may occur wherever the application "id(exp_1,exp_2)" (resp. "id(pat_1,pat_2)") would otherwise occur. On the other hand, non-infixed occurrences of id must be prefixed by the keyword "**op**". Infix status is cancelled by the **nonfix** directive. (*Note*: the tuple expression "(exp_1,exp_2)" is a derived

form of the numerically labelled record expression "$\{\#1{=}exp_1,\#2{=}exp_2\}$",
and a similar derived form exists for numerically labelled record patterns.
See Section 6.1.)

2.5   Comments

A comment is any character sequence within comment brackets (* *) in
which comment brackets are properly nested. An unmatched comment
bracket should be detected by the compiler.

2.6   Lexical analysis

Each item of lexical analysis is either a reserved word, a numeric label,
a special constant or an identifier; comments and formatting characters
separate items (except within string constants; see Section 2.3) and are
otherwise ignored. At each stage the longest next item is taken.

As a consequence of this simple approach, spaces or parentheses are
needed sometimes to separate identifiers and reserved words. Two examples
are

> `a:=`␣`!b`   or   `a:=(!b)`   but not   `a:=!b`
> (*assigning contents of b to a*)

> `~`␣`:int->int`   or   `(~):int->int`   but not   `~:int->int`
> (*unary minus qualified by its type*)

Rules which allow omission of spaces in such examples would also forbid
certain symbol sequences as identifiers; moreover, such rules are hard to
remember. It seems better to keep a simple scheme and tolerate a few
extra spaces or parentheses.

2.7   Delimiters

Not all constructs have a terminating reserved word; this would be verbose.
But a compromise has been adopted; **end** terminates any construct which
declares bindings with local scope. This involves only the **let**, **local** and
abstype constructs.

2.8   The bare syntax

The syntax of the bare language is presented in Table 1. The following
metasyntactic conventions are adopted:

Conventions

1. The brackets "<< >>" enclose optional phrases.

2. Repetition of iterated phrases is represented by "_"; this must not be confused with "...", a reserved word used in flexible record patterns.

3. For any syntax class s, we define the syntax class s_seq as follows:

$$s\_seq \quad ::= \quad s$$
$$(s_1, \_, s_n) \quad (n \geq 1)$$

4. Alternatives are in order of decreasing precedence.

5. L (resp. R) means left (resp. right) association.

The syntax of types binds more tightly that that of expressions, so type constraints should be parenthesized if not followed by a reserved word.

Each iterated construct (e.g. match, handler, ...) extends as far right as possible; thus parentheses may also be needed around an expression which terminates with a match, e.g. "**fn** *match*", if this occurs within a larger match.

3   Evaluation

3.1   Environments and values

Evaluation of phrases takes place in the presence of an ENVIRONMENT and a STORE. An ENVIRONMENT E has two components: a value environment VE associating values to variables and to value constructors, and an exception environment EE associating exceptions to exception names. A STORE S associates values to references, which are themselves values. (A third component of an environment, a type environment TE, is ignored here since it is relevant only to type-checking and compilation, not to evaluation.)

A *value* v is either a constant (a nullary constructor), a construction (a constructor with a value), a record, a reference, or a function value. A record value is a set of label-value pairs, written "$\{lab_1=v_1, \_, lab_n=v_n\}$", in which the labels are distinct; note that the order of components is immaterial. The labels lab_i in a record value must be either all identifiers, or else they must be the numeric labels #1, #2, _ , #n; the two kinds of label may not be mixed. A function value f is a partial function which, given a value, may return a value or a packet; it may also change the store as a side-effect.

An *exception* e, associated to an exception name exn in any exception environment, is an object drawn from an infinite set (the nature of e is immaterial, but see Section 3.8). A *packet* p=(e,v) is an exception e paired with a value v, called the *excepted* value. Neither exceptions nor packets are values.

Table 1: **The Syntax of the Bare Language**

EXPRESSIONS *exp*

```
aexp ::=
  var                          (variable)
  con                          (constructor)
  { lab₁=exp₁, _ ,             (record,n ≥ 0)
    labₙ=expₙ }
  ( exp )

exp ::=
  aexp                    (atomic)
  exp aexp             L  (application)
  exp : ty             L  (constraint)
  exp handle handler   R  (handle exc'ns)
  raise exn with exp      (raise exc'n)
  let dec in exp end      (local dec'n)
  fn match                (function)

match ::=
  rule₁ | _ | ruleₙ         (n ≥ 1)

rule ::=
  pat => exp

handler ::=
  hrule₁ || _ || hruleₙ     (n ≥ 1)

hrule ::=
  exn with match
  ? => exp
```

DECLARATIONS *dec*

```
dec ::=
  val vb                     (values)
  type tb                    (types)
  datatype db                (datatypes)
  abstype db                 (abstract
    with dec end              datatypes)
  exception eb               (exceptions)
  local dec in dec' end      (local dec'n)
  dec₁<<;>> _ decₙ<<;>>      (sequence, n ≥ 0)
```

```
PROGRAMS :  dec₁ ; _ decₙ ;
```

PATTERNS *pat*

```
apat ::=
  _                          (wildcard)
  var                        (variable)
  con                        (constant)
  { lab₁=pat₁, _ ,           (record,n ≥ 0) ᵃ
    labₙ=patₙ <<, ...>>}
  ( pat )

pat ::=
  apat                    (atomic)
  con apat             L  (construction)
  pat : ty             L  (constraint)
  var<<:ty>> as pat    R  (layered)
```

VALUE BINDINGS *vb*

```
vb ::=
  pat = exp                  (simple)
  vb₁ and _ and vbₙ          (multiple,n ≥ 2)
  rec vb                     (recursive)
```

TYPE BINDINGS *tb*

```
tb ::=
  <<tyvar_seq>> tycon = ty   (simple)
  tb₁ and _ and tbₙ          (multiple,n ≥ 2)
```

DATATYPE BINDINGS *db*

```
db ::=
  <<tyvar_seq>>tycon
    = constrs                (simple)
  db₁ and _ and dbₙ          (multiple,n ≥ 2)

constrs ::=
  con₁<<of ty₁>>| _ | conₙ<<of tyₙ>>
```

EXCEPTION BINDINGS *eb*

```
eb ::=
  exn<<:ty>><< =exn>>        (simple)
  eb₁ and _ and ebₙ          (multiple,n ≥ 2)
```

TYPES *ty*

```
ty ::=
  tyvar                      (type variable)
  <<ty_seq>>tycon            (type constr'n)
  { lab₁:ty₁, _ ,
    labₙ:tyₙ }               (record type,n ≥ 0)
  ty -> ty'               R  (function type)
  ( ty )
```

ᵃThe reserved word "..." is called the *record wildcard*. If it is absent, then the pattern will match any record with exactly those components which are specified; if it is present, then the matched record may also contain further components. If it occurs when n=0, then the preceding comma is omitted; "{...}" is a pattern which matches any record whatever.

Besides possibly changing S (by assignment), evaluation of a phrase returns a *result* as follows:

Phrase	Result		
Phrase	**Result**		
Expression	v	or	p
Value binding	VE	or	p
Type or datatype binding	VE		
Exception binding	EE		
Declaration	E	or	p

For every phrase except a **handle** expression, whenever its evaluation demands the evaluation of an immediate subphrase which returns a packet p as result, no further evaluation of subphrases occurs and p is also the result of the phrase. This rule should be remembered while reading the evaluation rules below. In presenting the rules, explicit type constraints (:*ty*) have been ignored since they have no effect upon evaluation.

3.2   Environment manipulation

We may write $\langle(id_1,v_1) \_ (id_n,v_n)\rangle$ for a value environment VE (the id_i being distinct). Then $VE(id_i)$ denotes v_i, $\langle\rangle$ is the empty value environment, and VE+VE' means the value environment in which the associations of VE' supersede those of VE. Similarly for exception environments. If E=(VE,EE) and E'=(VE',EE'), then E+E' means (VE+VE',EE+EE'), E+VE' means E+(VE',$\langle\rangle$), etc. This implies that an identifier may be associated both in VE and in EE without conflict.

3.3   Matching patterns

The matching of a pattern *pat* to a value v either *fails* or yields a value environment. Failure is distinct from returning a packet, but a packet will be returned when all patterns fail in applying a match to a value (see Section 3.4). In the following rules, if any component pattern fails to match then the whole pattern fails to match.

The following is the effect of matching a pattern *pat* to a value v, in each of the cases for *pat* (with failure if any condition is not satisfied):

_   :   the empty value environment $\langle\rangle$ is returned.

var   :   the value environment $\langle(var,v)\rangle$ is returned.

con<<*pat*>> :   if v = *con*<<v'>> then *pat* is matched to v', else failure.

> *var* **as** *pat* : *pat* is matched to v returning VE; then
> <(*var*,v)>+VE is returned.

{ lab_1=pat_1, _ , lab_n=pat_n, <<, ...>>} :
> if v={ lab_1=v_1, _ ,lab_m=v_m } , where $m \geq n$ if
> "..." is present and $m = n$ otherwise, then pat_i
> is matched to v_i returning VE_i, for each i; then
> VE_1+ _ +VE_n is returned.

3.4   Applying a match

Assume environment E. Applying a match "pat_1=>exp_1| _ |pat_n=>exp_n" to
value v returns a value or packet as follows. Each pat_i is matched to v
in turn, from left to right, until one succeeds returning VE_i; then exp_i
is evaluated in E+VE_i. If none succeeds, then the packet (ematch,()) is
returned, where ematch is the standard exception bound by predeclaration
to the exception name "match". But matches which may fail are to be
detected by the compiler and flagged with a warning; see Section 10(2).

Thus, for each E, a match denotes a function value.

3.5   Evaluation of expressions

Assume environment E=(VE,EE). Evaluating an expression *exp* returns a
value or packet as follows, in each of the cases for *exp*:

> *var*   :   the value VE(*var*) is returned.

> *con*   :   the value VE(*con*) is returned.

> *exp aexp*   :   *exp* is evaluated, returning function value
>   f; then *aexp* is evaluated, returning value
>   v; then f(v) is returned.

> { lab_1=exp_1, _ , lab_n=exp_n }:
>   the exp_i are evaluated in sequence, from
>   left to right, returning v_i respectively; then
>   the record { lab_1=v_1, _ , lab_n=v_n } is re-
>   turned.

> **raise** *exn* **with** *exp* :   *exp* is evaluated, returning value v; then
>   the packet (e,v) is returned, where e =
>   EE(*exn*).

exp **handle** *handler* : *exp* is evaluated; if *exp* returns a value v, then v is returned; if it returns a packet p = (e,v) then the handling rules of the *handler* are scanned from left to right until a rule is found which satisfies one of two conditions:

  1. it is of form "*exn* **with** *match*" and e=EE(*exn*), in which case *match* is applied to v;

  2. it is of form "? **=>** *exp'*", in which case *exp'* is evaluated.

If no such hrule is found, then p is returned.

let *dec* **in** *exp* **end** : *dec* is evaluated, returning E'; then *exp* is evaluated in E+E'.

fn *match* : f is returned, where f is the function of v gained by applying *match* to v in environment E.

3.6   Evaluation of value bindings

Assume environment E = (VE,EE). Evaluating a value binding *vb* returns a value environment VE' or a packet as follows, by cases of *vb*:

pat = *exp* : *exp* is evaluated in E, returning value v; then *pat* is matched to v; if this returns VE', then VE' is returned, and if it fails then the packet (ebind,()) is returned, where ebind is the standard exception bound by predeclaration to the exception name "bind".

vb_1 **and** _ **and** vb_n : $vb_1,\_,vb_n$ are evaluated in E from left to right, returning VE_1, _ ,VE_n; then VE_1+ _ $+VE_n$ is returned.

rec *vb* : *vb* is evaluated in E', returning VE', where E' = (VE+VE',EE). Because the values bound by "**rec** *vb*" must be function values (see 10(4)), E' is well defined by "tying knots" (Landin).

3.7 Evaluation of type and datatype bindings

The components VE and EE of the current environment do not affect the evaluation of type bindings or datatype bindings (TE affects their type-checking and compilation). Evaluation of a type binding just returns the empty value environment <>; the purpose of type bindings in the Core Language is merely to provide an abbreviation for a compound type. Evaluation of a datatype binding *db* returns a value environment VE' (it cannot return a packet) as follows, by cases of *db*:

$<<tyvar_seq>>tycon = con_1<< $ **of** $ty_1>> \mid $ _ $\mid con_n<<$**of** $ty_n>> :$
the value environment VE' = $<(con_1,v_1)$, _, $(con_n,v_n)>$ is returned, where v_i is either the constant value con_i (if "**of** ty_i" is absent) or else the function which maps v to $con_i(v)$. Other effects of this datatype binding are dealt with by the compiler or type-checker, not by evaluation.

db_1 **and** _ **and** db_n : db_1, _ , db_n are evaluated from left to right, returning VE_1, _ , VE_n; then VE' = VE_1+ _ $+VE_n$ is returned.

3.8 Evaluation of exception bindings

Assume environment E = (VE,EE). The evaluation of an exception binding *eb* returns an exception environment EE' as follows, by cases of *eb*:

$exn << =exn'>> $: EE' = $<(exn,e)>$ is returned, where

1. if *exn'* is present then e = EE(*exn'*); this is a *non-generative* exception binding since it merely re-binds an existing exception to *exn*;

2. otherwise e is a previously unused exception; this is a *generative* exception binding.

eb_1 **and** _ **and** eb_n : eb_1, _ ,eb_n are evaluated in E from left to right, returning EE_1, _ ,EE_n; then EE' = EE_1+_$+EE_n$ is returned.

3.9 Evaluation of declarations

Assume environment E = (VE,EE). Evaluating a declaration *dec* returns an environment E' or a packet as follows, by cases of *dec*:

val *vb*   :   *vb* is evaluated, returning VE'; then E' = (VE',<>) is returned.

type *tb*   :   E' = (<>,<>) is returned.

datatype *db*   :   *db* is evaluated, returning VE'; then E' = (VE',<>) is returned.

abstype *db* **with** *dec* **end** :

       db is evaluated, returning VE'; then *dec* is evaluated in E+VE', returning E'; then E' is returned.

exception *eb* :   *eb* is evaluated, returning EE'; then E' = (<>,EE') is returned.

local dec_1 **in** dec_2 **end** :

       dec_1 is evaluated, returning E_1, then dec_2 is evaluated in E+E_1, returning E_2; then E' = E_2 is returned.

dec_1<<;>> _ dec_n<<;>> :

       each dec_i is evaluated in E+E_1+ _ +E_{i-1}, returning E_i, for i = 1,2, _ ,n; then E' = (<>,<>)+E_1+ _ +E_n is returned. Thus when n = 0 the empty environment is returned.

Each declaration is defined to return only the *new* environment which it makes, but the effect of a declaration sequence is to accumulate environments.

3.10   Evaluation of programs

The evaluation of a program "dec_1 ; _ dec_n ;" takes place in the initial presence of the standard top-level environment ENV_0 containing all the standard bindings (see Section 5). For $i > 0$ the top-level environment ENV_i, present after the evaluation of dec_i in the program, is defined recursively as follows: dec_i is evaluated in ENV_{i-1} returning environment E_i, and then ENV_i = ENV_{i-1}+E_i.

4   Directives

Directives are included in ML as (syntactically) a subclass of declarations. They possess scope, as do all declarations.

There is only one kind of directive in the standard language, namely those concerning the infix status of value variables and constructors. Others, perhaps also concerned with syntactic conventions, may be included in extensions of the language. The directives concerning infix status are:

> **infix**<<r>> <<d>> id_1 _ id_n
>
> **nonfix** id_1 _ id_n

where d is a digit. The **infix** and **infixr** directives introduce infix status for each id_i (as a value variable or constructor), and the **nonfix** directive cancels it. The digit d (default 0) determines the precedence, and an infixed identifier associates to the left if introduced by **infix**, to the right if by **infixr**. Different infixed identifiers of equal precedence associate to the left. As indicated in Table 4 (page 409), the precedence of infixed application is just weaker than that of application.

While id has infix status, each occurrence of it (as a value variable or constructor) must be infixed or else preceded by **op**. Note that this includes occurrences of the identifier within patterns, even binding occurrences of variables.

Several standard functions and constructors have infix status (see Table 6) with precedence; these are all left associative except "::".

It may be thought better that the infix status of a variable or constructor should be established in some way within its binding occurrence, rather than by a separate directive. However, the use of directives avoids problems in parsing.

The use of local directives (introduced by **let** or **local**) imposes on the parser the burden of determining their textual scope. A quite superficial analysis is enough for this purpose, due to the use of **end** to delimit local scopes.

5 Standard bindings

The bindings of this section form the standard top-level environment ENV_0.

5.1 Standard type constructors

The bare language provides the record type "$\{lab_1:ty_1, \_ , lab_n:ty_n\}$" for each $n \geq 0$, and the infixed function-type constructor "->". Otherwise, type constructors are postfixed. The following are standard:

> Type *constants* (nullary constructors)   : unit,bool,int,real,string
> Unary type constructors   : list,ref

None of the identifiers ->, *, unit, bool, int, real, string, list, ref may be redeclared as type constructors. (* is used in the type of n-tuples, a derived form of record type.)

The constructors unit, bool and list are fully defined by the following assumed declaration

> **infixr** 5 ::
>
> **type** unit = {}
>
> **datatype** bool = true | false
>
>   **and** 'a list = nil | **op** :: **of** {#1: 'a, #2: 'a list}

The word "unit" is chosen since the type contains just one value "{}", the empty record. This is why it is preferred to the word "void" of ALGOL 68.

The type constants int, real and string are equipped with special constants as described in Section 2.3. The type constructor ref is for constructing reference types; see Section 7.

5.2   Standard functions and constants

All standard functions and constants are listed in Table 6. There is not a lavish number; we envisage function libraries provided by each implementation, together with the equivalent ML declaration of each function (though the implementation may be more efficient). In time, some such library functions may accrue to the standard; a likely candidate for this is a group of array-handling functions, grouped in a standard declaration of the unary type constructor "array".

Most of the standard functions and constants are familiar, so we need mention only a few critical points:

1. explode yields a list of strings of size 1; implode is iterated string concatenation (^). ord yields the ASCII code number of the first character of a string; chr yields the ASCII character (as a string of size 1) corresponding to an integer. The ordering relations <, >, <= and >= on strings use the lexicographic order; for this purpose, the newline character "\n" is identified with linefeed.

2. ref is a monomorphic function, but in patterns it may be used polymorphically, with type 'a -> 'a ref .

3. The character functions ord and chr, the arithmetic operators *, /, div, mod, + and - , and the standard functions floor, sqrt, exp and ln may raise standard exceptions (see Section 5.3) whose name in each case is the same as that of the function. This occurs for ord when the string is empty; for chr when the integer is not an ASCII code; and for the others when the result is undefined or out of range.

4. The values $r = a$ mod d and $q = a$ div d are determined by the condition $d * q + r = a$, where either $0 \leq r < d$ or $d < r \leq 0$. Thus the remainder takes the same sign as the divisor, and has lesser

magnitude. The result of arctan lies between $\pm pi/2$, and ln (the inverse of exp) is the natural logarithm. The value floor(x) is the largest integer $\leq$ x; thus rounding may be done by floor(x+0.5) .

5. Two multi-typed functions are included as quick debugging aids. The function print :*ty*->*ty* is an identity function, which as a side-effect prints its argument exactly as it would be printed at top-level. The printing caused by "print(*exp*)" will depend upon the type ascribed to this *particular* occurrence of *exp*; thus print is not a normal polymorphic function. The function makestring :*ty*->string is similar, but instead of printing it returns as a string what print would produce on the screen. Since top-level printing is not fully specified, programs using these two functions should not be ported between implementations.

5.3 Standard exceptions

All predeclared exception names are of type unit. There are three special ones: match, bind and interrupt. These exceptions are raised, respectively, by failures of matching and binding as explained in Sections 3.4 and 3.6, and by an interrupt generated (often by the user) outside the program. Note, however, that match and bind exceptions cannot occur unless the compiler has given a warning, as detailed in Section 10(2), (3), except in the case of a top-level declaration as indicated in 10(3).

The only other predeclared exception names are

ord chr * / div mod + - floor sqrt exp ln

Each name identifies the corresponding standard function, which is illdefined or out of range for certain arguments, as detailed in Section 5.2. For example, using the derived **handle** form explained in Section 8.2, the expression

3 div x **handle** div => 10000

will return 10000 when x = 0.

6 Standard derived forms

6.1 Expressions and patterns

The derived expressions and patterns are described in Table 2.

Each derived form may be implemented more efficiently than its equivalent form, but must be precisely equivalent to it semantically. The typechecking of each derived form is also defined by that of its equivalent form. The precedence among all bare and derived forms is shown in Table 4.

Table 2: Standard Derived Forms: Expressions and Patterns

DERIVED FORM	EQUIVALENT FORM

Types :
$ty_1 * \_ * ty_n$ $\qquad$ { #1:ty_1, _ , #n:ty_n }

Expressions :

() $\qquad$ { } $\hspace{2cm}$ (no space in "()")

(exp_1, _ , exp_n) $\qquad$ { #1=exp_1, _ , #n=exp_n } $\qquad$ $(n \geq 2)$

raise exn $\qquad$ **raise** exn **with** ()

case exp **of** $match$ $\qquad$ (**fn** $match$) (exp)

if exp **then** exp_1 **else** exp_2 $\qquad$ **case** exp **of** true=>exp_1 | false=>exp_2

exp **orelse** exp' $\qquad$ **if** exp **then** true **else** exp'

exp **andalso** exp' $\qquad$ **if** exp **then** exp' **else** false

(exp_1; _ ; exp_n; exp) $\qquad$ **case** exp_1 **of** (_) =>

$\qquad\qquad\qquad\qquad\qquad$ _ _

$\qquad\qquad\qquad\qquad\qquad$ _ _

$\qquad\qquad\qquad\qquad\qquad$ **case** exp_n **of** (_) => exp $\qquad$ $(n \geq 1)$

let dec **in** $\qquad$ **let** dec **in**
  exp_1; _ ; exp_n **end** $\qquad$ (exp_1; _ ; exp_n) **end**

while exp **do** exp' $\qquad$ **let val rec** f = **fn** () =>
$\qquad\qquad\qquad\qquad\qquad$ **if** exp **then** (exp'; f()) **else** ()
$\qquad\qquad\qquad\qquad\qquad$ **in** f() **end**

[exp_1 , _ , exp_n] $\qquad$ exp_1:: _ ::exp_n::nil $\qquad$ $(n \geq 0)$

Handling rules :
  exn => exp $\qquad$ exn **with** (_) => exp

Patterns :

() $\qquad$ { } $\hspace{2cm}$ (no space in "()")

(pat_1, _ , pat_n) $\qquad$ { #1=pat_1, _ , #n=pat_n } $\qquad$ $(n \geq 2)$

[pat_1, _ , pat_n] $\qquad$ pat_1:: _ ::pat_n::nil $\qquad$ $(n \geq 0)$

{ _, id<<:ty>><< **as** pat>>, _ } $\qquad$ { _, id=id<<:ty>><< **as** pat>>, _ }

The derived type "$ty_1 * \_ * ty_n$" is called an (n-)tuple type, and the values of this type are called (n-)tuples. The associated derived forms of expressions and patterns give exactly the treatment of tuples in the previous ML proposal [5].

The shortened **raise** form is only admissible with exceptions of type unit. The shortened form of handling rule is appropriate whenever the excepted value is immaterial, and is therefore (in the full form) matched to the wildcard pattern.

The final derived pattern allows a label and its associated variable to be elided in a record pattern, when they are the same identifier.

6.2   Bindings and declarations

A new syntax class *fb*, of function bindings, is introduced. Function bindings are a convenient form of value binding for function declarations. The equivalent form of each function binding is an ordinary value binding. These new function bindings must be declared by "**fun**", not by "**val**"; however, the bare form of value binding may still be used to declare functions, using **val** or **val rec** (see Table 3).

The last derived declaration (using "it") is only allowed at top-level, for treating top-level expressions as degenerate declarations; "it" is just a normal value variable.

7   References and equality

7.1   References and assignment

Following Cardelli, references are provided by the type constructor "ref". Since we are sticking to monomorphic references, there are two overloaded functions available at all monotypes *mty*:

1. ref : *mty* -> *mty* ref, which associates (in the store) a new reference with its argument value. "ref" is a constructor, and may be used polymorphically in patterns, with type 'a -> 'a ref .

2. **op** := : *mty* ref * *mty* -> unit , which associates its first (reference) argument with its second (value) argument in the store, and returns () as result.

The polymorphic contents function "!" is provided, and is equivalent to the function "**fn** (ref x) => x".

7.2   Equality

The overloaded equality function **op** = : *ety* * *ety* -> bool is available at all types *ety* which admit equality, according to the definition below. The

Table 3: **Standard Derived Forms: Bindings and Declarations**

DERIVED FORM	**EQUIVALENT FORM**

Function bindings fb :

$$var\ apat_{11}\ \_\ apat_{1n}\texttt{<<:ty>>}= exp_1$$
$$|\ \_\ \_$$
$$\_\ \_$$
$$|\ var\ apat_{m1}\ \_\ apat_{mn}\texttt{<<:ty>>}= exp_m$$

$var =$ **fn** x_1 => $\_$ **fn** x_n =>
    case $(x_1, \_ , x_n)$
    of $(\,apat_{11}, \_ , apat_{1n})$ => $exp_1\texttt{<<: }ty\texttt{>>}$
    $|\ \_\ \_$

    $\_\ \_$
    $|\ (apat_{m1}, \_ , apat_{mn})$ => $exp_m\ \texttt{<<:}ty\texttt{>>}$
    (where the x_i are new, and $m, n \geq 1$)

fb_1 **and** $\_$ **and** fb_n

vb_1 **and** $\_$ **and** vb_n
    (where vb_i is the equivalent of fb_i)

Declarations :

fun fb

val rec vb
    (where vb is the equivalent of fb)

exp

val it $= exp$

effect of this definition is that equality will only be applied to values which are built up from references (to arbitrary values) by value constructors, including of course constant values. On references, equality means identity; on objects of other types ety, it is defined recursively in the natural way.

The types which admit equality are as follows, assuming that abbreviations introduced by type bindings have first been expanded out:

1. A type ty admits equality iff it is built from arbitrary reference types by the record type construction and by type constructors which admit equality.

2. The standard type constructors bool, int, real, string and list all admit equality.

Thus for example, the type (int * 'a ref) list admits equality, but the types (int * 'a) list and (int -> bool) list do not.

A user-defined type constructor $tycon$, declared by a datatype binding db whose form is

$$<\!\!tyvar\_seq\!\!>\!\!tycon \,=\, con_1 <\!\!\text{of } ty_1\!\!>\; |\; \_\!\_ \;|\; con_n<\!\!\text{of } ty_n\!\!>$$

admits equality within its scope (but, if declared by **abstype**, only within the **with** part of its declaration) iff it satisfies the following condition:

3. Each construction type ty_i in this binding is built from arbitrary reference types and type variables, *either* by type constructors which already admit equality *or* by *tycon* or any other type constructor declared simultaneously with *tycon*, provided these other type constructors also satisfy the present condition.

The first paragraph of this section should be enough for an intuitive understanding of the types which admit equality, but the precise definition is given in a form which is readily incorporated in the type-checking mechanism.

8   Exceptions

8.1   Discussion

Some discussion of the exception mechanism is needed, as it goes a little beyond what exists in other functional languages. It was proposed by Alan Mycroft, as a means to gain the convenience of dynamic exception trapping without risking violation of the type discipline (and indeed still allowing polymorphic exception-raising expressions). Brian Monahan put forward a similar idea. Don Sannella also contributed, particularly to the nature of the derived forms (Section 8.2); these forms give a pleasant way of treating standard exceptions, as explained in Section 5.3.

The rough and ready rule for understanding how exceptions are handled is as follows. If an exception is raised by a **raise** expression

raise *exn* **with** *exp*

which lies in the textual scope of a declaration of the exception name *exn*, then it may be handled by a handling rule

exn **with** *match*

in a handler, but only if this handler is in the textual scope of the same declaration. Otherwise it may only be caught by the universal handling rule

? => *exp'* .

This rule is perfectly adequate for exceptions declared at top level; some examples in Section 8.4 below illustrate what may occur in other cases.

8.2   Derived forms

A handler discriminates among exception packets in two ways. First, it handles just those packets (e,v) for which e is the exception bound to the exception name in one of its handling rules; second, the match in this rule may discriminate upon v, the excepted value. Note however that, if a universal handling rule "? => *exp'* " is activated, then all packets are handled without discrimination. Thus "?" may be considered as a wildcard, matching any packet. It should be used with some care, bearing in mind that it will even handle interrupts.

A case which is likely to be frequent is when discrimination is required upon the exception, but not upon the excepted value; in this case, the derived handling rule

$$exn \texttt{ => } exp\,'$$

is appropriate for handling. Further, exceptions of type unit may be raised by the shortened form

raise *exn*

since the only possible excepted value is ().

8.3   An example

To illustrate the generality of exception handling, suppose that we have declared some exceptions as follows:

exception oddlist :int list **and** oddstring :string

and that a certain expression exp:int may raise either of these exceptions and also runs the risk of dividing by zero. The handler in the following **handle** expression would deal with these exceptions:

```
exp handle   oddlist      with   []          => 0
                            |    [x]          => 2*x
                            |    x::y::_      => x div y
         ||   oddstring    with   ""          => 0
                            |    s            => size(s)-1
         ||   div => 10000
```

Note that the whole expression is well-typed because in each handling rule the type of each match-pattern is the same as the exception type, and because the result type of each match is int, the same as the type of exp. The last handling rule is the shortened form appropriate for exceptions of type unit.

Note also that the last handling rule will handle div exceptions raised by exp , but will not handle the div exception which may be raised by "x div y" within the first handling rule. Finally, note that a universal handling rule

```
|| ? => 50000
```

at the end would deal with all other exceptions raised by exp .

8.4   Some pathological examples

We now consider some possible misuses of exception handling, which may arise from the fact that exception declarations have scope, and that each evaluation of a generative exception binding creates a distinct exception. Consider a simple example:

```
exception exn : bool;
fun f(x) =
    let exception exn:int in
        if x > 100 then raise exn with x else x+1
    end;
f(200) handle exn with true=>500 | false=>1000;
```

The program is well-typed, but useless. The exception bound to the outer exn is distinct from that bound to the inner exn; thus the exception raised by f(200), with excepted value 200, could only be handled by a handler within the scope of the inner exception declaration – it will not be handled by the handler in the program, which expects a boolean value. So this exception will be reported at top level. This would apply even if the outer exception declaration were also of type int; the two exceptions bound to exn would still be distinct.

On the other hand, if the last line of the program is changed to

```
f(200) handle ? => 500 ;
```

then the exception will be caught, and the value 500 returned. A universal handling rule (i.e. containing "?") catches any exception packet, even one exported from the scope of the declaration of the associated exception name, but cannot examine the excepted value in the packet, since the type of this value cannot be statically determined.

Even a single textual exception binding – if for example it is declared within a recursively defined function – may bind distinct exceptions to the same identifier. Consider another useless program:

```
fun f(x) =
    let exception exn in
        if p(x) then a(x) else
        if q(x) then f(b(x)) handle exn => c(x)
                else raise exn with d(x)
    end;
f(v);
```

Now if p(v) is false but q(v) is true, the recursive call will evaluate f(b(v)). Then, if both p(b(v)) and q(b(v)) are false, this evaluation will raise an exn exception with excepted value d(b(v)). But this packet will not be handled, since the exception of the packet is that which is bound to exn by the inner – not outer – evaluation of the exception declaration.

These pathological examples should not leave the impression that exceptions are hard to use or to understand. The rough and ready rule of Section 8.1 will almost always give the correct understanding.

9   Type-checking

The type discipline is exactly as in original ML, and here only a few points about type-checking will be discussed.

In a match "pat_1=>exp_1 | _ | pat_n=>exp_n", the types of all pat_i must be the same (ty say), and if variable var occurs in pat_i then all free occurrences of var in exp_i must have the same type as its occurrence in pat_i. In addition, the types of all the exp_i must be the same (ty' say). Then ty->ty' is the type of the match. The type of "**fn** $match$" is the type of the match.

The type of a handler rule "exn **with** $match$" is ty', where exn has type ty and $match$ has type ty->ty'. The type of a universal handling rule "? => exp" is the type of exp . The type of a handler is the type of all its handling rules (which must therefore be the same), and the type of "exp **handle** $handler$" is that of both exp and $handler$. The type of "**raise** exn **with** exp" is arbitrary, but exp and exn must have the same type. Exceptions may be polymorphic; any exn must have the same type at all occurrences within the scope of its declaration.

A type variable is only explicitly bound (in the sense of variable-binding in lambda-calculus) by its occurrence in the $tyvar\_seq$ on the left hand side of a simple type or datatype binding "<<$tyvar\_seq$>>$tycon$ = _", and then its scope is the right hand side. (This means for example that bound uses of 'a in both tb_1 and tb_2 in the type binding "tb_1 **and** tb_2" bear no relation to each other.) Otherwise, repeated occurrences of a type variable may serve to link explicit type constraints. The scope of such a type variable is determined by its first occurrence (ignoring all occurrences which lie within scopes already thus determined). If this first occurrence is in an **exception** declaration, then it has the same scope as the declared exception(s); otherwise, its scope is the smallest **val** (or **fun**) declaration in which it lies. For example, consider

fun G(f:'a->'b)(x:'a) =   **let val** y:'b = f(x)
                                and Id = (**fn** x:'c => x)
                 in (Id(x):'a, Id(y):'b) **end**

Here the scope of both 'a and 'b is the whole **fun** declaration, while the scope of 'c is just the **val** declaration. Note that this allows "Id" to be used polymorphically after its declaration. Moreover, type-checking must not further constrain a type variable within its scope. Thus for example the declaration

"**fun** Apply(f:'a->'b)(x:'a):'b = x"

– in which "x" has been written in error in place of "f(x)" – will be faulted since it requires 'a and 'b to be equated.

A simple datatype binding "<<*tyvar_seq*>>*tycon* = _ " is *generative*, since a new unique type constructor (denoted by *tycon*) is created by each textual occurrence of such a binding. A simple type binding such as "<<*tyvar_seq*>>*tycon* = *ty*", on the other hand, is *non-generative*; to take an example, the type binding " 'a couple = 'a * 'a " merely allows the type expression "*ty* couple" to abbreviate "*ty* * *ty*" (for any *ty*) within its scope. There is no semantic significance in abbreviation; in the Core Language it is purely for brevity, though in Modules non-generative type-bindings are essential in matching Signatures. However, the type-checker should take some advantage of non-local type abbreviations in reporting types at top-level; in doing this, it may need to choose sensibly between different possible abbreviations for the same type.

Some standard function symbols (e.g. =,+) stand for functions of more than one type; in these cases the type-checker should complain if it cannot determine from the context which is intended (an explicit type constraint may be needed). Note that there is no implicit coercion in ML, in particular from int to real; the conversion function real:int->real must be used explicitly.

10   Syntactic restrictions

1. No pattern may contain the same variable twice. No binding may bind the same identifier twice. No record type, record expression or record pattern may use the same label twice. In a record type or expression, either all labels must be identifiers or they must be the numeric labels #1, _ , #n for some n. The same applies to record patterns, except that some numeric labels may be absent if "..." is present.

2. In a match "pat_1=>exp_1 | _ | pat_n=> exp_n", the pattern sequence pat_1, _ , pat_n should be *irredundant* and *exhaustive*. That is, each pat_j must match some value (of the right type) which is not matched by pat_i for any $i < j$, and every value (of the right type) must be matched by some pat_i. The compiler must give warning on violation of this restriction, but should still compile the match. Thus the "match" exception (see Section 3.4) will only be raised for a match which has been flagged by the compiler. The restriction is inherited

by derived forms; in particular, this means that in the function bind-
ing "$var \; apat_1 \; \_ \; apat_n \; \texttt{<<:}ty\texttt{>>} = exp$" (consisting of one clause only),
each separate $apat_i$ should be exhaustive by itself.

3. For each value binding "$pat = exp$" the compiler must issue a report
   (but still compile) if either pat is not exhaustive or pat contains no
   variable. This will (on both counts) detect a mistaken declaration like
   "**val** nil $= exp$" in which the user expects to declare a new variable
   nil (whereas the language dictates that nil is here a constant pattern,
   so no variable gets declared). However, these warnings should not
   be given when the binding is a component of a top-level declaration
   val vb ; e.g. "**val** x::l $= exp_1$ **and** y $= exp_2$" is not faulted by the
   compiler at top level, but may of course generate a "bind" exception
   (see Section 3.6).

4. For each value binding "$pat = exp$" within **rec**, exp must be of the form
   "**fn** $match$". The derived form of value binding given in Section 6.2
   necessarily obeys this restriction.

5. In the left hand side "$\texttt{<<}tyvar\_seq\texttt{>>}tycon$" of a simple type or datatype
   binding, the $tyvar\_seq$ must contain no type variable more than once.
   The right hand side may contain only the type variables mentioned
   on the left. Within the scope of the declaration of $tycon$, any occurrence of $tycon$ must be accompanied by as many type arguments as
   indicated by the $\texttt{<<}tyvar\_seq\texttt{>>}$ in the declaration.

6. Assume temporarily that locally declared datatype constructors have
   been renamed so that no two textually distinct datatype bindings bind
   identically-named datatype constructors. Then, if the typechecker
   ascribes type ty to a program phrase p, every datatype constructor
   in ty must be declared with scope containing p. For example, if
   ty is ascribed to exp in "**let** dec **in** exp **end**" then ty must contain
   no datatype constructor declared by dec, since ty is also the type
   ascribed to the whole **let** expression.

7. Every global exception binding – that is, not localised either by **let**
   or by **local** – must be explicitly constrained by a monotype.

8. If, within the scope of a type constructor $tycon$, a type binding tb or
   datatype binding db binds (simultaneously) one or more type constructors $tycon_1, \_ , tycon_n$ then: (a) if the identifiers $tycon_i$ are all
   distinct from $tycon$, then their value constructors (if any) must also
   have identifiers distinct from those (if any) of $tycon$; (b) if any $tycon_i$ is
   the same identifier as $tycon$, then any value constructor of $tycon$ may
   be re-bound as a value constructor for one of $tycon_1, \_ , tycon_n$, but
   is otherwise considered unbound (as a variable or value constructor)

within the scope of tb or db, unless it is bound again therein. This constraint ensures that the scope of a type constructor is identical with the scopes of its associated value constructors, except that in an **abstype** declaration the scope of the value constructors is restricted to the **with** part.

11 Relation between the Core Language and Modules

The sister report [7] on ML Modules describes how ML declarations are grouped together into *Structures* which can be compiled separately. Structures, and the *Functors* which generate them, may not be declared locally within ML programs, but only at top-level or local to other Structures and Functors; this means that the Core Language is largely unaffected by their nature.

However, Structures and their components (types, values, exceptions and other Structures) may be accessed from ML programs via *qualified names* of the form

$$\text{id}_1. \_ .\text{id}_n.\text{id} \quad (n \geq 1)$$

where $\text{id}_1, \_ , \text{id}_n$ are Structure names, each id_i is the name of a component Structure of id_{i-1} for $1 < i \leq n$, and id is either a type constructor, a value constructor, a value variable, an exception name or a Structure name declared as a component of Structure id_n. Thus the syntax classes *tycon*, *con*, *var* and *exn* are extended to include qualified names. Further, the declaration

$$\textbf{open} \ \text{id}_1. \_ .\text{id}_n \quad (n \geq 1)$$

(where $\text{id}_1, \_ , \text{id}_n$ are as above) allows the components of the Structure $\text{id}_1. \_ .\text{id}_n$ to be named without qualification in the scope of the declaration.

Each Structure is equipped with a *Signature*, which determines the nature and type of each component, and this permits static analysis and type-checking for programs which use the Structure.

12 Conclusion

This design has been under discussion for over two years. In the conclusion (Section 11) of [5] we predicted that a few infelicities of design would emerge during the last year, and this has happened. But they are satisfyingly few. Use of the language by a wider community will probably raise further suggestions for change, but against this we must set the advantage of maintaining complete stability in the language. We shall adopt a policy of minimum change.

At the same time, *extensions* to ML – ones which preserve the validity of all existing programs – may be suggested either by practical need or by increased theoretical understanding. Examples of the latter may be the introduction of polymorphic assignment, or the extension of the equality predicate to a wider class of types. We hope that these extensions will be made when appropriate.

References

[1] M. Gordon, R. Milner and C. Wadsworth. *Edinburgh LCF*. Volume 78 of *Lecture Notes in Computer Science*, Springer Verlag, 1979.

[2] R. Burstall, D. MacQueen and D. Sanella. *HOPE: An Experimental Applicative Language*. Report CSR-62-80, Computer Science Dept, Edinburgh University, 1980.

[3] L. Cardelli. *ML under UNIX*. Technical Report, Bell Laboratories, Murray Hill, New Jersey, 1982.

[4] R. Milner. *A Proposal for Standard ML*. Report CSR-157-83, Computer Science Dept, Edinburgh University, 1983.

[5] R. Milner. *The Standard ML Core Language*. Report CSR-168-84, Computer Science Dept, Edinburgh University, 1984.

[6] R. Harper. *Standard ML Input/Output*. Technical Report, Computer Science Dept, Edinburgh University, 1985.

[7] D. MacQueen. *Modules for Standard ML*. Technical Report, Bell Laboratories, Murray Hill, New Jersey, 1985.

Table 4: **Syntax : Expressions and Patterns**

(See Section 2.8 for conventions and remarks)

$aexp$ ::=

<<**op**>>var	(variable)
<<**op**>>con	(constructor)
{ lab_1=exp_1, _ , lab_n=exp_n }	(record, $n \geq 0$)
()	(0-tuple)
(exp_1 , _ , exp_n)	(n-tuple, $n \geq 2$)
[exp_1 , _ , exp_n]	(list, $n \geq 0$)
(exp_1 ; _ ; exp_n)	(sequence, $n \geq 1$)

exp ::=

$aexp$		(atomic)
exp $aexp$	L	(application)
exp id exp'		(infixed application)
exp : ty	L	(constraint)
exp **andalso** exp'		(conjunction)
exp **orelse** exp'		(disjunction)
exp **handle** $handler$	R	(handle exception)
raise exn <<**with** exp>>		(raise exception)
if exp **then** exp_1 **else** exp_2		(conditional)
while exp **do** exp'		(iteration)
let dec **in** exp_1 ; _ ; exp_n **end**		(local declaration, $n \geq 1$)
case exp **of** $match$		(case expression)
fn $match$		(function)

$match$ ::=
    $rule_1$ | _ | $rule_n$ $(n \geq 1)$

$rule$ ::=
    pat => exp

$handler$ ::=
    $hrule_1$ || _ || $hrule_n$ $(n \geq 1)$

$hrule$ ::=
    exn **with** $match$
    exn => exp
    ? => exp

$apat$ ::=

_	(wildcard)
<<**op**>>var	(variable)
con	(constant)
{ lab_1=pat_1, _ , lab_n=pat_n <<, . . .>>}	(record,$n \geq 0$) [a]
()	(0-tuple)
(pat_1 , _ , pat_n)	(tuple, $n \geq 2$)
[pat_1 , _ , pat_n]	(list, $n \geq 0$)
(pat)	

pat ::=

$apat$		(atomic)
<<**op**>>con $apat$	L	(construction)
pat con pat'		(infixed construction)
pat : ty	L	(constraint)
<<**op**>>var<<:ty>> **as** pat	R	(layered)

---

[a] If $n = 0$ then omit the comma; "{. . .}" is the pattern which matches any record. If a component of a record pattern has the form "id=id<<:ty>><<**as** pat>>", then it may be written in the elided form "id<<:ty>><<**as** pat>>".

Table 5: **Syntax : Types, Bindings, Declarations**

(See Section 2.8 for conventions)

$ty ::=$

$tyvar$	(type variable)
$\mathtt{<<}ty\_seq\mathtt{>>}tycon$	(type construction)
$\{\ lab_1{:}ty_1,\ \_\ ,\ lab_n{:}ty_n\ \}$	(record type, $n \geq 0$)
$ty_1\ *\ \_\ *\ ty_n$	(tuple type, $n \geq 2$)
$ty_1\ \mathtt{->}\ ty_2$ $\qquad$ R	(function type)
$(\ ty\ )$	

$vb ::=$

$pat = exp$	(simple)
vb_1 **and** $\_$ **and** vb_n	(multiple, $n \geq 2$)
rec vb	(recursive)

$fb ::=$

$\mathtt{<<op>>}var\ apat_{11}\ \_\ apat_{1n}\mathtt{<<:}ty\mathtt{>>} = exp_1$	(clausal function,
$\quad\mid\ \_\ \_$	$\quad m, n \geq 1$) [a]
$\quad\mid\ \mathtt{<<op>>}var\ apat_{m1}\ \_\ apat_{mn}\mathtt{<<:}ty\mathtt{>>} = exp_m$	
fb_1 **and** $\_$ **and** fb_n	(multiple, $n \geq 2$)

$tb ::=$

$\mathtt{<<}tyvar\_seq\mathtt{>>}tycon = ty$	(simple)
tb_1 **and** $\_$ **and** tb_n	(multiple, $n \geq 2$)

$db ::=$

$\mathtt{<<}tyvar\_seq\mathtt{>>}tycon = constrs$	(simple)
db_1 **and** $\_$ **and** db_n	(multiple, $n \geq 2$)

$constrs ::=$

$\mathtt{<<op>>}con_1\mathtt{<<of\ }ty_1\mathtt{>>}\ \mid\ \_$	
$\quad\mid\ \mathtt{<<op>>}con_n\mathtt{<<of\ }ty_n\mathtt{>>}$	($n \geq 1$)

$eb ::=$

$exn\mathtt{<<:}ty\mathtt{>><<}\ =exn'\mathtt{>>}$	(simple)
eb_1 **and** $\_$ **and** eb_n	(multiple, $n \geq 2$)

$dec ::=$

val vb	(value declaration)
fun fb	(function declaration)
type tb	(type declaration)
datatype db	(datatype declaration)
abstype db **with** dec **end**	(abstract type declaration)
exception eb	(exception declaration)
local dec **in** dec' **end**	(local declaration)
exp	(top-level only)
dir	(directive)
$dec_1\mathtt{<<;>>}\ \_\ dec_n\mathtt{<<;>>}$	(declaration sequence, $n \geq 0$

$dir ::=$

infix$\mathtt{<<r>>}\ \mathtt{<<d>>}\ id_1\_\ id_n$	(declare infix, $0 \leq d \leq 9$)
nonfix $id_1\ \_\ id_n$	(cancel infix)

---

[a] If var has infix status then op is required in this form; alternatively var may be infixed in any clause. Thus, at the start of any clause, "op $var\ (apat, apat')$ $\_$" may be written "$(apat\ var\ apat')$ $\_$"; the parentheses may also be dropped if "$:ty$" or "$=$" follows immediately.

Table 6: **Predeclared Variables and Constructors**

In the types of these bindings, "num" stands for either int or real, and
"nums" stands for integer, real or string (the same in each type). Similarly
"ty" stands for an arbitrary type, "mty" stands for any monotype, and
"ety" (see Section 7.2) stands for any type admitting equality.

nonfix		infix
nil	: 'a list	**Precedence 7 :**
map	: ('a->'b) -> 'a list	/ : real * real -> real
	-> 'b list	div : int * int -> int
rev	: 'a list -> 'a list	mod : " " "
		* : num * num -> num
true,false	: bool	
not	: bool -> bool	**Precedence 6 :**
		+ : " " "
~	: num -> num	- : " " "
abs	: num -> num	^ : string * string -> string
floor	: real -> int	
real	: int -> real	**Precedence 5 :**
sqrt	: real -> real	:: : 'a * 'a list -> 'a list
sin,cos,arctan	: real -> real	@ : 'a list * 'a list
exp,ln	: real -> real	-> 'a list
		Precedence 4 :
size	: string -> int	= : ety * ety -> bool
chr	: int -> string	<> : " " "
ord	: string -> int	< : nums * nums -> bool
explode	: string -> string list	> : " " "
implode	: string list -> string	<= : " " "
		>= : " " "
ref	: mty -> mty ref	
!	: 'a ref -> 'a	**Precedence 3 :**
		o : ('b->'c) * ('a->'b)
print	: ty -> ty	-> ('a->'c)
makestring	: ty -> string	:= : mty ref * mty -> unit

Special constants: as in Section 2.3.
Notes:

1. The following are constructors, and thus may appear in patterns:

   nil true false ref :: and all special constants.

2. Infixes of higher precedence bind tighter. "::" associates to the right;
   otherwise infixes of equal precedence associate to the left.

3. The meanings of these predeclared bindings are discussed in Section 5.2.

13   Changes to the ML Core Language

The following changes are made to the Core Language of Standard ML, from April 1987. The Core Language report is referred to as MLCore.

13.1   Numeric record labels

The numeric record labels, hitherto #1 #2 _ , are now to be written 1 2 _ , i.e. without the prefix # . The restrictions on use of numeric labels are removed; they may be mixed with non-numeric record labels in record types, patterns and expressions, and are not required to be an initial subsequence of the integers. Thus any finite set of labels is now admissible in a record type. Note that the tuple type $ty_1* \_ *ty_n$ is still the type $1{:}ty_1, \_ , n{:}ty_n$; tuple types are, as before, just those whose labels are some permutation of the integers $1 \_ n \ (n \geq 2)$.

13.2   Selector functions

For each record label *lab* (numeric or otherwise), the selector function #*lab* is introduced; it is a derived form, whose equivalent form is

$$\mathbf{fn} \ \{ \ lab{=}\text{x}, \dots \} => \text{x}$$

Thus—just as for the equivalent form—the type of each occurrence of #*lab* must be deducible from the context; sometimes an explicit type constraint may be required for this purpose.

13.3   Abbreviations in datatype bindings

A new form of datatype binding is introduced, with the form

$$db \ \mathbf{withtype} \ tb \qquad\qquad (*)$$

A simple example of a datatype declaration using this form is

> **datatype** ('a,'b)tree = tip **of** 'a
> | node **of** 'b * ('a,'b)forest
> **withtype** ('a,'b)forest = ('a,'b)tree list

The type abbreviations introduced by **withtype** may be used both in the datatype binding and later; thus, the above example is equivalent to

> **datatype** ('a,'b)tree = tip **of** 'a
> | node **of** 'b * ('a,'b)tree list;
> **type** ('a,'b)forest = ('a,'b)tree list

In the new form ($*$) *tb* is not interpreted recursively; that is, if *tb* binds a type constructor *tycon*, uses of *tycon* in a right-hand side within *tb* will not refer the present binding but to an earlier one. On the other hand *db* is (as usual) interpreted recursively; the effect of the new form is to allow the abbreviations in *tb* to mediate the recursion of *db*.

Datatype bindings can only occur following **datatype** or **abstype**, so we can define the new form by giving equivalent forms for the two derived forms

> **datatype** *db* **withtype** *tb*
>
> **abstype** *db* **withtype** *tb* **with** *dec* **end**

Their equivalent forms are as follows:

> **datatype** *db'*; **type** *tb*
>
> **abstype** *db'* **with type** *tb*; *dec* **end**

where *db'* is obtained from *db* by simultaneously expanding out the abbreviations defined by *tb* .

A restriction is that **withtype** may appear at most once in any datatype binding. The new form also inherits the general restriction (10(1) in ML-Core) that no binding may bind the same identifier twice.

13.4   Polymorphic equality (The following replaces Section 7.2 of MLCore)

An important subclass of types consists of the class *ety* of equality types, or eqtypes, which we now define. In giving the definition we assume that all type abbreviations have been expanded out.

First we determine the type constructors which admit equality, which we shall also call eqtype constructors, as follows:

1. The standard type constructors unit, bool, int, real, string, list, ref and the record-type constructors are all eqtype constructors.

2. If datatype constructors $tycon_1, \_ , tycon_n$ are simultaneously declared in a datatype binding, then they are eqtype constructors provided that every type ty which occurs as a right-hand side in this binding is built from arbitrary reference types and type variables using only eqtype constructors and $tycon_1, \_ , tycon_n$ themselves.

Thus the only reason that a type constructor may not admit equality is if, in its declaration or in the declaration of any type constructor on which it depends, the function-type constructor $->$ is used without being enclosed in the reference-type constructor ref . However, an eqtype constructor declared by **abstype** only admits equality in the "with" part of its declaration. We denote an eqtype constructor by *etycon* .

To allow polymorphic eqtypes, we introduce (as a subclass of *tyvar*) the class *etyvar* of eqtype variables, represented by identifiers beginning with two or more primes ('), e.g. "a , "b . Eqtype variables may only appear in explicit type constraints or in specifications, not in type or datatype bindings. (They will also occur as the result of type-checking.). Their significance is that they may only be instantiated to eqtypes. The syntax of eqtypes *ety* is as follows, assuming that all type abbreviations have been expanded out:

ety ::=

etyvar	(eqtype variable)
$<< ety_seq >> etycon$	(eqtype construction)
ty ref	(arbitrary reference type)
$\{lab_1:ety_1, \_ ,lab_n:ety_n\}$	(record eqtype, $n > 0$)

The infixed equality and inequality predicates (= and <>) are provided with polymorphic type "a * "a − > bool .

13.5   Polymorphic assignment

The infixed assignment function := is now given the polymorphic type 'a ref * 'a − > unit . This extension has been shown to be sound by Mads Tofte. However, the reference function ref still has the monomorphic types mty − > mty ref in expressions (though polymorphic in patterns, with type 'a − > 'a ref). It is hoped to find a robust and easily understood relaxation of this restriction in the near future.

13.6   Polymorphic exceptions

It is necessary to introduce a restriction on the use of polymorphic exceptions, due to an unsoundness recently discovered by MacQueen. The restriction is as follows:

> If an exception *exn* is declared with a polymorphic type, or if such a type is inferred for it by the type checker, then no handler of *exn* may occur within a function expression which lies within the scope of the declaration of *exn*.

Thus the following is forbidden:

let exception *exn* : 'a **in** _ (**fn** _ **handle** *exn* _) _ **end**

Note that there is no restriction on occurrences of **raise** expressions, nor upon handlers of monomorphic exceptions.

Standard ML Input/Output

Robert Harper [*]

1   Introduction

This document describes the Standard ML [1] character stream input/output system. The primitives defined below are intended as a simple basis that may be compatibly superseded by a more comprehensive I/O system that provides for streams of arbitrary type or a richer repertoire of I/O operations. The I/O primitives are organized into two modules, one for the basic I/O primitives that are required to be provided by all implementations, and one for extensions to the basic set. An implementation may support any, all, or none of the functions in the extended I/O module, and may extend this module with new primitives. If an implementation does not implement a primitive from the set of extensions, then it must leave it undefined so that unsupported features are recognized at compile time.

The fundamental notion in the SML I/O system is the (finite or infinite) character stream. There are two types of stream, `instream` for input streams, and `outstream` for output streams. These types are provided by the implementation of the basic I/O module. Interaction with the outside world is accomplished by associating a stream with a *producer* (for input streams) or a *consumer* (for output streams). The notion of a producer and a consumer is purely metaphorical. Their realization is left to each implementation; the SML programmer need be aware of their existence only insofar as it is necessary to imagine the source (or sink) of characters in a stream. For instance, ordinary disk files, terminals, and processes are all acceptable as producers or consumers. A given implementation may support a range producers and consumers; all implementations must allow disk files to be associated with input and output streams.

Streams in SML may be finite or infinite; finite streams may or may not have a definite end. A natural use of an infinite stream is the connection of an `instream` to a process that generates an infinite sequence, say of prime numbers represented as

---

[*]Reprinted by permission from Robert Harper.

numerals. Most often streams are finite, though not always terminated. Ordinary disk files are a good example of producers of finite streams of characters. Processes as producers give rise to the notion of an unterminated finite stream — a process may at any time refuse to supply any more characters to a stream, a condition which is, of course, undetectable. All subsequent input requests will therefore wait forever. Primitives are provided for detecting the end of an input stream and for terminating an output stream.

The stream types provided by the basic I/O module are abstract, and as such have no visible structure. However, it is helpful to imagine that each stream has associated with it a buffer that mediates the interaction between the ML system and the producer or consumer associated with that stream, and a control object, which is used for device-specific mode-setting and control. A typical example of the use of the control object is to modify the character processing performed by a terminal device driver.

In the spirit of simplicity and generality, this proposal does not treat such implementation-dependent details as the resolution of multiple file access (both within and between processes), and the names of files and processes. The window between the SML system and the operating system is limited to two primitives, each of which takes a string parameter whose interpretation is implementation-specific. One convention must be enforced by all implementations — end of line is represented by the single newline character, \n, regardless of how it is represented by the host system. However, since end of file is a condition, as opposed to a character, the means by which this condition is indicated on a terminal is left to the implementation.

2   Basic I/O Primitives

The fundamental I/O primitives are packaged into a structure BasicIO with signature BASICIO (see Figure 1). A structure matching this signature (and having the semantics defined below) must be provided by every SML implementation. It is implicitly open'd by the standard prelude so that these identifiers may be used without the qualifier BasicIO.

The type instream is the type of input streams and the type outstream is the type of output streams. The exception io_failure is used to represent all of the errors that may arise in the course of performing I/O. The value associated with this exception is a string representing the type of failure. In general, any I/O operation may fail if, for any reason, the host system is unable to perform the requested task. The value associated with the exception should describe the type of failure, insofar as this is possible.

```
signature BASICIO = sig
  (* Types and exceptions *)
  type instream
  type outstream
  exception io_failure: string

  (* Standard input and output streams *)
  val std_in: instream
  val std_out: outstream

  (* Stream creation *)
  val open_in: string -> instream
  val open_out: string -> outstream

  (* Operations on input streams *)
  val input: instream * int -> string
  val lookahead: instream -> string
  val close_in: instream -> unit
  val end_of_stream: instream -> bool

  (* Operations on output streams *)
  val output: outstream * string -> unit
  val close_out: outstream -> unit
end
```

Figure 1: Basic I/O Primitives

The standard prelude binds std_in to an instream and binds std_out to an outstream. For interactive ML processes, these are expected to be associated with the user's terminal. However, an implementation that supports the connection of processes to streams may associate one process's std_in with another's std_out.

The open_in and open_out primitives are used to associate a disk file with a stream. The expression open_in(s) creates a new instream whose producer is the file named s and returns that stream as value. If the file named by s does not exist, the exception io_failure is raised with value "Cannot open "^s. Similarly, open_out(s) creates a new outstream whose consumer is the file s, and returns that stream.

The input primitive is used to read characters from a stream. Evaluation of input(s,n) causes the removal of n characters from the input stream s. If fewer than n characters are currently available, then the ML system will block until they become available from the producer associated with s.[1] If the end of stream is reached while processing an input, fewer than n characters may be returned. In particular, input from a closed stream returns the null string. The function lookahead(s) returns the next character on instream s without removing it from the stream. Input streams are terminated by the close_in operation. This primitive is provided primarily for symmetry and to support the reuse of unused streams on resource-limited systems. The end of an input stream is detected by end_of_stream, a derived form that is defined as follows:

```
val end_of_stream(s) = (lookahead(s)="")
```

Characters are written to an outstream with the output primitive. The string argument consists of the characters to be written to the given outstream. The function close_out is used to terminate an output stream. Any further attempts to output to a closed stream cause io_failure to be raised with value "Output stream is closed".

3   Extended I/O Primitives

In addition to the basic I/O primitives, provision is made for a some extensions that are likely to be provided by many implementations. The structure ExtendedIO consists of an extensible set of operations that are commonly used but are either too complex to be considered primitive or to be implementable on all hosts. Its signature appears in Figure 2.

The function execute is used to create a pair of streams, one an instream and one an outstream, and associate them with a process. The string argument to execute is the (implementation-dependent) name of the process to be executed. In the case that the process is an SML program, the instream created by execute is connected to the std_out stream of the process, and the outstream returned is connected to the process's std_in.

The function flush_out ensures that the consumer associated with an outstream has received all of the characters that have been written to that stream. It is provided primarily to allow the ML user to circumvent undesirable buffering characteristics that may arise in connection with terminals and other processes. All output streams are flushed when they are closed, and in many implementations

---

[1]The exact definition of "available" is implementation-dependent. For instance, operating systems typically buffer terminal input on a line-by-line basis so that no characters are available until an entire line has been typed.

```
signature EXTENDEDIO = sig
  val execute: string -> instream * outstream
  val flush_out: outstream -> unit
  val can_input: instream * int -> bool
  val input_line: instream -> string
  val open_append: string -> outstream
  val is_term_in: instream -> bool
  val is_term_out: outstream -> bool
end
```

Figure 2: Extended I/O Primitives

an output stream is flushed whenever a newline is encountered if that stream is connected to a terminal.

The function can_input takes an instream and a number and determines whether or not that many characters may be read from that stream without blocking. For instance, a command processor may wish to test whether or not a user has typed ahead in order to avoid an unnecessary prompt. The exact definition of "currently available" is implementation-specific, perhaps depending on such things as the processing mode of a terminal.

The input_line primitive returns a string consisting of the characters from an instream up through, and including, the next end of line character. If the end of stream is reached without reaching an end of line character, all remaining characters from the stream (*without* an end of line character) are returned.

Files may be open for output while preserving their contents by using the open_append primitive. Subsequent output to the outstream returned by this primitive is appended to the contents of the specified file.

Basic support for the complexities of terminal I/O are also provided. The pair of functions is_term_in and is_term_out test whether or not a stream is associated with a terminal. These functions are especially useful in association with std_in and std_out because they are opened as part of the standard prelude. A terminal may be designated as the producer or consumer of a stream using the ordinary open_in and open_out functions; an implementation supporting this capability must specify a naming convention for designating terminals. Terminal I/O is, in general, more complex than ordinary file I/O. In most cases the ExtendedIO module provided by an implementation will have additional operations to support mode control. Since the details of such control operations are highly host-dependent, the functions that may be provided are left unspecified.

Acknowledgements

The Standard ML I/O system is based on Luca Cardelli's proposal [2], and on a simplified form of it proposed by Kevin Mitchell and Robin Milner. The final version was prepared with the help of Dave MacQueen, Dave Matthews, Robin Milner, Kevin Mitchell, and Larry Paulson.

References

[1] Robin Milner, *The Standard ML Core Language*, Edinburgh University.

[2] Luca Cardelli, *Stream Input/Output*, AT&T Bell Laboratories.

Appendix C

Syntax Charts for a Subset of Standard ML

In this appendix, syntax charts for the part of ML used in this book are given. However, the ultimate document describing the syntax of ML is the ML Report; the charts are given only because they are most often easier to read and understand for a beginner. More details about syntax charts are given in Chapter 9.

To simplify the charts, all boxes are omitted. The information they give the reader is instead given by the use of different fonts. All words occurring in small capital letters, as for instance DECLARATION, are non-terminal symbols that refer to some other chart (except in the chart for real constants, where the letter E is a terminal symbol). Words in small italic letters are non-terminal symbols not described in any other chart; they should be self-explanatory, though. The remaining symbols are terminal symbols that can occur in ML programs.

The alternatives in a chart are given in order of decreasing precedence, so upper branches should be chosen before lower branches, if several of them apply. The letters "L" and "R" are used to denote left and right associativity, respectively. The string "0-9 LR" is used to indicate that the precedence and associativity depend on how the described identifier has been defined.

The main syntax charts describe the constructions PROGRAM, DECLARATION, TYPE, IDENTIFIER, EXPRESSION, PATTERN, MATCH, and SPECIAL CONSTANT. The remaining charts are auxiliary charts used to increase readability. For all charts, spaces, formatting characters, and comments can occur between all symbols, except within identifiers and constants.

PROGRAM

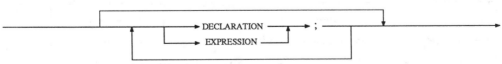

DECLARATION

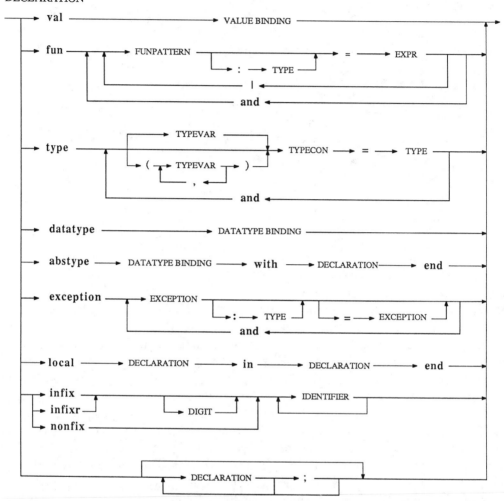

VALUE BINDING

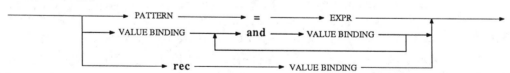

FUNPATTERN

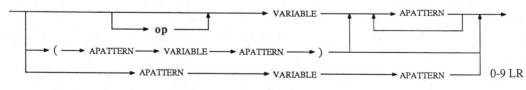

DATATYPE BINDING

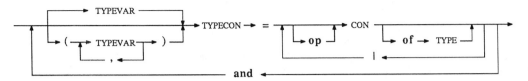

TYPE

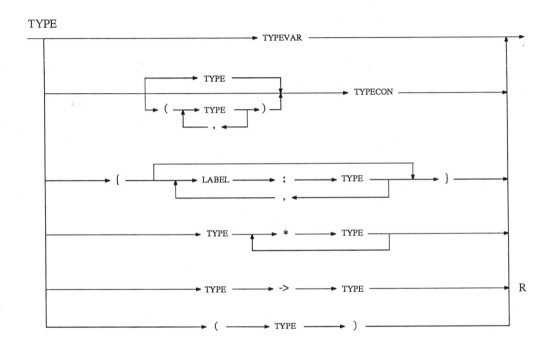

R

VARIABLE, TYPECON, EXCEPTION, LABEL, CON (CONSTRUCTOR)

IDENTIFIER

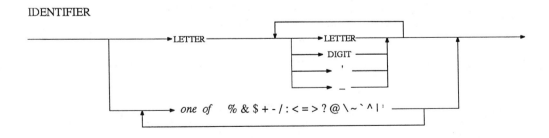

TYPEVAR

ATOMIC EXPRESSION

APATTERN (ATOMIC PATTERN)

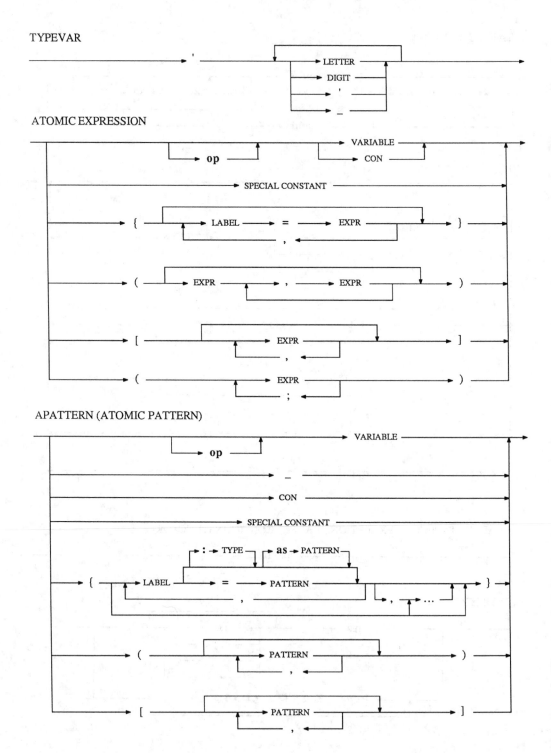

EXPR (EXPRESSION)

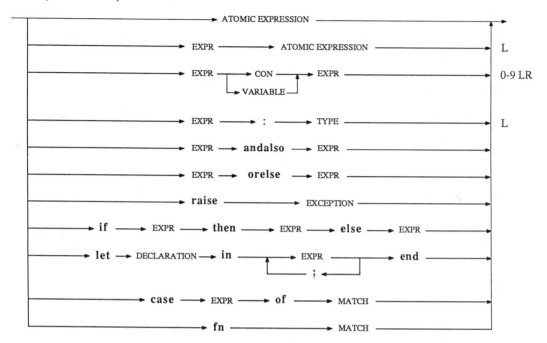

PATTERN

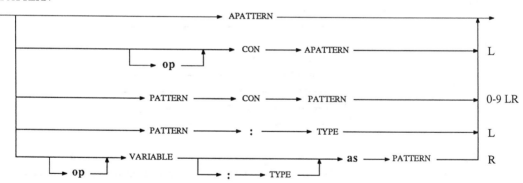

MATCH

RULE

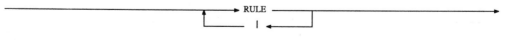

SPECIAL CONSTANT

INTEGER CONSTANT

REAL CONSTANT

STRING CONSTANT

LETTER

one of   ABCDEFGHIJKLMNOPQRSTUVWXYZabcdefghijklmnopqrstuvwxyz

DIGIT

one of   0123456789

Appendix D

Predefined Functions

The definitions below are candidates for the inclusion as predefined functions in an ML system. For completeness, most standard functions and operators are included. For some functions, a simple version is first given as a comment, and, then, an efficient version is given. All functions are referred to from the index.[1]

```
(* ----------------------------- Exceptions ------------------------------ *)

exception hd and tl and reduce1 and last and findone and fromto and index and
          take and drop and cut and lookup and combine and ** and power and
          integer and fac and digitval and for and iter and have and getint and
          getlist;

(* -------------------- General functions and combinators -------------------- *)

(* use is a predefined system command *)              (* string list -> unit *)

(* makestring is an overloaded standard function *)          (* 'a -> string *)

fun load file = use[file];                                   (* string -> unit *)

fun I a = a;                                                     (* 'a -> 'a *)

fun K a b = a;                                              (* 'a -> 'b -> 'a *)

fun C f x y = f y x;                    (* ('a -> 'b -> 'c) -> 'b -> 'a -> 'c *)

fun Y f x = f (Y f) x;                  (* (('a -> 'b) -> 'a -> 'b) -> 'a -> 'b *)

fun curry f x y = f(x, y);              (* ('a * 'b -> 'c) -> 'a -> 'b -> 'c *)

fun uncurry f (x, y) = f x y;           (* ('a -> 'b -> 'c) -> 'a * 'b -> 'c *)
```

---

[1]If you want an electronic copy of the definitions, the author will try to send them to you over the network, if you send your electronic mail address to "...!mcvax!enea!chalmers!wikstrom", "...wikstrom@chalmers.se", or "...wikstrom@chalmers.csnet".

```
(* o is a standard operator (prec 3) *)(* ('a -> 'b) * ('c -> 'a) -> 'c -> 'b *)

infixr 3 oo;                          (* ('a -> 'b) * ('c -> 'd -> 'a) ->     *)
fun (f oo g) x y = f(g x y);          (*                   'c -> 'd -> 'b *)

(* -------------------------- Tuple functions ------------------------- *)

(* #1, #2, ..., #i, ... are *)     (* 'a1 * 'a2 * ... * 'ai * ... 'an -> 'ai *)
(* standard tuple selectors *)

(* #id is a standard record selector, *)
(* if id is a label in the record     *)

fun fst (x, _) = x;                                       (* 'a * 'b -> 'a *)

fun snd (_, y) = y;                                       (* 'a * 'b -> 'b *)

fun pair x y  = (x, y);                              (* 'a -> 'b -> 'a * 'b *)

fun swap(x, y) = (y, x);                             (* 'a * 'b -> 'b * 'a *)

(* -------------------------- List functions ------------------------- *)

(* :: is a standard operator (prec 5) *)        (* 'a * 'a list -> 'a list *)

(* @  is a standard operator (prec 5) *)     (* 'a list * 'a list -> 'a list *)
infixr 5 @;

fun cons x xs = x :: xs;                        (* 'a -> 'a list -> 'a list *)

fun hd nil      = raise hd                            (* 'a list -> 'a *)
  | hd (x :: _) = x;

fun tl nil      = raise tl                          (* 'a list -> 'a list *)
  | tl (_ :: xs) = xs;

fun null nil = true                                 (* 'a list -> bool *)
  | null  _  = false;

fun last nil       = raise last                      (* 'a list -> 'a *)
  | last (x :: nil) = x
  | last (_ :: xs)  = last xs;

fun append l m = l @ m;                 (* 'a list -> 'a list -> 'a list *)

fun postfix x xs = xs @ [x];            (* 'a -> 'a list -> 'a list *)

(* val hangon = C postfix *)           (* 'a list -> 'a -> 'a list *)
fun hangon xs x = xs @ [x];
```

```
(* fun len nil        = 0             *)                    (* 'a list -> int *)
(*  | len (_ :: xs) = 1 + len xs; *)
local fun len' n nil        = n
        | len' n (_ :: xs) = len' (n+1) xs
in fun len xs = len' 0 xs end;

(* map is a standard function *)          (* ('a -> 'b) -> 'a list -> 'b list *)


(* rev is a standard function *)                   (* 'a list -> 'a list *)

fun filter p nil        = nil            (* ('a -> bool) -> 'a list -> 'a list *)
  | filter p (x :: xs) =
      if p x then x :: filter p xs
      else            filter p xs;

fun findone p nil        = raise findone      (* ('a -> bool) -> 'a list -> 'a *)
  | findone p (x :: xs) =
      if p x then x
      else findone p xs;

fun find p nil        = nil              (* ('a -> bool) -> 'a list -> 'a list *)
  | find p (x :: xs) =
      if p x then [x]
      else find p xs;

fun reduce f u nil        = u        (* ('a -> 'b -> 'b) -> 'b -> 'a list -> 'b *)
  | reduce f u (x :: xs) =
      f x (reduce f u xs);
val foldr = reduce;

fun redleft f u nil        = u       (* ('a -> 'b -> 'a) -> 'a -> 'b list -> 'a *)
  | redleft f u (x :: xs) =
      redleft f (f u x) xs;
val foldl = redleft;

fun reduce1 f nil        = raise reduce1       (* ('a -> 'a -> 'a) ->     *)
  | reduce1 f (x :: nil) = x                   (*          'a list -> 'a *)
  | reduce1 f (x :: xs)  = f x (reduce1 f xs);

fun listrec f u nil        = u           (* ('a -> 'a list -> 'b -> 'b) ->     *)
  | listrec f u (x :: xs) =              (*               'b -> 'a list -> 'b *)
      f x xs (listrec f u xs);

val flat = reduce append nil;                      (* 'a list list -> 'a list *)
```

```
fun fromto n m =                               (* int -> int -> int list *)
      if     n > m + 1 then raise fromto
      else if n = m + 1 then nil
      else n :: fromto (n + 1) m;

infix 5 --;
val op -- = uncurry fromto;                    (* int * int -> int list *)

fun genlist state next 0 = nil                 (* 'a -> ('a -> 'a) ->     *)
  | genlist state next n =                      (*           int -> 'a list *)
      state :: genlist (next state) next (n-1);

fun duplicate x 0 = nil                        (* 'a -> int -> 'a list *)
  | duplicate x n = x :: duplicate x (n-1);

fun index n nil     = raise index              (* int -> 'a list -> 'a *)
  | index 1 (x :: _) = x
  | index n (_ :: xs) = index (n-1) xs;

fun take 0 xs       = nil                       (* int -> 'a list -> 'a list *)
  | take n nil      = raise take
  | take n (x :: xs) = x :: take (n-1) xs;

fun drop 0 xs       = xs                         (* int -> 'a list -> 'a list *)
  | drop n nil      = raise drop
  | drop n (x :: xs) = drop (n-1) xs;

fun cut 0 xs        = (nil, xs)                  (* int -> 'a list ->        *)
  | cut n nil       = raise cut                  (*         'a list * 'a list *)
  | cut n (x :: xs) =
      let val (ys, zs) = cut (n-1) xs
      in (x :: ys, zs) end;

fun mem nil       a = false                      (* ''a list -> ''a -> bool *)
  | mem (x :: xs) a = a = x orelse mem xs a;

fun count nil       a = 0                        (* ''a list -> ''a -> int  *)
  | count (x :: xs) a =
      if a = x then 1 + count xs a
      else              count xs a;

fun duplicates nil     = false                   (* ''a list -> bool *)
  | duplicates (x :: xs) = mem xs x orelse
                            duplicates xs;

fun remdupl nil      = nil                        (* ''a list -> ''a list *)
  | remdupl [x]      = [x]
  | remdupl (x :: xs) = if mem xs x then remdupl xs
                         else       x :: remdupl xs;
```

```
fun interleave a nil              = [[a]]              (* 'a -> 'a list ->    *)
  | interleave a (xxs as x :: xs) =                    (*          'a list list *)
      (a :: xxs) :: map (cons x) (interleave a xs);

fun perms nil        = [nil]                           (* 'a list -> 'a list list *)
  | perms (x :: xs) =
      flat (map (interleave x) (perms xs));

(* ---------- Lists as sets ---------- *)

fun union s t =                            (* ''a list -> ''a list -> ''a list *)
      s @ filter (not o mem s) t;

fun intersection s t =                     (* ''a list -> ''a list -> ''a list *)
      filter (mem s) t;

fun difference s t =                       (* ''a list -> ''a list -> ''a list *)
      filter (not o mem t) s;

(* ---------- Lists as tables ---------- *)

fun delete k nil             = nil         (* ''a -> (''a * 'b) list -> *)
  | delete k ((k', i) :: ps) =             (*        (''a * 'b) list    *)
      if k = k' then  delete k ps
      else (k', i) :: delete k ps;

fun insert k i ps =                        (* ''a -> 'b -> (''a * 'b) list -> *)
      (k, i) :: delete k ps;               (*              (''a * 'b) list    *)

fun lookup k nil = raise lookup            (* ''a -> (''a * 'b) list -> 'b *)
  | lookup k ((k', i) :: ps) =
      if k = k' then i
      else lookup k ps;

(* ---------- Lists and pairs ---------- *)

fun split nil          = (nil, nil)        (* ('a * 'b) list ->       *)
  | split ((x, y) :: xys) =                (*        'a list * 'b list *)
      let val (xs, ys) = split xys
      in (x :: xs, y :: ys) end;

fun combine(nil, nil) = nil                (* 'a list * 'b list ->    *)
  | combine(nil, ys)  = raise combine      (*         ('a * 'b) list *)
  | combine(xs,  nil) = raise combine
  | combine(x :: xs, y :: ys) =
      (x, y) :: combine(xs, ys);

fun allpairs xs ys =                       (* 'a list * 'b list ->    *)
      flat(map (fn x => map (pair x) ys) xs);  (*        ('a * 'b) list *)
```

```sml
(* ---------- List sorting ---------- *)

fun merge nil ys : int list   = ys        (* int list -> int list -> int list *)
  | merge xs   nil            = xs
  | merge (x :: xs) (y :: ys) =
      if x <= y then x :: merge      xs (y :: ys)
      else              y :: merge (x :: xs)      ys;

fun sort nil = nil                               (* int list -> int list *)
  | sort [x] = [x]
  | sort xs  = let val (ys, zs) = cut (len xs div 2) xs
               in merge (sort ys) (sort zs) end;

(* ------------------------- Boolean functions -------------------------- *)

(* = and <> are polymorphic standard *)         (* ''a * ''a -> bool *)
(* operators (prec 4) *)

(* <, >, <=, and >= are overloaded *)           (* int    * int    -> bool *)
(* standard operators (prec 4)      *)          (* real   * real   -> bool *)
                                                (* string * string -> bool *)

(* not is a standard function *)                        (* bool -> bool *)

fun eq  x y  =  x = y;                          (* ''a -> ''a -> bool *)

fun neq x y  =  x <> y;                         (* ''a -> ''a -> bool *)

infix 4 ==;
fun x == y = if x = y          then true        (* real * real -> bool *)
             else if x+y = 0.0 then false
             else abs((x-y)/(x+y)) < 1E~15;

val eq'r = curry op ==;                         (* real -> real -> real *)

fun conj x y = x andalso y;                     (* bool -> bool -> bool *)

fun disj x y = x orelse  y;                     (* bool -> bool -> bool *)

fun conjl nil      = true                       (* bool list -> bool *)
  | conjl (x :: xs) = x andalso conjl xs;
val all = conjl;

fun disjl nil      = false                      (* bool list -> bool *)
  | disjl (x :: xs) = x orelse disjl xs;
val some = disjl;

fun forall nil p       = true                   (* 'a list ->            *)
  | forall (x :: xs) p = p x andalso forall xs p; (* ('a -> bool) -> bool *)
```

```
fun exists nil p       = false                    (* 'a list ->              *)
  | exists (x :: xs) p = p x orelse exists xs p;  (*  ('a -> bool) -> bool *)
```

```
(* ------------------------- Number functions ------------------------- *)
```

```
(* + and - are overloaded standard *)               (* int  * int  -> int  *)
(* operators (prec 6)            *)                  (* real * real -> real *)
```

```
(* * is an overloaded standard operator (prec 7) *)  (* int  * int  -> int  *)
                                                     (* real * real -> real *)
```

```
(* div and mod are standard operators (prec 7 *)     (* int  * int  -> int  *)
```

```
(* / is a standard operator (prec 7) *)              (* real * real -> real *)
```

```
(* abs and ~ are overloaded standard functions *)       (* int  -> int  *)
                                                        (* real -> real *)
```

```
(* sqrt, sin, cos, arctan, exp, ln *)                   (* real -> real *)
(* are standard functions *)
```

```
fun tan x = sin x / cos x;                              (* real -> real *)
```

```
fun cot x = cos x / sin x;                              (* real -> real *)
```

```
fun add'i x y : int  = x + y;                       (* int  ->  int ->  int *)
val add = add'i;
```

```
fun add'r x y : real = x + y;                       (* real -> real -> real *)
```

```
fun subtract'i x y : int = y - x;                   (* int  -> int  -> int  *)
val subtract = subtract'i;
```

```
fun subtract'r x y : real = y - x;                  (* real -> real -> real *)
```

```
fun times'i x y : int  = x * y;                     (* int  -> int  -> int  *)
val times = times'i;
```

```
fun times'r x y : real = x * y;                     (* real -> real -> real *)
```

```
fun over'i x y : int  = y div x;                    (* int  -> int  -> int  *)
```

```
fun over'r x y : real = y / x;                      (* real -> real -> real *)
val over = over'r;
```

```
fun invert x = 1.0 / x;                                 (* real -> real *)
```

```
fun sq'i x : int  = x * x;                              (* int  -> int  *)
val sq = sq'i;
```

```
fun sq'r x : real = x * x;                              (* real -> real *)

val succ = add 1;                                       (* int  -> int  *)

val pred = subtract 1;                                  (* int  -> int  *)

fun divides   n i = n mod i = 0;                 (* int -> int -> bool *)

fun hasfactor n i = i mod n = 0;                 (* int -> int -> bool *)

val even = hasfactor 2;                                 (* int  -> bool *)

val odd  = not o even;                                  (* int  -> bool *)

infixr 8 **;
(* fun i ** n = if      n < 0 then raise **    *)      (* int * int -> int  *)
(*              else if n = 0 then 1           *)
(*              else i * i ** (n-1);           *)
fun i ** n = if      n < 0 then raise **
                else if n = 0 then 1
                else let val k = i ** (n div 2)
                     in if even n then k * k else i * k * k
                     end;

fun power x y = if      x <  0.0 then raise power    (* real -> real -> real *)
                else if y == 0.0 then 1.0
                else exp(y * ln x);
infixr 8 **' ;
val op **' = uncurry power;                        (* real  * real -> real *)

(* The values of maxint and minint are implementation dependent *)
val maxint = 2**30;                                              (* int *)
val minint = ~(2**30-1);                                         (* int *)

val pi = 3.14159265358979323844;                                 (* real *)

fun log x = ln x / ln 10.0;                             (* real -> real *)

fun log2 x = ln x / ln 2.0;                             (* real -> real *)

(* floor is a standard function *)                      (* real -> int  *)

(* real is a standard function *)                       (* int  -> real *)

fun round x = floor(x + 0.5);                           (* real -> int  *)

fun ceiling x = if real(floor x) = x then floor x       (* real -> int  *)
                else                  floor(x + 1.0);
```

```
fun integer x = if x > real maxint orelse x < real minint    (* real -> bool *)
                then raise integer
                else real(round x) == x;

fun fac n = if      n < 0 then raise fac                      (* int  -> int  *)
            else if n = 0 then 1
            else n*fac(n-1);

val sum'i = foldl add 0;                              (* int  list -> int  *)
val sum   = sum'i;

val sum'r = foldl add'r 0.0;                          (* real list -> real *)

val prod'i = foldl times 1;                           (* int  list -> int  *)
val prod   = prod'i;

val prod'r = foldl times'r 1.0;                       (* real list -> real *)

fun sigma f k l  =                    (* (int -> int ) -> int -> int -> int  *)
      sum  (map f (k -- l));

fun sigma'r f k l =                   (* (int -> real) -> int -> int -> real *)
      sum'r(map f (k -- l));

fun max'i (x : int ) y  = if x > y then x else y;    (* int  -> int  -> int  *)
val max = max'i;

fun max'r (x : real) y  = if x > y then x else y;    (* real -> real -> real *)

fun min'i (x : int ) y  = if x < y then x else y;    (* int  -> int  -> int  *)
val min = min'i;

fun min'r (x : real) y  = if x < y then x else y;    (* real -> real -> real *)

local fun gcd' n m = if m = 0 then n
                     else gcd' m (n mod m);
in fun gcd n m = gcd' (abs n) (abs m) end;            (* int -> int -> int *)

fun factors n = filter (divides n) (2 -- n div 2);    (* int -> int list *)

fun prime n = null(find (divides n)                    (* int -> bool *)
                   (2 -- round(sqrt(real n))));

(* ---------- Random numbers ---------- *)

fun random seed = let val x = seed * 147.0             (* real -> real *)
                  in x - real(floor x) end;

fun randlist n seed = genlist seed random n;    (* int -> real -> real list *)
```

```
fun randint i j seed =                          (* int -> int -> real -> int *)
      floor(seed * real(j - i + 1)) + i;

fun randintlist i j n seed =                    (* int -> int -> int ->      *)
      map (randint i j) (randlist n seed);      (*          real -> int list *)
```

```
(* --------------------- Character and string functions --------------------- *)

(* ^ is a standard operator (prec 6) *)        (* string * string -> string *)

(* size and ord are standard functions *)                 (* string -> int *)

(* chr is a standard function *)                           (* int -> string *)

(* explode is a standard function *)                 (* string -> string list *)

(* implode is a standard function *)                 (* string list -> string *)
```

```
fun digit c    = c >= "0" andalso c <= "9";              (* string -> bool *)

fun lowercase c = c >= "a" andalso c <= "z";             (* string -> bool *)

fun uppercase c = c >= "A" andalso c <= "Z";             (* string -> bool *)

fun letter c    = lowercase c orelse uppercase c;        (* string -> bool *)

fun digitval d  = if digit d then ord d - ord "0"        (* string -> int  *)
                  else raise digitval;
```

```
(* --------------------------- Iterating functions --------------------------- *)

fun until p next state =                (* ('a -> bool) -> ('a -> 'a) -> 'a -> 'a *)
      if p state then state
      else until p next (next state);
```

```
fun for n m next state =                (* int -> int ->                      *)
      if      n > m + 1 then raise for  (* (int * 'a -> 'a) -> 'a -> 'a *)
      else if n = m + 1 then state
      else for (n + 1) m next (next(n, state));

fun iter n next state =                 (* int -> ('a -> 'a) -> 'a -> 'a *)
      if n < 0 then raise iter
      else if n = 0 then state
      else iter (n - 1) next (next state);
(* --------------------- Input and output functions --------------------- *)

(* print is a standard command *)                         (* 'a -> 'a *)
```

```
(* std_in  is a standard instream *)                          (* instream  *)
(* std_out is a standard outstream *)                         (* outstream *)

(* open_in   is a standard command *)            (* string -> instream  *)
(* open_out  is a standard command *)            (* string -> outstream *)
(* close_in  is a standard command *)             (* instream  -> unit *)
(* close_out is a standard command *)             (* outstream -> unit *)

(* input  is a standard command *)         (* instream  * int    -> string *)
(* output is a standard command *)         (* outstream * string -> unit   *)

(* lookahead     is a standard command *)        (* instream -> string *)
(* end_of_stream is a standard command *)        (* instream -> bool   *)

fun skip s = if lookahead s = " "  orelse       (* instream -> unit *)
                lookahead s = "\n" orelse
                lookahead s = "\t"
             then (input(s, 1); skip s)
             else ();

fun have s c = if c = lookahead s then input(s, 1)      (* instream ->    *)
                 else (output(std_out, "Did not get " ^ c);   (* string   ->    *)
                    raise have);                        (*          string *)

local fun getint' s n =
             if digit(lookahead s)
             then getint' s (10 * n + digitval(input(s, 1)))
             else n
     fun getposint s = if digit(lookahead s)
                       then getint' s 0
                       else raise getint
in fun getint s =                                       (* instream -> int *)
        (skip s; if lookahead s = "~"
                 then (input(s, 1); ~(getposint s))
                 else getposint s)
end;

local fun convert 0 = ""
       | convert n = convert(n div 10) ^
                     chr(ord "0" + n mod 10)
in fun putint s 0 = output(s,"0")               (* outstream -> int -> unit *)
     | putint s n =
         if n < 0 then (output(s, "~");
                        putint s (~n))
         else output(s, convert n);
end;
```

```
(* getstring does not handle escape sequences *)
local fun getchars s = if lookahead s = "\"" then ""
                       else input(s, 1) ^ getchars s
in fun getstring s = (skip s; have s "\"";                    (* instream -> string *)
                      let val str = getchars s
                      in (have s "\""; str) end)
end;

fun putstring s str =                              (* outstream -> string -> unit *)
      output(s, "\"" ^ str ^ "\"");

fun getpair get1 get2 s =                          (* (instream -> 'a) ->      *)
      (skip s; have s "(";                         (* (instream -> 'b) ->      *)
       let val e1 = get1 s                         (*  instream ->     'a * 'b *)
       in skip s; have s ",";
          let val e2 = get2 s
          in skip s; have s ")"; (e1, e2) end
       end);

fun putpair put1 put2 s (x, y) =           (* (outstream -> 'a -> 'b) ->      *)
      (output(s, "("); put1 s x;           (* (outstream -> 'c -> 'd) ->      *)
       output(s, ","); put2 s y;           (*  outstream -> 'a * 'c   -> unit *)
       output(s, ")"));

local fun getelements get s =
              (skip s;
               if      lookahead s = "]" then nil
               else if lookahead s = "," then
                       (input(s, 1);
                        get s :: getelements get s)
               else raise getlist)
in fun getlist get s =                             (* (instream -> 'a) -> *)
        (skip s; have s "["; skip s;               (*  instream -> 'a list *)
         if lookahead s = "]"
         then (have s "]"; nil)
         else let val xs = get s :: getelements get s
              in (have s "]"; xs) end)
end;

local fun putlist' put s nil        = ()
       | putlist' put s [x]         = put s x
       | putlist' put s (x :: xs) =
             (put s x; output(s, ", ");
              putlist' put s xs)
in fun putlist put s xs =                           (* (outstream -> 'a -> unit) ->   *)
        (output(s, "[");                            (*  outstream -> 'a list ->  unit *)
         putlist' put s xs;
         output(s, "]"))
end;
```

Index

abs 28, 32, 98
absolute magnitude 75
abstr 300
abstract data type 298, 352
abstract machine 113, 339, 353
abstract syntax 290, 329, 352
abstract syntax tree 290, 352
abstraction 4, 9, 38, 45, 197, 327, 347, 354
abstraction barrier 252
abstype 300
accumulating parameter 245
accumulator 17
accuracy 31
ackermann 248
Ackermann's function 239
Ada xiii
add 184, 433
adjacency list 317
algebra 223
Algol xiii
algorithm 7, 11, 12, 45, 59, 347
all 432
allpairs 431
alphanumeric identifier 36, 202, 385
alternative pattern 141
ALU 16
analyser 351
and 154
andalso 76, 398
append 155, 172, 195, 428
application 48, 350
applicative evaluation order 80, 353
arc 317
architecture 18
arcsin 54
argument 48, 50, 350
argument type 43, 349
arithmetic 6, 7
arithmetic expression 8, 108, 286
arity 100
as 143
ASCII code 85, 376
assembler 19
assembly language 19
assignment 38
associativity 26, 110, 207

atomic expression 424
atomic pattern 424
attribute 258
automatic programming 337
axiom 116, 353

Babbage, Charles 11
backslash 87
backspace 86
Backus, John 19, 109
bag 307, 318
balanced tree 278
base case 168, 354
basic operation 12
BASIC xiii, 20
batch mode 20
bell 86
bigint 27
bignum 27
binary code 282
binary digit 7
binary number system 7
binary operator 24
binary search tree 311
binary tree 275
binding 3, 120, 349
binomial coefficient 163
bit 7
black box 45, 299
BNF grammar 109, 290, 319
body 47, 52
bool 71, 136, 395
Boole, George 71
boolean expression 76
bottom-up design 339, 354
bottom-up testing 101, 341
bound variable 124, 350
branching recursion 235
branching structure 275
bubble sort 247
bug 68, 341
byte 17

C 427
calculation 9
canonical element 301

439

canonical expression 24, 26, 93, 114, 348
cardinality 309
carriage return 86
cartesian product 93
case 148, 398
case analysis 70, 80, 147, 354
case expression 147, 398
category 5
ceiling 83, 434
char 86
character 84, 179, 376
characteristic function 312
choice 12, 70
chr 376, 396
Church, Alonzo xiii, 20
circular definition 164
circular type 271
class 5
close_in 416
close_out 416
closure 120, 125, 178, 315, 350
COBOL xiii
code 85
code reading 341
code word 86, 282, 376
coding 353
combinator 199, 297, 350
combine 214, 431
combining principle 12, 106
command 320, 348
command interpreter 327
comment 343, 387
commutativity 156, 205
comparison operator 70, 99
compiler 19, 347
complex arithmetic 103, 268
complexity 160, 201, 237, 355
compose operator 193, 428
composite object 92
composition 55, 315
computability 20
computation 9, 11, 26, 60, 353
computation rule 14
computer 15, 347
con 135
concatenation 88
concept 3, 347
conclusion 116
concrete constructor 299
concrete data type 250, 352
concrete syntax 290, 329, 352
condition controlled iteration 246, 351
conditional equation 61
conditional expression 71, 80, 118, 398
conj 195, 432

conjl 432
conjunction 76, 398
connected graph 319
cons 152, 195, 428
constant 9, 38, 139, 349
constructor 93, 135, 140, 152, 153, 251, 351
constructor constant 253, 351
constructor function 253, 351
consumer 320
context dependence 111
control character 86
convergence 246
correctness proof 65
cot 433
count 174, 430
course-of-values recursion 232, 351
CPU 16
curried function 186, 188, 191, 194, 205, 350
curry 188, 427
cut 430
cycle 319

data 2, 347
data abstraction 251, 261, 298, 354
data object 135
data structure 92, 226
data type 5, 24, 251, 351
data type binding 393
datatype 135
datatype declaration 134
datum 2, 347
de Morgan's laws 78
debugging 66, 68, 175, 340, 341
declaration 36, 121, 127, 349, 393, 422
declaration sequence 130
declarative property 14
decoding tree 282
decomposition 63, 147
decomposition into cases 81, 354
delayed evaluation 140
delete 431
delimiter 387
denotation 7
derivation rule 116, 354
derivative 247
dictionary 382
difference 431
differentiation 247, 294
digit 7
digit 91, 436
digitval 87, 436
dimension 29
direct-access file 306
directed graph 317
directive 206, 394

disj 195, 432
disjl 432
disjoint patterns 144
disjoint sets 315
disjunction 76, 398
div 24, 396
divide and conquer 236, 355
divides 195, 434
domain 43, 182, 314, 349
double recursion 235
drop 183, 430
duality 78
duplicate 182, 430
duplicates 430
dynamic binding 126

edge 317
efficiency 160, 223, 225, 237, 244, 342
Egyptian triangle 310
else 71
encapsulation 73
end 129, 131
end_of_stream 321, 416
enumeration type 135
environment 3, 39, 118, 349, 388
environment store 118
eq 195, 432
equality 74, 75, 99, 136, 399
equality relation 273
equality type 173
equation 61, 223
equivalence relation 315
error handling 154
error message 66
escape sequence 87
Euclid's algorithm 240
Eulerian circuit 319
evaluation 9, 294, 388, 391
even 74, 434
exception 25, 154, 388, 397, 401
exception 154
exception binding 393
executable specification 337
execution error 68
exhaustive pattern 144, 405
exists 222, 309, 433
exp 32, 396
experimental system development 336, 355
explode 180, 396
explorative programming 355
exponent 30
exponential function 55, 199
exponentiation 27, 101, 208
expression 120, 348, 425
extensible language 127, 135

f91 249
fac 160, 181, 435
factorial 160
factors 216, 435
failure 25
false 71, 136, 395
fib 235, 244
Fibonacci number 235, 244
file 228, 254
filter 215, 429
find 216, 429
findone 429
finite set 309
fixed-point numeral 30
flat 172, 429
floating-point numeral 30
floor 34, 396
fn 48, 52
foldl 220, 429
foldr 429
for 244, 436
forall 222, 309, 432
forest 289
form feed 86
formal differentiation 294
formula 9
FORTRAN xiii, 19
free representation 352
free type 352
free variable 124, 350
fromto 159, 195, 430
fst 97, 428
full binary tree 277, 284
fun 48, 52, 399
function 42, 123, 349
function application 52, 123, 350
function binding 400
function body 47
function declaration 48
function expression 51, 115, 350
function object 51, 123
functional abstraction 46, 349, 354
functional argument 189
functional language 20, 348
functional programming 1

gcd 240, 435
general binary tree 286
general recursion 238, 351
genlist 209, 430
getint 324, 437
getlist 438
getpair 325, 438
getstring 438
grammar 104, 109, 290, 352

graph 43, 45, 317, 319

Hamiltonian circuit 319
hangon 428
hasfactor 195, 434
have 325, 437
hd 155, 428
hermit 136, 140
Heron formula 129
hidden function 305
hiding 131
hierarchical structure 92
hierarchy 5
higher order concept 4
higher order function 184, 350
high-level language 19, 348
Hilbert curve 334
history recursion 233
HOPE xiii, 380
Huffman code 284
hypotenuse 29

I 199, 427
identifier 36, 202, 348, 385, 423
identity element 156, 218
identity function 90, 199
if 71, 398
imperative language 297, 348
imperative programming 12
implementation 65, 302, 355
implementation descriptor 300, 355
implode 180
in 129, 131
indentation 72, 343
index 182, 430
induction 167
induction hypothesis 168
inductive case 354
inductive step 168
infinite set 312
infix 206
infix application 49
infix directive 269, 386, 394
infix notation 203, 350
infix operator 206
infixed construction 152
infixr 207
information 2, 347
information hiding 131, 344
inorder 280
input 320, 415
input 321, 416
insert 431
instream 416
instruction 17

int 24, 395
integer 23, 272
integer 75, 435
integer constant 385, 426
integer division 24
integration 198
interactive system 20, 23
interleave 224, 431
interpretation 2
interpreter 113, 296, 334, 347
interrupt 25
intersection 226, 431
interval arithmetic 318
invariant 226
invert 75, 195, 433
io_failure 416
irrational number 30
isomorphism 272
ISWIM xiii, 21
it 40, 400
iter 243, 436
iteration 106, 110, 243, 351
iterative design 336, 354

K 200, 427
K byte 17

labelled tree 278
labelled tuple 258
lambda calculus xiii, 20, 202
language 108, 347
language level 348
last 156, 173, 428
layered pattern 143
layout 343
lazy evaluation 79, 140, 216, 353
lazy language xiv
LCF xiii
leaf tree 281
left associative 26
len 157, 166, 429
let 129, 398
letter 91, 436
lexical analysis 352, 387
lexical structure 104, 352
lexicographic order 89, 214
life-cycle 335
line feed 86
linear recursion 235, 235, 351
linear structure 302
linearly recursive type 269
LISP xiii, 21, 282
list 150, 269
list 150, 269, 395
list generator 159, 209

list reducer 157, 217
list searching 215
list template 157
list transformer 213
listrec 429
ln 32, 396
load 427
local 131
local declaration 129, 398
local scope 128
log 434
log2 434
logarithm 55
logic programming 337
lookahead 321, 416
lookup 227, 431
lowercase 91, 436

machine code 348
magic square 231
makestring 90, 397, 427
map 191
mapping 44
match 144, 350, 425
mathematical induction 354
mathematical notation 200
matrix 227
max 188, 435
maxint 434
maxreal 33
McCarthy, John 21
mean value 196
meaning 7
median 175
mem 430
members 309
merge 177, 432
merge sort 248
method 12, 59
min 435
minint 434
ML xiii
ML program 23
ML system 23
mod 24, 396
modelling 10, 134, 250
module 338, 407
modulo operator 24
multiple binding 133, 400
multiple recursion 174, 182, 233
mutual recursion 235

name 3, 120
named type 257
naming 139, 343

naming convention 57, 135
national character 87
natural correspondence 289
natural number 168, 181, 270
negation 77
neq 195, 432
nested expression 73
nested recursion 239
Neumann von, John 16
new line 28
Newton iteration 246
nil 151, 269, 395
node 275, 317
nonfix 206
nonfix directive 386, 394
non-free type 272
non-regular type 261
non-terminating computation 118
normal evaluation order 80, 353
not 141
null 152, 428
number 6
number controlled iteration 243, 351
number system 7
numeral 6, 24, 30, 105

octal number system 35
odd 75, 434
of 148, 253
op 204
open 321
open expression 350
open_in 416
open_out 416
operand 24, 49, 52, 350
operating system 21
operation 44
operational property 14
operational semantics 113, 353
operator 8, 24, 49, 52, 202, 350
operator expression 24, 24, 117
optimal code 284
optimization 342, 355
optional part 110
ord 86, 376, 396
order concept 162, 355
ordered sequence 303
ordered tree 276
ordinal 86
orelse 76, 398
output 320, 415
output 321, 416
outstream 416
over 433
overflow 27, 33, 117

overloaded function 98, 350

pair 92
pair 195, 428
pair constructor 93, 140
palindrome 160, 180, 248
parameter 38, 47, 50, 52, 350
parentheses expression 115
parser generator 294
parsing 291, 352
partial correctness 241, 355
partial function 154, 182, 349
partial order 303
partial recursive function 239, 351
partially applicable function 184, 350
partition 315
Pascal xiii
Pascal's triangle 201, 210
path 276
pattern 425
pattern matching 96, 138, 152, 251, 254, 259,
         349, 390
perfect number 230
performance requirement 302, 353
perms 224, 431
permutation 224
pi 30, 434
pi 35, 201
polar coordinates 253
polymorphic equality 413
polymorphic function 97, 350
polymorphism 153
polytype 151, 265, 350
positional number system 7
postfix 195, 428
postfix notation 264
postorder 280
power 101, 434
powerset 233
pragmatics 104, 347
precedence 26, 78, 107, 109, 208
pred 434
predefined function 29
predicate 153, 251, 260, 351
predicate logic 336
prefix application 49
prefix code 282
prefix notation 203, 350
premise 116
preorder 280
prime 202
prime 217, 435
prime number 216
primitive recursion 222, 232, 277, 351
principle of induction 167

print 90, 397, 436
problem 59
problem decomposition 354
problem solving 1, 59
procedural abstraction 46, 349
procedure 45, 349
prod 158, 435
producer 320
production 109
program 8, 11, 23, 40, 121, 347, 384, 394, 421
program derivation 340, 354
program layout 343
program maintenance 338
program proving 66, 355
program store 113
program verification 65
programming 1, 353
programming in the large 338
programming in the small 338
programming language 18
programming methodology 335
prompt 23
putint 437
putlist 325, 438
putpair 438
putstring 438

quantifier 309
queens problem 241
queue 262, 270
quicksort 236
quote 84
quotient type 273, 301, 352

raise 154
raise exception 154
randint 436
randintlist 436
randlist 435
random 211, 435
random number 210
random walk 213, 231
range 43, 314, 349
rapid prototyping 336, 354
rational number 29, 318
readability 40, 343
read-eval-print loop 23
real 31, 34, 395
real constant 385, 426
real number 29
rec 178, 399
record 92, 258
record selector 260
record wild card 259
rectangular coordinates 253

recursion 15, 61, 106, 164, 201, 232
recursion assumption 170, 171
recursive binding 177
recursive case 354
recursive decomposition 166, 354
recursive definition 171
recursive type 269
redleft 429
reduce 218, 429
reduce1 429
reducer 157, 277, 279
reduction 25, 53, 72, 114
reduction machine 113, 353
reduction rule 14
redundant pattern 144, 405
referential transparency 320, 348
refinement 69
reflexive relation 315
regular data type 251, 352
relation 42, 313, 349
relational operator 71, 88
relative accuracy 31
relative magnitude 75
remdupl 430
repetition 12
representation type 299
reserved word 384
result type 349
reusable program 338
rev 156, 171, 245
rewrite rule 14
right associative 26
root 276
roots 102, 103
round 34, 54, 434
round2 64
routine 45
rule 145, 350, 425
run-time error 67

SASL xiii
scalar product 174, 227
Scheme xiii
scientific notation 30
scope 39, 348
scope rule 127
seed 210
selector 97, 153, 251, 260, 351
selector function 412
self-referential definition 164, 178
semantics 9, 104, 112, 347, 353
sequence 12
sequence expression 175, 322, 398
sequential decomposition 63, 354
sequential file 304

series 197
set 5, 226, 307
set abstraction 308
shortest path length 319
side effect 348, 90, 175, 320
sieve of Eratosthenes 230
sigma 197, 435
significant digit 74
signum 70
Simpson formula 199
simulation 211
sine function 201
size 88
skip 324, 437
SML xiii
snd 98, 428
software 21
software crisis 20
software engineering 335
some 432
sort 176, 219, 225, 432
sorting 236, 247, 248
space 28
space complexity 161, 355
special constant 385, 426
specification 13, 60, 69, 266, 302, 335, 353
split 215, 431
sq 57, 433
sqrt 32, 396
square root 32
stack 167, 272
standard data type 136
standard deviation 183, 195
standard environment 122, 395
standard function 28, 32, 155
standard stream 321, 416
stand_dev 196
state 120, 348
static binding 126
std_in 416
std_out 416
step-wise refinement 62, 267, 354
Stirling's formula 103
stream 320, 415
strict evaluation order 80, 353
strict language xiv
string 84, 179
string 395
string constant 385, 426
structural induction 170, 274, 354
structured growth 340, 354
structured program 344
substitution 53
subtract 433
succ 434

successor function 168, 181, 270
sum 158, 435
sum1to 48
summation of series 197
swap 428
symbol 2
symbolic identifier 202, 385
symmetric relation 315
syntax 9, 104, 347, 352
syntax analysis 352
syntax chart 105, 352
syntax error 67

table 45, 227, 316
tabulation 86
tail recursion 243, 245, 351
take 183, 430
tan 433
template 157, 170, 171, 172, 173, 174, 277
temporary binding 128
terminal symbol 106
termination 234
testing 65, 66, 69, 340, 355
then 71
theorem proving 240
three-valued logic 252
throw-away programming 336
time complexity 161, 355
times 433
tip 275
tl 155, 428
top-down design 62, 69, 101, 241, 250, 267,
         339, 354
top-level 40, 127
total correctness 241, 355
total function 154, 349
total order 303
towers of Hanoi 237
tracing 175
transfer function 86
transitive closure 315
transitive relation 315
tree 275, 289
tree traversal 280, 287
trick coding 18
trigonometrical function 54
true 71, 136, 395
truncation 33
truth table 78
truth value 71
tuple 92, 100, 151
type 5, 24, 251, 347, 351, 423
type 257
type binding 393
type checking 56, 404

type completeness 95
type constant 263, 351
type constraint 55, 143
type constructor 93, 351
type declaration 257
type deduction 56, 67
type error 67
type expression 265
type function 263, 351
type variable 98, 173, 202, 264, 350, 424
typed language 250

unary operator 28
uncurry 427
undefined value 240
underbar 202
undirected graph 317
union 226, 431
union type 255
unit 29, 256
unit 136, 140, 395
universal relation 314
universe 308
until 246, 436
updating 229
uppercase 91, 436
use 69, 427

val 37, 52, 399
valid 300
valid representation 306
validation 61, 69, 336, 353
value 9, 114, 348, 388
value binding 133, 392
value declaration 37, 105
variable 9, 38, 120, 121, 139, 349
vector 227
verification 66, 69, 340, 355
view 262
VLSI 18
vocabulary examiner 326
von Neumann, John 16

well-structured program 333, 344, 355
wild card 99, 139, 259
with 300
word 17

Y 201, 427